LIBRARY OF NEW TESTAMENT STUDIES

592

formerly the Journal for the Study of the New Testament Supplement series

Editor
Chris Keith

Editorial Board
Dale C. Allison, John M. G. Barclay, Lynn H. Cohick,
R. Alan Culpepper, Craig A. Evans, Robert Fowler, Simon J.
Gathercole, Juan Hernández Jr., John S. Kloppenborg, Michael
Labahn, Matthew V. Novenson, Love L. Sechrest, Robert Wall,
Catrin H. Williams, Brittany E. Wilson

Relating the Gospels

Memory, Imitation and the Farrer Hypothesis

Eric Eve

LONDON • NEW YORK • OXFORD • NEW DELHI • SYDNEY

T&T CLARK
Bloomsbury Publishing Plc
50 Bedford Square, London, WC1B 3DP, UK
1385 Broadway, New York, NY 10018, USA
29 Earlsfort Terrace, Dublin 2, Ireland

BLOOMSBURY, T&T CLARK and the T&T Clark logo are trademarks of Bloomsbury Publishing Plc

First published in Great Britain 2021
This paperback edition published 2022

Copyright © Eric Eve, 2021

Eric Eve has asserted his right under the Copyright, Designs and Patents Act, 1988, to be identified as Author of this work.

All rights reserved. No part of this publication may be reproduced or transmitted in any form or by any means, electronic or mechanical, including photocopying, recording, or any information storage or retrieval system, without prior permission in writing from the publishers.

Bloomsbury Publishing Plc does not have any control over, or responsibility for, any third-party websites referred to or in this book. All internet addresses given in this book were correct at the time of going to press. The author and publisher regret any inconvenience caused if addresses have changed or sites have ceased to exist, but can accept no responsibility for any such changes.

A catalogue record for this book is available from the British Library.

Library of Congress Cataloging-in-Publication Data
Names: Eve, Eric, author.
Title: Relating the gospels : imitation, memory, and the Farrer hypothesis / Eric Eve.
Description: London ; New York : T&T Clark, 2021. | Series: The library of New Testament studies, 2513-8790 ; 592 | Includes bibliographical references and index. | Summary: "Relating the Gospels examines the synoptic problem and argues that the similarities between the gospels of Matthew and Luke outweigh the objections commonly raised against the theory that Luke used the text of Matthew in composing his gospel"–Provided by publisher.
Identifiers: LCCN 2020044222 (print) | LCCN 2020044223 (ebook) | ISBN 9780567681102 (hardback) | ISBN 9780567681119 (pdf) | ISBN 9780567681140 (epub)
Subjects: LCSH: Bible. Gospels–Criticism, interpretation, etc. | Synoptic problem.
Classification: LCC BS2555.52 .E95 2021 (print) | LCC BS2555.52 (ebook) | DDC 226/.066–dc23
LC record available at https://lccn.loc.gov/2020044222
LC ebook record available at https://lccn.loc.gov/2020044223

ISBN:	HB:	978-0-5676-8110-2
	PB:	978-0-5676-9906-0
	ePDF:	978-0-5676-8111-9
	ePUB:	978-0-5676-8114-0

Series: Library of New Testament Studies, ISSN 2513-8790, volume 592

Typeset by Integra Software Services Pvt. Ltd.

Contents

Abbreviations		vi
1	Introduction	1
2	Models, memory and Markan priority	5
	Elite, oral and scribal composition	5
	Memory	11
	The evangelists' purpose	15
	Markan priority	20
	Implications and working hypotheses	25
3	Transformational techniques	29
	Progymnasmata	29
	Compositional practices in previous Synoptic Problem scholarship	32
	Reordering and rearrangement	42
	Literary imitation	55
4	Significant similarities	75
	Significant verbal similarities in the triple tradition	75
	Significant verbal similarities in the double tradition	85
	Significantly similar beginnings	89
	Conclusion	114
5	Difficult differences	117
	Infancy and resurrection narratives	117
	Alternating primitivity	120
	Luke's non-use of Matthean additions to Mark	126
	Unpicking or 'minor disagreements'	131
	Conclusion	143
6	The order objection	145
	The problem	145
	Matthew's order	146
	Luke's order	159
	Conclusion	198
7	Conclusion	205
	Retrospect	205
	Known unknowns	205
	Prospects	210
Bibliography		211
Index of References		226
Index of Authors		245

Abbreviations

2DH	Two Document Hypothesis
2GH	Two Gospel Hypothesis
AB	Anchor Bible
Aen.	Virgil, *Aeneid*
AJS	*American Journal of Sociology*
Apion	Josephus, *Against Apion*
Ant	Josephus, *Jewish Antiquities*
Arion	*Arion: A Journal of Humanities and the Classics*
BBR	*Bulletin for Biblical Research*
BPC	Biblical Performance Criticism
BETL	Bibliotecha ephemeridum theologicarum lovaniensum
BICS	*Bulletin of Institute of Classical Studies*
BS	Bulletin Supplement
BTCB	Brazos Theological Commentary on the Bible
CBSS	Continuum Biblical Studies Series
CBQ	*Catholic Biblical Quarterly*
CCS	Cambridge Classical Studies
CEQ	James M. Robinson, Paul Hoffmann and John S. Kloppenborg, *The Critical Edition of Q: Synopsis Including the Gospels of Matthew and Luke, Mark and Thomas with English, German and French Translations of Q and Thomas* (Hermeneia; Minneapolis: Fortress, 2000)
CL	*Christianity and Literature*
CS	Luke's Central Section
CSML	Cambridge Studies in Medieval Literature
EA	Exclusive Agreement (of two Synoptic Gospels against the third)
EC	*Early Christianity*
Ep.	Seneca, *Epistulae morales*
ETL	*Ephemerides theologicae Lovanienses*

ExpTim	*Expository Times*
FH	Farrer Hypothesis
GRBS	*Greek, Roman and Byzantine Studies*
HTR	*Harvard Theological Review*
HVA	High verbatim agreement
IA	Inclusive Agreement (of all three Synoptic Gospels)
Il.	Homer, *Iliad*
Inst.	Quintilian, *Institutio oratoria*
JBL	*Journal of Biblical Literature*
JHS	*Journal of Hellenic Studies*
JQR	*Jewish Quarterly Review*
JR	*The Journal of Religion*
JSJ	*Journal for the Study of Judaism in the Persian, Hellenistic and Roman Period*
JSNT	*Journal for the Study of the New Testament*
JSNTSup	Journal for the Study of the New Testament, Supplements
LCL	Loeb Classical Library
Life	Josephus, *Life* (Autobiography)
LNTS	Library of New Testament Studies
LVA	Low verbatim agreement
LXX	Septuagint
MDLATC	*Materiali e discussioni per l'analisi dei testi classici*
Migr. Abr.	Philo, *De Migratione Abrahami* (*On the Migration of Abraham*)
MPH	Matthean Posteriority Hypothesis
NIGTC	The New International Greek Testament Commentary
NovT	*Novum Testamentum*
NovTSup	Novum Testamentum, Supplements
NTGL	The New Testament and Greek Literature
NTM	New Testament Monographs
NTS	*New Testament Studies*
Od.	Homer, *Odyssey*
OECGT	Oxford Early Christian Gospel Texts

OT	*Oral Tradition*
PBM	Paternoster Biblical Monographs
PCNT	Paideia Commentaries on the New Testament
PTMS	Pittsburgh Theological Monograph Series
QiM	Alan Kirk, *Q in Matthew: Ancient Media, Memory, and Early Scribal Transmission of the Jesus Tradition* (LNTS, 564; London: Bloomsbury T&T Clark, 2016)
RBS	Resources for Biblical Study
SAC	Studies in Antiquity & Christianity
SBL	Society of Biblical Literature
SF	*Social Forces*
SM	Sermon on the Mount
SNTSMS	Society for New Testament Studies Monograph Series
SNTW	Studies of the New Testament and Its World
SP	Sacra Pagina
Spec. Leg.	Philo, *De specialibus legibus* (*On the Special Laws*)
SS	Semeia Studies
STAC	Studien und Texte zu Antike und Christentum
STNJT	*Studia Theologica – Nordic Journal of Theology*
TPAPA	*Transactions and Proceedings of the American Philological Association*
TPINTC	TPI New Testament Commentaries
TS	*Theological Studies*
TUMSR	Trinity University Monograph Series in Religion
TynBul	*Tyndale Bulletin*
UWSLL	University of Wisconsin Studies in Language and Literature
Vit. Mos.	Philo, *De vita Mosis* (*Life of Moses*)
VPT	Voices in Performance and Text
War	Josephus, *The Jewish War*
WBC	Word Biblical Commentary
WTG	Eric Eve, *Writing the Gospels: Composition and Memory* (London: SPCK, 2016)

1

Introduction

How are the Gospels of Matthew, Mark and Luke related to one another? Since the mid-nineteenth century the dominant position had been that Matthew and Luke made independent use of Mark and Q (the hypothetical source that supposedly accounts for the so-called double tradition, the material common to Matthew and Luke not found in Mark). But dissenters from this Two Document Hypothesis (2DH) have long been proposing alternative theories, not least the Two Gospel Hypothesis (2GH) and the Farrer Hypothesis (FH), both of which do away with the need to postulate Q by proposing, in the first case, that Luke used Matthew and Mark then used the other two, and in the second, that Matthew used Mark and Luke then used the other two.[1] The debate between competing theories has increasingly come to turn on not just why the later evangelists would have treated their sources in the manner the theories require but how they could have done so given the writing technologies available to them and the source-utilization techniques employed by other ancient authors.[2] It is often suggested that such considerations favour the 2DH[3]; this book, however, will argue that it is the Farrer Hypothesis that makes better sense of the data.[4]

---

[1] The Griesbach Hypothesis (the earliest version of the 2GH) predated the 2DH; the FH also has pre-twentieth-century precursors.

[2] F. Gerald Downing has been something of a pioneer in this area in a series of articles many of which will be discussed in Chapters 3 and 5, although the need to address some of these questions was already adumbrated by William Sanday, 'The Conditions under Which the Gospels Were Written, in Their Bearing upon Some Difficulties of the Synoptic Problem' in William Sanday (ed.), *Oxford Studies in the Synoptic Problem* (Oxford: Clarendon, 1911), 3–26. Other substantial contributions in this area include R.A. Derrenbacker, *Ancient Compositional Practices and the Synoptic Problem* (BETL, 186; Leuven: Peeters-Leuven, 2005), and Alan Kirk, *Q in Matthew: Ancient Media, Memory, and Early Scribal Transmission of the Jesus Tradition* (LNTS, 564; London: Bloomsbury T&T Clark, 2016) (henceforth *QiM*), together with a number of the essays in P. Foster, A. Gregory, J.S. Kloppenborg, J. Verheyden (eds), *New Studies in the Synoptic Problem: Oxford Conference, April 2008: Essays in Honour of Christopher M. Tuckett* (BETL, 239; Leuven: Peeters, 2011). The present author's previous book, *Writing the Gospels: Composition and Memory* (London: SPCK, 2016) (henceforth *WTG*), also looks at ancient compositional techniques in relation to the composition of the gospels but only sketches the possible implications for the Synoptic Problem.

[3] Notably in the work of Gerald Downing, Robert Derrenbacker and Alan Kirk, which will be discussed in Chapter 3.

[4] It thus responds to a challenge issued by advocates of the 2DH, for example Derrenbacker, *Compositional Practices*, 258, 'As a new generation of FGH advocates work through their theory, the compositional conventions of writers in the Greco-Roman world need to become part of their discussion'; and Kirk, *QiM*, 307, n. 28, commenting on John C. Poirier and Jeffrey Peterson (eds), *Marcan Priority without Q: Explorations in the Farrer Hypothesis* (LNTS, 455; London: Bloomsbury T&T Clark, 2015), 'Anyone hoping to find engagement with ancient media realities in the most recent set of FGH essays … will be disappointed.'

In doing so we shall need to revisit a number of well-ploughed fields, both for the sake of completeness and to counter arguments that advocates of the 2DH continue to deploy. But we shall also explore some fresher pastures, in relation to memory use, literary imitation and the influence of Matthew's order on Luke's.[5]

As defended here, the FH is not a denial that other sources may have been involved in the composition of Matthew and Luke, particularly if by 'sources' we mean not only written documents but also oral tradition and collective memory. But it is a denial that one of those sources was Q, in the sense of the hypothetical document required by the 2DH. It is conceivable that Luke used Matthew and Mark and that Matthew and Luke also had a common source in addition to Mark, but that common source would be something other than the 2DH Q. Moreover, such a Three Document Hypothesis would be difficult to test, since the reconstruction of its hypothetical common source would lack the relatively tight constraints that inform attempts to reconstruct Q.[6] The hypothetical third source would be in danger of becoming sufficiently flexible to accommodate any apparent difficulties, thereby rendering any 3DH potentially unfalsifiable. This does not make such a hypothesis untrue, but it may render it unfruitful. In general, while the existence of hypothetical lost written sources cannot be excluded *a priori*, it seems better to make as little use of them as possible and to first see if we can do without them; other sources may have existed, but the possibility of our reliably reconstructing them seems remote. In any case, the aim here is not to account for every factor that may have gone into the composition of the Synoptic Gospels but to argue where those three gospels fit into the process.

Suggested solutions to the Synoptic Problem cannot hope to reconstruct precisely what actually happened. There are too many unknowns. The texts of any gospels available to Matthew and Luke will not have been identical to those printed in modern critical editions of the New Testament, but we can never know precisely what they were, which means that the significance of detailed differences and similarities in wording is subject to the uncertainties of textual reconstruction. Moreover, while we can discuss the working methods of the gospel authors on the basis of appropriate ancient analogies, we can never know for certain precisely how the evangelists went about their tasks. All we can do is construct the most economic available hypothesis that plausibly explains the surviving data, where economy relates not just to the number of documents involved but to the compositional methods demanded of the evangelists.

---

[5] The role of memory is not in itself a novel insight, see, e.g., Andrew Gregory, 'What Is Literary Dependence?' in Foster, *New Studies*, 87–114, here 95–103. The discussion of the role of memory in gospel composition has been substantially advanced by Kirk, *QiM*, which appeared in the same year as Eve, *WTG*. The potential importance of literary imitation as a mode of gospel composition has been identified, for example, by Dennis MacDonald, Thomas Brodie and Adam Winn (for further bibliography, see Chapter 3), although its application to the Synoptic Problem has so far been slight. Some of the details of the argument concerning Luke's order in Chapter 6 also appear in M.D. Goulder, *Luke: A New Paradigm* (JSNTSup, 20; Sheffield: Sheffield Academic Press, 1989), but in the rather different context of a process involving reverse scrolling through Matthew by Luke, which the present study does not envisage.

[6] Although such attempts are not without their problems: see Eric Eve, 'Reconstructing Mark: A Thought Experiment' in Mark Goodacre and Nicholas Perrin (eds), *Questioning Q* (London: SPCK, 2004), 89–114, and Nicholas Perrin, 'The Limits of a Reconstructed Q' in Goodacre, *Questioning Q*, 71–88.

Rather than attempting an objective evaluation of every conceivable solution to the Synoptic Problem, the present study will confine itself to comparing the viability of the Farrer Hypothesis with that of its principal competitor, the Two Document Hypothesis. Sometimes the argument may thus turn not so much on whether the FH can provide a totally watertight explanation of every potential difficulty, but whether it can provide one at least as plausible as that offered by the 2DH; a potential difficulty for the FH cannot select in favour of the 2DH if it is an equal or worse difficulty for the 2DH.

In Chapter 2 we shall begin by sketching out a general picture of how the gospel writers may have worked. In Chapter 3 we shall explore the techniques ancient authors typically employed in reworking their sources. The following three chapters will argue that the reasons for supposing that Luke did know Matthew outweigh those for supposing he did not. Chapter 4 will identify a number of similarities between these two gospels that suggest Luke used Matthew. Chapter 5 will counter four of the principal arguments that have been urged against such dependence. Chapter 6 will address the weightiest argument, the alleged difficulty of envisaging how and why Luke would have dispersed and rearranged so much of the material he found in Matthew. Finally, Chapter 7 will sum up the conclusions of this study and review some of the issues that remain.

2

Models, memory and Markan priority

A solution to the Synoptic Problem is more likely to command respect if it fits ancient compositional methods. In the present chapter we shall therefore look at some different models of ancient literary composition and the working methods they entail.[1] We shall leave a more detailed examination of transformational techniques (the kinds of things ancient authors typically did with their source material) to the following chapter. In the present one we shall also briefly discuss Markan priority, both because it makes sense to address this early on and because thinking through the implications of Matthew's and Luke's use of Mark will help crystallize the preceding discussion.

Elite, oral and scribal composition

If you ask someone how they envisage the gospel writers working, they might well describe them sitting at a desk, pen in hand, writing on a papyrus scroll open in front of them while referring to other written sources lying in convenient reach on their desktop.[2] But this picture is quite inappropriate. We now recognize that writing desks were not in use as early as the first century, that many authors preferred to dictate their works rather than act as their own scribes and that ancient authors did not routinely work in the kind of splendid scholarly isolation favoured by modern ones.[3] We should not, however, overcorrect for such anachronisms by overstating the oral component of first-century culture.[4]

We also need to be wary of assuming that elite authors (which the evangelists were not) provide the best models for understanding the composition of the gospels.

---

[1] This both summarizes and builds upon *WTG*.
[2] So Richard C. Beaton, 'How Matthew Writes' in Markus Bockmuehl and Donald A. Hagner (eds), *The Written Gospel* (Cambridge: Cambridge University Press, 2005), 116–34 (116); cf. the equally anachronistic picture in Burton L. Mack, *A Myth of Innocence: Mark and Christian Origins* (Philadelphia: Fortress, 1988), 321–3.
[3] For notable correctives to the naïve view, see Sanday, 'Conditions'; Derrenbacker, *Compositional Practices*; Werner H. Kelber, *Imprints, Voiceprints & Footprints of Memory: Collected Essays of Werner Kelber* (RBS, 74; Atlanta: SBL, 2013).
[4] Larry W. Hurtado, 'Oral Fixation and New Testament Studies? "Orality," "Performance" and Reading Texts in Early Christianity', *NTS* 60 (2014), 321–40; cf. Rafael Rodríguez, 'Reading and Hearing in Ancient Contexts', *JSNT* 32 (2009), 151–78; Paul S. Evans, 'Creating a New "Great Divide": The Exoticization of Ancient Culture in Some Recent Applications of Orality Study to the Bible', *JBL* 136 (2017), 749–64.

They may, however, provide a convenient starting point. Elite authors, at least Roman ones, typically employed slaves (or other assistants) to do much of their donkey work, including reading to them, assisting with their research (e.g. by taking notes from archives), taking down a first draft from dictation and perhaps doing some initial polishing of that draft before presenting it to the author for further correction and then finally making one or more fair copies. Composition might take place in several stages. First, a research phase in which the author gathered his (or occasionally her) material and made or dictated notes. Then the composition of a rough draft, usually (though not exclusively) via dictation. Often this rough draft might be an attempt to get the material in order prior to the application of any literary (or rhetorical) polish. The author might then apply this polish at a subsequent stage when dictating a second draft. At some point he might try out a draft on a circle of friends to glean suggestions and feedback. He might then annotate his draft for his secretary (slave or freedman scribe) to make a final fair copy which would form the archetype for 'publication'. Although there was a commercial book trade, publication generally meant the formal reading of the work before an invited audience and/or the distribution of a small number of copies to a few friends in the hope that they in turn would make more copies so that the work would eventually circulate through their network. While some works may have been intended primarily for private perusal and some were used that way, more typically an elite literary work would be received through listening to it being read aloud, for example to an invited audience or as a form of highbrow entertainment at an elite dinner party.[5]

The study of the works of elite historians suggests that although they may well have consulted a number of works in the course of their research, in the course of composition they generally preferred to follow only one source at a time. This did not prevent their switching from one source to another in the course of their own work, but in writing up any particular episode they would choose one source and largely stick to that for the basis of their own composition, perhaps also including the odd detail they happened to remember from their reading of other sources, or from oral tradition, or from their own background knowledge. In doing so, however, elite authors tended to avoid borrowing the wording of their sources, instead seeking to retell the material in their own words.

Following one source at a time did not necessarily mean having eye contact with that source. Some passages in Plutarch, for example, seem to have been prone to memory errors that suggest that Plutarch had first read the account he intended to use and then put it aside while dictating his version from memory. Moreover, a passage in which Pliny the Younger mentions his own working methods (*Letters* 9.36.1–3) suggests that he did what Quintilian and other teachers recommended, namely composing a section of material in his head and then dictating the well-ordered contents of his mind to a scribe.[6]

---

[5] Rex Winsbury, *The Roman Book: Books, Publishing and Performance in Classical Rome* (London: Bristol Classical Press, 2009), 95–110, 113; Jocelyn Penny Small, *Wax Tablets of the Mind: Cognitive Studies of Memory and Literacy in Classical Antiquity* (Abingdon: Routledge, 1997), 35–40.

[6] *WTG*, 53–8; C.B.R. Pelling, 'Plutarch's Method of Work in the Roman Lives', *JHS* 99 (1979), 74–96, here 92–4; cf. David J. Neville, 'The Phantom Returns: Delbert Burkett's Rehabilitation of Proto-Mark', *ETL* 84 (2008), 135–73, here 168–9; Sharon Lea Mattila, 'A Question Too Often Neglected', *NTS* 41 (1995), 199–217, here 213–15.

How far this generalized description of elite working methods can be applied to the evangelists is another matter. The evangelists are unlikely to have had access to squads of slaves and research assistants, but it is possible that analogous roles could have been played by volunteers from their church communities. We know, for example, that Paul dictated at least some of his letters, so it is by no means implausible that other church leaders could also call on secretarial assistance. Again, the evangelists presumably had circles of friends and colleagues on whom they could have tried out their rough drafts for discussion and feedback. It is most unlikely that Matthew or Luke squirreled themselves away with a copy of Mark until emerging with a manuscript of their own gospel penned in total solitude; it is far more likely that the people who wrote the gospels had discussed their source material and how they proposed to use it with friends and colleagues for some time before beginning the formal process of composition. The writing of the gospels was unlikely to have been any less a socially embedded collaborative enterprise than the writing of elite literature.[7]

The gospels nevertheless differ from elite literary productions in a number of important respects. They were not written for elite edification or entertainment but to be used in the worship of the church and for the encouragement and instruction of believers. Neither were they written to enhance the literary reputation of their authors, who remain anonymous behind their compositions. Moreover, the evangelists were far less scrupulous than elite authors about recycling the wording of their sources and did not paraphrase their sources to anything like the extent of elite Graeco-Roman historians; in comparison with elite compositions what is surprising about parallel passages in the gospels is not the degree to which they differ but the degree to which they agree. Again, the gospels were not written to the same literary standard as elite literature; as Alan Kirk observes, the gap between cultivated Greek style and that of the evangelists suggests they belonged to different social settings, leading Kirk to question (against the views of several other scholars) whether the evangelists would have had access to an elite rhetorical education or whether rhetorical handbooks might be wholly reliable guides to how they worked. He acknowledges that the evangelists put their own stamp on their material to some extent, but their only partial digestion of their sources suggests that they should perhaps be seen as tradents (transmitters of tradition) rather than authors, the distinction being that a tradent is immersed in a tradition while an author maintains a greater critical distance from his sources, although there is a continuum between the two. We shall later explore whether Kirk may be over-correcting, but the point remains that while there may be some similarities between the working methods of the evangelists and their elite contemporaries, there are also likely to have been significant differences.[8]

A very different model of gospel composition views the gospels not as literary texts but as oral-traditional works passed on and gradually modified by a succession of

---

[7] Cf. Richard Last, 'Communities That Write: Christ-Groups, Associations, and Gospel Communities', *NTS* 58 (2012), 173–98.
[8] See *WTG*, 53–9, and *QiM*, 29–41.

traditional storytellers.[9] In favour of this model is the apparent oral style particularly of Mark and the fact that some folklorists and experts on oral epic poetry have seen an analogy between the kinds of variations found between the Synoptic Gospels and those found in different performances of oral tradition. But as a general thesis about the composition of the gospels the oral-compositional model runs into a number of difficulties. It overestimates the extent to which the first-century Roman Empire was an oral culture and underestimates the extent to which writing had penetrated many layers of society.[10] It can give no adequate account of how the gospels came to be written down in relatively fixed and distinct versions.[11] And it largely sidesteps the evidence that have led the great majority of scholars to postulate the existence of some kind of literary relationship between Matthew, Mark and Luke.[12]

A third model of ancient text production, drawing on the work of scholars such as Richard Horsley, Jan Assmann, Loveday Alexander, Alan Kirk and Gerald Downing, may be termed the scribal, school or scholarly model. Such a scribal or scholarly model can be derived partly from the education of ancient Near Eastern scribes and partly from the cultivation of tradition in Hellenistic schools. In the former, the purpose of literary composition was not elite entertainment but the education of scribes, who would copy out and learn a great deal of material by heart (often by oral recitation) not simply to acquire basic literacy but, more importantly, as part of their enculturation into the scribal ethos of their society. Some more experienced scribes might then contribute to this process by producing educational material of their own (often in the form of wisdom literature, although the same process could extend to other genres). Such scribes would see themselves not as authors in the sense of authorities producing new material in their own name, but rather as conduits of older tradition in whose name they wrote, while in fact making their own contribution by bringing

---

[9] So, with many variations, Albert B. Lord, 'The Gospels as Oral Traditional Literature' in William O. Walker (ed.), *The Relationships among the Gospels: An Interdisciplinary Dialogue* (Trinity University Monograph Series in Religion, 5; San Antonio: Trinity University Press, 1978), 33–91; Pieter J.J. Botha, *Orality and Literacy in Early Christianity* (BPC, 5; ed. H.E. Hearon and P. Ruge-Jones; Eugene, OR: Cascade, 2012), esp. 163–90; Antoinette Clark Wire, *The Case for Mark Composed in Performance* (BPC, 3; Eugene, OR: Cascade, 2011); Joanna Dewey, 'The Survival of Mark's Gospel: A Good Story?', *JBL* 123 (2004), 495–507; Joanna Dewey, 'The Gospel of Mark as Oral Hermeneutic' in Tom Thatcher (ed.), *Jesus, the Voice and the Text: Beyond the Oral and the Written Gospel* (Waco: Baylor University Press, 2008), 71–87.

[10] So Hurtado, 'Oral Fixation'.

[11] For a fuller discussion and critique, see *WTG*, 60–72, and cf. *QiM*, 9–28.

[12] For a useful summary, see Gregory, 'Literary Dependence', 87–107. T.M. Derico, *Oral Tradition and Synoptic Verbal Agreement: Evaluating the Empirical Evidence for Literary Dependence* (Cambridge: James Clarke, 2017), has questioned the argument that the extent of verbal agreement between Synoptic parallels shows that the relationship between them must be literary rather than oral, claiming that it is often backed up by little more than scholarly intuition. But while Derico questions some of the evidence that is offered for supposing that extended verbal agreement suggests literary dependence, he does not dispose of all of it, and he does not address the argument from the degree of common order in the Synoptic Gospels. Moreover, the example he supplies of verbal parallels occurring in Jordanian oral-traditional narratives about the twentieth-century missionary Roy Whitman is neither sufficiently similar to the Jesus tradition nor transmitted under relevantly similar circumstances. Derico makes no claim that his arguments disprove the existence of a literary relationship between the Synoptic Gospels, and it would seem they do not.

the material up to date. Since they had so thoroughly imbibed the tradition they saw themselves as representing, their own compositions often resembled them in register and phraseology, but what might look to a modern reader like a tissue of literary allusions would in fact be the recycling of traditional modes of expression and thought that had been thoroughly internalized.[13]

The Hellenistic School model envisages authors building upon collections of saying and anecdotes about the founder (of some philosophical or technical school in a profession such as medicine or building), but the end result might be similar. In particular the practical and educational ends served by both the scribal model and the school model were arguably closer in many respects to the purposes of early Christian literature such as the gospels than were the aims of much elite literature. Both scribal and technical literature were also more like the Synoptic Gospels in terms of their willingness to borrow the wording of sources.[14]

This scribal/school model bears some resemblance to the 'midrash' model Michael Goulder propounded for Matthew[15] but has been more thoroughly explored in Kirk's 'scholar' model. Kirk recognizes that attempts to privilege orality at the expense of writing in antiquity are overdone, but also highlights the dangers of over-correcting for this exaggerated orality thesis by exaggerating the role of literacy.[16] In place of what he regards as various inadequate models, Kirk proposes the use of a media-interface or oral-derived model, in which there is constant interaction between the spoken and written registers, so that orality and literacy are jointly constitutive of written texts.[17]

---

[13] See *WTG*, 73–8; Jan Assmann, *Religion and Cultural Memory* (tr. Rodney Livingstone; Stanford, CA: Stanford University Press, 2006), 113–17; Richard A. Horsley, *Scribes, Visionaries and the Politics of Second Temple Judea* (Louisville–London: Westminster John Knox, 2007), 90–108; David M. Carr, *Writing on the Tablet of the Heart: Origins of Scripture and Literature* (Oxford: Oxford University Press, 2005), 40–1; *QiM*, 60–73.

[14] Loveday Alexander, 'Luke's Preface in the Context of Greek Preface-Writing', *NovT* 28 (1986), 48–74; Loveday Alexander, 'Memory and Tradition in the Hellenistic Schools' in Werner H. Kelber and Samuel Byrskog (eds), *Jesus in Memory: Traditions in Oral and Scribal Perspectives* (Waco: Baylor University Press, 2009), 113–53; F. Gerald Downing, 'Writers' Use or Abuse of Written Sources' in Paul Foster, Andrew Gregory, John S. Kloppenborg and J. Verheyden (eds), *New Studies in the Synoptic Problem* (BETL, 139; Leuven: Leuven University Press, 2011), 523–48, here 524–36.

[15] M.D. Goulder, *Midrash and Lection in Matthew* (Eugene, OR: Wipf and Stock, 2004; original publication London, SPCK, 1974), 3–27, envisages Matthew as a scribe; the following chapter, pp. 28–69, describes what Goulder there describes as the 'midrashic method', although it rapidly becomes apparent that what Goulder has in mind is scribal text production through particular methods of scriptural interpretation rather than later rabbinic midrash. In the face of criticism from Philip. S. Alexander, 'Midrash and the Gospels' in Christopher M. Tuckett (ed.), *Synoptic Studies: The Ampleforth Conferences of 1982 and 1983* (JSNTSup, 7; Sheffield: JSOT Press, 1984), 1–18, Goulder later dropped the term 'midrash', instead referring to 'embroidering', by which he meant '(1) to elaborate the stories in scripture, for doctrinal or edifying purposes, and (2) to use a technique of association for this end' – see Goulder, *Luke*, 123–8.

[16] *QiM*, 11–14, 16–20; cf. my attempt to make similar points in Eve, *WTG*, 1–4, 24–6, 67–72. *QiM* and *WTG* both came out in 2016. Kirk and I take opposing views on the Synoptic Problem, but there is some convergence of the views we independently came to on compositional models. Kirk frequently appears as a conversation partner in the present study, although it has not always been possible to do full justice to every nuance of his thought in the space available.

[17] *QiM*, 11–12, 21.

Kirk insists that putting something in writing makes a difference: it allows the material to be coherently organized according to some unifying editorial policy within a framework supplied by a particular genre. The act of writing also causes any traditional material employed to be filtered through the scribal mentality of the writer, so that it becomes stamped with scribal patterns and habits. It allows the material to be arranged in stable relationships; items that were originally separate (or separable) are placed in a fixed arrangement. Moreover, writing allows the stable juxtaposition of different types of material. This allows the creation of durable networks of meaning among the parts that make up the work, so that, for example, it becomes possible to create argumentative patterns that would be unlikely to survive in purely oral transmission. Writing solidifies tradition in stable artefacts that organize the material in ways that may prompt fresh use of it in the tradition.[18]

Kirk observes that, in addition to the differences noted earlier, the evangelists' investment in their source material is very different from that of elite historians.[19] He accordingly proposes that Hellenistic scribes and Graeco-Roman scholars might provide better parallels. While some scribes received only a rudimentary training in basic literacy and performed only low-level clerical functions, other ancient Near Eastern scribes were of higher status and might also be scholars. A comparable class of people could be found in Greece and Rome. Such persons had more advanced literate and scholarly abilities, and often pursued their scholarship alongside more mundane activities such as school-teaching. The school tradition discussed by Loveday Alexander included persons of this sort, and Kirk follows Alexander in proposing that scholars of this type might provide a closer analogue to the working methods of the evangelists.[20]

It is unclear whether any of these models provide a perfect fit to the evangelists. While the scribal model may be a reasonably good fit for Matthew, it is perhaps only a partial fit for Luke. The gospels seem to be more rhetorically aware and more narratively elaborate than the typical products of scribes and schools. It is by no means straightforward to determine the educational and social levels of the evangelists, who were, on the one hand, capable of quite sophisticated narrative composition employing recognized rhetorical techniques, but who, on the other, wrote in relatively unsophisticated koine Greek and show no signs of enjoying the elite status that would

---

[18] *QiM*, 21–8; cf. Erhardt Güttgemanns, *Candid Questions Concerning Gospel Form Criticism: A Methodological Sketch of the Fundamental Problems of Form and Redaction Criticism* (PTMS, 26; tr. William G. Doty; Pittsburgh, PA: Pickwick Press, 1979), 277–90; and Werner H. Kelber, *The Oral and the Written Gospel: The Hermeneutics of Speaking and Writing in the Synoptic Tradition, Mark, Paul and Q* (VPT; Bloomington: Indiana University Press, 1997), 105–16.

[19] *QiM*, 59; cf. *WTG*, 124. In Luke's case, note the argument of David P. Moessner, 'Luke as Tradent and Hermeneut', *NovT* 58 (2016), 259–300, that the force of παρηκολουθηκότι at Lk. 1.3 is to claim not that the author has thoroughly researched his material but that he has both 'experienced familiarity with' and 'informed competence in' the traditions with which he is working; his principal credential for writing is thus his long-term familiarity with the tradition of which he aims to be both tradent and interpreter.

[20] *QiM*, 60–73; cf. Alexander, 'Memory and Tradition in the Hellenistic Schools', 113–53; Horsley, *Scribes*, 90–108; *WTG*, 16–19, 73–8.

be the normal prerequisite for a full rhetorical education.²¹ It is probably best to take an eclectic approach, seeing the composition of the gospels as drawing on elements of both the elite and the scribal models, perhaps, in Luke's case, as the result of a scholarly or technical author trying his hand at a more literary composition, supported by at least the rudiments of a rhetorical education, or perhaps of someone who had gained experience from acting as literary assistant to an elite author.²²

Memory

The composition of the gospels will have depended heavily on both the individual memory of the evangelists and the collective memory of their communities. While these two facets of memory thoroughly interpenetrate in practice, it will be convenient to treat each in turn.

Memorization formed a central part of pre-modern education across a wide range of cultures ranging from ancient Mesopotamia to at least the end of the European Middle Ages; the ancient world developed and taught a number of memory techniques which it bequeathed to the medieval one.²³ Because virtuosity with memory was valued for its own sake and because reading materials were relatively inaccessible and cumbersome to use, but perhaps even more to enculturate the next generation into the values of their society, educated persons were expected to learn a considerable body of texts by heart (often verbatim, though for some texts and some purposes memory of gist might suffice). Pre-modern authors thus often worked primarily from

---

[21] Estimates of Luke's literary competence vary. For example, John Moles, 'Luke's Preface: The Greek Decree, Classical Historiography and Christian Redefinitions', *NTS* 57 (2011), 461–82, Heather M. Gorman, 'Crank or Creative Genius? How Ancient Rhetoric Makes Sense of Luke's Order' in John C. Poirier and Jeff Peterson (eds), *Marcan Priority without Q: Explorations in the Farrer Hypothesis* (LNTS, 455; London: Bloomsbury T&T Clark, 2015), 62–81, and Michael W. Martin, 'Progymnastic Topic Lists: A Compositional Template for Luke and Other Bioi?', *NTS* 54 (2008), 18–41, all highlight features of Luke's writing they believe point to his advanced rhetorical training and high level of literary competence. This is disputed by Osvaldo Padilla, 'Hellenistic παιδεία and Luke's Education: A Critique of Recent Approaches', *NTS* 55 (2009), 416–37, on the basis both of Luke's composition of speeches and of the absence of classical allusions in his work, although Padilla allows that a rhetorical education gained in Jewish circles might be more focused on Moses and David than Homer and Demosthenes. In common with Steve Reece, '"Aesop," "Q" and "Luke,"' *NTS* 62 (2016), 357–77, here 367–9, Padilla nevertheless allows that Luke probably underwent a primary and secondary education but then had a technical rather than rhetorical tertiary one. This resembles the position of Loveday Alexander, *The Preface to Luke's Gospel: Literary Convention and Social Context in Luke 1.1–4 and Acts 1.1* (SNTSMS, 78; Cambridge: Cambridge University Press, repr. Paperback 2005 edn, 1993), esp. 169–86, 210–11. Sean A. Adams, 'Luke and *Progymnasmata*: Rhetorical Handbooks, Rhetorical Sophistication and Genre Selection' in Matthew Ryan Hauge and Andrew Pitts (eds), *Ancient Education and Early Christianity* (LNTS, 533; London: Bloomsbury T&T Clark, 2016), 137–54, takes a similar view while cautioning that the *Progymnasmata* straddled the secondary and tertiary levels of education.

[22] That such persons existed is suggested, for example, by Josephus, *Apion*, 1.50, mentioning assistants who helped him with his Greek in composing the *Jewish War*.

[23] Carr, *Writing*, esp. 27–8, 71–5, 96–9, 125, 135–7, 156, 180–2, 208–9, 228–30, 236–7, 247–8; Mary Carruthers, *The Book of Memory: A Study of Memory in Medieval Culture* (CSML; Cambridge: Cambridge University Press, 2nd edn, 2008), 89–92, 172–86; Frances A. Yates, *The Art of Memory* (London: Pimlico, 1992), 17–92; Small, *Wax Tablets*, 81–116.

their memory of their sources.²⁴ In the absence of modern scholarly habits of precise citation and quotation, they had no need to keep looking them up, but could usually rely on their memory to be good enough for the purpose on hand. Ancient authors could and did consult written texts in the course of conducting their research, and it is hardly likely that every written text was considered worth memorizing, but to be considered well-educated someone would generally be expected to have good memory command of texts that were considered culturally important. Furthermore, having a good memory meant not simply the ability to retain and regurgitate considerable quantities of text (although it would, of course, require that) but also the ability to process the remembered text in memory and combine it with other material to produce one's own compositions.

Thus, as Kirk notes, memory competence gave mastery of a store of materials that one could draw upon to formulate new writing and speech; it enabled the activation of a tradition, leading to the scribal use of mastered tradition as a source for the composition of new works that in turn became part of that tradition.²⁵ As Kirk expresses it:

> Scribal transmission of a cultural work was conceived not merely on technical lines of textual reproduction but on moral lines as the authentic realization of a normative tradition. Authenticity in manuscript transmission was a moral category, an ethical commitment to the tradition ... The scribal obligation to preserve and transmit a normative tradition conjoined with the didactic obligation to make it responsive to contemporary contexts. Transmission and cultivation converged; it is the differential interaction of these two vectors that is constitutive of manuscript tradition, giving rise to its patterns of variation and agreement.²⁶

Scribal exegesis could be seen as the creative redeployment of traditional elements whereby scribes employed memory to assemble traditions into new combinations. Scribes acting as tradents were thus competent not only in written but also in oral, memory-based tradition, and indeed many surviving manuscript traditions appear to have needed (or at least to have had) an ongoing oral tradition to supplement them.²⁷

Kirk insists that scribal memory would be constrained by the logical ordering of its written sources, meaning that there were limits on the possible reordering of source material. But while it is eminently reasonable to take account of psychological and cultural constraints on the scribal use of memory, one may question whether Kirk's view is unduly restrictive.

The key issue here is how memory retrieval and cueing operate. It is easy enough to envisage Matthew or Luke using Mark from memory when they are following Mark's

---

[24] Mattila, 'Question', 214–15.
[25] WTG, 73–8, 81–6; QiM, 93–9.
[26] QiM, 117.
[27] QiM, 110–22. For an example of the interplay of oral and written traditions, see Martin S. Jaffee, *Torah in the Mouth: Writing and Oral Tradition in Palestinian Judaism, 200 BCE–400 CE* (Oxford: Oxford University Press, 2001).

order through the use of forward sequential cueing, the mechanism that allows people to recite a poem or text in its original order.[28] But this is not the only possible retrieval mechanism. Retrieval operates by progressing from one or more *cues* to the *target memory* (the item one wishes to recall). Cues enable retrieval through *associations* or *links* (which link one memory to another), and retrieval can be achieved by a variety of cues. There are no restrictions on the kinds of mnemonic link that can be made, although some will be far stronger than others, and there are a number of factors that can either strengthen or weaken the effectiveness of potential cues.[29] A mundane example given by Baddeley et al. concerns the different cues to remembering I ate peas with my dinner last night. I might be prompted by the question 'What did you eat last night?' or by the question 'When did you last eat peas?' or by the smell of peas or by the radio playing the same music I was listening to when dining on peas or by seeing a plate of peas (or, no doubt, by numerous other cues).[30]

At least some people in antiquity were well able to retrieve material in a non-linear fashion. According to Mary Carruthers, 'One accomplishment which always seems to have been greatly admired by both ancient and medieval writers was the ability to recite a text backwards as well as forward, or to skip around it in a systematic way without getting confused.' She goes on to cite the example of one Simplicius, who could, on demand, supply all the penultimate verses in each book of Virgil from memory or move forwards or backwards in memory through Cicero's orations.[31] Carruthers goes on to point out that 'the proof of a good memory lies not in the simple retention and regurgitation even of large amounts of material. Rather, it is the ability to move it around instantly, directly, and securely that is admired'.[32] While the evangelists may not have equalled the memory virtuosity of the examples Carruthers cites, we should not be too quick to restrict what memory could achieve.[33]

New Testament and Jewish authors could on occasion cite and allude to widely scattered parts of the Old Testament. For example, Paul summoned a catena of biblical citations at Rom. 3.10-18 to make the point that all alike are under sin and retrieved the opening of Psalm 32 at Rom. 4.7-8 to argue that righteousness does not come from works.[34] In the *Migration of Abraham*, Philo was able to weave a substantial allegorical commentary on a couple of verses of Genesis drawing on material from scattered locations throughout the Pentateuch (as we shall see in Chapter 3); it is hard to see how this could have been achieved other than by some form of non-

---

[28] David C. Rubin, *Memory in Oral Traditions: The Cognitive Psychology of Epic, Ballads, and Counting-out Rhymes* (Oxford: Oxford University Press, 1995), esp. 39-193; Alan Baddeley, Michael W. Eysenck and Michael C. Anderson, *Memory* (Hove: Psychology Press, 2009), 170; Eric Eve, *Behind the Gospels: Understanding the Oral Tradition* (London: SPCK, 2013), 100-2.

[29] *WTG*, 94-5; Baddeley et al., *Memory*, 165-80.

[30] Baddeley et al., *Memory*, 165-6. With the smell of peas, compare Marcel Proust's memory associations with the smell of a madeleine, discussed as an example of (involuntary) associative memory by Daniel L. Schacter, *Searching for Memory: The Brain, the Mind, and the Past* (New York: Basic Books, 1996), 26-8, 120-1.

[31] Carruthers, *Book of Memory*, 21, citing Augustine, *De natura et origine animae* 4.7.9 on Simplicius.

[32] Carruthers, *Book of Memory*, 21-2.

[33] Cf. the discussion in Gregory, 'Literary Dependence', 95-103.

[34] For the Romans 4 example in the light of rabbinic exegesis, see Steve Moyise, *The Old Testament in the New: An Introduction* (CBSS; London: Continuum, 2001), 25.

sequential associative cueing. Moreover, at least four of the seven interpretative rules attributed to Hillel (argument from analogy, extension from one biblical texts to topically related texts, extension by derivation from two biblical texts and derivation from something similar in another passage) would seem to rely on non-sequential associative linking.[35]

Kirk's apparent insistence that a writer's memory could *only* access material by employing the 'organizational network of cues' constituted by 'habituated narrative sequences' and 'conventional moral *topoi*' and '*topoi*-sequences' thus needs qualifying (and Kirk does to some extent qualify it himself).[36] We shall return to this issue in Chapter 3, but for now we should note that while it is impossible to assess the evangelists' precise mnemonic abilities, we should probably reckon on their lying somewhere between that of the memory virtuosi and the mere ability to follow sequential cues.[37]

In any case, it seems unlikely that either Matthew or Luke would have produced their complete gospels in one go on the basis of their own unaided individual memories alone. It seems far more likely that the process of composition involved more than one draft, and that it may also have involved some degree of note-taking and assistance from collaborators.[38]

Also important is collective memory. This refers primarily to the means by which a group configures its past in the service of group identity and orientation towards its future. Such means may include oral traditions, ways of behaving, commemorative rituals and ceremonies (such as the Lord's Supper) and written texts. Collective memory is thus primarily a process rather than a thing, but by extension it can also refer to the content of commonly held beliefs about the past and to the way that past is evaluated. This may often include the reputation of salient heroes and villains who embody either the values the community stands for or those to which it is opposed. It will likely include stories that explain how and why the community came into being, what it stands for and where it should aspire to be going, providing guidance for behaviour and orientation for values.

Collective memory (like individual memory) has a complex relation to the actual past. It is neither the same thing as history (which involves a more deliberate and methodical reflection on the past) nor wholly divorced from it. Theories of collective memory that see it as largely a present construction based on no more than fragments of the real past are problematic. Collective memory is better seen as an ongoing dialogue between the past and the present, in which the past is viewed through the frameworks of present needs and perceptions, while those same frameworks have been

---

[35] Günter Stemberger, *Introduction to the Talmud and Midrash* (tr. Markus Bockmuehl; Edinburgh: T&T Clark, 2nd edn, 1996), 18–20.
[36] Alan Kirk, 'Memory, Scribal Media, and the Synoptic Problem' in Paul Foster, Andrew Gregory, John S. Kloppenborg and J. Verheyden (eds), *New Studies in the Synoptic Problem* (BETL, 139; Leuven: Leuven University Press, 2011), 459–82, here 463. Kirk cites Rubin, *Memory*, 90–101, 143, 293, in support of his position, but Rubin's concern is to explain how serial cueing might be facilitated, not to rule out other kinds of cueing.
[37] See also the discussion in *WTG*, 93–9.
[38] *WTG*, 145–6.

inherited from the past, so that past and present constantly reshape each other. Many aspects of the past continue to impinge on the present and thus cannot be ignored by either history or memory. Individual people may be suggestible to some degree and individual memories are undoubtedly shaped and reshaped by their social contexts, but there are limits to how far people can be systematically misled about their own pasts. The past also continues to live on in its physical remains, social institutions and historical effects. And yet there is often more than one way in which the past, including the reputation of salient individuals, can be understood and constructed in the present. The collective memory with which the evangelists had to do was thus not simply a fund of useful information about Jesus; it was also part of the cognitive, conative and affective stream of tradition in which they swam and from which they imbibed.

Collective memory is something that would have both empowered and constrained the evangelists. It would have empowered them insofar as it provided traditions on which they could draw and with which they could rely on their own work resonating; it would have constrained them insofar as their gospels would have needed to resonate with existing collective memory to be accepted as authoritative. That does not mean that the evangelists could not attempt to challenge and remould collective memory, but it constrains the ways in which they could do so. In particular the Jesus they presented had to be recognizably the same Jesus their target audience were already familiar with, and his words and deeds would have to be at least broadly congruent with how that Jesus was already understood. A change in circumstances might nevertheless bring about a change in the way the tradition was interpreted and evaluated, so that a narrative that reconfigured previous interpretations towards current circumstances might well get a ready hearing. This does not mean that the evangelists would have been confined merely to reacting to changes in circumstances; they were not merely passive vehicles of shifts in community memory, and it is reasonable to suppose that they had their own agendas. But it does mean that they had to reckon with the existing tradition, effectively making them part-tradents as well as part-authors.[39]

The evangelists' purpose

Writing a gospel would not be a trivial undertaking under the conditions of antiquity. It would nevertheless confer a number of advantages over purely oral transmission. By

---

[39] On collective memory in relation to the gospels, see further *WTG*, 103–24; Samuel Byrskog, 'A New Quest for the *Sitz im Leben*: Social Memory, the Jesus Tradition and the Gospel of Matthew', *NTS* 52 (2006), 319–36; Barry Schwartz, 'Where There's Smoke, There's Fire: Memory and History' in Tom Thatcher (ed.), *Memory and Identity in Ancient Judaism and Early Christianity: A Conversation with Barry Schwartz* (Semeia Studies, 78; ed. G.O. West; Atlanta: SBL, 2014), 7–37; Alan Kirk and Tom Thatcher, 'Jesus Tradition as Social Memory' in Alan Kirk and Tom Thatcher (eds), *Memory, Tradition, and Text: Uses of the Past in Early Christianity* (SBL SS, 52; Leiden; Boston: Brill, 2005), 25–42; Alan Kirk, 'Social and Cultural Memory' in Kirk and Thatcher (eds), *Memory, Tradition, and Text*, 1–24; Chris Keith, 'Social Memory Theory and Gospels Research: The First Decade (Part One)', *EC* 6 (2015), 354–76; Chris Keith, 'Social Memory Theory and Gospels Research: The First Decade (Part Two)', *EC* 6 (2015), 517–42.

committing one's account of Jesus to writing, one had a far better chance of preserving it through time and disseminating it across space. Whereas each occasion on which a story of Jesus was retold orally would tend to reshape it to suit the occasion and the audience, a narrative committed to manuscript would remain relatively stable, allowing the particular interpretation of the Jesus tradition inscribed in that manuscript (and subsequent copies of the manuscript) to endure.

Jan Assmann has suggested that as the time from an originating event grows longer *communicative memory* (i.e. memory passed on by word of mouth from the original witnesses) must give way to *cultural memory* if memory of the originating event is to survive. Such a transformation may often be precipitated by a *Traditionsbruch* (rupture in tradition), typically occurring forty years or so after the originating events.[40] In societies with writing, cultural memory generally depends on the production of written texts, since these are far more effective in solidifying collective memory than the rehearsal of oral traditions at festivals and rituals. The purely oral propagation of cultural memory requires the presence of a competent performer who is expert in the relevant tradition together with a receptive audience at particular festivals. Where, however, cultural memory is mediated by written texts, all that is needed is a copy of the text and someone competent to read it aloud. Written texts are therefore far more efficient at solidifying cultural memory since performances of them are far more readily available.[41]

Assmann further suggests that cultural texts have two kinds of function, *formative* and *normative*. The formative function is to provide an account of origins that explains to a community what it is, how it got that way and what it stands for. The normative function is to explain how members of that community should behave and what values they should espouse.[42] The gospels might reasonably be described as formative and normative texts designed to promote, explain and cement Christian identity and provide guidance for Christian living.

This does not, however, explain why more than one gospel should have been written. Yet circumstances change and collective memory is often contested memory. If Matthew, Mark, Luke and John (together with the authors of the many apocryphal gospels) wrote different texts, it is most probably because they had different convictions about how Christian identity should be understood. Moreover, once one gospel had been written, anyone who wanted to promote a different vision of the matters it covered would need to produce another written text to compete with it.

---

[40] Jan Assmann, *Cultural Memory and Early Civilization: Writing, Remembrance, and Political Imagination* (tr. David Henry Wilson; Cambridge: Cambridge University Press, 2011), 34–41; cf. Werner H. Kelber, 'The Works of Memory: Christian Origins as MnemoHistory – A Response' in Alan Kirk and Tom Thatcher (eds), *Memory, Tradition, and Text: Uses of the Past in Early Christianity* (SBL Semeia Studies, 52; ed. G.A. Yee; Leiden; Boston: Brill, 2005), 221–48, here 244, reprinted in Kelber, *Imprints*, 265–96 (290).

[41] Assmann, *Religion*, 103–14; Chris Keith, 'Prolegomena on the Textualization of Mark's Gospel: Manuscript Culture, the Extended Situation, and the Emergence of the Written Gospel' in Tom Thatcher (ed.), *Memory and Identity in Ancient Judaism and Early Christianity: A Conversation with Barry Schwartz* (SS, 78; Atlanta: SBL, 2014), 161–86; *WTG*, 26–8.

[42] Assmann, *Religion*, 38, 104.

I previously argued that Luke and Matthew intended not only to compete with but to replace their predecessor gospels.[43] Matthew incorporated so much of Mark into his own composition as to render Mark virtually redundant. On the other hand, Luke used rather less of Mark. Presumably Mark was one of the 'many' narratives earlier writers had attempted which Luke now thought he could improve upon by offering his own orderly account (Lk. 1.1-4). If Luke stopped short of explicitly criticizing his predecessors, criticism is nevertheless implied by the assumption that Luke thought he could do better (otherwise, he would have no reason to write). But 'doing better' could in principle mean writing something Luke considered better suited to his target audience (a Gentile church becoming aware of its separation from historic Israel, say) rather than a desire to displace his predecessors altogether. Rather than setting out to replace Matthew and Mark, then, it may be better to see FH Luke as intending to compete with or emulate them.[44] John may be even further from intending to displace his predecessors (presumably the Synoptic Gospels), aiming instead to supplement them while presupposing some knowledge of them in his target audience.

Either way, Matthew and Luke probably had different attitudes towards their sources from that of an elite historian. For example, when Josephus, a writer with whom Luke is frequently compared, employed the Septuagint as his principal source for the first half of his *Jewish Antiquities* it was hardly with the intent of displacing or competing with his Greek Bible, any more than Philo intended to replace or compete with the Pentateuch with his Lives of Abraham, Joseph, and Moses or his expositions of the Pentateuchal laws. Graeco-Roman writers will often have used sources for the information they contained, and presumably will often have hoped to improve on them in terms of literary polish, but they would seldom have been concerned to suppress or subvert their message in the interests of constructing community identity in a different way; often their primary aims were to inform and entertain (and to enhance their own literary standing in the course of so doing), not to shape and solidify the cultural memory of a relatively new minority group. And while Philo and Josephus were working with centrally important cultural texts that were strongly embedded in the collective memory of their people (though not necessarily that of the target audience for whom they were writing), this would seldom be the case with the sources employed by elite Graeco-Roman historians and biographers. It follows that Matthew and Luke might not handle their sources in the manner typical of elite Graeco-Roman authors. As already noted, the evangelists will have been at least part-tradents as well as part-authors.

While the evangelists may thus have had many purposes in common, they will also have differed. This is not the place for a lengthy discussion of the aims of each

---

[43] *WTG*, 29–32; in part following David C. Sim, 'Matthew's Use of Mark: Did Matthew Intend to Supplement or to Replace His Primary Source?', *NTS* 57 (2011), 176–92; John C. Poirier, 'Delbert Burkett's Defence of Q' in John C. Poirier and Jeff Peterson (eds), *Marcan Priority without Q: Explorations in the Farrer Hypothesis* (LNTS, 455; London: Bloomsbury T&T Clark, 2015), 191–225, here 208–9.

[44] *Pace* Poirier, 'Delbert Burkett's Defence', 208–9, this may be closer to the position of Eric Franklin, *Luke: Interpreter of Paul, Critic of Matthew* (JSNTSup, 92; Sheffield: JSOT, 1994), 169–73.

individual evangelist, but it will be helpful to offer a brief sketch of why Matthew and Luke may have been motivated to improve on the work of their predecessors.

While Mark's Gospel has fascinated many modern readers, the very indeterminacies that might appeal to postmodern sensibilities could well have proved frustrating to ancient ones. The seemingly truncated ending with the woman fleeing in silent terror from the Empty Tomb at Mk 16.8 is the most obvious example. The existence of subsequent additions to Mark's ending indicates that Matthew and Luke would not have been the only ancient readers of Mark to find it less than satisfactory. Mark makes it clear that the death of Jesus was part of the divine plan, central to Jesus' role as Son of Man, Messiah and Son of God, thereby countering the scandal of a crucified Messiah, and Matthew and Luke are in sufficient agreement with Mark on this that they can employ his gospel as the basis of their own. But beyond that Mark's intent is not always clear. His Christology can be interpreted in more than one way, while so much of Jesus' relatively limited teaching in Mark seems focused on the need for cross-bearing discipleship that Markan audiences may have been left wondering how they were meant to *live* as Christians. Both Matthew and Luke may well have felt that Mark failed to give an adequately rounded view of Christian discipleship and Matthew in particular seems to have felt Mark's narrative left too many gaps and ambiguities, since his changes to Mark often take the form of tying up Markan loose ends.

Matthew appears to have been a Christian Jew writing primarily for other Christian Jews. His attitude towards Gentiles is ambivalent: while he promotes the Gentile mission (Mt. 28.19-20), he does so on the basis of converts obeying Jesus' commands, which he presents as Messianically interpreted Torah (5.17-20). Elsewhere he tends to use the term 'Gentiles' disparagingly (5.47; 6.7, 32; 18.17) and maintains that the earthly Jesus gave priority to Israel (10.5-6). He assumes his audience will practise Jewish forms of piety (6.1-18) and that they will pay the temple tax or the *fiscus Judaicus* that replaced it (17.24-27). Matthew's Jesus offers his own interpretation of the Torah, which is to exceed the righteous of the scribes and Pharisees (5.20), against whom he engages in particularly fierce polemic, probably because Matthew sees them as types for the Jewish leadership of his own day. This suggests that Matthew and his principal target audience belonged to a form of Christian Judaism that has been disowned by formative (or early rabbinic) Judaism and was now recruiting from the wider Gentile world. Matthew's Gospel attempts to present his own group as true Israel, inheriting all the promises of the Law and the Prophets, in contradistinction to a mainstream Judaism that (in his view) has gone astray through the hypocrisy of its leaders and rejection of its Messiah. Among Matthew's main emphases are first, that contrary to superficial appearances, Jesus really is Jesus' expected Messiah since he indeed fulfils the relevant prophecies; second, that despite what other Jews might say, it is Matthew's group who now constitute true Israel since it is they who follow the true interpretation of Israel's Torah; and third, that while one's eternal destiny rests upon obedience to Jesus' stringent commands, God is willing to be merciful to those who exhibit mercy.

There is much in both Mark and Matthew that FH Luke would have found valuable, allowing him to use both earlier gospels as major sources for his own work. But Luke's perspective is different from Matthew's. Whereas Matthew appears to be a Jew writing primarily for other Jews (while encouraging them to welcome Gentile believers), Luke seems to be a Gentile addressing a mainly Gentile church that is coming to terms with being an entity separate from historic Israel. Luke concurs with Matthew in emphasizing continuity with what has gone before, but he constructs this continuity differently. Matthew's community is seen as true Israel through its adherence to the Messianically interpreted Torah, while Gentiles are viewed as outsiders who might potentially be brought into the fold. Luke's community is viewed as the successor to an Israel that has largely rejected its Messiah and so has forfeited its place in God's scheme of salvation history. The Church Luke envisages is characterized by repentance and acceptance of the offer of salvation, not by any residual loyalty to the Torah, except in the attenuated sense of embracing Israelite monotheism, rejecting idolatry and adopting appropriate standards of ethical behaviour. Luke shares with Matthew the perception of the Church as a continuation of the story of God's dealings with Israel and a fulfilment of promises and prophecies made to Israel, but his perspective on Israel is that of a non-Israelite.

If FH Luke understood Matthew along the lines suggested here, he could well have felt ambivalent towards it. Matthew contained a great deal of material that was valuable for Christian life and practice (as its widespread reception by the Church demonstrates), but its perspectives on matters such as Israel, Gentiles and the Torah could well have appeared problematic to a Luke concerned to provide a largely Gentile audience with assurance or security (ἀσφάλειαν – Lk. 1.4) about their place in the people of God. For all its virtues, Matthew's Gospel did not construct and confirm Christian identity the way Luke wanted it understood. In particular, although the Torah had its place in the piety of devout Israelites, Luke wanted to play down any suggestion that it laid any continuing obligations on Gentiles (Acts 15). This in itself would require a radical reshaping of Matthew's Sermon on the Mount, along with the suppression of any other material devoted to the finer details of Torah observance, which Luke would have deemed irrelevant to his target audience. Moreover, Luke's decision to write a second volume would have impacted on what he included in his first. Given that the start of the Gentile mission was to mark a significant turning point in Acts, Luke might reasonably want to avoid anticipating it too far in his gospel. Similarly, Luke's presentation of the post-ascension Jesus reigning from heaven in Acts might lead to his downplaying any Matthean tendency to superimpose the Risen Christ upon the earthly Jesus.

Matthew's Gospel subsequently proved highly popular in the (predominantly Gentile) Church, without its Jewish perspective apparently providing any great obstacle to its use. But FH Luke was writing at a time when the relatively new Gentile church was less sure of either its identity or its legitimacy. It would be in such a situation that Luke perceived the need for a gospel better suited than Matthew to the needs of his target audience.

Markan priority

The FH and the 2DH concur that Mark's Gospel was used as a source by both Matthew and Luke, so there is little need to justify Markan priority at length here.[45] Since, however, Markan priority is a fundamental assumption throughout this study it may be worth reviewing it briefly and going on to discuss some of its implications.

Many of the earlier arguments for Markan priority have long been recognized as inconclusive, although some of them continue to be suggestive. Mark is roughly coextensive with the material common to all three Synoptic Gospels and generally agrees with either Luke or Matthew in the ordering of that material. Earlier advocacy of Markan priority took this to indicate that Luke and Matthew must therefore have used Mark as a source, but such patterns of agreement are logically compatible with any sequence of dependence (e.g. defenders of the 2GH would argue that the common material and ordering came about through Mark's conflation of Matthew and Luke). It might seem more natural to envisage Matthew and Luke expanding Mark with additional material than to think of Mark truncating Matthew and Luke at both ends and omitting so much valuable teaching material while often expanding his narratives, but the latter is not inconceivable. One can at least imagine a Mark who wanted to produce a short, fast-paced, dramatic narrative suitable for performance in one sitting and who therefore cut out most of the sayings material and added additional narrative touches. It is less clear, however, why such a Mark should work from both Matthew and Luke since the desired result could have been arrived at more easily by simply abbreviating one or the other.

Again, while it is not impossible for an author to write less well (or more colloquially) than his sources,[46] Mark's Greek is the least literary of the three Synoptic Gospels, and it seems more likely that both Matthew and Luke improved on it in than that Mark composed his gospel in a more colloquial register on the basis of their accounts.[47]

---

[45] For defences of Markan priority, see, e.g., Mark Goodacre, *The Case against Q: Studies in Markan Priority and the Synoptic Problem* (Harrisburg, PA: Trinity Press International, 2002), 19–45; G.M. Styler, 'Excursus IV: The Priority of Mark' in C.F.D. Moule (ed.), *The Birth of the New Testament* (London: A&C Black, 3rd edn, 1981), 285–316; John S. Kloppenborg Verbin, *Excavating Q: The History and Setting of the Sayings Gospel* (Edinburgh: T&T Clark, 2000), 11–54; W.D. Davies and Dale C. Allison, *A Critical and Exegetical Commentary on the Gospel according to Saint Matthew* (ICC; Edinburgh: T&T Clark, 1988), vol. 1, 97–114; Eric Eve, 'The Synoptic Problem without Q?' in Paul Foster, Andrew Gregory, John S. Kloppenborg and J. Verheyden (eds), *New Studies in the Synoptic Problem* (BETL, 139; Leuven: Leuven University Press, 2011), 551–70, here 553–6; Craig A. Evans, 'The Two Source Hypothesis' in Stanley E. Porter and Bryan R. Dyer (eds), *The Synoptic Problem: Four Views* (Grand Rapids, MI: Baker Academic, 2016), 27–45, here 28–35, and, classically, Burnett Hillman Streeter, *The Four Gospels: A Study of Origins Treating of the Manuscript Tradition, Sources, Authorship, & Dates* (London: Macmillan, 1926), 157–69.

[46] E.P. Sanders and Margaret Davies, *Studying the Synoptic Gospels* (London: SCM, 1989), 72.

[47] Nicholas A. Elder, *The Media Matrix of Early Jewish and Christian Narrative* (LNTS, 612; London: Bloomsbury T&T Clark, 2019), 61–93, 145–65, makes a strong case for identifying oral linguistic residues in Mark that Matthew and Luke redact in a more literary direction. Alex Damm, *Ancient Rhetoric and the Synoptic Problem: Clarifying Markan Priority* (BETL, 252; Leuven: Peeters, 2013), 59–60, argues that an author would be more likely to adapt source material to better conform to rhetorical convention, which he goes on to argue more plausibly explains what Matthew and Luke would have done with Mark than the other way around.

An important argument for Markan priority is the evidence of editorial fatigue and resultant inconcinnities in Matthew and Luke. For example, at Mt. 20.20-21 the mother of James and John appears out of nowhere to ask Jesus to give her sons the places of honour when he comes into his kingdom. She then disappears back into nowhere when Jesus addresses his reply to her two sons (Mt. 20.22-23), as he does in Mark (10.35-40) where the mother never puts in an appearance at all. This looks suspiciously like Matthew's clumsy attempt to avoid these two disciples making this inappropriate request for themselves. The existence of examples of this sort is easiest to explain if Mark was a source for Matthew and Luke.[48]

The term 'editorial fatigue' might be taken to suggest an editor working with a source open in front of him and attempting to edit it in much the way we would a modern printed text. If, as suggested here, Matthew and Luke were not so much editing Mark by sight but reworking him from memory, then editorial fatigue needs re-envisaging as a form of memory error.[49] It might in any case be easier to imagine an author working from memory making errors of this sort than one who has his source text constantly before his eyes. Aspects of the remembered text could easily be overlooked in the course of mental recomposition, leading to the minor infelicities that occur from time to time in the later texts.

Perhaps the greatest difficulty for Markan posteriority (on the 2GH), however, is the implausibility of the procedure it attributes to Mark. 2GH Mark would have to be capable of the close comparison of two documents (either by eye or from memory) to work out their common order and wording (where it is common) and to reconcile or conflate it (where it is not). Yet the Mark who is capable of this extraordinarily sophisticated literary effort ends up writing less sophisticated Greek than either of his sources, which makes him appear a strangely self-contradictory figure. Moreover, even when presented with coherent accounts of such pericopae as the Temptation and the Beelzebul Controversy, in both his sources he apparently chooses to abbreviate them, in the former case to the point of cryptic obscurity, while nevertheless adding a mass of extraneous detail to stories such as those of the Gerasene Demoniac. Admittedly a 2GH Mark with good memory command of both his sources could produce a degree of perhaps accidental verbal conflation in the course of his own composition, but even if this is allowed, the other difficulties remain.

An even greater difficulty attends the Mark envisaged by Delbert Burkett, who has to conflate up to five sources, the two principal ones being Proto-Mark A and Proto-Mark B (which are each derived from an original Proto-Mark).[50] Even though Burkett's Mark seldom has to conflate so many sources at once, the procedure attributed to him is both suspiciously awkward and suspiciously wooden. Burkett's Mark is modelled on Tatian, but whereas Tatian had a plausible motive to attempt the harmonization of four gospels that were seen as authoritative, it is far from clear why Mark should carry

---

[48] See Mark Goodacre, 'Fatigue in the Synoptics', *NTS* 44 (1998), 45–58, here 45–54; and Styler, 'Priority of Mark', 293–8, 304–9.
[49] *WTG*, 100–1.
[50] Delbert Burkett, *Rethinking the Gospel Sources: From Proto-Mark to Mark* (New York: T&T Clark, 2004), 224–66.

out the close conflation of two versions of Proto-Mark together with three further minor sources.[51]

Burkett is attempting to argue that none of the canonical gospels is directly dependent on any of the others. His arguments against the priority of canonical Mark partly relate to divergences of order in the triple tradition, especially in Matthew chapters 8 and 9,[52] but he mainly relies on indications of Markan redaction supposedly absent from Matthew and Luke, in particular Matthew's and Luke's avoidance of innocuous Markan terms such as πολύς, πάλιν, ἴδε and φημί.[53] A similar argument is mounted against Mark's and Luke's use of Matthew.[54] Both Alan Kirk and David Neville have criticized Burkett, arguing in particular that statistics of words apparently avoided by a later evangelists do not tell the whole story; one must also take particular compositional and redactional contexts into account.[55] For example, it is not that Matthew and Luke systematically avoid characteristic Markan words such as πολύς and πάλιν when otherwise copying Mark; it is rather that these terms often fall victim to the later evangelists' substantial rewriting or abridgement of their source. One might further object that Matthew's and Luke's consistent suppression of, say, a characteristically Markan φημί in favour of λέγω is not obviously any odder than canonical Mark's suppression of Proto-Mark's λέγω in favour of φημί where it occurs in his sources (which would be implied by Burkett's view).

While Kirk appears to dismiss Burkett's work altogether, Neville ends up cautiously allowing that Burkett has made the case for a redactional layer in canonical Mark unknown to Matthew and Luke, while suggesting that Burkett should first have considered the case for a single Proto-Mark before multiplying hypothetical sources.[56] Given Neville's detailed critique of Burkett, this conclusion is perhaps surprising, but in light of Neville's suggestion that a single Proto-Mark might suffice, it may amount to little more than a recognition that the copies of Mark used by Matthew and Luke are unlikely to have contained a text identical to modern reconstructions of canonical Mark.

Neville's more extended discussion emphasizes the point more fully than Kirk's briefer one, but both critics concur in seeing Burkett as (wrongly) relying on a 'copy-and-edit' model of composition rather than envisaging the evangelists as composing from memory.[57] Both critics thus tacitly acknowledge that Burkett's case against Markan priority would gain more traction if the evangelists were seen primarily as compiler-copyists closely following their written sources. From this it follows that the thesis of Markan priority suggests a model of composition in which writers relied on their long-term or short-term memory of what they had gleaned from their sources

---

[51] Cf. Neville, 'The Phantom Returns', 149.
[52] Burkett, *Rethinking*, 60–74.
[53] Burkett, *Rethinking*, 7–42
[54] Burkett, *Rethinking*, 43–59.
[55] Alan Kirk, 'Orality, Writing, and Phantom Sources: Appeals to Ancient Media in Some Recent Challenges to the Two Document Hypothesis', NTS 58 (2012), 1–22, here 11–16; Neville, 'The Phantom Returns'.
[56] Neville, 'The Phantom Returns', 167–73.
[57] Kirk, 'Phantom Sources', 15–16; Neville, 'The Phantom Returns', 149, 159–60, 168–9.

to compose their own version, rather than working from constant eye contact with a manuscript.[58]

On the understanding of composition adumbrated here, Mark's Gospel would not be some text Matthew or Luke just happened across and decided to use as a source for their own efforts; it is far more likely that both later evangelists would have gained considerable intimacy with Mark's Gospel before they started planning their own works. Matthew and Luke would have obtained excellent memory command of Mark, to the extent that either of them could have recited much of it without the support of a written text (although they will have needed the support of a written text to acquire that level of proficiency in the first place). Whether such a recital from memory would have been word perfect is another matter; absolute verbatim accuracy may not have been needed, although it seems likely that much of Mark's wording would have been reproduced along with all the gist (as is suggested by the extent to which Matthew and Luke often reproduce Mark's wording).

It is, of course, impossible for us to know precisely how Matthew and Luke interacted with Mark's text, but the following seem plausible. First, since Matthew and Luke presumably belonged to the literate minority in their respective communities, it is possible that they were responsible for making the copies of Mark their communities used and conceivable that they made copies of Mark for their own use. Copying out the text, which would normally have involved dictating it to themselves as they wrote, would have been one way to help them learn it. Second, it seems likely that Matthew's and Mark's prior interaction with Mark will have gone well beyond committing it to memory. For as long as Mark remained the primary written narrative account of Jesus' ministry available to them, it is likely that Matthew and Luke would have preached on it, taught from it, discussed it with friends and colleagues, deeply pondered it and generally internalized it as a central part of their tradition.

Third, it is also likely that neither evangelist's use of Mark will have been entirely uncritical. For example, it could well be that when Matthew or Luke recited Mark from memory or made a copy from a manuscript, they made a number of minor improvements as they went, such as replacing καί with δέ or an historical present with an aorist, in accord with their own habitual modes of speaking and writing. Such relatively minor changes might then have become part of the text of Mark they remembered when coming to write their own gospels, without their constantly having to make conscious editorial changes at the point of written composition.[59]

Fourth, it is conceivable that the two later evangelists made more substantial changes to the way they rendered the text as they preached on it, read it aloud or recited it. For example, if Matthew preached on a section of Mark he found ambiguous or obscure, it might be that he expanded on it in the course of his preaching. If, for example, he

---

[58] Neville, 'The Phantom Returns', 168.
[59] Moreover, users of Mark may have regarded it more as a rough draft than a polished, 'published' work whose literary integrity had to be fully respected; see Matthew D.C. Larsen, *Gospels before the Book* (New York: Oxford University Press, 2018). Larsen's contention that Mark was simply a set of notes is undermined by the extent to which Larsen is forced to concede the existence of Markan structure, but this does not negate the argument that Mark may have been perceived as a rough draft.

was aware of Jewish accusations that the disciples had stolen the body from the Empty Tomb, he may well have incorporated (or invented) a tradition about the guard on the tomb (Mt. 28.11-15). Or again, faced with Mark's cryptically brief Temptation Story (Mk 1.12-13) Matthew may already have been in the habit of expanding on it before he ever came to pen his gospel, as he may already have been in the habit of expanding Mark's account of the Beelzebul Controversy (Mk 3.22-30 || Mt. 12.22-32) with (some of) the additional material he found in tradition, another source, or his own invention, in order, say, to fill in some of the gaps he perceived in Mark's presentation of Jesus' argument.[60]

These particular suggestions are admittedly speculative and none of them will be relied upon in what follows; their role is purely illustrative. They nonetheless illustrate the kind of thing that may have happened on the understanding of composition outlined above. The process by which Matthew, say, arrived at the final text of his gospel (not least those parts of it that are dependent upon Mark) will have been rather more complex than a simplistic (print-culture) model of literary dependence might suggest. Moreover, some of these processes may already have taken place before Matthew or Luke began actually composing their gospels. To talk of Matthew and Luke 'reworking' or 'rewriting' their sources rather than merely 'editing' them is an attempt to capture something of this complexity, but since the full details of such reworking are now irrecoverable, we shall inevitably end up effectively using a somewhat simplified model in what follows, often arguing as if Matthew and Luke were simply modifying their predecessor texts as they wrote.

The final issue to consider is whether Matthew or Luke would have made any use of a physical manuscript of Mark at all (in the sense of having eye contact with it) in the course of composing their own gospels. Clearly, there is no way we can know what they actually did, but it seems plausible that they would have kept a copy of Mark to hand. Even if they had near-perfect memory command of Mark, it may have been convenient for them to refresh their memories from a manuscript of Mark when they were using Mark in Mark's order and could simply scroll forward through the text. It seems less likely, however, that they would have maintained eye contact with a manuscript of Mark while mentally composing their own version of a Markan section. As David Neville says, 'A genuine author working with source material is unlikely to have consulted his source(s) every few words, but to have read through a passage or sequence of passages, put the source(s) aside, then composed.'[61] In addition to the conclusions from the Burkett–Kirk–Neville debate outlined above, three further features of the text would seem to support this view: first, the phenomenon that James Dunn has called attention to, namely that the wording of parallel passages in the triple tradition is often quite disparate (thus suggesting that something other than

---

[60] Eric Eve, 'The Devil in the Detail: Exorcising Q from the Beelzebul Controversy' in John C. Poirier and Jeff Peterson (eds), *Marcan Priority without Q: Explorations in the Farrer Hypothesis* (LNTS, 455; London: Bloomsbury T&T Clark, 2015), 16–43; cf. Damm, *Ancient Rhetoric*, 246–56.

[61] Neville, 'Phantom Returns', 149; cf. the suggestion in Pelling, 'Plutarch's Method', 92, that 'an author, immediately before narrating an episode, would *reread* one account, and compose with that version fresh in his mind' (emphasis original); see also *WTG*, 57–8.

straight copying took place);[62] second, the occurrence of editorial fatigue, if that is to be explained as a species of memory error; and third, on the FH, the incidence of minor agreements of Matthew and Luke against Mark (more on which is discussed in Chapter 4), which are easier to explain as Luke employing Mark from memory and unconsciously conflating his text with that of Matthew's than by Luke working from a copy of Mark open in front of him and consciously deciding to incorporate odd fragments of Matthew's wording.

Implications and working hypotheses

To summarize: Matthew's and Luke's principal sources would have been texts with which they were already thoroughly familiar and with which they had already thoroughly engaged. The gist of these texts, and certain parts of them (such as memorable aphorisms, striking sayings, vivid images and passages that chimed particularly with community concerns), would have been well embedded in the collective memory of their target audiences, a fact both evangelists would have had to reckon with in their own compositions. The evangelists would not have been writing for purely archival, entertainment or literary reputational purposes but rather to shape and solidify the cultural memory of their target audience in ways they considered appropriate, in part as a response to circumstances and in part in accordance with their own views. In all probability, the evangelists will have dictated (or possibly inscribed) their compositions having first mulled over them in their own minds and in conversation with friends and colleagues as part of an ongoing process of oral and memory-based cultivation of the texts. These companions could have continued to support the evangelists' work by offering secretarial support and constructive criticism. Depending on the resources available the process of composition probably went through several stages, including note-taking, discussion and multiple drafts.[63] A similar process of revision could have continued after the evangelists produced what they considered to be their first finished copies and almost certainly did so in the process of subsequent scribal copying.

Throughout this process, both the community's collective memory and the earlier sources employed would have acted as both resource and constraint. On the one hand, they would have provided the evangelists with a fund of material they could use, a tradition of interpretation on which they could call and a body of knowledge and assumptions they could rely on their target audience sharing. On the other hand, that

---

[62] James D.G. Dunn, 'Altering the Default Setting: Re-envisaging the Early Transmission of the Jesus Tradition', *NTS* 49 (2003), 139–75; James D.G. Dunn, *Jesus Remembered* (Grand Rapids; Cambridge: Eerdmans, 2003), 216–24. Dunn uses his observations to argue for the influence of oral tradition to explain some sets of Synoptic parallels, but the literary paradigm he sets out to oppose is more a print paradigm way of working with texts than the memory and manuscript model argued here. For critiques of Dunn's conclusions, see John S. Kloppenborg, 'Variation and Reproduction of the Double Tradition and an Oral Q?', *ETL* 83 (2007), 53–80; Kirk, 'Memory', 469–70; Eve, *Behind*, 108–15; *WTG*, 128–30.

[63] The note-taking need not have consisted primarily of excerpting from written sources; it may have comprised notes of oral tradition, community discussions and other factors that could have entered into the final composition.

same body of shared knowledge, assumptions and evaluations would restrict how far the evangelists could reshape their material while still producing something likely to have the desired effect on their target audience. One strategy might be to use familiar-sounding material but to relocate it into contexts that subtly altered its meaning, as FH Luke would have done with much of Matthew. Another could be to alter the thrust of familiar material by more or less subtle changes to its wording. Yet another would be to incorporate fresh material that appeared sufficiently congruent with what was familiar to be accepted. Overarching all these would be the deployment of both familiar and new material in a similar-but-different frame. Whether the evangelists were trying to reshape or to solidify their communities' sense of identity (and it would probably have been a bit of both), their compositions would need to present a Jesus that appeared congruent with what their target audience already knew.

We have suggested that when Matthew and Luke composed their gospels, their primary access to Mark is most likely to have been from memory, probably supported by occasional reference to a physical manuscript. A final question to consider is whether the same is likely to have applied to Luke's use of Matthew (on the FH) or to both the later evangelists' use of Q (on the 2DH). It may seem tempting to relate the answer to this question to the variation in the degree of verbal agreement in the double tradition, from virtually verbatim (e.g. in the teaching of John the Baptist at Mt. 3:7b-10 || Lk. 3.7b-9) to virtually none (e.g. in the Parable of the Talents/Pounds at Mt. 25.14-30 || Lk. 19.11-27). Derrenbacker has observed that on the 2DH Matthew tends to deviate more from Q's wording where he diverges from Q's order, which implies a similar correlation between FH Luke and Matthew (since any such correlation would be based on the relative ordering of the double tradition material in Matthew and Luke).[64] One way of explaining this might be that FH Luke had eye contact with Matthew in the high verbal agreement (HVA) passages but was relying on his memory of Matthew for the low verbal agreement (LVA) ones. But this is by no means assured, since in principle HVA passages could be ones Luke had learned off by heart because he particularly liked the way they were phrased (or whose wording was particularly prized by his target audience) while LVA passages could be ones Luke chose to substantially rewrite even though he had the text of Matthew open in front of him. The same could equally apply to 2DH Matthew's and Luke's of Q.

It is best, therefore, not to make any *a priori* assumptions that the presence or absence of HVA is an indicator of eye contact with a source or reliance on memory. This is not to deny that such a correlation might exist, but if so, it would only be a tendency, not a rule. It may turn out, for example, that FH Luke's wording is often closer to Matthew's where Luke appears to be using Matthean material in Matthean sequence, and it would then be plausible to suppose that Luke's consultation of a manuscript of Matthew in such cases could be part of the explanation for this. This is very different, however, from using degrees of verbal agreement as indicators of memory versus manuscript use.

In sum, then, our working hypothesis is that Luke and Matthew worked primarily from memory of their sources, but may have refreshed their memory from written

---

[64] Derrenbacker, *Compositional Practices*, 238; cf. *WTG*, 133.

copies of their sources when it was convenient to do so (mainly when they were following a source in the order of that source). Although we cannot exclude the possibility that the evangelists may on occasion have dictated (or even inscribed) particular passages while maintaining eye contact with a written source, this is unlikely to have been their normal practice, which we shall assume to have been to compose from either short-term or long-term memory.

There is one final point to emphasize. The evangelists' precise educational level has proved hard to pin down; they display some knowledge of quite sophisticated rhetorical techniques while writing in relatively unsophisticated koine Greek from an apparently non-elite social station. It is equally hard to pin down a precise analogy to their compositions, which bear partial similarities to those of ancient historians, biographers, technical writers, scribes and scholars, while resisting total assimilation to any of them. We therefore need to be open to a corresponding degree of eclecticism in envisaging their working methods.

The next chapter will progress from this rather abstract account of compositional models to more concrete details of how ancient authors transformed what they found in their sources.

3

Transformational techniques

Progymnasmata

One way to find out how ancient authors typically treated their sources is to ask what they were taught to do. Evidence for this survives in the *Progymnasmata*, preliminary exercises in composition that formed the initial stages of a rhetorical education, including literary composition. One may question whether the evangelists would have had access to a progymnastic education, but the *Progymnasmata* outline compositional techniques that were widespread at the time the gospels were written, and several recent studies have illustrated how the evangelists employed the compositional techniques taught in the *Progymnasmata* and employed by their Jewish and Graeco-Roman contemporaries.[1]

A number of progymnastic textbooks survive from antiquity, the earliest being that of Aelius Theon, probably dating from the first century CE.[2] Theon's exercises concerned *chreia* (a brief pointed saying or action attributed to a named individual), then *fable* (a fictional story conveying a truth), *narrative* (an account of real or imaginary events), *topos* ('language amplifying something that is acknowledged to be either a fault or a brave deed'),[3] *ecphrasis* (description), *prosopeia* (composition of a speech suitable to a particular person in particular circumstances), *encomium* and *invective* (speeches or writings praising or denouncing some person or thing), *syncrisis* (a comparison of two persons or things), *thesis* (an argument in favour of a general proposition), *law*, *paraphrase*, *elaboration* ('language that adds what is lacking in thought and expression')[4] and *contradiction*. This mixes categories, since some exercises (such as chreia and fable) concern types of source material with which the student might

---

[1] In addition to Mikeal C. Parsons and Michael Wade Martin, *Ancient Rhetoric and the New Testament* (Waco, TX: Baylor University Press, 2018), see Damm, *Ancient Rhetoric*, esp. 16–17; Michael R. Licona, *Why Are There Differences in the Gospels? What We Can Learn from Ancient Biography* (New York: Oxford University Press, 2017), and Adams, 'Luke and *Progymnasmata*'.

[2] For English translations and brief accompanying explanations, see George A. Kennedy, *Progymnasmata: Greek Textbooks of Prose Composition and Rhetoric* (Atlanta: SBL, 2003). For a recent defence of a first-century date for Theon, see Parsons and Martin, *Ancient Rhetoric*, 11–12 n.19.

[3] Theon, *Exercises*, 6 (7) [106]; cited at Kennedy, *Progymnasmata*, 42. Numbers in parentheses refer to chapter numbers in Spengel (where these differ from Kennedy's) while numbers in square brackets indicate pages in Spengel's edition (see Kennedy, *Progymnasmata*, p. 3).

[4] Theon, *Exercises*, 16 [110]; cited at Kennedy, *Progymnasmata*, 71.

work, others (such as ecphrasis, prosopeia and encomium) are types of material the student might be asked to produce, while others (such as paraphrase and elaboration) are techniques for transforming source material. Moreover, although such techniques are left until the end, they are presupposed in the earlier exercises as ways the student might work on source material such as chreiai and fable: 'Chreias are practiced by restatement, grammatical inflection, comment, and contradiction, and we expand and compress the chreia, and in addition (at a later stage in study) we refute and confirm.'[5]

In sum, the exercises train the student to transform source material by grammatical adjustment (e.g. varying number and case), paraphrase (saying the same thing in different words), compression and expansion or elaboration (which may include explanatory comment).[6] The example Theon gives of expanding a chreia is worth citing in full:

> For example, this chreia is brief: 'Epaminondas, dying childless, said to his friends, "I leave two daughters, the victory at Leuctra and that at Mantinea."' We expand it as follows: 'Epaminadas [*sic*], the general of the Thebans, was, you should know, a great man in peacetime, but when war with Lacedaimonians came to his fatherland he demonstrated many shining deeds of greatness. When serving as Boeotarch at Leuctra, he defeated the enemy; and conducting a campaign and contending on behalf of his country, he died at Mantinea. When he had been wounded and his life was coming to an end, while his friends were bewailing many things, including that he was dying childless, breaking into a smile he said, "Cease your weeping, my friends, for I have left you two immortal daughters: two victories of my country over Lacedaimonia, one at Leuctra, the elder, the younger just begotten by me at Mantinea."'[7]

The expansions Theon suggests here are of three different kinds. First, there is mere verbal padding, such as the lengthening of Epaminondas' originally pithy saying with phrases such as 'you should know'. Second, there are circumstantial details presumably intended to add vividness, such as the wailing of the friends and the dying general's smile. Finally, there is the addition of substantive information, for example that Epaminondas was a Theban general engaged in war against Lacedaimonia who served as Boeotarch and was fatally wounded at Mantinea; it is this final type of material that serves to clarify the point of the original chreia. Presumably, Theon has not simply made all this up, so some additional source of information is implied. Although Theon nowhere specifies what this additional source is, it may well be general background knowledge he expects students to possess. This background knowledge in turn represents memory of material (written or otherwise) that has been combined with the chreia set for the expansion exercise.

The various techniques outlined above were not designed merely to encourage change for the sake of change but to equip students with the means to improve on their

---

[5] Theon, *Exercises*, 3 (5) [101]; cited at Kennedy, *Progymnasmata*, 19.
[6] Cf. Licona, *Differences*, 13–14.
[7] Theon, *Exercises*, 3 (5) [103–4]; cited at Kennedy, *Progymnasmata*, 21–2.

sources, not least in pursuit of rhetorical goals. For speeches, this would especially by enhancing the arrangement, clarity and propriety of their source material (where 'propriety' denotes the appropriateness of one's style and content to the context in which they are being deployed).[8] For narrative the chief virtues would be clarity, conciseness and credibility,[9] the pursuit of which could involve any of the transformational techniques we have seen (e.g. one might either abbreviate in the interests of conciseness or expand in the interests of clarity or credibility).[10]

Synoptic parallels contain many examples of the techniques Theon teaches (not only in chreiai). For example, in the Healing of the Paralytic (Mk 2.1-12 || Mt. 9.2-8 || Lk. 5.17-26) Matthew substantially abbreviates Mark, while Luke paraphrases (although both the later evangelists are relatively conservative with Jesus' sayings). Matthew's version of the Beelzebul Controversy (Mt. 12.22-32) is an elaboration of the Markan version (Mk 3.22-30), whether on the basis of Q, additional traditions known to Matthew or simply what Matthew considered necessary for clarification.[11] Other examples of Matthean expansion might include the addition of Peter's walking on the sea to the Markan account (Mt. 14.28-31) or of Jesus' amplified response to Peter's Confession (Mt. 16.17-19). The explanatory addition at Mt. 16.12 to the puzzling saying about the leaven taken from Mk 8.14-21 may be a closer parallel to Theon's example, as may Luke's elaboration of the Transfiguration account at Lk. 9.31-32.

The Synoptic Gospels exemplify several types of material similar to those covered in Theon's exercises. The gospel pronouncement stories are closely related to chreia.[12] Parables are a particular form of fable;[13] just as Theon suggests that a fable can be concluded with a gnomic comment,[14] so we sometimes find proverbial sayings or explanatory comments tacked on to the end of parables (e.g. Lk. 13.30; 14.11 = 18.14b; 15.7, 10; 16.9). The Gospels and Acts are full of narratives (such as the birth stories, miracle stories, passion account) and contain speeches by various characters that could qualify as examples of prosopeia. The gospels as a whole could be seen (at least in part) as encomia of Jesus, while they contain within them several examples of invective against the Jewish leadership (e.g. Matthew 23). While the gospel narratives tend to be sparing in detail, Parsons and Martin find examples of ecphrasis in Jesus' baptism, the transfiguration, Jesus' clothing in the trials before Herod and Pilate and Pentecost.[15] Given the narrative genre of the gospels one might not expect much by way of formal argumentation, but, where Jesus engages in debate, there are some brief examples of what could be regarded as thesis and contradiction (e.g. Jesus' teaching on divorce

---

[8] Damm, *Ancient Rhetoric*, 3-80. Damm's study focuses on the adaptation of chreia in the composition of speeches and so may not be directly applicable to other types of material in the gospels.
[9] Theon, *Exercises*, 5 (4) [79]; cited at Kennedy, *Progymnasmata*, 29; cf. Parsons and Martin, *Ancient Rhetoric*, 76-7.
[10] Parsons and Martin, *Ancient Rhetoric*, 93, 104.
[11] See Eve, 'Devil', 21-32, and cf. Damm, *Ancient Rhetoric*, 246-64.
[12] Parsons and Martin, *Ancient Rhetoric*, 17-44.
[13] Parsons and Martin, *Ancient Rhetoric*, 45-70; Matthew Ryan Hauge, 'Fabulous Parables: The Storytelling Tradition in the Synoptic Gospels' in Matthew Ryan Hauge and Andrew Pitts (eds), *Ancient Education and Early Christianity* (LNTS, 533; London: Bloomsbury T&T Clark, 2016), 89-105.
[14] Theon, *Exercises*, 4 (3) [75]; cited at Kennedy, *Progymnasmata*, 26.
[15] Parsons and Martin, *Ancient Rhetoric*, 126-8.

at Mk 10.2-12), and at least some of Jesus' longer speeches have been shaped with rhetorical conventions in mind.[16] Finally, Luke and John in particular could be said to contain a syncrisis between Jesus and John the Baptist (Lk. 1–2; 3.2-22; 5.33-39; 7.18-35; 16.16; Jn 1.6-9, 19-28; 3.22–4.3), though admittedly not exactly in the form envisaged by Theon; nevertheless, several of elements Theon suggests should figure in a comparison of persons (birth, office, reputation, actions) do occur in Luke.[17]

This brief review would seem to justify Downing's view:

> Particularly important are discussions of elementary education and examples that have survived of elementary exercises. The procedures are always so similar that it would be absurd to suppose without massive supporting evidence that the NT evangelists could have learned to write Greek and cope with written source material at all while remaining outside the pervasive influence of these common steps toward literacy.[18]

Difficulties remain in identifying the precise educational level of the evangelists and reconciling their relatively unsophisticated Greek with the signs of their having undergone at least the preliminary stages of a rhetorical (and not merely clerical) education. We may nevertheless accept the main point that both Downing and Licona are making, namely that the *Progymnasmata* provide a good guide to compositional techniques likely to have been available to the evangelists.

This conclusion only takes us so far, however. For one thing, the *Progymnasmata* shed little light on what is arguably the most contentious aspect of the Synoptic Problem, namely the problem of order (how the 2DH Matthew could have reordered Q or the FH Luke reordered Matthew, to the extent seemingly required). For another, although it is reasonable to assume that the *Progymnasmata* describe techniques the evangelists could employ, this does not entail that they would have been restricted to these techniques; techniques taught in preliminary exercises are likely to fall short of those available to mature writers. It is thus necessary to examine not only what student writers were taught to do but what experienced writers actually did.

Compositional practices in previous Synoptic Problem scholarship

Discussion of the Synoptic Problem has been fruitfully advanced by comparisons of the compositional methods required of the evangelists on competing source-critical theories with those exemplified by other ancient writers. Several New Testament

---

[16] For examples, see Damm, *Ancient Rhetoric*.
[17] Theon, *Exercises*, 10 (9) [112–13]; cited at Kennedy, *Progymnasmata*, 52–3. Parsons and Martin, *Ancient Rhetoric*, 265–9, regard Luke's comparison here as an extended one of a broadly conventional type, albeit continued beyond Luke's Infancy Narrative into discontinuous sections of the gospel, although Adams, 'Luke and *Progymnasmata*', 149–51, complains that Luke does not stick closely enough to Theon's prescriptions for his comparison to count as a formal *syncrisis*.
[18] F. Gerald Downing, 'Compositional Conventions and the Synoptic Problem', *JBL* 107 (1988), 69–85, here 71; cf. Licona, *Differences*, 14.

scholars have made contributions in this area; here there will be space to review only three of the most salient.

F. Gerald Downing has been something of a pioneer in this field. His first major contribution comes in a pair of articles that investigate Josephus' use of sources[19] and apply his findings to Luke's likely method of working on the basis that his intentions and tendencies are often identical to those of Josephus (in the *Jewish Antiquities*).[20]

Downing finds that in his use of *Aristeas*, which is closer to his style than is the Septuagint, Josephus generally paraphrases, often making changes for the sake of avoiding reproducing the wording of his source. He sometimes omits or changes material for theological reasons, but most of his changes seem to be changes for change's sake.

When it comes to the biblical material, which Josephus has undertaken to translate faithfully without alteration, he omits material to remove discrepancies, duplicates, interruptions and whatever might appear too magical, theologically inappropriate or apologetically awkward. Josephus also makes a number of additions for the purposes of harmony and continuity (tidying up the narrative), underlining the role of prophecy and providence, emphasizing piety and moral uplift, apologetics, interest and clarity. Although Downing does not explicitly state the point, such additions fit comfortably under the rubric of elaboration noted above in relation to the *Progymnasmata*.[21] Josephus creates no major events (as opposed to speeches, which he handles much more freely), either purely from imagination or by 'midrashic exposition'. The one exception to this, Moses' military campaign in *Ant*. 2, appears in Artapanus (thus providing Josephus with the warrant of a source).

Josephus also rearranges material, generally for the sake of harmony and continuity, to make the narrative more coherent. In particular, he brings together material on the basis of topic, person, place or event for the sake of thematic coherence. He also carries out a small amount of straightforward conflation of parallel accounts, often for similar reasons (to produce a smoother and more coherent narrative overall). Where his sources (Samuel–Kings and Chronicles) 'conflict in a fairly straightforward fashion over some major matter, Josephus follows the older and fuller source'.[22] Only in the two instances where his sources conflict in detail does Josephus compose his own fresh account on the basis of items selected from his sources rather than attempting to harmonize and conflate the parallel accounts. In summary, Downing finds that

> the keynote of Josephus' method is still 'simplicity', and simplicity seems to be a major part of his aim. Where his sources are straightforward he is happy just to paraphrase; where a single source seems illogical, he tidies it up; and if he has two

---

[19] Specifically, Josephus' use of the *Letter of Aristeas* at *Ant*. 12 and of Joshua–Judges at *Ant*. 5, the legal/hortatory material of Exodus and Deuteronomy at *Ant*. 4, and of the parallel narratives in Samuel–Kings and Chronicles.
[20] F. Gerald Downing, 'Redaction Criticism: Josephus' Antiquities and the Synoptic Problem I', *JSNT* 8 (1980), 46–65; F. Gerald Downing, 'Redaction Criticism: Josephus' Antiquities and the Synoptic Problem II', *JSNT* 9 (1980), 29–48.
[21] Damm, *Ancient Rhetoric*, 55–8, likewise views elaboration as a technique for enhancing 'clarity, beauty, propriety and force'.
[22] Downing, 'Redaction Criticism I', 62.

sources that will not readily combine, he makes up a third account of his own, blithely ignoring large parts of both. But it remains a 'version', quite clearly. There is no major invention, no major allusiveness.[23]

In the second article, Downing applies what he has ascertained about Josephus' methods to the composition of the gospels, particularly Luke. He begins by suggesting that since Luke's aims, intentions and characteristic interests are so similar to Josephus' it is reasonable to suppose that he employed the same compositional methods (as opposed, for example, to composition based on midrash and the lectionary as proposed by Michael Goulder and John Drury, which Downing believes is not evidenced elsewhere).[24] Downing then proceeds to argue that, on the assumption that Luke's working methods were essentially the same as Josephus', Luke's use of Mark and Q is much easier to explain than is Luke's use of Matthew and Mark or Mark's of Matthew and Luke. Among the difficulties with the FH that Downing identifies, three in particular stand out.

First, Downing argues that since Josephus does not invent whole episodes, Luke cannot have invented his entire Infancy Narrative from scratch, 'even from scriptural meditation, or haggadic legends attached to other figures'.[25] If one is then left wondering where (on any theory of Synoptic relations) Luke's Infancy Narrative can have come from, Downing adds: 'That is not to say that the Infancy Narrative could not have grown from very small beginnings before reaching Luke'.[26] He does not, however, illustrate such a process of growth from other examples or explain how such an appropriate introduction to Luke's Gospel might result. Be that as it may, Downing's main contention is that Luke cannot have known Matthew's Infancy Narrative, since, if he had, he would have conflated more of it with his own source. Downing acknowledges that there are some points of contact (such as Jesus' Davidic descent and virginal conception) between the two accounts but no incidents or phrases.[27] Nevertheless, Downing's insistence that FH Luke should have taken over more of Matthew's account is in some tension with his later finding that 'where [Plutarch's sources] entirely disagree, he simply follows one',[28] since following Plutarch's practice would have permitted Luke to follow his own Infancy Narrative source in preference to Matthew.

Second, Downing objects that Luke's radical compression of Matthew's Sermon on the Mount and scattering of many of its fragments across his central section are unlike anything in Josephus.[29]

Third, Downing argues that FH Luke would have to have followed a laborious procedure unparalleled in any other ancient author by 'unpicking' Matthew from Mark

---

[23] Downing, 'Redaction Criticism I', 64.
[24] Downing, 'Redaction Criticism II', 32, criticizing Goulder, *Midrash*.
[25] Downing, 'Redaction Criticism II', 34.
[26] Downing, 'Redaction Criticism II', 34.
[27] Downing, 'Redaction Criticism II', 33–4, 42.
[28] Downing, 'Compositional Conventions', 81.
[29] Downing, 'Redaction Criticism II', 36.

(i.e. taking over what Matthew adds to or changes in Mark while avoiding what he has in common).[30] We shall return to this point in Chapter 5.

Downing's contribution is undoubtedly valuable, but it is also open to criticism. First, while it is clearly useful to take Josephus as a parallel to Luke, Downing overstates the similarities between their aims, intentions and interests (especially when he calls them 'identical'). Josephus undertakes to give an accurate rendering of the Jewish Scriptures (his principal source for the first half of his *Jewish Antiquities* – *Ant.* 1.5, 17); Luke makes no such undertaking but promises rather to provide an orderly account of what predecessors have also attempted to narrate (Lk. 1.1-4). Josephus is expounding to outsiders what he regards as the ancient roots of his people and their religion; Luke is providing a normative and formative text to guide, solidify and legitimate a far more recently created group. These aims are not identical, and a comparison of Josephus' variant accounts of his own Galilean ministry at *War* 2.566–3.63 and *Life* 28-413 might suggest greater flexibility in his treatment of more recent material in which he is personally invested.[31] Moreover, Downing himself acknowledges that while both authors paraphrase, Luke is much readier than Josephus to take over the wording of his sources unchanged, and although Luke is the most literary of the evangelists, his Greek prose lacks the polish of Josephus'.[32] Downing suggests that this may be because Luke showed an even greater respect for his sources than Josephus showed for scripture and that achieving Josephus' level of polish would have been a waste of effort, but the first of these explanations seems unlikely (given that Josephus' sources were already regarded as scriptural while Luke's were not and that the degree of verbal agreement varies widely)[33] and the second undermines Downing's contention that Luke and Josephus were addressing similar audiences for similar purposes.

Second, Downing's demonstration that 2DH Luke's use of Mark and Q could have been carried out by methods akin to Josephus' use of his sources is only an argument in favour of the 2DH if a similar demonstration is offered of 2DH Matthew's use of Mark and Q, which Downing fails to provide. Since Q is reconstructed on the assumption that Luke and Matthew made independent use of Mark and Q and that the order of Q is better represented by Luke, it will obviously appear that 2DH Luke could have straightforwardly combined Mark and Q; but unless the 2DH can account for Matthew's reordering and conflation of Mark and Q in an equally satisfactory way the argument is circular. Moreover, Downing's argument here is vulnerable to the counter-argument that FH Luke would principally be reordering sayings material, rather than the kind

---

[30] Downing, 'Redaction Criticism II', 42–5.
[31] Tessa Rajak, *Josephus: The Historian and His Society* (London: Duckworth, 1983), 144–73, argues that these two accounts are not so much mutually contradictory as shaped for different purposes. The point is not that Josephus' accounts of his own antics provides a direct analogy to the evangelists' use of sources, but that it illustrates how the same source material can be substantially reshaped to fit different aims, for which see also C.B.R. Pelling, 'Plutarch's Adaptation of His Source-Material', *JHS* 100 (1980), 127–40. One might also be forgiven for wondering if some of what Josephus wrote about himself may illustrate a greater capacity for imaginative embellishment than Downing finds in the *Antiquities* (e.g. *War* 3.351–4, 387–91; *Life* 208–11).
[32] Downing, 'Redaction Criticism II', 33.
[33] See Mattila, 'Question', 209–10.

of narrative material Downing focuses on in Josephus, and that a fairer comparison might be with, say, Josephus' use of Pentateuchal material in *Ant.* 3–4.[34]

Much of Downing's other work in this area revolves around the related problems of unpicking and conflation as objections to the FH and 2GH.[35] The 'unpicking' objection will be addressed in Chapter 5; at this point we may simply agree that detailed and deliberate unpicking of the type Downing attributes to FH Luke (of Matthean from Markan material) is unlikely to be something much attempted by ancient authors (while denying that FH Luke would have attempted it).

In his 1988 article Downing extends his work on conflation from Josephus to Plutarch (and, more briefly, Livy), but comes to much the same conclusion: ancient authors did occasionally employ conflation, but only of a very simple kind, by which Downing means the (sometimes arbitrary) combination of complete elements (as opposed, say, to individual words and phrases) from two different but broadly parallel accounts, without the kind of critical appraisal of source material a modern historian might apply.[36] The remainder of the article then focuses not on examples of unduly complex conflation that either the 2GH Mark or the FH Luke would have to have performed but on an amplification of the unpicking argument by citing examples of ready-made conflation (i.e. agreements in their sources) they declined to follow.[37] While Downing's discussion of conflation could provide grounds for objecting to the procedure adopted by 2GH Mark, it is less clear that it impacts any more on FH Luke than on 2DH Matthew.

More recently Downing has directed his attention to a puzzle he noted in his comparison of Luke and Josephus, namely that the evangelists appear much readier than other ancient authors to borrow much of the wording of their sources unaltered. He suggests that a parallel to the evangelists' verbatim borrowing of source material might be found in *Fachprosa*, relatively sophisticated writing on technical subjects such as medicine.[38] As Downing notes, this would support Loveday Alexander's suggestion of a school setting for the transmission of the Jesus tradition and the composition of the gospels.[39] This seems a promising line of enquiry, but the notion that the evangelists are closer to technical writers than to elite historians and biographers is in some tension with Downing's earlier contention that Luke's aims, objectives and thus methods were identical to those of Josephus.

Robert Derrenbacker begins his investigation by surveying what five ancient writers (Arrian, Dionysius, Cassius Dio, the author of 2 Maccabees and Philostratus)

---

[34] Mark Goodacre, 'On Choosing and Using Appropriate Analogies: A Response to F. Gerald Downing', *JSNT* 26 (2003), 237–40, here 239–40.

[35] F. Gerald Downing, 'Towards the Rehabilitation of Q', *NTS* 11 (1964), 169–81; Downing, 'Compositional Conventions'; F. Gerald Downing, 'Disagreements of Each Evangelist with the Minor Close Agreements of the Other Two', *ETL* 80 (2004), 445–69; F. Gerald Downing, 'Writers' Use or Abuse' in Foster et al., *New Studies*, 536–45; F. Gerald Downing, 'Plausibility, Probability and Synoptic Hypotheses', *ETL* 93 (2017), 445–69.

[36] Downing, 'Compositional Conventions', 72–82. More recently Licona, *Differences*, has compared how similar material is dealt with in parallel passages in Plutarch and in the gospels and similarly finds that the evangelists are employing much the same compositional conventions as Plutarch.

[37] Downing, 'Compositional Conventions', 82–5.

[38] Downing, 'Writers' Use or Abuse', 524–36.

[39] Alexander, 'Luke's Preface', 59–70; Alexander, 'Memory and Tradition'; see also *WTG*, 77–8.

said about their use of sources in their prefaces. From this survey Derrenbacker derives the following 'compositional criteria' (or preferred methods of working): (1) a preference for eyewitness source material; (2) frequent use of oral sources along with written ones; (3) choice of the more plausible source where two sources disagree; (4) use of ὑπομνήματα (preliminary notes or rough drafts) in the production of ancient texts; (5) the multifaceted nature of the adaptation of source material (meaning that adaptation might involve some combination of subtraction, addition, and alteration); (6) the abbreviation of sources, say to produce an epitome of a longer work (which generally proceeded by consistently abbreviating every episode, rather than including some episodes in full and dropping others completely as the 2GH Mark would have done); and (7) the interlacing of *legomena* (sayings and anecdotes) among narrative material culled from other (written) sources.[40]

Item (5) in this list substantially agrees with both Downing's results and what can be gathered from the *Progymnasmata*, but on the face of it item (3) may be in some tension with Downing's view that where sources disagree an ancient author would always either attempt to conflate them (if this could be managed simply) or else write his own account borrowing more or less randomly from his sources. This apparent discrepancy may partly be due to the fact that while Downing is looking at what Josephus (and subsequently Plutarch) actually did, Derrenbacker is summarizing what ancient authors (or at least Arrian and Lucian) claim to be or advise doing, although Downing also remarks that 'where [Plutarch's sources] entirely disagree, he simply follows one.'[41]

Derrenbacker goes on to examine how a number of ancient authors worked based on an analysis of texts in relation to their identifiable sources, taking as his examples the parallel accounts of Diodorus, Strabo and Arrian on India and Josephus' account of the period of the monarchy, for which he explicitly builds on Downing's work.[42] His principal conclusions are (1) the authors examined tend to follow one source at a time, meaning that although they may alternate between sources for complete episodes, there is no micro-conflation of sources within individual episodes (beyond the occasional simple conflation of the sort that Downing identifies);[43] (2) the authors tend to adopt the wording of the source they are following; (3) none of the authors examined carries out any radical reordering of their sources.[44]

The detailed discussion that lies behind these conclusions qualifies both them and some of those Derrenbacker derived from his study of prefaces. For example, Derrenbacker finds Arrian and Strabo making use of secondary sources within individual pericopae (contrary to what his first summary statement might suggest), although such secondary additions tend to come at the end of pericopae (thereby justifying the denial of substantial conflation).[45] Again, contrary to his earlier conclusion about the abbreviation of sources, Derrenbacker concedes that Diodorus

---

[40] Derrenbacker, *Compositional Practices*, 52–76, esp. 75–6.
[41] Downing, 'Compositional Conventions', 81.
[42] Derrenbacker, *Compositional Practices*, 77–117.
[43] So also Mattila, 'Question', 199–206.
[44] Derrenbacker, *Compositional Practices*, 116–17.
[45] Derrenbacker, *Compositional Practices*, 86.

may have abbreviated Ephorus by selective extraction of material rather than by abbreviating each episode, so that selective extraction as a means of epitomization was a technique available to ancient authors after all.[46]

That said, Derrenbacker's detailed study of a selection of passages from Josephus largely supports Downing's, to which Derrenbacker adds those of Christopher Begg's redaction-critical study of Josephus, which comes to similar conclusions.[47] Derrenbacker points out that Josephus was probably drawing from a larger range of sources than Downing supposes, but he nevertheless concurs with Downing that Josephus is probably the most appropriate analogy for the composition of the Synoptic Gospels.[48] He further notes that while Josephus normally includes events that are attested by both the Deuteronomic Historian and the Chronicler, there are occasional exceptions where he omits such doubly attested material (e.g. 2 Sam. 23.8-35 || 1 Chron. 11.10-47 and 2 Sam. 7.18-29 || 1 Chron. 17.16-27). Moreover, while the Deuteronomic Historian and the Chronicler generally agree in their order of events, in at least one instance where they do not Josephus reworks the order of both (*Ant.* 7.53-89).[49]

Downing's conclusion that Josephus' method of conflation is a simple one is confirmed by Derrenbacker and amplified by the observation that Josephus tends to alternate between his sources in extended blocks; that is, not only does Josephus largely avoid alternating between sources within any given pericope, but he also tends not to alternate between them pericope by pericope, preferring to follow several pericopae (in Derrenbacker's examples, between two and seventeen) in one source before switching to the other. It is in this context that Derrenbacker observes that Josephus follows the wording of the source whose order he is following, which might indeed be expected if he has one source in front of him at a time (or even if he is following one source in memory at a time), although since Josephus paraphrases quite thoroughly, the verbal connections Derrenbacker finds are slight.[50] Derrenbacker's summary of Begg's findings also largely supports Downing's conclusions: Josephus largely tries to include the material peculiar to all his sources, and he adapts his sources using the four editorial techniques of omission (particularly of duplicate material), rearrangement, modification and addition.[51]

Derrenbacker proceeds to apply these findings to the 2GH, FH and 2DH. He finds the 2GH problematic partly on account of the mechanical difficulty of the number of passes Luke would have made through Matthew's discourses (difficult enough with a codex, near impossible with a scroll) but even more importantly because the micro-conflation within individual pericopae that Mark would need to have performed is contrary to what is known of the working methods of the ancient authors reviewed.[52] Derrenbacker next turns to Michael Goulder's version of the FH.[53] Derrenbacker finds

---

[46] Derrenbacker, *Compositional Practices*, 91–2.
[47] Christopher Begg, *Josephus' Account of the Early Divided Monarchy* (BETL, 108; Leuven: Leuven University Press, 1993).
[48] Derrenbacker, *Compositional Practices*, 100–1.
[49] Derrenbacker, *Compositional Practices*, 101–3.
[50] Derrenbacker, *Compositional Practices*, 100–13.
[51] Derrenbacker, *Compositional Practices*, 113–16.
[52] Derrenbacker, *Compositional Practices*, 144–66.
[53] In particular in Goulder, *Midrash*, and Goulder, *Luke*.

Goulder's characterization of Matthew as midrash on Mark to be problematic on a number of grounds but otherwise sees his account of Matthew's adaptation of Mark as relatively unproblematic.[54] He is less sanguine about Goulder's proposals for Luke's use of Matthew. For one thing, although Goulder's Luke technically conforms to ancient compositional practice by following one source at a time and relying on memory to supplement it, in using Matthew he is prone to reproducing the remembered passage more accurately than the passage he is meant to have open in front of him, thus effectively moving between the two just for the sake of brief words or phrases.[55] Derrenbacker also objects to Goulder's proposal that Luke was working backwards through a scroll of Matthew, partly because Luke's movements through Matthew would have to include forward as well as backward movements but mainly because the process of going backwards through a scroll while going forwards through individual pericopae is one that is hard to imagine technically, as well as lacking adequate motivation or parallel in the methods of other ancient authors.[56] Derrenbacker concedes that the mechanical problems faced by Goulder's Luke would be eased if Luke used a codex of Matthew rather than a scroll (as Derrenbacker goes on to propose for Matthew's use of Q), but still finds Luke's proposed reverse contextualization of Matthew 16-25 at Lk. 13.22-18.8 hard to swallow, while a more random utilization of Matthew in this section would leave the FH Luke open to Streeter's charge of crankiness.[57] Derrenbacker finally turns his attention to Mark Goodacre's defence of the FH and finds it 'technically and mechanically feasible in light of ancient compositional techniques' but objects that 'descriptions of what Luke is doing with his sources on the FGH are not always compelling literary or artistic descriptions'.[58] Derrenbacker's final verdict on the FH is nevertheless reserved rather than dismissive:

> If the FGH is to remain a credible theory on Synoptic relationships, its advocates need to take these observations into question, and seriously reevaluate some of the ways in which the specifics of the theory are described in light of the compositional conventions of the Greco-Roman world.[59]

Last of all, Derrenbacker evaluates the 2DH in the light of ancient compositional practices. He finds Luke's proposed use of Mark and Q to be largely unproblematic but acknowledges that Matthew's use of Mark and Q is harder to explain, on account both of the extent to which 2DH Matthew would need to have reordered much of the material he took from Q and of a number of occasions (notably in Mark-Q overlap passages) where it appears that Matthew (and occasionally Luke) must have performed micro-conflation of Mark and Q within the scope of an individual pericope.

---

[54] Derrenbacker, *Compositional Practices*, 182–8.
[55] Derrenbacker, *Compositional Practices*, 190–5.
[56] Derrenbacker, *Compositional Practices*, 195–8.
[57] Derrenbacker, *Compositional Practices*, 195–200.
[58] Derrenbacker, *Compositional Practices*, 201–2, citing John S. Kloppenborg, 'On Dispensing with Q?: Goodacre on the Relation of Luke to Matthew', *NTS* 49 (2003), 210-36, here 226-31, and Christopher M. Tuckett, *Q and the History of Early Christianity* (Edinburgh: T&T Clark, 1997), 16-31.
[59] Derrenbacker, *Compositional Practices*, 202.

Derrenbacker offers two proposals to alleviate these difficulties: first, that Matthew may have had access to Q in the form of a codex (thereby facilitating random access) and second, that Matthew and Luke sometimes employed their memory of their sources when they did not have eye contact with them, thereby enabling Matthew to draw on his memory of Q when using it out of sequence and explaining the apparent instances of micro-conflation: when Matthew or Luke was primarily following Q (say) the occasional reminiscence of Mark might influence their text.[60] Against the first of these proposals it might be objected that although a codex might make random access easier than a scroll, the *scriptio continua* format of the text it contained would still make random access to fragments of Q quite challenging. Derrenbacker's second proposal, concerning memory, appears sound. Finally, Derrenbacker (parenthetically) implies that the incidence of micro-conflation of Mark and Q on the 2DH is significantly less than that of Mark and Matthew on the FH, but nowhere substantiates this with any examples of FH Luke's alleged micro-conflation of Matthew and Mark.[61] Derrenbacker may be thinking of the numerous Matthew-Luke agreements against Mark in the triple tradition (on the basis that these would all constitute micro-conflations by FH Luke); if so, this point will be addressed in the next chapter. But unless it can be shown that Luke's alleged micro-conflation must have been more on the scale of 2GH's Mark than that of 2DH's Matthew, presumably the memory explanation offered for 2DH Matthew will serve as well for FH Luke.

Alan Kirk also regards micro-conflation as atypical of ancient authors. In Kirk's view, the memory of a source dealt in 'cognitive units' which were 'the smallest whole units of discourse', meaning 'a coherent, intelligible sequence of words and phrases'. This entails that while such whole units might be moved around, they could not readily be decomposed into smaller lexical units which could then be shuffled around at will and conflated.[62] He gives as an example the difficulty of conflating his nine-digit U.S. social security number with his nine-digit Canadian social security number.[63] Kirk's point can probably be explained in terms of memory (or digit) span: human working memory is normally limited to a handful of items, which may be individual words or digits, but could be meaningful chunks of information, which can allow working memory to hold much more.[64] Moving around whole units (meaningful chunks) in memory is relatively straightforward because there are likely to be relatively few of them, whereas if larger meaningful units are decomposed into smaller lexical ones the number of such small units will quickly exceed working memory capacity, making it much harder to shuffle them.

Kirk nevertheless acknowledges that small-scale conflation can sometimes occur but suggests that it is then 'likely a matter of reminiscence'.[65] How 'reminiscence' differs from memory is left undefined; presumably the former is inadvertent and the latter deliberate. Here, Kloppenborg's distinction between micro-conflation (through

---

[60] Derrenbacker, *Compositional Practices*, 253–5.
[61] Derrenbacker, *Compositional Practices*, 240–1
[62] *QiM*, 146; *WTG*, 94.
[63] *QiM*, 146, n. 278; cf. the analogous example at *WTG*, 94.
[64] Baddeley et al., *Memory*, 20–2, suggest a memory span of six or seven items.
[65] *QiM*, 146.

visually consulting multiple sources), harmonization and assimilation (through memory) may be pertinent.[66] One may also wonder how far the small-scale conflation of decomposed elements differs from the procedure Kirk attributes to the composition of Mt. 4.23–5.2 from Mk 1.21; 1.32-34; 1.39; 3.7-13 and 6.6. Kirk points out that much of this passage consists of Markan stock phrases, typical actions and generalized geographical references, and so proposes that Matthew's memory competence of Mark 'provides him with a lexical inventory to compose from'.[67] Presumably what Kirk means, then, is not that Mt. 4.23–5.2 was composed on the deliberate basis of precisely the Markan passages he lists but that these passages exemplify the kinds of Markan stock phrases Matthew had absorbed and now employed. This seems fair enough, and it accords with aspects of the scribal model of composition outlined in Chapter 2.[68] The boundary between scribal-memorial composition on the base of a lexical inventory and small-scale conflation of decomposed elements may seem not altogether distinct, but it remains most unlikely that an ancient author would attempt the deliberate micro-conflation of sources without some compelling reason.[69]

In common with Derrenbacker, Kirk recognizes that Matthew's use of Mark and Q poses a potential problem for the 2DH and proposes memory as an important part of the solution. Much of his contribution in this area has already been covered in Chapter 2. In terms of transformational techniques Kirk further advances the discussion by examining how a selection of ancient scholarly writers went about reordering their source material as a model for how Matthew (and hence, by implication, any other evangelist) may have done so. We shall examine his findings below.

Downing, Derrenbacker and Kirk have usefully identified many of the transformational techniques that the evangelists are likely to have shared with their contemporaries, such as expansion, compression, paraphrase, omission, addition, clarification and at least some degree of rearrangement, many of which can also be derived from the *Progymnasmata*.[70] While there was also a clear tendency to follow one source at a time, it is less clear how strictly this was adhered to; clearly both some degree of alternation and some degree of conflation occurred, although typically not at a pericope-by-pericope level in the first case or a word-by-word level in the second. The remainder of this chapter will explore whether ancient authors might sometimes go beyond the techniques identified so far. We shall begin with the question of reordering.

---

[66] John S. Kloppenborg, 'Macro-Conflation, Micro-Conflation, Harmonization and the Compositional Practices of the Synoptic Writers', *ETL*, 95, 4 (2019), 629–43, here 629.
[67] *QiM*, 231, 239–41.
[68] And also at *WTG*, 73–8.
[69] James W. Barker, 'Ancient Compositional Practices and the Gospels: A Reassessment', *JBL* 135 (2016), 109–21, here 110–19, suggests several examples of micro-conflation occurring both before and after the composition of the gospels, citing 4Q41, the Greek Minor Prophets Scroll and the Diatessaron, and going on to cite the textual tradition of the gospels and the micro-conflation of Mk 14.12 and Isa. 9.6-10 at Mt. 13.13-14. It may, however, be questioned whether these examples exhibit deliberate micro-conflation (as opposed to assimilation or harmonization in memory); see the critique of Barker in Kloppenborg, 'Macro-Conflation' and cf. Mattila, 'Question', 204–6.
[70] Craig S. Keener, *Christobiography: Memory, History and the Reliability of the Gospels* (Grand Rapids, MI: Eerdmans, 2019), 261–327, also contains a valuable discussion of literary techniques in ancient biographies, in which category he includes the gospels, but Keener's book appeared too late for me to engage with here.

Reordering and rearrangement

On any of the leading Synoptic source-utilization theories, at least one of the evangelists must have substantially reordered at least one of his sources. On either the FH or the 2GH, Luke has rearranged a great deal of Matthew's material (most notably distributing a large part of the Sermon on the Mount across his central section), whereas on the 2DH, Matthew must have performed a similarly extensive rearrangement of Q and to a lesser extent Mark, notably in Matthew 5–9. Neither FH Luke's rearrangement of Matthew nor 2DH Matthew's rearrangement of Q fits comfortably with the transformational techniques reviewed so far. The present section will therefore explore possible precedents for this kind of reordering.[71]

Since Kirk locates the evangelists, particularly Matthew, in the realm of scholarly composition, it is to other examples of ancient scholarly literature that he turns for comparable examples of rearrangement. His investigation proceeds in two stages, first by examining three examples and then by giving a theoretical account of how the sort of rearrangement he finds there might be facilitated by the memory-manuscript fusion of ancient scribal practice.

Kirk's first example is taken from the Homer lexicon of Apollonius Sophista (an Alexandrian scholar who worked in the first century CE). This contains a list of words from Homer's epics in roughly alphabetical order (i.e. ordered by the first two, or occasionally three, letters), each followed by a short definition and an appropriate quotation (or quotations) from Homer. Apollonius is reckoned to have used a number of sources, including an earlier Homer lexicon by Apion, a commentary on the *Odyssey* by Heliodorus, a 'polysemantic' source (which sets out various different shades of meaning for each word) and a tradition of Homer commentary known at the D scholia.[72]

Kirk is primarily interested in how Apollonius uses Heliodorus' *Odyssey* commentary as a source for words not found in the *Iliad*. Kirk's principal finding is that under each initial letter pair, Apollonius appends blocks of Odyssean word entries (taken from Heliodorus) to the list of Iliadic ones, with the Odyssean words within each such block appearing in the order in which they (or at least the appended quotations containing them) occur in the *Odyssey*. Thus, for example, the block of Odyssean words beginning αγ- follows the corresponding block of Iliadic words and works forward through the *Odyssey* from ἀγακλυτά (*Od*. 3.388) to ἀγέρθη (*Od*. 24.349), with the intervening ten entries running more or less in the order of their occurrence in the *Odyssey*. Heliodorus' commentary naturally follows the narrative sequence of the *Odyssey*, and Apollonius preserves this relative order of material within each of his Heliodorus blocks.[73]

This is not quite the full story, however, since many of the words that appear in the *Odyssey* also appear in the *Iliad*. Where Apollonius wishes to employ Heliodorus' treatment of such words, he simply tacks the Heliodoran material onto the end of the corresponding entry in the appropriate Iliadic block with some introductory formula

---

[71] On which see also Barker, 'Compositional Practices', 119–21.
[72] *QiM*, 73–4.
[73] *QiM*, 74–6.

such as 'as Heliodorus says', without, however, otherwise altering the existing Iliadic entry. Kirk suggests that this procedure is analogous to Matthew's use of Mark and Q: 'Where Markan pegs exist, Matthew conflates Q material with Markan materials; where such pegs are lacking he brings the Q material separately in blocks.'[74]

One might question this analogy on the grounds that Matthew's Gospel is a very different kind of writing from a Homer lexicon, and that Matthew lacks the clear alphabetic principle of arrangement employed by Apollonius. One might also probe Kirk's assertion that Apollonius' memory command of the *Odyssey* would have aided his use (also from memory) of Heliodorus' commentary,[75] since it is not entirely obvious how knowing the *Odyssey* off by heart would have enabled rapid sequential access to all the words in the *Odyssey* commencing with αγ- (say) via the commentary. The point is presumably that since the order of the commentary follows the narrative order of the *Odyssey*, secure knowledge of the latter would aid memory access to the former. But Apollonius would still be left with the far from trivial task of scanning Heliodorus' commentary for words corresponding to each letter pair, and it is far from obvious that this would be much faster, less laborious, but no less reliable to do in memory than by scanning a manuscript of Heliodorus. One suspects the task might be more manageable via at least one intermediate written step, such as inscribing all the material relating to words beginning with each individual letter in turn onto wax tablets or papyrus notes and then extracting the letter pairs from such notes.[76] Indeed, Kirk subsequently goes on to remark that 'it is absurd to think, for example, that Apollonius Sophista drafted his *Homer Lexicon* wholly in memory', although he still thinks memory was essential to his project.[77] But even allowing for these reservations, one can see the point Kirk is making: here is an example of a scholarly author (whom Kirk takes to be broadly analogous to the evangelists' literary milieu) combining Source B with Source A in a manner that results in a quite particular procedure for rearranging the contents of Source B: either by affixing matter to pegs supplied in Source A or by preserving the relative order of B material within blocks of B.

The Apollonius example is complicated by his employment of more than two sources. The other source Kirk mainly discusses is the 'polysemantic source', identifiable by its use of the pattern ἐπὶ μὲν ... ἐπὶ δὲ ... ἐπι δὲ ... κτλ to set out alternative shades of meaning for a word. Apollonius occasionally interpolates entries from this source into his alphabetic sequence, either individually or in blocks.[78]

Kirk's final observation on Apollonius is that he 'is a *compiler* and *consolidator* of a scholarly lexical tradition'. That is to say that for the most part he appears content merely to assemble previous scholarly material into his own arrangement, only occasionally offering his own opinion.[79] The explicit lesson Kirk draws from this is that Apollonius'

---

[74] *QiM*, 77.
[75] *QiM*, 77.
[76] Cf. Francis Watson, *Gospel Writing: A Canonical Perspective* (Grand Rapids, MI; Cambridge: Eerdmans, 2013), 170, and John C. Poirier, 'The Roll, the Codex, the Wax Tablet and the Synoptic Problem', *JSNT* 35 (2012), 3–30, here 19–24.
[77] *QiM*, 144.
[78] *QiM*, 74–5, 78.
[79] *QiM*, 78–9.

work was not an attempt to suppress predecessors or putative rivals; implicitly Kirk seems to be emphasizing the very limited creative input of this kind of scholarly writer.

From Apollonius' *Homer Lexicon* Kirk moves on to a collection of interrelated florilegia, collections of chreiai, maxims and the like attributed to noteworthy persons and arranged topically under various headings. Kirk suggests that this material is analogous to that which 2DH Matthew would have taken from Q. The florilegia he examines span several centuries in their source utilization: the tenth-century Byzantine *Antonius* and *Melissa Augusta* both used the *Maximus*, which in turn drew from the ninth-century *Corpus Parisinum* (*CP*); the *CP* in its turn drew on three older sources, including the fifth-century compiler Stobaeus, while Stobaeus used Pseudo-Plutarch and Arius Didymus.

An examination of these various examples shows a tendency to preserve the order of sayings within individual *topoi* (the topics or headings under which the material was arranged) while varying the order of topoi. Beyond this broad generalization, various types of rearrangement may be observed. So, for example, the *Antonius* frequently distributes items from a unified topos in the *Maximus* across three or four different topoi, while retaining the relative order of the *Maximus* sayings within their new locations. This was probably achieved by making multiple passes through the *Maximus* to gather up appropriate items for each of the *Antonius*' sub-topoi. On the other hand, the compiler of the *Maximus* repeatedly scanned *CP* to cycle his materials into seventy-one moral topoi. This often results in the relocation of *CP* sayings and occasionally in giving them a different purpose. It also produces a consistent agreement in *relative* order between the *Maximus* and the *CP* (its source) within the sequence of sayings under each individual topos. Stobaeus (an important source for *CP*) takes over but adapts the conventional topos/rubric design of his source, carrying out changes in order and making additions within that sequence. He introduces some rubrics of his own and rearranges the rubric order of Ps.-Plutarch, but at the same time he maintains a steady forward movement through his source (although he inverts the order of Ps.-Plutarch Books 4 and 5).[80] Changes in topos order are more frequent nearer the beginning of his work. Within each rubric Stobaeus generally follows the sequence of his source, though with transpositions and additions from other sources. Overall Stobaeus follows – as he generally does within each rubric – Ps.-Plutarch's order, thus creating extensive agreement in relative order, though he not infrequently transposes order within these sequences or, less often, pulls materials forward from a different rubric.

In general, then, these florilegia exemplify rearrangement of source material by means of a broad forward movement through one's source(s), possibly employing multiple forward scans to collect items for inclusion under one's own topos scheme, thereby generating a pattern of 'forward sequential agreements'. In Kirk's view, not

---

[80] The notion of steady forward movement through a source may need some refinement. The table and discussion at *QiM*, 81–4, shows the *Melissa Augustana* varying considerably from the macro-structure (sequence of topoi rubrics) of the *Maximus*, which would make steady forward movement difficult to trace in this instance (so it cannot be taken as a universal). Moreover, where any two sequences contain some items in a common order, it will always be possible to represent one as steadily moving through the other while reordering the material that is not in the common sequence. In the main, though, Kirk's other examples bear out the point he is making reasonably well.

only is this method of rearrangement the most common and economical available, it is pretty much how Matthew used Q. Matthew's source-utilization strategy also resembles that of the *CP*, which also has to integrate narrative material (*chreia*) with sayings material and does so by integrating material on the topical peg principle and then using the remainder of the materials from the DIE (Democritus/Isocrates/Epictetus, another of his sources, organized by moral topoi) after using those that have a peg in Stobaeus.[81] Unlike Matthew, however, the florigelia lack any overall narrative arc; this would seem to be a non-trivial difference.

Having illustrated *how* a number of ancient scholarly authors incorporate their sources into their own different arrangements of the material, Kirk goes on to discuss *why* they might be restricted to such methods. As noted in Chapter 2, Kirk lays considerable stress on the scribal use of memory. But he is also keen to argue that memory command of a written text does not mean that anything goes. Inscription in writing results in standardized organization of material. A tightly knit sequence of argumentation depends on the written medium for its transmission. 'The cognitive fusion of memory and manuscript bears upon source-critical analysis in an important way. It entails that a source, in its utilization, cannot casually be dissolved into orality and its elements reconstituted or rearranged willy-nilly.'[82]

Kirk's point is that the ability to recall and access the contents of a text depends on the mnemonic arrangement of the material it contains: a fixed arrangement suitable for memory retrieval relies on schematic cueing. Narrative provides one such *schema*, in that the narrative logic of a sequence of events greatly aids the recalling of events in that sequence. Topoi sequences provide another type of schema (particularly where the topoi employed are broadly conventional and thus already part of the user's mental apparatus). They also provide a convenient means both of chunking material into individual items that short-term memory can deal with and of providing a mental indexing scheme for search and retrieval. In order to retrieve a particular saying, one first moves to the topos heading under which it is located, then works through the items under that topos until one finds it. For this to work efficiently requires not merely some kind of taxonomic arrangement but also a coherent, systematic one – for example, not merely a ragbag of sayings about friendship but an argumentative sequence whose internal logical aids sequential memory retrieval. It is precisely the ability of the written medium to create substantial stable coherent sequences that makes manuscripts an appropriate support for memorizing the material they contain. According to Kirk, what is thereby stored in the memory of a manuscript is thus not a mere jumble of items that can be retrieved at whim but a highly organized set of materials that can be retrieved only according to the systematic connections provided by the coherent arrangement of the underlying written text. Memory retrieval relies on the activation of the appropriate cues, and for manuscripts accessed in memory, the most efficient cueing system is sequential forward movement through the text.[83]

---

[81] *QiM*, 79–92.
[82] *QiM*, 128.
[83] *QiM*, 131–45.

Kirk describes one way in which the memory-manuscript interface may well have worked, but one may question whether this is the only way in which it could do so.[84] The forward sequential movement through sources preserving the relative order of transposed materials in the examples Kirk examines might simply represent the most efficient method of dealing with that kind of material in the absence of any compelling reasons for doing anything different. Other things being equal, it probably is easier to run forwards through a familiar sequence than in some other order. But that does not make other forms of retrieval impossible (as noted in Chapter 2). While for most of us it is considerably harder to recite the alphabet backwards than forwards, with a bit of effort and concentration many people could manage it, and plucking arbitrary random letters out of the sequence is no problem at all, just as many people familiar with Matthew's Gospel can retrieve individual sayings such as 'Blessed are the peacemakers, for they shall be called sons of God' or 'You are Peter, and on this rock I will build my church' without needing any particular retrieval strategy. Whether such examples constitute cogent objections to Kirk's argument is a matter to which we shall return.

A different question is whether using a different comparator would yield different results. We have already noted in passing Josephus' use of the Pentateuch at *Ant.* 3-4; it may be even more instructive to look how Philo of Alexandria reorders material he takes from scripture. While none of Philo's works provides an exact parallel to FH Luke's use of Matthew, a brief look at three of them suggests that the rearrangement of source material FH Luke would need to have performed was not obviously beyond the reach of ancient authors.

Perhaps the closest parallel to a gospel in Philo's writings is his *Life of Moses*, which for all its evident differences from the gospels at least has in common that it presents the *bios* of a religiously foundational figure.[85] Although we could probably guess what Philo's sources were, he is quite explicit about them:

> But I will disregard their malice, and tell the story of Moses as I have learned it, both from the sacred books (Βίβλων τῶν ἱερῶν), the wonderful monuments of his wisdom that he left behind him, and from some of the elders of the nation (ἀπὸ τοῦ ἔθνους πρεσβυτέρων); for I always interwove what I was told with what I read (τὰ γὰρ λεγόμενα τοῖς ἀναγινωσκομένοις), and thus believed myself to have closer knowledge than others of his life's history.
>
> (*Vit. Mos.* 1.4).

This passage indicates that Philo used a mix of oral and written sources, and that the latter were the five books of Moses. The oral material was presumably used from memory and may thus be regarded as part of the cultural memory of Philo's community. Philo may also have accessed the Pentateuch largely from memory, not least since he speaks of *learning* from both the oral and the written material, and because he says

---

[84] Compare the discussion in *WTG*, 92–102.
[85] Cf. Philip L. Shuler, 'Philo's Moses and Matthew's Jesus: A Comparative Study in Ancient Literature' in David T. Runia (ed.), *The Studia Philonica Annual* (Atlanta: Scholars, 1990), vol. 2, 86–103, and (for Luke and Philo), Maren R. Niehoff, *Philo of Alexandria: An Intellectual Biography* (New Haven: Yale University Press, 2018), 130, 140–1, 168.

he 'always interwove' both types of material and that doing so resulted in his having 'closer knowledge than others' of Moses' life.[86]

Philo may thus be somewhat analogous to Luke in writing about a central founder figure on the basis of collective memory (including various oral traditions) and a number of written sources (four or five in the case of Philo, since each book of the Pentateuch would be on a separate scroll).[87] Philo's treatment of Moses' life remains largely faithful to the biblical text, interspersed with a number of further traditions some of which are paralleled in later Midrash together with some quasi-philosophical reflections of his own.[88] His principal sources are Exodus and Numbers, with occasional forays into Genesis and Leviticus, and some material based on Deuteronomy at the end.

Philo arranges his *Life of Moses* into four consecutive sections describing Moses as first king, second legislator, third priest and fourth prophet.[89] The first of these sections broadly follows the order of the biblical narrative from Genesis 47 to Number 23 with occasional transpositions, presumably in the interests of constructing a smoother narrative. So, for example, the description of Moses' ancestry at *Vit. Mos.* 1.7, based partly on material in Exod. 6.16-21, is brought forward to the start of the narrative, just after the summary of Genesis 47 at *Vit. Mos.* 1.5-6 but before *Vit. Mos.* 1.8 narrates Pharaoh's order to kill the Israelite male children as described in Exod. 1.15-16, 22. Philo also recounts how the Jews came to Egypt as a result of famine (*Vit. Mos.* 1.34 based on Genesis 47) and became subject to cruel forced labour (*Vit. Mos.* 1.36-8 based on Exod. 1.8-14; 5.6-19), in between his versions of Exod. 2.10a and 2.11-12 at *Vit. Mos.* 1.18 and 1.44, respectively. At *Vit. Mos.* 1.96-139 he reorders the ten plagues of Exod. 7.14–12.32 into a scheme of his own devising[90] and at *Vit. Mos.* 1.197-211 he shows some tendency to combine and conflate the parallel accounts of manna, quails and water from the rock found in Exod. 16.13-31; 17.2-7 and Num. 11.7-9, 31-32, and possibly Num. 20.2-13 (though it is far from clear that he uses any of the details from Numbers 20). Apart from that Philo adds some material of his own, often in the form of moralizing commentary on the narrative, and omits all the legislative material in Exodus 20 to Numbers 10 and Numbers 15–19 (and anywhere else it occurs). Overall, though, Philo largely follows the biblical account, making his treatment of the biblical narrative in Exodus and Numbers not dissimilar to Luke's treatment of

[86] Harry A. Wolfson, *Philo: Foundations of Religious Philosophy in Judaism, Christianity and Islam* (Cambridge, MA: Harvard University Press, rev. edn, 1968), vol. 1, 95–6, suggests that Philo had long experiencing of preaching about this material in synagogue worship. Niehoff, *Philo*, 173–91, envisages the young Philo as heavily engaged with Alexandrian scholarly exegesis.

[87] Niehoff, *Philo*, 130, 243, further sees parallels between the engagements with specifically Roman discourse in Philo's *Exposition* and Luke's writings.

[88] E.g., for midrashic parallels to the accounts of Moses' miracle working in Philo, see Eric Eve, *The Jewish Context of Jesus' Miracles* (JSNTSup, 231; Sheffield: Sheffield Academic Press, 2002), 56–7, nn.7-9, 68, n. 21. For Philo's modelling of Moses on the ideal Stoic-Cynic philosopher, see Carl R. Holladay, *Theios Aner in Hellenistic Judaism: A Critique of the Use of This Category in New Testament Christology* (Missoula, MT: Scholars Press, 1977), 103–98.

[89] Erwin R. Goodenough, *By Light, Light: The Mystical Gospel of Hellenistic Judaism* (New Haven: Yale University Press, 1935), 180–98.

[90] According to Philo, *Vit. Mos.* 1.96-7, God distributed the miracles among Moses, Aaron and himself according to the elements involved. For a discussion of how this scheme obliges Philo to rearrange the biblical sequence of the ten plagues, see Gerhard Delling, 'Wunder-Allegorie-Mythus bei Philon von Alexandreia' in *Gottes ist der Orient* (Festschrift O. Eissfeldt; Berlin: Evangelische Verlagsanstalt, 1959), 42–68, here 43–4; cf. *Exod. R.* 12.4 and Eve, *Jewish Context*, 66–7.

Mark's narrative (except that Luke omits rather more of Mark) or Josephus' of the Deuteronomic History.

The second section, dealing with Moses as legislator at the start of *Vit. Mos.* 2, in fact has very little on the law of Moses, since Philo deals with this elsewhere (see below). It instead contains Philo's view on why Moses is the best of legislators interspersed with references to the Sabbath Law (Exod. 20.8-11 *et passim*; *Vit. Mos* 2.21-2), the Day of Atonement (Lev. 23.27-32; *Vit. Mos.* 2.23-4), the Flood and the destruction of Sodom as examples of punishments (Gen. 6.5–7.24; 19.24-29; *Vit. Mos.* 2.53-6), the deliverance of Lot (Gen. 19.1-23; *Vit. Mos.* 2.57-8) and the deliverance of Noah (Gen. 6.12–9.1; *Vit. Mos.* 2.59-65).

The third and fourth sections, on Moses as priest and prophet, range over the Pentateuch so liberally that Philo's rearrangement of his biblical sources is best shown in a pair of tables (3.1 and 3.2, both referring to *Vit. Mos.* 2):

Table 3.1 Moses as Priest

66	Moses possessed the qualities of priesthood
67-70	Moses maintained a state of purity for lawgiving at Sinai (Exod. 24.18; 34.28; Deut. 9.9)
71-6	Moses instructed on the building of the sanctuary
77-86	Details of the construction (Exod. 26.18-37)
88	Significance of the materials chosen for construction
89-93	Plan of the Tabernacle (Exod. 27.9-18)
94	Furniture for the Tabernacle: the altar (Exod. 40.6, 29)
95-7	The ark (Exod. 25.10-22)
98-100	Symbolism of the ark
101	The altar of incense (Exod. 30.1-6)
102-3	The candlestick (Exod. 25.31-40)
104	The table (Exod. 25.23-30; salt on it Lev. 24.7 LXX)
105-8	Explanation of furniture and required attitude of worshippers
109-16	High priestly vestments (Exod. 28.1-39)
117-35	Explanation of the vestments' symbolism
136-48	Brazen laver (Exod. 38.8; 38.26-27 LXX)
139-40	Symbolic significance of the laver
141-2	Selection of priests (Aaron and his sons) (Exod. 28.1)
143-52	Installation of priests (Exod. 29.1-37; Lev. 8)
153-9	Additional sacrifices after installation (Lev. 9 [esp. v.24])
159-60	Various daily sacrifices
161-73	The reason for choosing the Levites: the Golden Calf (Exod. 32)
174	Distinction between Priests and attendants, leading to strife (Num. 16.1-3)
175-9	The budding of Aaron's rod (Num. 17)
180	The fruit of the rod were nuts (Num. 17.8)
180-6	The significance of the nuts as indicating a type of virtue

In this section Philo substantially reorders the material he uses, although in doing so he creates a perfectly coherent section of his own, starting with the qualities of Moses as a priest, then going on through the construction of the sanctuary, the furnishing of the sanctuary and the selection and appointment of priests.[91] Although Philo presents this material in his own way and adds his own comments and ideas, the amount of detail

Table 3.2 Moses as Prophet

187	Introduction; having discussed Moses under first three heads Philo will now go on to discuss him as prophet
188-91	Three types of prophecy, of which only the second two will be narrated here
192	Examples in which the divine voice laid down the law by question and answer
193-202	Stoning of a mixed-race (Jewish-Egyptian) man for blasphemy (**Lev. 24.10-14**)
203	New statute against cursing the name of God (**Lev. 24.15-16**)
204-8	Exposition of the statute
209-12	Proper use of the Sabbath (in part Exod. 20.8-11; 31.13-17; 35.2-3; Lev. 23.3; Deut. 5.12-15)
213-20	Stoning of man gathering sticks on the Sabbath (**Num. 15.32-36**; see LXX)
213	Visible voice (**Exod. 20.18 LXX**)
217	Moses knew the matter deserved death (**Exod 31.14; 35.2**)
219	Prohibition of lighting fire on the Sabbath (**Exod. 35.3**, possibly also implied in Exod. 16.23)
221	Transition from punishment of impiety to other kinds of issue
222-32	Provisions for the keeping of Passover by persons with corpse impurity (**Num. 9.1-14**)
233	Transition to next example
234-45	Right of daughters to inherit; order of inheritance after that (**Num. 27.1-11**)
246	Transition to next type of prophecy
247-55	Moses at the Red Sea (**Exod. 14**)
252	'They sink like lead into the depths' (alluding to **Exod. 15.10, 5**)
256-7	The songs of Moses, Israel and Miriam (**Exod. 15.1-21**)
258-69	Provisions for the Manna (**Exod. 16.4-8; 13b-30**)
270-4	The Golden Calf (**Exod. 32**)
275-87	Korah's rebellion (**Num. 16.1-4, 28-35**)
288-9	Moses' farewell blessings of the tribes (**Deut. 33**)
290-1	The death of Moses (Moses knows the story before he dies!) (**Deut. 34**)
292	Conclusion

---

[91] According to Goodenough, *By Light*, 189–92, Philo's rearrangement of the biblical narrative in this section may in part have been to deal with the problem that in the Pentateuch it is Aaron rather than Moses who is given the leading priestly role, while Philo wishes to emphasize Moses' superiority in this role.

taken from the biblical text backs up his claim to be using scripture as a source and so displays an ability to substantially reorder his sources or at least Exodus. Towards the end (175–86) Philo more or less follows a section of Numbers in sequence, and he seems largely to have used one source at a time (Exodus then Leviticus then Numbers). It is more difficult to detect a consistently forward movement in the material taken from Exodus, although the bulk of what he takes from Exodus could be gathered up in two forward passes.

The section on Moses as Prophet is a bit more complex to describe. Bold type indicates where Philo has more clearly employed a biblical source. The section begins with four examples taken from Leviticus (24.10-16) and Numbers (15.32-36, 9.1-14, 27.1-11), the second of which has allusions to at least three passages in Exodus (Exod. 20.18, 31.14, 35.2). The remaining examples of Moses' prophetic prowess occur in canonical order but are widely spaced apart in the source texts (Exodus 14; Exod. 15.1-21; Exod. 16.4-8, 13b-30; Exod. 32; Num. 16.1-4, 28-35; Deuteronomy 33–34). There is thus less (though still some) evidence of Philo reordering his source material in this section, but rather more evidence of his ability to select passages from his source texts out of their immediate context.[92]

Overall, there are some notable similarities between Philo's use of his sources and Luke's use of his. In both cases the source's narrative order is largely retained, with just the occasional transposition. In both cases there is a large central section or sections in which legal and some other material (in one case) and sayings and some other material (in the other) are placed in a sequence of the writer's own devising that is at considerable variance from that in which it occurs in the author's source text(s). Both authors return to the order of their sources to narrate the last days of their respective subjects.

It might nevertheless be objected that these parallels between Philo and Luke are far from perfect, and that in particular, Philo's reordering of Pentateuchal material is rather less extensive than FH Luke's reordering of Matthean material. To address the second objection, we may turn to a work in which Philo deals more extensively with legal material. In *Spec. Leg.* (*Special Laws*) Philo gives his own account of the legal material in the Pentateuch, rearranged in a schema of his own devising (derived from Jewish tradition), namely to use the Ten Commandments as headings under which to place the other material (*Spec. Leg.*1.1).[93] Philo paraphrases rather than quotes the legal material he refers to and intersperses it with explanations of his own devising, so it is not always apparent which particular passage of scripture he has in mind. For example, at *Spec. Leg.* 1.1-12 Philo starts out with a discussion of circumcision; passages such as Gen. 17.10-14 and Lev. 12.3 would be relevant to this topic but it is far from clear that Philo is referring to any specific passage. In many cases, though, it is reasonably clear what biblical passage Philo is reflecting. The order of Pentateuchal material that

---

[92] Goodenough, *By Light*, 192–7, observes that Philo here arranges his material by different kinds of prophecy; there is thus some analogy with Kirk's recycling according to topos.

[93] Peder Borgen, *Philo of Alexandria: An Exegete for His Time* (NovTSup, 86; Leiden: Brill, 1997), 60, 71–2. On the first book of *De Specialibus Legibus* and its relation to *De Vita Mosis*, see Goodenough, *By Light*, 107–12. On Philo's originality in employing the Ten Commandments as heads for expounding the Torah (in a predominantly Roman Stoic context), see Niehoff, *Philo*, 151–4.

results at *Spec. Leg.* 1.1-100 is set out in Table 3.3; biblical references in bold indicate where Philo's source seems clear; those in ordinary type indicate passages that might be relevant but where it is less clear which specific passage(s), if any, Philo had in mind.

Table 3.3 *Special Laws* 1.1-100

1-12	Circumcision; the discussion is general (explaining the custom) and does not appear to reference any specific texts, although Gen. 17.10-14; Lev. 12.3 would be relevant, while the linking of circumcision with the heart at 6 presumably references Deut. 10.16; 30.6
13-14	Sovereignty of God (by implication Exod. 20.3; Deut. 5.7)
15	Sun, moon and stars not to be worshipped (**Deut. 4.19**)
16-20	Exposition of above
21-2	Prohibition of gods of gold and silver (by implication Exod. 20.4-5; Deut. 5.8-9, explicitly **Exod. 20.23**)
23-4	Exposition in terms of not loving money
25	Don't make idols that melt (**Lev. 19.4**)
26-7	The vanity of wealth and riches
28-9	Other types of false gods appealing to the imagination through music and art
30	Moses insisted that God is the creator of all things
31	Life is maintained through clinging to God (**Deut. 4.4**)
32-5	Argument for the existence of God
36-40	The nature of God's essence
41-50	God revealed himself to Moses (**Exod. 33.13-23**)
51	Embracing truth in purity; 'proselytes' (Lev. 9.33-34; Deut. 10.19)
52	Newcomers to be treated with goodwill (**Lev. 19.34**)
53	Don't revile gods (**Exod.** 22.28; **22.27** [LXX])
54-5	Summary punishment of those who abandon God (Deut. 17.2-7; cf. Deut. 13.12-18)
56-7	The good example of Phineas (**Num. 25.1-13**)
58	Condemnation of people who brand themselves (**Lev. 19.28**; cf. Lev. 21.2; Deut. 14.1)
59	Banishment of false opinion
60	Prohibition of various forms of divination, etc. (**Deut. 18.10-12**)
61-3	Further explanation of this prohibition
64-5	Promise of a true prophet (**Deut. 18.15-18**)
66	Regulations for Temple worship
67-8	There should be only one temple (**Deut. 12.5-7, 11-14, 17-18**)
69-70	People come from all over to go to the temple
71-3	Description of the Temple (Lev. 16.29-34)
74-5	No trees are planted in temple grounds (**Deut. 16.21**)
76	Temple revenues do not come from landed estates
77-8	But from offering of the first-fruits (**Exod. 30.12-16**)

79	The Levites are the priestly tribe on account of their zeal on one occasion (**Exod. 32.25-29**)
80	Priests must be without deformity or blemish (**Lev. 21.17-21; 22.4**)
81	Because man was made in the image of God (**Gen. 1.27**)
82-3	Regulations for the dress of priests (**Exod. 28.40-43**)
84-97	The High Priest's dress (**Lev. 16.4; Exod. 28.4-39**)
98-100	Priests offering sacrifices should not drink wine (**Lev. 10.8-11**)

There is some parallel here with the examples Kirk examines, in that Philo is recycling legal material into topoi-sequences of his own devising.[94] Even from Table 3.3 it is apparent that Philo is hardly constrained by the order of his sources here and seems quite able to jump between them, so that here Philo is in principle combining material from five separate scrolls, though in practice it seems more likely that he would have been working largely from memory. But however Philo went about it, it seems clear from this example that an author roughly contemporary with the evangelists was well able to reorder source material quite radically; it is hard to discern any consistent forward movement through his sources here, even with a reasonable number of multiple forward scans.[95]

It may, however, be objected that since Philo thoroughly paraphrases his source material, while the evangelists preserve much of its actual wording, the foregoing parallel is less than exact. To address this point, we shall turn to the opening of the *Migration of Abraham*, where Philo offers an allegorical exegesis of Gen. 12.1-3. In the course of doing so he references a large number of other biblical (mainly Pentateuchal) passages and often quotes them.[96] The sequence of references in *Migr* 1-100 is set out in Table 3.4.

Here there are occasionally small clusters taken from roughly contiguous source material, but in the main Philo roams across the Pentateuch with sovereign freedom. Philo's ordering of biblical material here is hardly due to successive forward scans, but appears rather due to his own train of thought. Moreover, he appears well able to glean material from the Pentateuch (and 1 Samuel) to fit that train of thought without being constrained to follow the sequential topical or narrative logic of his sources, except perhaps within those occasional small clusters.

It may, however, be objected that the composition of the *Migration of Abraham* is not a true analogy to the composition of Luke, since while Philo is using a series of quotations and allusions interspersed in a commentary of his own devising, Luke is

---

[94] Or at least in part, perhaps, that of the Jewish tradition he is following; see Borgen, *Philo*, 59-61; and Harry Austryn Wolfson, *Philo: Foundations of Religious Philosophy in Judaism, Christianity and Islam* (Cambridge, MA: Harvard University Press, 1947), vol. 2, 201.

[95] Borgen, *Philo*, 78, suggests that Philo's *Exposition of the Laws of Moses* (*On the Creation, On Abraham, On Joseph, On the Decalogue, On the Special Laws 1-4; On the Virtues; On Rewards and Punishments*) broadly follows the biblical chronology, so in a broader sense Philo does follow the order of his sources, but it remains the case that he does not do so locally in *Special Laws*.

[96] On Philo's method of intertextual allegorical commentary in its Alexandrian context, not least in relation to the *Migration of Abraham*, see Niehoff, *Philo*, 181-5.

Table 3.4 Biblical Passages Cited in *Migration of Abraham* 1–100

1	Gen. 12.1-3
3	Gen. 3.19
5	Gen. 28.17
8	Exod. 34.12; (10.28; 23.21)
12	Gen. 12.1
13	Gen. 13.9
15	Exod. 2.23
17	Gen. 50.25
18	Gen. 50.24
19	Gen. 39.7; 40.8; (39.1 LXX)
20	Gen. 41.41; 40.15
21	Gen. 39.8-9, 12; 42.18; 45.28
22	Gen. 50.19; 45.7-8
25	Exod. 12.11
27	Gen. 31.3
29	Gen. 26.2
36	Exod. 15.25
37	Gen. 2.9
38	1 Sam. 9.9
42	Gen. 1.31
43	Gen. 12.1
44	Gen. 15.6; Deut. 34.4
47	Exod. 20.18; 20.22
48	Deut. 4.12
53	Gen. 12.2
54	Exod. 1.9
56	Deut. 4.6-7
60	Deut. 7.7-8
61	Exod. 23.2 LXX
62	Deut. 20.1
64	Lev. 11.42
66	Gen. 3.14
67	Lev. 8.21, 29
68	Num. 14.11-12
69	Deut. 23.1-2
74-5	(Cain and Abel; Gen. 4.1-8)
76	Exod. 4.10

78-9	Exod. 4.14
81	Exod. 4.15-16
83	Exod. 7.12, 20-22; 8.7
84	Exod. 7.1
85	Exod. 7.12; 8.19; 32.16; 8.18
86	Gen. 12.2
94	Gen. 25.5-6
95	Gen. 30.13
97	Exod. 35.22-3; 38.26 LXX
99	Num. 21.30 LXX

constructing a narrative almost entirely out of his source materials (assuming the bulk of his L material did in fact come from one or more sources). But while Philo and Luke were clearly working under different constraints, it remains the case that at least one first-century author was able to employ source material well out of its original context and order, without being confined to the kind of forward movement and preservation of relative order exhibited by Kirk's scholarly writers. In particular, Philo does not appear to have been operating under any cognitive constraints to follow the coherent arrangement of his sources.

That said, there is an important distinction between what Philo is doing and what Kirk's examples are doing. We should distinguish between occasional random access, selective rearrangement and systematic rearrangement. Occasional random access is the ability to pluck the odd piece of material from its original context and place it elsewhere, a feat that no one will regard as problematic. At the opposite extreme, systematic rearrangement is the process of taking the bulk of Source A and incorporating it in a different sequence into text B. Selective rearrangement lies between the two; it consists of taking a number of items from Source A and placing them in a different arrangement in text B. With this distinction in place it becomes apparent that the Philonic examples illustrate selective rearrangement whereas Kirk's examples concern systematic rearrangement. It is plausible that systematic rearrangement will be more constrained by the considerations Kirk advances than selective rearrangement, since systematic rearrangement has to find a place for all the material to be incorporated into the new work, which in turn implies the need for a systematic approach to gathering up this material. What the Philonic examples then show is that the same constraints do not necessarily apply to selective rearrangement.

Systematic rearrangement is the appropriate strategy for 2DH Matthew to use, since 2DH Matthew has to incorporate the whole of Q into his gospel. It is less clear, however, that it is so appropriate for FH Luke, who does not incorporate the whole of Matthew (of which the double tradition material accounts for only about a quarter).[97]

---

[97] Matthew contains 1,070 verses of which 241 are represented in Q, based on the table at James M. Robinson, Paul Hoffmann and John S. Kloppenborg, *The Critical Edition of Q: Synopsis Including the Gospels of Matthew and Luke, Mark and Thomas with English, German and French Translations of Q and Thomas* (Hermeneia, Minneapolis; Leuven: Fortress Press; Peeters Publishers, 2000), ix–xii (henceforth *CEQ*).

Thus while the examples drawn from Philo do not negate Kirk's findings, they at least qualify the extent to which they can determine the constraints on FH Luke.

We shall return to this issue in Chapter 6, which will examine Kirk's proposals for 2DH Matthew's rearrangement of Mark and Q and then propose how FH Luke may have worked with Matthew's order.

Literary imitation

By giving students models and examples to work from, writers of *Progymnasmata* were both encouraging students to learn through imitation and training them how to imitate. Imitation was by no means confined to students, however; in one form or another literary (or rhetorical) imitation was a widely practised ancient compositional technique.

Georg Knauer proposed that Virgil's imitative use of Homer might be understood as analogous to the New Testament's typological relation to the Old.[98] Reversing this analogy could suggest taking Virgil's imitation of Homer as a model for the gospels' use of the Old Testament. While epic poetry may seem too remote from the genre of the gospels for this to be plausible, Knauer points out that both Homer and the Jewish Scriptures were the most salient cultural texts for the respective subsequent writers to draw on. It has in any case long been recognized that the evangelists made use of earlier sacred texts through quotation, reference, allusion, rewriting and so-called 'midrash'.[99] These kinds of intertextuality at least approximate, and often constitute, forms of imitation. But while there has been a growing recognition that the practice of literary/rhetorical imitation may have much to offer for our understanding of the evangelists' techniques, there has to date been only limited application of this insight to the Synoptic Problem.[100]

In its earliest sense (as found, for example, in Plato and Aristotle) 'imitation' (*imitatio* in Latin or μίμησις in Greek) referred to the imitation of reality in art and

---

[98] Georg Nicolaus Knauer, 'Vergil's *Aeneid* and Homer', *GRBS* 5 (1964), 61–84, here 82.

[99] On 'Midrash' as a possible model, see, e.g., Goulder, *Midrash*, 28–69; John Shelby Spong, *Resurrection: Myth or Reality? A Bishop's Search for the Origins of Christianity* (San Francisco: HarperSanFrancisco, 1994), 3–22; Marie Noonan Sabin, *Reopening the Word: Reading Mark as Theology in the Context of Early Judaism* (Oxford: Oxford University Press, 2002), 34–51. For criticisms of the use of the term 'midrash' in this context, see, e.g., Alexander, 'Midrash'; and Raymond E. Brown, *The Birth of the Messiah: A Commentary on the Infancy Narratives in Matthew and Luke* (London: Geoffrey Chapman, 1977), 557–62.

[100] Brad McAdon, *Rhetorical Mimesis and the Mitigation of Early Christian Conflicts: Examining the Influence That Greco-Roman Mimesis May Have in the Composition of Matthew, Luke, and Acts* (Eugene, OR: Pickwick, 2018), argues *inter alia* for a mimetic relationship between Luke and Matthew. I only became aware of McAdon's book at a relatively stage in writing this one, so I have been unable to engage with it fully here. Dennis R. MacDonald, 'The Synoptic Problem and Literary Mimesis: The Case of the Frothing Demoniac' in Foster, *New Studies*, 509–21, represents an explicit attempt to apply literary imitation to the Synoptic Problem, but only insofar as MacDonald sees Matthew and Luke taking over elements of Mark's imitation of Euripides' *Hercules furens* at Mk 9.14-19. Gary N. Knoppers, 'The Synoptic Problem? An Old Testament Perspective', *BBR* 19 (2009), 11–34, contains a helpful discussion of how imitation might shed light on parallel narratives in both the OT and the NT. Further examples of the application of literary imitation to gospel criticism will be encountered below.

literature and hence (following Aristotle) to the means of representing reality (or an imagined reality) in narrative or drama. In later rhetorical discourse 'imitation' came to refer to the imitation of prior literary models in one's own composition.[101] The first sense can shade into the second via the imitation of the techniques and characteristic themes of one's predecessors; that is, one's own representation of reality (imitation in sense one) may proceed through imitation of earlier representations, either through imitation of particular models (our second sense) or through imitation of techniques gleaned from a range of earlier models via one's literary and rhetorical education (a sense midway between the other two). In Andrew Pitts' terminology, literary imitation can also be either 'external' (imitating the style, language or arrangement of one's model) or 'internal' (reworking its content).[102]

Imitation in its rhetorical sense was not so much a particular technique as a mode of appropriating earlier material. It was widely practised in antiquity and was closely related to emulation (*aemulatio* or ζῆλος), the competitive (but generally respectful) attempt to equal or surpass the model(s) being emulated.[103] As a first approximation, imitation can be defined as the creative reworking of a previous text, or of a number of previous texts, from which one was meant to draw the best features and qualities. It was not mere copying, nor was it mere slavish repetition of what had been said before. Neither was it plagiarism, from which it could be distinguished not least by making it clear what models were being employed through the tenor of one's writing, so that one's target audience could discern what was being imitated, and also by avoiding mere copying or paraphrase without any further transformation of the material.[104] The impression of plagiarism was also often mitigated by the use of multiple models. Thus, 'Horace refers to flitting around and gathering all the best models to patch together into a better whole (*Odes* 4.2)',[105] while Seneca (*Ep.* 84) likens the writer to a bee gathering material to make honey: 'One ought to imitate the bees, he concludes, taking ideas from reading, but also applying one's own genius.'[106] Virgil's imitation 'is not pastiche

---

[101] For this distinction and a discussion of 'imitation' in the first sense, see Octavian D. Baban, *On the Road Encounters in Luke-Acts: Hellenistic Mimesis and Luke's Theology of the Way* (PBM; Milton Keynes: Paternoster, 2006), 73–118; see also Andrew W. Pitts, 'The Origins of Greek Mimesis and the Gospel of Mark: Genre as a Potential Constraint in Assessing Markan Imitation' in Matthew Ryan Hauge and Andrew Pitts (eds), *Ancient Education and Early Christianity* (LNTS, 533; London: Bloomsbury T&T Clark, 2016), 107–136, here 118–19.

[102] Pitts, 'Origins', 120, 127.

[103] For a more nuanced discussion of the relation between imitation and emulation, see Adriana Maria Schippers, 'Dionysius and Quintilian: Imitation and Emulation in Greek and Latin Literary Criticism' (PhD Dissertation; Leiden, 2019), 19–61.

[104] Tim Whitmarsh, *Greek Literature and the Roman Empire: The Politics of Imitation* (Oxford: Oxford University Press, 2001), 26–89; D.A. Russell, 'De Imitatione' in David West and Tony Woodman (eds), *Creative Imitation and Latin Literature* (Cambridge: Cambridge University Press, 1979), 1–16; Thomas L. Brodie, 'Luke 7,36–50 as an Internalization of 2 Kings 4,1–37: A Study in Luke's Use of Rhetorical Imitation', *Biblica* 64 (1983), 457–85, here 459–62.

[105] Ellen Finkelpearl, 'Pagan Traditions of Intertextuality in the Greco-Roman World' in Dennis R. MacDonald (ed.), *Mimesis and Intertextuality in Antiquity and Christianity* (SAC; Harrisburg, PA: Trinity Press International, 2001), 78–90, here 83.

[106] Finkelpearl, 'Pagan Traditions', 83; cf. Karl Olav Sandnes, '*Imitatio Homeri*? An Appraisal of Dennis R. MacDonald's "Mimesis Criticism"', *JBL* 124 (2005), 715–32, here 725–8; Carruthers, *Book of Memory*, 237–8; *WTG*, 85–6.

but creative writing within a tradition'.[107] It 'is described variously as a process of inspection, contemplation, wrestling, pioneering, digesting, honey-making, a process of being impregnated by the old text, so that the old text and the author combine to produce something quite new'.[108] Paradoxically, then, imitation was often the means by which Greek and Roman authors strove to be creative and original, through the transformations they wrought on the sources imitated.

Based mainly on his reading of Longinus, D.A. Russell suggests five principles of successful imitation:

(i) The object must be worth imitating.
(ii) The spirit rather than the letter must be reproduced.
(iii) The imitation must be tacitly acknowledged, on the understanding that the informed reader will recognize and approve the borrowing.
(iv) The borrowing must be 'made one's own', by individual treatment and assimilation to its new place and purpose.
(v) The imitator must think of himself as competing with his model, even if he knows he cannot win.[109]

That imitation of appropriate models was inculcated in literate education is indicated, for example, by Quintilian (*Inst.* 10.1-2).[110] It may, however, be questioned how relevant it is for the composition of the gospels, not least on account of their genre and the probable educational level of their authors.[111] We shall nevertheless argue that it was a technique potentially available to the evangelists and probably employed by Luke.[112]

To begin with, imitation was by no means confined to epic poetry and often crossed genres. Tony Woodman points to a straightforward instance of imitation in prose historiography in Tacitus, where, he maintains, *Annals* 1.61-2 is largely an imitation of *Histories* 2.70. The account of Germanicus' visit to the site of the catastrophic Roman defeat in the Teutoborg forest at *Annals* 1.61-2 appears to be an imitation of the account of the far more recent visit of Vitellius to the site of the first battle of Cremona at *Histories* 2.70, an imitation, moreover, that also contains several echoes of Virgil (*Aen.* 8.196-7; 10.850; 12.36). Woodman similarly proposes that the account of Caecina's subsequent attempt to establish a camp in the face of German opposition at *Annals* 1.64-5 imitates an account of an earlier battle with the Germans at *Histories* 5.14.2–5.15.2. In each

---

[107] Ian M. le M. Du Quesnay, 'From Polyphemus to Corydon: Virgil, Eclogue 2 and the Idylls of Theocritus' in David West and Tony Woodman (eds), *Creative Imitation and Latin Literature* (Cambridge: Cambridge University Press, 1979), 35–70, here 37.
[108] Brodie, 'Luke 7,36–50', 462.
[109] Russell, 'De Imitatione', 15.
[110] Teresa Morgan, *Literate Education in the Hellenistic and Roman Worlds* (CCS; Cambridge: Cambridge University Press, 2007), 251–3; Dennis R. MacDonald, *The Gospels and Homer: Imitation of Greek Epic in Mark and Luke-Acts* (NTGL, 1; Lanham, MD: Rowman & Littlefield, 2015), 3–4.
[111] Damm, *Ancient Rhetoric*, XXXIII, n. 81, suggests that one should rather focus on techniques used in the composition of ancient biography, which he regards as closest to the genre of the gospels, and cf. the caution displayed in this regard by Pitts, 'Origins', 129–36.
[112] See also the discussion of imitation in McAdon, *Rhetorical Mimesis*, 17–47, 255–82.

case Woodman suggests that Tacitus is engaged in 'substantive imitation', by which he means supplying the details of an incident of which he has a bare notice from those of which he has a fuller account in order to make his work more entertaining. Woodman also notes that elsewhere *Annals* 1 contains several imitations of Livy, who in turn is recognized to have imitated Homer, Herodotus and Thucydides.[113] That historians employed imitation is also indicated by Lucian's complaint about their often doing so inappropriately.[114]

According to Thomas Brodie:

> Literary dependence occurred not only within particular genres, as when one epic poet imitated another, but also between genres that were quite diverse. Homeric epic, for instance, was imitated and adapted by both historiography and drama. In a very different mode of crossing from one genre to another, Vergil's Latin epic poetry was summarized into Greek prose.
> Likewise in biblical composition; there are many well-known instances of literary dependence within particular genres ... In biblical composition, as in the broader world of writing, literary dependence is not confined within a particular genre.[115]

Moreover, literary imitation was by no means unknown to biblical writers. The use of the Deuteronomic History by the Chronicler or the various examples of 'rewritten bible' might be seen as a form of imitation, while the story of David and Goliath at 1 Samuel 17 might be viewed as (ironically) imitating ancient Near Eastern epic.[116] A more substantial example is the book of Tobit, which Dennis MacDonald and George Nickelsburg see as imitating both Homer and Genesis (among other influences such as Job and Ahikar).[117] In particular MacDonald proposes that Tobias' travels on behalf of his father in Tobit imitate Telemachus' quest for news of his long-absent father in *Od.* 1-4, 15. For example, both Telemachus and Tobias are aided by a supernatural figure – the goddess Athene or the angel Raphael – in the guise of a relative or family friend, both encounter wedding feasts in the course of their journeys, both have to beg their hosts to be sent home, and there is a similar sequence of events overall. Of

---

[113] Tony Woodman, 'Self-Imitation and the Substance of History: Tacitus, *Annals* 1.61-5 and *Histories* 2.70, 5.14-15' in David West and Tony Woodman (eds), *Creative Imitation and Latin Literature* (Cambridge: Cambridge University Press, 1979), 143-56. Cf. the discussion of imitation in Greek historiography in Pitts, 'Origins', 119-29.

[114] McAdon, *Rhetorical Mimesis*, 281-2, citing Lucian, *How to Write History*, 15.

[115] Thomas L. Brodie, 'Towards Tracing the Gospels' Literary Indebtedness to the Epistles' in Dennis R. MacDonald (ed.), *Mimesis and Intertextuality in Antiquity and Christianity* (Studies in Antiquity & Christianity; Harrisburg, PA: Trinity Press International, 2001), 104-16, here 107.

[116] Sergey Frolov and Allen Wright, 'Homeric and Ancient Near Eastern Intertextuality in 1 Samuel 17', *JBL* 130 (2011), 451-71.

[117] Dennis R. MacDonald, 'Tobit and the *Odyssey*' in Dennis R. MacDonald (ed.), *Mimesis and Intertextuality in Antiquity and Christianity* (SAC; Harrisburg, PA: Trinity Press International, 2001), 11-40, and George W.E. Nickelsburg, 'Tobit, Genesis, and the *Odyssey*: A Complex Web of Intertextuality' in MacDonald (ed.), *Mimesis and Intertextuality*, 41-55. See also Anne M. O'Leary, *Matthew's Judaization of Mark Examined in the Context of the Use of Sources in Greco-Roman Antiquity* (LNTS, 323; ed. M. Goodacre; London: T&T Clark, 2006), 58-70, who discusses Tobit's use of Genesis, Deuteronomy and Homer as an example of Jewish rewriting of sources.

particular note is the incidental appearance of Tobias' dog, given that domesticated dogs following their owners around rarely appear in Jewish texts (Tob. 5.16; 11.4; cf. *Od.* 2.11; 17.62 where Telemachus is followed by a pair of dogs).[118] While accepting MacDonald's case, Nickelsburg argues that some features of Tobit are better explained as an imitation of the journey of Jacob in which he gains a bride (Gen. 27.42–35.29), partly contaminated with Isaac's briefer journey to the same end in Genesis 24.

There is little (surviving) ancient reflection on what sort of transformative techniques imitation might employ. Thomas Brodie suggests:

> The actual practice of imitating or emulating involved a considerable range of techniques of adaptation. Among the most basic were those of compression (or abbreviation) and expansion. A more complex technique was that of fusing and dividing. In this process characters or actions which in the source were quite distinct, in the new text were fused into one. Or alternatively single elements of the source text were divided in the process of rewriting. Other techniques could be mentioned but the choice would be selective.[119]

Abbreviation and expansion are techniques we have already met. Fusing is related to what is elsewhere called *contamination*, the process by which elements from one narrative are introduced into another or 'the fusing of incidents, scenes, or plots from two or more Greek originals'.[120]

One important difference between imitation and the types of ancient source utilization usually attributed to ancient historians, biographers and scholar-tradents is that imitative techniques can be employed to create a narrative about different characters and events from those in the source text, as, for example, when Virgil takes incidents and characters from the *Iliad* and *Odyssey* to create his epic poem about Aeneas. Moreover, the imitator is not confined to merely recycling material from his models; there is nothing to stop fresh elements being introduced into the text (even if many apparently fresh elements draw from a general cultural stock). The *Aeneid* is by no means simply a mangled version of Homer with some of the names changed. And while Virgil may seem far removed from the evangelists, he provides a particularly useful example of imitative techniques both because no one doubts that he was imitating Homer and because there is an abundance of scholarship on how he went about it.[121]

The *Iliad* concerns a small segment of the Trojan War, in which the Greek leader Agamemnon so upsets the Greek hero Achilles that the latter refuses to fight until his friend Patroclus is killed in battle by the Trojan champion Hector, leading first to Achilles' slaying of Hector and then to a brief moment of reconciliation when

---

[118] MacDonald, 'Tobit and the *Odyssey*', 35
[119] Brodie, 'Luke 7,36–50', 462.
[120] George Converse Fiske, *Lucilius and Horace: A Study in the Classical Theory of Imitation* (Madison: 1920), 50.
[121] See also the discussion of Virgil's imitation of Homer in Adam Winn, *Mark and the Elijah-Elisha Narrative: Considering the Practice of Greco-Roman Imitation in the Search for Markan Source Material* (Eugene, OR: Pickwick, 2010), 11–33, and McAdon, *Rhetorical Mimesis*, 25–34.

Hector's father, the Trojan king Priam, dares to visit Achilles' camp to collect his son's corpse. The first half of the *Odyssey* narrates Telemachus' journeying to find news of his long-absent father followed by Odysseus' long-delayed return home from Troy and his various adventures along the way; the second half narrates what happens when Odysseus returns home to Ithaca and takes his revenge on the suitors who have been trying to win the hand of his faithful wife Penelope while eating him out of house and home. The first half of the *Aeneid* tells of the escape of Aeneas (a relatively minor Trojan hero in the *Iliad*) from the sack of Troy and his voyage across the Mediterranean (via various adventures) to Italy, where he is destined to found what will in time become the Roman people. The second half narrates how the goddess Juno (who holds an implacable hatred for the Trojans) stirs up an otherwise unnecessary war of the local Latins against the Trojan newcomers after the Latin king offers his daughter Lavinia in marriage to Aeneas, to which Turnus, who regards Lavinia as his promised bride, strongly objects.

Initially, it may appear that the first half of the *Aeneid*, in which Aeneas travels from Troy to Italy, imitates the *Odyssey* while the second half, in which Aeneas fights a war in Italy, imitates the *Iliad*, but while this is not wholly incorrect, it is an excessively rough approximation. Imitation of the *Odyssey* continues well into the second half of the *Aeneid*, while the first half contains scenes imitating the *Iliad* (e.g. the games for Anchises at *Aen.* 5.42-603 imitate the games for Patroclus at *Il.* 23.226-897). Moreover, Virgil often contaminates one Homeric scene with another (e.g. Aeneas' visit to Evander at *Aen.* 8.102-584 contaminates Telemachus' visit to Nestor in *Od.* 3.1-484 with that to Menelaus at *Od.* 4.1-619).[122] But Virgil doesn't simply borrow details from one Homeric scene while imitating another. The *Aeneid* illustrates fusion of actions and characters throughout. Thus Aeneas is not simply another Odysseus[123] or another Achilles,[124] he is both rolled into one with elements of Telemachus and an idealized Augustus. Similarly, Lavinia is both Helen (the woman over whom a war is fought) and Penelope (whose suitors must be overcome). If that suggests that Turnus may be another Paris or another Odyssean suitor, he is introduced instead as another Achilles, but is then slain like Hector when Aeneas finally takes on Achilles' role, thus exemplifying division (of the *Iliad*'s Achilles among two leading actors in the *Aeneid*) along with the fusion of several roles in the person of Turnus.[125] That in turn suggests that Virgil is not simply lifting a scene here from the *Odyssey* and another there from the *Iliad*, but often combining the two, so that Aeneas' arrival in Italy to fight another Trojan War (with clear echoes of the *Iliad*) is simultaneously Odysseus' return to Ithaca to reclaim his wife and defeat the suitors for her hand. Indeed, rather than seeing Virgil as alternately mining first the *Odyssey* and then the *Iliad* for materials to imitate in his

---

[122] Knauer, 'Vergil's *Aeneid*', 65.
[123] Francis Cairns, *Virgil's Augustan Epic* (Cambridge: Cambridge University Press, 1989), 177–214, esp. 184–94.
[124] L.A. MacKay, 'Achilles as Model for Aeneas', *TPAPA* 88 (1957), 11–16; Katherine Callen King, 'Foil and Fusion: Homer's Achilles in Vergil's Aeneid', *MDLATC* 9 (1982), 31–57.
[125] Knauer, 'Vergil's *Aeneid*', 66, 76.

own composition, one might more subtly see him as viewing the *Odyssey* as already an imitation of the *Iliad* and then reading the former through the lens of the latter.[126]

Homer was not Virgil's only source. Virgil was also familiar both with subsequent epic poetry (such as Apollonius' *Argonautica*) and with the tradition of scholarly interpretation and criticism of Homer (not least among Alexandrian scholars).[127] The *Aeneid* further displays knowledge of the contents of the now lost Epic Cycle: the *Cypria* (the prequel to the *Iliad*), the *Aethiopis* (the immediate sequel to the *Iliad*), the *Ilias parva*, or 'Little Iliad', the *Ilious persis* (or 'Sack of Troy') and the *Nostoi* (or 'Returns', i.e. of the other Greek heroes from the Trojan War apart from Odysseus), and possibly of the non-Trojan parts of the Cycle as well.[128] Moreover, the legend of Aeneas' flight from Troy to Italy ultimately leading to the founding of Rome was hardly Virgil's creation, and he was presumably familiar with many of its earlier forms.[129]

This use of multiple sources and traditions does not, however, result in some kind of monstrous hybrid, as if the *Aeneid* were a Frankenstein's monster mashed together out of disparate elements. Although Virgil regarded the poem as still unfinished at the time of his death, he had succeeded in composing an epic with its own integrity. The *Aeneid* imitates the *Iliad* and the *Odyssey*, but it does merely rehash them, just as Virgil's Aeneas combines elements of Achilles, Odysseus and Telemachus while transcending all three. Consistently termed *pius*, Virgil's Aeneas is depicted as morally superior to his Homeric prototypes and ultimately concerned not with his own agenda but with the divine destiny that will lead to the founding of Rome.

Two passages near the start of the *Aeneid* may serve to provide a more detailed view of how Virgil works.[130] The first, *Aen.* 1.81-143, narrates a storm at sea involving Aeneas and his companions after they have set out from Troy. Here Virgil draws primarily on the account of Odysseus' shipwreck at *Od.* 5.291-387, after Odysseus has left Calypso's isle on a raft. Both accounts feature storm blasts from various winds, divine interventions to both cause and end the storm, people swimming and planks in the sea, and similar cries from the protagonist wishing he had perished at Troy. Virgil also seems to have borrowed a couple of details from the storm and shipwreck at *Od.* 12.403-19, such as the helmsman and sailors being thrown into the sea. The storms occur in similar contexts in Homer and Virgil. After the destruction of his raft in *Od.* 5, Odysseus comes ashore at the land of the Phaeacians, where he meets first Nausicáa and subsequently her parents Alcinous and Arete, to whom he narrates his adventures up to that point, including the storm in *Od.* 12. As a result of this storm, Odysseus

---

[126] Edan Dekel, *Virgil's Homeric Lens* (New York: Routledge, 2012), 1-2, 19-21.
[127] Ralph Hexter, 'On First Looking into Vergil's Homer' in Joseph Farrell and Michael C.J. Putnam (eds), *A Companion to Vergil's Aeneid and Its Tradition* (Chichester: Wiley-Blackwell, 2010), 26-36.
[128] Ursula Gärtner, 'Virgil and the Epic Cycle' in Marco Fantuzzi and Christos Tsagalis (eds), *The Greek Epic Cycle and Its Ancient Reception: A Companion* (Cambridge: Cambridge University Press, 2015), 543-64; for the Epic Cycle in general, see the other essays in the same volume, esp. Fantuzzi and Tsagalis, 'Introduction: Kyklos, the Epic Cycle and Cyclic Poetry' in Fantuzzi and Tsagalis, *Greek Epic Cycle*, 1-40; and Ingrid Holmberg, 'The Creation of the Ancient Greek Epic Cycle', *OT* 13 (1998), 456-78.
[129] Sergio Casali, 'The Development of the Aeneas Legend' in Joseph Farrell and Michael C.J. Putnam (eds), *A Companion to Vergil's Aeneid and Its Tradition* (Chichester: Wiley-Blackwell, 2010), 37-51; Anonymous, 'The Aeneas-Legend from Homer to Virgil', *BICS, BS 52: Roman Myth and Mythography*, 34.S52 (July 1984), 12-24.
[130] Cf. the discussion of Virgil's imitation of Homer in McAdon, *Rhetorical Mimesis*, 25-34.

fetches up on an island called Ogygia, where he encounters Calypso, who keeps him as an object of her passion for seven years. Odysseus finally leaves Calypso's isle on the raft that Poseidon shatters in the storm at *Od.* 5.291-387. After the storm in Book 1 of the *Aeneid*, Aeneas and his men land at Carthage, where Aeneas meets Dido, to whom he narrates his adventures to date and who also becomes his lover. Dido thus combines the roles of Calypso and Alcinous (as well as Homer's Circe and Apollonius' Medea).

The storm in the Aeneid is caused through the agency of Aeolus, who controls the winds, as he is said to do at *Od.* 10.1-55.[131] Aeolus' appearance in the Aeneid storm thus underlines a contrast between Odysseus and Aeneas. In the Odyssey Aeolus' winds are let loose to destructive effect through the folly of Odysseus' companions, none of whom will make it home. In the Aeneid, Aeolus acts at the bidding of Juno's malice; Aeneas and his companions are blameless. Such contrast and reversal is another common technique in literary imitation, often called positivization, the portraying of characters or events in one's own narrative in a better light than those they are modelled on.

Poseidon's role is inverted between the two texts. In the *Odyssey*, it is Poseidon who causes the storm that destroys Odysseus' raft, mainly because he is furious with Odysseus for blinding his son, the Cyclops Polyphemus. In Virgil, however, it is Neptune – the Roman equivalent of Poseidon – who comes to Aeneas' rescue by stilling the storm, even more emphatically than Athene does in the *Odyssey*. Neptune's ostensible reason for intervening is that he resents Juno and Aeolus interfering in his realm, but according to Homer this wouldn't be the first time the god of the sea has intervened on Aeneas' behalf. At *Il.* 20.273-352, Poseidon rescues Aeneas from certain death at the hand of Achilles, while Hera (the equivalent of the Roman Juno) and Athene declare their unremitting hostility to the Trojans – a hostility that Juno continues to display in *Aeneid* 1 even while Neptune comes to the rescue again. Moreover, at *Il.* 20.302-8 Poseidon utters the prophecy that gave rise to the Aeneas legend. This suggests that *Il.* 20 is yet another hypotext alluded to by the storm scene in the *Aeneid*. This further illustrates *contaminatio* – or conflation – of multiple hypotexts into a single account.

Book Two of the *Aeneid* begins Aeneas' narration to Dido of the events leading up to his arrival on her shores and covers the reception of the wooden horse and the subsequent fall of Troy. In Homer, these events are described much more briefly in Demodocus' song at *Od.* 8.486-520,[132] but Aeneas' account parallels the events more fully described in the *Iliou persis*. Ursula Gärtner points out that there are so many extant accounts of the fall of Troy that faced with such 'a near-insoluble tangle of sources' we cannot confidently determine whether Virgil was drawing directly on the *Iliou persis*, but that we should regard him as engaged in rivalling the cyclic tradition at this point; Virgil's originality lay in narrating the fall of Troy from a Trojan viewpoint (specifically, that of Aeneas).[133]

---

[131] For the use of *Od.* 10.1–468 in *Aen.* 1, see Knauer, 'Virgil's *Aeneid*', 70–1.
[132] For a more nuanced discussion of the relation of Virgil to Homer here, see Dekel, *Virgil's Homeric Lens*, 86–8.
[133] Gärtner, 'Virgil and the Epic Cycle', 551.

The second passage we shall examine here, *Aen.* 2.469-558,[134] describes how Achilles' son Pyrrhus (also called Neoptolemus) leads a rush into King Priam's palace, slaughtering as he goes and finally killing Priam among the altars. At Pyrrhus' first appearance in this scene he is likened to a snake (*Aen* 2.469-75):

Just before the entrance-court and at the very portal is Pyrrhus, proudly gleaming in the sheen of brazen arms: even as when into the light comes a snake, fed on poisonous herbs (*mala gramina*), whom cold winter kept swollen underground, now, his slough cast off, fresh and glistening in youth (*positis novus exuviis nitidusque iuventa*), with uplifted breast he rolls his slippery length (*convolvit sublato pectore terga*), towering towards the sun and darting from his mouth a three-forked tongue (*arduus ad solem, et linguis micat ore trisculis*)![135]

The principal source of this snake imagery is the battle between Hector (Priam's son) and Achilles (Pyrrhus' father), where it describes Hector's defensive posture at *Il.* 22.93-6:

And as a serpent of the mountain awaiteth a man at his lair, having fed upon evil herbs (κακὰ φάρμακα), and dread wrath hath entered into him, and terribly he glareth as he coileth him about within his lair; even so Hector in his courage unquenchable would not give ground, leaning his bright shield against the jutting wall.[136]

In the *Iliad*, Priam's son Hector is likened to a snake when he is about to be attacked and killed by Achilles. In the *Aeneid*, Achilles' son Pyrrhus is likened to a snake as he is about to go on a rampage that culminates in his slaying Hector's father Priam. Here Virgil's adaptive imitation of Homer goes beyond mere borrowing to a kind of ironic reversal. According to E.J. Kenney, Homer is not Virgil's only source at this point: Kenney suggests that the sloughing of the skin and other details are drawn from Nicander, *Theriaca*, 31-4, 137-8, 389-92, and that Virgil further imitates himself by drawing on *Georgics* 3.426 (*convolvens sublato pectore terga*), 437 (*positis novus exuviis nitidusque iuventa*), 439 (*arduus ad solem, et linguis micat ore trisculis*) which is in turn based on *Theriaca* 359-72.[137] Virgil's imitation here is thus many-layered.

Soon after this passage Virgil draws on another Iliadic image in likening the incursion into the palace to a river bursting its banks, *Aen.* 2.494-9:

---

[134] The discussion here is based largely on those in E.J. Kenney, 'Iudicium Transferendi: Virgil, *Aeneid* 2.469-505 and Its Antecedents' in T. West and D. Woodman (eds), *Creative Imitation and Latin Literature* (Cambridge: Cambridge University Press, 1979), 103-20; and Dekel, *Virgil's Homeric Lens*, 66-75.
[135] This and all subsequent translations from the *Aeneid* are those of H. Ruston Fairclough in the LCL edition.
[136] Translation by A.T. Murray in the LCL.
[137] Kenney, 'Iudicium Transferendi', 105-9.

Force finds a way; the Greeks, pouring in, burst a passage, slaughter the foremost, and fill the wide space with soldiery. Not with such fury, when a foaming river, bursting its barriers, has overflowed and with its torrent overwhelmed the resisting banks, does it rush furiously upon the fields in a mass and over all the plains sweep herds and folds.

As Kenney notes, whereas the snake image is applied to the violence of an individual, that of the torrent is applied to the violence of a group. Its Homeric prototype occurs at *Il.* 5.87-9 where, however, it is applied to the individual Greek warrior Diomedes routing scores of Trojans:

For he stormed across the plain like unto a winter torrent at the full, that with its swift flood sweeps away the embankments; this the close-fenced embankments hold not back, neither do the walls of the fruitful vineyards stay its sudden coming when the rain of Zeus driveth it on; and before it in multitudes the fair works of men fall in ruin. Even in such wise before Tydeus' son were the thick battalions of the Trojans driven in rout, nor might they abide him for all they were so many.

Both the *Iliad* and the *Aeneid* liken the unstoppable force of human violence to the irresistible destructive force of a flood, but whereas in Homer the image is applied to one Greek hero routing large numbers of armed foes in the heat of battle, in Virgil it is applied to a band of Greeks wreaking havoc in a domestic setting by slaughtering people unable to defend themselves. Once again Kenney argues that the *Iliad* is not the only source Virgil has in mind at this point, since he was also drawing on Lucretius, *de rerum natura*, 1.280-9 (which was itself modelled on the Iliadic simile).[138]

Once Pyrrhus comes face to face with Priam, the Trojan king reminds the Greek warrior that the latter's father showed respect and decency by allowing him to retrieve Hector's corpse (referring to the events narrated in *Il.* 24.469-692). Pyrrhus responds by sarcastically telling the old king to take news of him (Pyrrhus) to his father Achilles and then dispatches him to the underworld by burying his sword in Priam's side. The reader familiar with Homer will, however, be aware that it is not Priam but Odysseus who is destined to bring news of Pyrrhus to Achilles in Hades, and that the portrait Odysseus paints of Achilles' son (*Od.* 11.504-40) is rather more flattering than that being offered by Aeneas to Dido. To such a reader either Aeneas or Odysseus must now appear to be an unreliable narrator.[139]

A great deal more could be said on this passage, but enough has been said to illustrate the point. If Virgil were simply imitating Homer by following him one epic at a time in sequence, at this point he would (roughly speaking) be paralleling *Od.* 8.486-520, but he in fact draws on a substantial range of other sources, including similes taken from *Il.* 22.93-6 and 5.87-89, an oblique allusion to *Od.* 11.465-540, and a wide range of non-Homeric material besides (not least from something like the *Iliou persis*), often conflating (ideas and phrases, if not words) as he goes and creating a great deal

---

[138] Kenney, 'Iudicium Transferendi', 109–10.
[139] Dekel, *Virgil's Homeric Lens*, 71–2.

of subtle intertextual meaning as a result, potentially impacting the way Homer is read as much as the interpretation of Virgil. This goes considerably beyond the operations of compression, expansion, paraphrase and rearrangement that are said to be the principal source-utilization techniques of Graeco-Roman authors or, at least, of elite historians and biographers.

As should by now be apparent, imitation is not one single transformational technique, rather it is a mode of source utilization in which a number of such techniques may be employed. These can be hard to pin down, since, as David West and Tony Woodman put it, 'the imitator moveth as he listeth and therefore … there is no set grammar of comparison for the critic to apply'.[140] As a mode of creative re-writing, imitation cannot be reduced to a neat set of mechanical operations. Clearly, the kinds of transformation that occur in imitation include those discussed earlier in this chapter, such as paraphrase, compression, elaboration and some reordering and conflation. It may be helpful to summarize what further transformational techniques have now been uncovered. These include:

1. Transformation of events and characters into a different narrative concerning different events and characters. For example, Homer's Achilles and Odysseus become Virgil's Aeneas, the journey home to Ithaca becomes the journey to Italy, Telemachus' travels on behalf of his father become Tobias' travels on behalf of his.
2. The creative addition and transformation of elements not directly taken from the imitated hypotext. For example, Neptune's rebuke to Aeolus in Virgil's storm scene.
3. Fusion and splitting of elements, characters and roles. For example, Aeneas combines elements of both Odysseus and Achilles, while Achilles is split between Aeneas and Turnus, who in turn ends up in the role of Homer's Hector.
4. The construction of a narrative out of more than one imitated hypotext. For example, Tobit's use of both Genesis and the *Odyssey* (along with Deuteronomy and the Ahiqar legend).
5. Replacing a more negative element in the hypotext with a more positive one ('positivization'). For example, Aeneas is constantly presented as dutiful (*pius*) in contrast to the wily self-interested Odysseus or the vengeful Achilles.[141]
6. Although it is not obviously illustrated in any of the examples above, Brodie also lists 'internalization', by which he means shifting the focus from an external, physical aspect to an internal, mental one.[142]
7. Contamination of one scene with elements of another. For example, the lightning, the effect of the wind on the rigging and the fate of other crew members in Virgil's

---

[140] 'Epilogue' in David West and Tony Woodman (eds), *Creative Imitation and Latin Literature* (Cambridge: Cambridge University Press, 1979), 195–200, here 200.
[141] Which makes it all the more shocking when the *Aeneid* ends with Aeneas' vengeful killing of Turnus. For a specific example of the Aeneas/Achilles contrast as positivization, see Thomas L. Brodie, *The Birthing of the New Testament: The Intertextual Development of the New Testament Writings* (NTM 1; Sheffield: Sheffield Phoenix Press, 2004), 11. For further examples of positivization in other ancient authors, see O'Leary, *Matthew's Judaization*, 31–7, 52, 54–6.
[142] Brodie, *Birthing*, 11–12.

storm are taken from *Od.* 12.403-419 rather than the principal passage being imitated at *Od.* 5.291-387, while the figure of Aeolus is borrowed from *Od.* 10.1-55.

The final item raises the question whether examples of imitative techniques should qualify what has been said about the limited use of conflation and the implausibility of ancient authors unpicking material from one context to use in another. The example from *Aen.* 2.469-558 is particularly pertinent, since there Virgil unpicks the snake and flood similes from their narrative contexts at *Il.* 22.93-6 and 5.87-9 to redeploy them his account of the sack of Troy (in this case apparently relying on his audience to recognize the original Iliadic contexts for these transpositions to have their full effect). What is being 'unpicked' here, however, is not a couple of words or a phrase but a complete image (or, in Kirk's terminology, a complete cognitive unit). The matter is, however, complicated by the fact that in Virgil the snake image is further conflated with details from other sources. The application of the snake image and the phrase 'poisonous/evil herbs' (*mala gramina*/κακὰ φάρμακα) are drawn from Homer; the snake's hibernation and sloughing of its skin are drawn from Nicander; while lines 473–5 have been borrowed from Virgil's own *Georgics* 3.426, 437, 439. Moreover, in Kenney's view, this is all done to establish a subtle and complex web of allusions to emphasize Neoptolemus' malevolence.[143] This is still not word-by-word micro-conflation, but it does suggest an ability to select elements from various sources and combine them in fresh ways that goes beyond the more basic conflation envisaged by Downing and Derrenbacker. It is more sophisticated than anything that needs to be attributed to FH Luke, but does suggest that the kind of limited unpicking of complete sense units from Matthean narrative contexts that would need to be attributed to FH Luke was not beyond the range of techniques available to ancient authors.

A second issue is how imitation is to be distinguished from related forms of intertextuality such as allusion,[144] re-writing and composition on the basis of familiar tropes, such as might take place in a scribal or literary tradition. The short answer is that there are no hard and fast boundaries between any of these, but rather a continuum in which one shades into another. Virgil's use of Homer might be taken as a paradigm case of imitation which other forms of intertextuality might more closely or distantly resemble (although Virgil employs the other forms of intertextuality as well).

As a first approximation, it may be said that imitation is more a matter of deliberate literary artifice employed as a way of generating meaning, whereas scribal composition is more concerned with the transmission and updating of tradition. But there is surely some fuzziness at the borders. Even if one sees Ben Sira, say, as primarily a scribe composing on the basis of the wisdom traditions available to him, it would not be totally outrageous to describe him as engaged in the imitation of previous wisdom texts. Conversely, while Virgil is clearly engaged in deliberate mimesis of Homer, he is doing so within a long tradition of scholarly exegesis and criticism of Homer, which he surely embodies (and so transmits) just as much as a more modest writer in some scholarly or scribal school. This does not annul the distinction between artistic mimesis and scribal-traditional composition, but it does suggest some kind of overlap (and

---

[143] Kenney, 'Iudicium Transferendi', 106–9.
[144] On which point, see Finkelpearl, 'Pagan Traditions', 78–82.

family resemblance) between the two, such that it may be better to think in terms of literary imitation and scribal-traditional composition lying at two ends of a continuum rather than as two wholly distinct phenomena having nothing at all in common.

This continuum also encompasses what Goulder earlier termed 'midrash' and what has more recently been termed 'biblical rewriting'.[145] This refers to a mode of intertextuality that is more creative than redaction, is intended as interpretative rather than literary and which can be seen in other Jewish texts (such as Chronicles reworking of Samuel–Kings and various examples of 'rewritten bible' such as *Jubilees* or the first half of Josephus' *Jewish Antiquities*). Overall, then, one might see a spectrum of source utilization stretching from copying, through redaction ('copy and edit') and rewriting to literary imitation.

A final question, also about what constitutes imitation, is how one decides whether text A may be plausibly regarded as an imitation of hypotext B. This can be hard to pin down, given that imitation can shade into allusion, that it can be more or less systematic (in trying to use the whole or only the part of the source), more or less creative (in the amount of invention it combines with material taken or transformed from the source) and more or less transformative (shading from a rewriting of precisely the same story to something with only a subtle relation to the original), and that similarities between accounts do not always indicate a relationship of direct imitation.[146] Nevertheless, the following list of indicators, culled from the proposals of three different NT scholars, may provide a useful guide:[147]

1. *Availability of Proposed Hypotext*: The text an author is said to have imitated must have been available to that author, so it must have been written earlier than the imitating text and be plausibly familiar to the author. In the case of the evangelists, the main hypotexts of interest will be the OT and the earlier Synoptic Gospels, so this criterion should be unproblematic for the FH provided one thinks Luke was written sufficiently after Matthew.[148]
2. *Accessibility of Proposed Hypotext to the Target Audience*: To the extent that a successful imitation aims to be recognized as such, its success depends on its target audience recognizing the hypotexts that have been imitated. The implied audiences of

---

[145] Mogens Müller, 'The New Testament Gospels as Biblical Rewritings', *STNJT* 68 (2014), 21–40; cf. Mogens Müller, 'Acts as Biblical Rewriting of the Gospels and Paul's Letters' in Mogens Müller and Jesper Tang Nielsen (eds), *Luke's Literary Creativity* (LNTS, 573; London: Bloomsbury T&T Clark, 2016), 96–117, and several of the other essays in *Luke's Literary Creativity*, e.g., Lukas Borman, 'Rewritten Prophecy in Luke-Acts' (pp. 121–43); Joseph M. Lear Jr., 'Luke's Use of the Old Testament in the Sending of the Seventy(-Two): A Compositional Study' (pp. 160–82); and Marianne Bjelland Kartzow, 'Rewritten Stereotypes: Scripture and Cultural Echo in Luke's Parable of the Widow and the Judge' (pp. 208–24).

[146] The storm-stilling at Mk 4.35-41 and *Aen*. 1.81-156 provides an interesting case in point. Although one could make a case for it, it seems unlikely that Mark is imitating Virgil here, not least because there are more plausible models for him to have employed (notably Jon. 1.3-16 and Ps. 107.23-32).

[147] Adapted from Dennis R. MacDonald, 'Introduction' in Dennis R. MacDonald (ed.), *Mimesis and Intertextuality in Antiquity and Christianity* (SAC; Harrisburg, PA: Trinity Press International, 2001), 1–9, here 2–3; Winn, *Mark*, 30–3; and O'Leary, *Matthew's Judaization*, 20–3. Compare the more succinct list in McAdon, *Rhetorical Mimesis*, 46.

[148] On which, see David Landry, 'Reconsidering the Date of Luke in Light of the Farrer Hypothesis' in John C. Poirier and Jeffrey Peterson (eds), *Marcan Priority without Q: Explorations in the Farrer Hypothesis* (LNTS, 455; London: Bloomsbury T&T Clark, 2015), 160–90.

Matthew and Luke will both have been familiar with the OT, and it is at least plausible that the target audience of later gospels will have been familiar with earlier ones.

3. *Status of Proposed Hypotext*: A model should be worthy of imitation, so that a proposed hypotext is more plausible if it is one that would carry weight with its target audience. Again, this condition is likely to be fulfilled where the proposed hypotexts are taken from the OT and earlier gospels.
4. *Similarity of Structure*: Imitation of a hypotext is more likely if the imitating text and the hypotext share a similar order of events (or other elements).
5. *Similarities in Narrative Details and Actions.*
6. *Verbal Similarities*: While not required, any verbal echoes of the hypotext will tend to support the existence of a relationship with the imitating text.
7. *Density of Parallels*: The more similarities between the two texts there are, the stronger the case for seeing a relationship between them.
8. *Distinctiveness of Parallels:* The similarities in points 4–7 above are more likely to indicate a direct relationship between texts if the features appealed to are distinctive (as opposed, say, to common expressions or tropes).
9. *Thematic Congruence*: In the presence of other positive indicators, A is far more likely to be an imitation of B if A and B are about the same kind of thing. For example, that *Aen.* 1.81-156 is related to *Od.* 5.291-387 and 12.406-53 is made more plausible by the fact that all these passages are concerned with life-threatening storms at sea followed by arrival at a strange land. Similarly, other things being equal, Luke's Infancy Narrative is more plausibly related to Matthew's Infancy Narrative and/or various OT birth and infancy narratives than it is, say, to the Chronicler's story of a new temple and post-exilic restoration.[149]
10. *Intelligibility of Differences*: There is more likely to be a direct mimetic relationship between two texts if the later text's changes to its model are reasonably explicable in terms of the later author's goals and interests.

While meeting all ten criteria would be jointly sufficient for establishing an imitative relationship between texts, it is not necessary. Since imitations may be more or less obvious or subtle, complete or partial and close or free, some measure of judgement is inevitably required in any individual case. That said, the existence of clear-cut cases of A imitating B is likely to enhance the plausibility of less clear instances of A's imitation of B.

A number of scholars have argued for Luke's (and Mark's) imitation not only of scripture but of Homer and other Greek authors.[150] Not everyone will be convinced by

---

[149] The latter proposal comes from Brodie, *Birthing*, 521–35, and Louis T. Brodie, 'A New Temple and a New Law', *JSNT* 5 (1979), 21–45.

[150] E.g., in relation to scripture, Winn, *Mark*, 51–119; Brodie, *Birthing* (and other items cited above); Brodie, 'New Temple'; Brodie, 'Luke 7,36–50'; Louis T. Brodie, 'Towards Unraveling the Rhetorical Imitation of Sources in Acts: 2 Kgs 5 as One Component of Acts 8,9–40', *Biblica* 67 (1986), 41–67; Brodie, 'Towards Tracing'; Louis T. Brodie, 'Towards Unravelling Luke's Use of the Old Testament: Luke 7.11–17 as an *Imitatio* of 1 Kings 17.17–24', *NTS* 32 (1986), 247–67; in relation to Greek literature, see Chris Shea, 'Imitating Imitation: Vergil, Homer and Acts 10: 1–11:18' in Jo-Ann A. Brant, Charles W. Hedrick and Chris Shea (eds), *Ancient Fiction: The Matrix of Early Christian and Jewish Narrative* (Atlanta: SBL, 2005), 37–60; Dennis R. MacDonald, 'The Shipwrecks of Odysseus and Paul', *NTS* 45 (1999), 88–107; MacDonald, *Gospels and Homer*; Dennis R. MacDonald, *Luke and Vergil: Imitations of Classical Greek Literature* (NTGL, 2; Lanham, MD: Rowman & Littlefield, 2014).

all the parallels proposed, but the proposal is by no means implausible in itself, since it is hard to see how anyone in the first-century Roman Empire could become reasonably literate in Greek without encountering Homer.[151]

Many of the examples of Luke and Mark imitating Homer that MacDonald proposes are unconvincing,[152] but it only takes one of them to be reasonably convincing to show that imitation is a technique Luke employed, and MacDonald makes a good case for seeing the storm and shipwreck at Acts 27.13-44 as an imitation of those at *Od.* 5.282-463 (of Odysseus alone on a raft swimming ashore on the land of the Phaeacians), *Od.* 12.403-53 (of the shipwreck in which all of Odysseus' remaining companions are drowned leaving him alone to wash up on Ogygia (Calypso's isle) and *Od.* 14.299-319 (one of Odysseus' lying tales). MacDonald identifies a number of words Luke uses that are either rare or hapaxes in the New Testament while occurring in the Odyssey (and to some extent) in other Greek literature. These include such nautical terms as λιμήν, 'harbour' (Acts 27.12; *Od.* 5.418; 12.305), πρῷρα, 'prow' (Acts 27.30, 41; *Od.* 12.230), κυβερνήτης, 'pilot' or 'helmsman' (Acts 27.11; Rev. 18.17; *Od.* 9.78; 12.152, 217, 412), πέλαγος, 'open sea' (Acts 27.5; Mt. 18.6; *Od.* 5.330, 335), πηδάλιον, 'rudder' (Acts 27.40; Jas 3.4; *Od.* 5.255, 270, 315), πρύμνη, 'stern' (Acts 27.29, 41; Mk 4.38; *Od.* 12.411) and ναῦς, 'ship' (Acts 27.41; elsewhere the NT uses πλοῖον of any water-borne craft). While all these terms appear in classical Greek as well as Homer, the combination of terms (though not the precise phrase) in ἐπέκειλαν τὴν ναῦν, 'they ran the ship aground', at Acts 27.41 is more distinctive to Homer (e.g. *Od.* 9.146-50, 546-7; 11.20; 12.5-6).[153]

---

[151] Ronald F. Hock, 'Homer in Greco-Roman Education' in Dennis R. MacDonald (ed.), *Mimesis and Intertextuality in Antiquity and Christianity* (SAC; Harrisburg, PA: Trinity Press International, 2001), 56–77; Quintilian, *Inst.* 1.8.5; 10.1.46-50. See also J. Duncan M. Derrett, 'Homer in the New Testament', *ExpTim* 121 (2009), 66–9.

[152] Margaret M. Mitchell, 'Homer in the New Testament?', *JR* 83 (2003), 244–60, cogently argues that MacDonald's suggestions of a wholescale imitation of Homer by Mark do not stand up to critical scrutiny, aptly noting, for example, that 'many of MacDonald's interpretations of particular passages are forced or contorted, rendered on the basis of inconsistent application of interpretive principle' (p. 252). Mitchell nonetheless concedes that the search for Homeric influence on the NT may nevertheless be a worthwhile exercise, suggesting, for example, the possibility of a Homeric allusion in the mention of Zeus and Hermes at Acts 14.8-18 (p. 257). Sandnes, 'Imitatio Homeri', 728-32, further argues that Mark does not sufficiently advertise his alleged emulation of Homer for this to be taken as his intention. See also the discussion in Craig S. Keener, *Acts: An Exegetical Commentary* (Grand Rapids, MI: BakerAcademic, 2012), vol. 1, 83–4, 87, and the reviews of *Does the New Testament Imitate Homer? Four Cases from the Acts of the Apostles*, by Dennis R. MacDonald, by Stan Harstine *JBL* 124 (2005), 383–5, Jennifer K. Berenson Maclean, *CBQ* 70 (2008), 381–2, and Luke Timothy Johnson, *TS* 66 (2005), 489–90, and *CL* 54 (2005), 285–7. Johnson makes the important point that by the time Luke wrote, Greek literature was so thoroughly impregnated with Homer that Luke may often have been working with some more immediate intertext. Keener is not hostile to the possibility that Greek literature influenced Luke, but objects to making the supposed Homeric (or other Greek) parallel the sole or dominant hypotext for Luke. For a balanced assessment of the strengths and weaknesses of MacDonald's proposals, see also Winn, *Mark*, 34–50; as Winn justly observes, too many of MacDonald's alleged parallels between Mark and Homer are 'unpersuasive'.

[153] MacDonald, 'Shipwrecks', 94–5; F.F. Bruce, *The Acts of the Apostles: The Greek Text with Introduction and Commentary* (London: Tyndale Press, 1951), 467, also sees the archaic ναῦς as 'plausibly ascribed to Homeric reminiscence', but while noting the Homeric echo of ηὔχοντο ἡμέραν at Acts 27.29, states (p. 463), 'Much of the language of the *Odyssey* became part of a literary tradition in nautical matters' and regards this storm scene in Acts as 'also indebted' to Jon. 1.4-16 (p. 451). Craig S. Keener, *Acts: An Exegetical Commentary* (Grand Rapids, MI: BakerAcademic, 2015), vol. 4, pp. 3651–2, sees Luke as 'directly evoking Greek literary traditions' at Acts 27.41 but talks of him borrowing literary language rather than imitating Homer.

As well as noting a number of verbal reminiscences between Acts 27 and the *Odyssey* 14 pseudo-shipwreck,[154] MacDonald traces a number of thematic similarities between the shipwreck suffered by Paul and those narrated in *Odyssey* 5 and 12. In all three stories the voyagers set out to a fair wind, but there are intimations of trouble ahead (either from the sailors, in Homer, or from the narrator, in Acts). Both in Homer and in Acts the good sailing conditions soon end, while in both the traditional name of a wind is used along with the stock images of wind, waves and darkness. In both the sailors take the standard measures such as jettisoning cargo and taking in sails to mitigate the risks but end up losing any hope of survival. Each of the three storms result in the destruction of a vessel, but in each of the three at least one person survives to arrive on shore.

As MacDonald acknowledges, none of these elements is particularly distinctive since one might expect to find any of them in an account of a shipwreck.[155] But there are some more distinctive elements. Both Paul (at Acts 27.23-26) and Odysseus (at *Od*. 5.333-52) are reassured by a supernatural helper (an angel in the first case, the goddess Ino in the second). Admittedly their roles are different, but they do both talk about reaching land and promise survival on account of fate or divine necessity. Again, Odysseus reaches land by first clinging to a plank from his shattered raft and then swimming for the shore (*Od*. 5.365-464), while these modes of transport are divided between Paul's companions, some of whom swim while others cling to fragments of the shattered ship (Acts 27.43-44). The similarities continue once Paul and Odysseus come ashore. Both need protection against the cold (Acts 28.2; *Od*. 5.465-93); in Acts a fire is used, at *Od*. 5.489-91 Odysseus covers himself with leaves, and fire is mentioned only as a simile; both receive kind assistance from the locals (Acts 28.2; *Od*. 6.110-249), both are likened to gods after an initially more negative evaluation (Acts 28.6; *Od*. 6.241-3) and both are subsequently given hospitality by the local ruler (Acts 28.7; *Od*. 7.154-78 *et seq*.) before finally being helped on their way with gifts (Acts 28.10; *Od*. 13.1-92) and arriving at their respective destinations without further incident (Acts 28.11-14; *Od*. 13.93-124). While many of the elements shared between Acts 27–28 and the *Odyssey* might be stock elements of any story of shipwreck and survival, MacDonald argues that the density of parallels (along with a number of other intertextual indicators) show that Luke must be imitating Homer here.[156]

Some caution may be in order concerning the nature of this imitation. Susan Praeder has argued that Acts 27.1–28.16 share themes, techniques and vocabulary with a substantial range of ancient literature dealing with sea-voyages, storms and shipwrecks, and that writing storm scenes was part of a first-century rhetorical training.[157] Praeder acknowledges that the phrase ἐπέκειλαν τὴν ναῦν must be a reminiscence of the *Odyssey*,[158] but that does not entirely settle the question whether Luke set out specifically to imitate Homer, or whether he is consciously or unconsciously recycling a Homeric phrase picked up in the course of learning to write storm scenes as part of his literary education. The other correspondences with the *Odyssey* noted above do

---

[154] MacDonald, 'Shipwrecks', 96, n. 48.
[155] MacDonald, 'Shipwrecks', 97–9.
[156] MacDonald, 'Shipwrecks', 99–106.
[157] Susan Marie Praeder, 'Acts 27: 1–28:16:Sea Voyages in Ancient Literature and the Theology of Luke-Acts', *CBQ* 46 (1984), 683–706.
[158] Praeder, 'Sea Voyages', 701.

seem to indicate its influence on Luke, but it is probably not the sole influence; here we have a case where imitation in sense two (imitation of a particular model) becomes hard to distinguish from imitation in the intermediate sense (imitation of a tradition of themes and techniques), not least because the putative Homeric model is the point of origin for much of the tradition that follows. But on balance it seems likely that Luke is to some extent imitating Homer here, even if partially along the lines Praeder suggests (through reminiscence of a writing exercise).

In principle, Luke's reason for this imitation could be similar to the substantive imitation carried out by Tacitus, namely to create a lively and entertaining tale out of a bare notice (conceivably, all Luke knew was that Paul had been shipwrecked, cf. 2 Cor. 11.25).[159] It is, however, unlikely that this would have been his principal purpose, since Luke clearly uses this section of Acts to further his theological interests, and it may well be that his story of salvation from shipwreck is intended to be both symbolic of Luke's wider concern with salvation and indicative of the divine necessity of Paul's arriving safely in Rome according to God's plan and purpose.[160]

MacDonald suggests that Luke has set out to Christianize Homer by exalting Paul and his God in contrast to Odysseus and the arbitrary antics of the Greek gods.[161] If so, Luke's imitation of Homer starts to resemble Virgil's in purpose as well as technique. Like Virgil, Luke retains the effects of various winds, people swimming and planks in the sea. In some respects, Paul's landing on Malta is closer to Odysseus' arrival at the land of the Phaeacians than is Aeneas' arrival at Carthage. Yet Paul, like Aeneas but unlike Odysseus, rescues his companions and not just himself; Paul and Aeneas are both presented as morally superior to Odysseus, though Luke takes this positivization further by having Paul state his confidence in divine deliverance (Acts 27.21-26), compared with the panicky cries uttered by the protagonists in Homer and Virgil. That said, the account of the shipwreck in Acts feels more distant from the world of the *Odyssey* than does the storm scene in the *Aeneid*, in part because Acts is not epic poetry, in part because Paul is a very different kind of hero from either Odysseus or Aeneas and in part because Luke's theological and ideological framework is further removed from the mythological framework of both epics than either is from the other. Moreover, Luke may have had additional sources, such as some account of what occurred in Paul's shipwreck (or, at least, accounts of other contemporary shipwrecks on which to draw for verisimilitude).[162] If Luke is imitating Homer here, the result

---

[159] Cf. Troy M. Troftgruben, 'Slow Sailing in Acts: Suspense in the Final Sea Journey (Acts 27:1-28:15)', *JBL* 136 (2017), 949-68.

[160] Robert C. Tannehill, *The Narrative Unity of Luke-Acts: A Literary Interpretation* 2: *The Acts of the Apostles* (Philadelphia: Fortress, 1990), 330-43; cf. Praeder, 'Sea Voyages', 695-706; Keener, *Acts*, vol. 4, 3566-70.

[161] MacDonald, 'Shipwrecks', 106-7.

[162] Cf. Keener, *Acts*, vol. 4, 3556-66, who argues that the account of the shipwreck in Acts is based on an eyewitness account, while allowing that Luke 'may have derived some of his vocabulary from Greek literary tradition' and that Homer's sea storms (*Od.* 5.291-473; 12.402-25) were often used as models. That said, Keener cites with apparent approval the argument of F.F. Bruce to the effect that 'Luke drew on the literary tradition of storms and shipwrecks established as early (in extant sources) as the *Odyssey*', and it is by no means impossible that Luke could be employing literary imitation of Homer to describe a real event. Keener also considers the possibility that Luke may be employing Jonah typology here, but finds the parallels 'not very compelling', while allowing that there may be some value in seeing a contrasting Jonah allusion 'so long as we do not make literary imitation of Jonah Luke's primary purpose'.

is something further removed from Homer than Virgil's imitation. It is nonetheless noteworthy that Luke employs many of the same techniques.

This raises the question whether Luke may have been emulating Virgil by imitating Homer. Luke need not have been intimately acquainted with the *Aeneid* in Latin to be aware of its existence and to have some conception of its storyline and its relation to Homer. The *Aeneid* quickly became one of the most celebrated pieces of Latin literature of its day and was certainly known about by at least some Greek-speaking Jews (*Sib. Or.* 11.140-71) as well as being available in a Greek prose translation. Moreover, Luke might plausibly have intended Luke-Acts as in part a Christian response to Virgil's epic celebrating the triumph of Roman rule, even if the *Aeneid* is rather more ambivalent than that.[163] Both works tell of the emergence of a new people from the ruins of the old. In both, the new people maintain some aspects of the religion of the old but abandon their name and their language. Both narratives are driven by prophecy and the impulse of fate or divine necessity towards the eschatological establishment of an everlasting kingdom of peace. In both, a protagonist sails from the eastern Mediterranean with Rome as the ultimate goal via various adventures on the way. Both end on an abrupt note, with Paul preaching while a prisoner in Rome and Aeneas killing Turnus, but both endings signal that the way is now open to the promised future.[164] It is suggestive that Luke introduces the name Aeneas into his narrative at Acts 9.33-34, immediately after Paul's conversion; might this be to indicate an analogy between the two?[165] Clearly Luke does not imitate the *Aeneid* at the detailed level of individual pericopae; any resemblance would rather be at the level of overall thrust, particularly in Acts.[166] But Luke's imitation of Virgil is not the main point at issue here; the point is the general plausibility of Luke's employing imitation as a mode of source utilization.[167]

---

[163] Adam Parry, 'The Two Voices of Virgil's "Aeneid"', *Arion* 2 (1963), 66–80.

[164] Marianne Palmer Bonz, *The Past as Legacy: Luke-Acts and Ancient Epic* (Minneapolis: Fortress, 2000), 25–9, 181–93; MacDonald, *Luke and Vergil*, 1–5.

[165] Most commentators appear to attach little or no significance to the name Aeneas here in Acts, but Michael Kochenash, 'You Can't Hear "Aeneas" without Thinking of Rome', *JBL* 136 (2017), 667–85, argues that the name Aeneas was less common in the first century than is often supposed, so that the associations of the Aeneas legend (though not necessarily Virgil's version of it) would inevitably signal the narrative's drive towards Rome.

[166] Keener, *Acts*, vol. 1, 83–7, criticizes Bonz (and MacDonald) for suggesting that Luke-Acts might be seen as a prose epic and questions whether Luke can be seen as imitating Virgil (while accepting that Luke certainly imitates the LXX). Keener nevertheless acknowledges that Luke-Acts and the *Aeneid* can fruitfully be seen as sharing the function of 'foundation stories' but argues that function is not the same as genre, and that Luke's preface (Lk 1.1-4) stands in the way of seeing Luke-Acts a prose epic (a point that Bonz indeed appears to stumble over).

[167] MacDonald is hardly alone in suggesting the use of mimesis in Acts. Other proposals include McAdon, *Rhetorical Mimesis*, 181–246, who argues that Acts 7.58–15.30 is a mimetic transformation of Galatians 1–2; Michael Kochenash, 'The Scandal of Gentile Inclusion: Reading Acts 17 with Euripides' *Bacchae* in Mark Glen Bilby, Margaret Froelich and Michael Kochenash (eds), *Classical Greek Models of the Gospels and Acts: Studies in Mimesis Criticism* (Claremont, CA: Claremont Press, 2018), 124–44, Ilseo Park, 'Acts 2 as an Intertextual Map: Moving from Dionysian to Platonic Identity' in Bilby et al., *Classical Greek Models*, 113–24, and Courtney Friesen, *Reading Dionysus: Euripides' Bacchae and the Cultural Contestations of Greeks, Jews, Romans, and Christians* (STAC, 95; Tübingen: Mohr Siebeck, 2015), 207–34, who all argue for Acts' imitation of Euripides' *Bacchae*, with Park, 'Acts 2', and Rubén E. Dupertuis, 'The Summaries of Acts 2, 4 and 5 and Plato's Republic' in Jo-Ann A. Brant, Charles W. Hedrick and Chris Shea (eds), *Ancient Fiction: The Matrix of Early Christian and Jewish Narrative* (Atlanta: SBL, 2005), 275–96, arguing for Acts' imitation of Plato.

We shall examine a possible instance of Lukan imitation in the next chapter in connection with his Infancy Narrative. In the meantime, this chapter has shown that the kinds of transformational techniques employed in literary imitation go beyond both the basics taught in the *Progymnasmata* and those identified in the work of scholars such as Downing, Derrenbacker and Kirk. In addition, our rapid survey of Philo's use of the Pentateuch indicates that ancient authors' capacity to employ source material out of its original sequence may be greater than has sometimes been allowed. In neither case does this mean that absolutely anything goes when it comes to how Luke may have employed his sources; the point is rather that he could have used a wider range of techniques than is sometimes allowed for while still remaining in the ambit of contemporary compositional practices.

4

Significant similarities

Matthew and Luke clearly differ, but they also resemble each other. The issue is whether the similarities outweigh the differences. This is not simply a matter of counting; the question is rather whether the quality and extent of the similarities are such to suggest that Luke's dependence on Matthew (in addition to Mark) looks more plausible than their independent use of Mark and Q. This chapter will argue that they are, pending examination of the alleged differences in the chapters that follow.

Matthew and Luke are similar in the way they both expand on Mark. Both the later evangelists add similar material, along with other material of their own, and both of them insert infancy narratives at the beginning and resurrection narratives at the end. These general points are, however, not particularly troublesome for the 2DH. Given access to Mark, Q and other material of their own, it is not that surprising that Matthew and Luke should both combine them. Assuming Matthew and Luke were familiar with the conventions of the Graeco-Roman *bios*, it is not so much of a coincidence that they should both choose to begin by giving details of Jesus' birth and family (which would have been considered the appropriate way to situate their hero) and to conclude with strange events occurring just after his death (also a conventional move). These general resemblances remain and may support the case for Luke's dependence on Matthew, but more striking similarities are needed to establish it.

We shall therefore begin by discussing the agreements of Matthew and Luke against Mark in the triple tradition. We shall next examine the degree of verbatim agreement in the double tradition. Finally, we shall explore the considerable extent of Matthew-Luke agreement over the first four chapters of Matthew, arguing for Luke's extensive use of Matthew and providing contextualized examples of the types of Matthew-Luke agreement previously discussed.[1]

Significant verbal similarities in the triple tradition

If Matthew and Luke were independently using Mark and Q, one would not expect there to be too many agreements of Matthew and Luke against Mark. They might

---

[1] Many of these similarities could be taken as also indicating Matthew's possible use of Luke, for which see especially Robert K. MacEwen, *Matthean Posteriority: An Exploration of Matthew's Use of Mark and Luke as a Solution to the Synoptic Problem* (LNTS, 501; London: Bloomsbury T&T Clark, 2015). Occasional indications of Luke's use of Matthew being the more likely direction of dependence will be noted as they arise, but MacEwen's arguments merit detailed engagement beyond the scope of the present study.

occasionally make similar changes to Mark, and some apparent agreements of Matthew and Luke against Mark could arise through the assimilation of the text of one gospel to the other in the process of scribal copying. Defenders of the 2DH can further appeal to the use of Q to explain Matthew-Luke agreements in some triple tradition passages or to the hypothesis of a Proto-Mark or Deutero-Mark to explain others.[2] The FH nevertheless maintains that there are too many Matthew-Luke agreements for such explanations to plausibly account for all of them, especially given the extent of some of the agreements and the lack of any manuscript evidence for many of the alleged textual assimilations.

Traditionally, these agreements have been divided into 'major agreements' and 'minor agreements'. The term 'major agreements' (described on the 2DH as 'Mark-Q overlaps') refers to sets of parallels in the triple tradition where Matthew and Luke agree in adding substantially similar material to the account found in Mark or where Matthew otherwise becomes the middle term. The clearest examples are the teaching of John the Baptist (Mt. 3.11-12 || Mk 1.7-8 || Lk. 3.16-17), the Temptation (Mt. 4.1-11 || Mk 1.12-13 || Lk. 4.1-13), the Beelzebul Controversy (Mt. 12.22-32 || Mk 3.22-30 || Lk. 11.14-22), the Mission Charge (Mt. 10.5-16 || Mk 6.7-13 || Lk. 9.2-5; 10.1-12) and the Parable of the Mustard Seed (Mt. 13.31-32 || Mk 4.30-32 || Lk. 13.18-19).[3]

In deploying the category of Mark-Q overlap, the 2DH concedes that the substantial Matthew-Luke agreements in these pericopae must be due to at least one evangelist's use of a second source in addition to Mark but proposes that the second source is Q rather than Matthew. One might explain 2DH Matthew's apparently close conflation of Mark and Q in these passages on the assumption that he was employing both texts from memory. More awkward is (a) the need to postulate that Mark and Q happen to agree on including versions of just these passages and (b) the extent of the verbal agreement between Mark and Q they apparently contain. Should it become necessary to postulate Mark's dependence on Q or Q's on Mark, the whole 2DH edifice would start to crumble, since in principle Q might contain the whole of Mark and we would never know it. Mark-Q overlaps would only become apparent when Mark chose to abbreviate Q, but not where Mark chose to copy Q or expand on Q, as he might equally well have done.[4]

Even if one accepts that Mark and Q might easily overlap in the manner required, one may question whether Mark-Q overlap provides the best explanation of this set of agreements or whether it is simply an ad hoc epicycle created to preserve the 2DH. On the face of it, these major agreements undermine the 2DH claim that FH Luke fails to take over Matthew's additions to Mark by providing clear instances where he does just that.[5] Some 2DH advocates nevertheless argue that far from helping the

---

[2] For a survey of the study of the minor agreements, see Frans Neirynck, *The Minor Agreements of Matthew and Luke against Mark with a Cumulative List* (BETL, 37; Leuven: Leuven University Press, 1974), 11–48. See also Streeter, *Four Gospels*, 295–331.

[3] Sanders and Davies, *Studying*, 78–81; Streeter, *Four Gospels*, 305. Streeter, *Four Gospels*, 186–8, also includes the Baptism, although *CEQ*, 18–19, regards this as uncertain.

[4] E.P. Sanders, 'The Overlaps of Mark and Q and the Synoptic Problem', *NTS* 19 (1972), 453–65, here 454–7; Eve, 'Reconstructing Mark', 112.

[5] See Eve, 'Devil', 16–43, and Mark Goodacre, 'Taking Our Leave of Mark-Q Overlaps: Major Agreements and the Farrer Theory' in Mogens Müller and Heike Omerzu (eds), *Gospel Interpretation and the Q-Hypothesis* (LNTS, 573; ed. London: Bloomsbury T&T Clark, 2018), 201–22, here 207–10.

FH, these passages pose a major difficulty for it, since (it is claimed) in these passages Luke tends to retain Matthew's wording except where it agrees with Mark's, so that Luke would appear to have deliberately 'unpicked' Matthew from Mark, a difficult, unprecedented and seemingly pointless procedure. We shall rebut this objection in Chapter 5. Assuming that rebuttal is successful, the major agreements constitute significant similarities between Matthew and Luke that favour the FH over the 2DH, being indicative of passages where Luke follows Matthew in preference to Mark.[6]

The term 'minor agreements' denotes smaller agreements in wording of Matthew and Luke against Mark, sometimes of a single word, sometimes of several words in combination, where no Q parallel is thought to exist. That said, it is questionable how far the Matthew-Luke agreements should be divided into 'major' and 'minor'. The term 'minor agreement' suggests something of only minor import. It also lumps very different types of agreement together while artificially separating the more substantial 'minor' agreements from the category of major agreements, whereas there is in fact a continuous spectrum of agreements from occurrences of δέ for καί, through agreements of notable words such as ὕστερον against ἔσχατον (Mt. 22.27 || Mk 12.22 || Lk. 20.32), agreements of phrases such as τῇ τρίτῃ ἡμέρᾳ ἐγερθῆναι against μετὰ τρεῖς ἡμέρας ἀναστῆναι (Mt. 16.21 || Mk 8.31 || Lk. 9.22) or ὃν λαβὼν ἄνθρωπος against ὃς ὅταν (Mt. 13.31 || Mk 4.31 || Lk. 13.19), agreements in complete clauses such as τίς ἐστιν ὁ παίσας σε (Mt. 26.68 || Mk 14.65 || Lk. 22.64) or αὐτὸς ὑμᾶς βαπτίσει ἐν πνεύματι ἁγίῳ καὶ πυρί against αὐτὸς δὲ βαπτίσει ὑμᾶς ἐν πνεύματι ἁγίῳ (Mt. 3.11 || Mk 1.8 || Lk. 3.16), through the common addition of longer blocks of material such as Mt. 3.7-10 || Lk. 3.7-9 in the course of John's preaching or Mt. 12.27-28 || Lk. 11.19-20 in the course of the Beelzebul Controversy to virtually the entire substance of the Temptation Story.[7]

We shall therefore adopt the terminology of *inclusive* and *exclusive* agreements proposed by Werner Kahl.[8] In Kahl's terminology an *inclusive* agreement (IA) is one shared by all three Synoptic evangelists, while an *exclusive* agreement (EA) is an agreement of any two of them against the third. If one counts only form-identical words, then there are 1,852 IAs, 1,908 Mark-Matthew EAs (or EA[Mk-Mt]), 1,039 EA[Mk-Lk] and 637 EA[Mt-Lk].[9] What is immediately striking about these figures is that the quantity of EA[Mt-Lk] is a substantial proportion (61.3 per cent) of EA[Mk-Lk]; or, if one counts EAs and IAs together, in the triple tradition, Luke shares 2,489 form-identical words with Matthew as against 2,891 with Mark. These precise figures could be affected by textual variants and subjective judgements about what is to be taken as agreeing with what, but it is striking that while Luke agrees with Matthew less than he does with Mark, the extent of the agreement is of a similar order of magnitude.

---

[6] On why these major agreements favour Luke's use of Matthew rather than vice versa, see Goodacre, 'Taking Our Leave', 218–21.
[7] Goodacre, *Case*, 163–4; Goodacre, 'Taking Our Leave', 209–13; Werner Kahl, 'Inclusive and Exclusive Agreements – Towards a Neutral Comparison of the Synoptic Gospels, Or: Minor Agreements as Misleading Category' in Mogens Müller and Jesper Tang Nielsen (eds), *Luke's Literary Creativity* (LNTS, 550; London: Bloomsbury T&T Clark, 2016), 44–78 (50–2).
[8] Kahl, 'Inclusive and Exclusive Agreements', 53.
[9] Kahl, 'Inclusive and Exclusive Agreements', 54, based on the figures given by A.M. Honoré, 'A Statistical Study of the Synoptic Problem', *NovT* 10 (1968), 95–147, here 96.

A substantial number of EA^(Mt-Lk) could plausibly arise from changes made by two independent authors improving the same base text, such as replacing καί with δέ or the historic present with the aorist. Whether all such agreements can be dismissed as coincidental is another matter, since even EA^(Mt-Lk) that look individually trivial may become significant in conjunction with others.[10] Far more awkward for the 2DH are a number of EA^(Mt-Lk) outside the likely extent of Q that are not so easily dismissed as either trivially coincidental or the effect of textual assimilation.

The most notorious of these is the common addition by Matthew and Luke of τίς ἐστιν ὁ παίσας σε ('who is it that struck you?') to Mark's account of the mockery of Jesus before the Sanhedrin at Mt. 26.68 || Mk 14.65 || Lk. 22.64.[11] A common 2DH explanation of this striking agreement is that it is a secondary interpolation into Matthew via textual assimilation, resulting in a clumsy Matthean text in which the attendants spit on Jesus' face rather than blindfolding him, rendering the question about who struck him pointless. But there is no extant manuscript of Matthew that lacks the relevant words.[12] To appeal to conjectural emendation to save the 2DH might be fair enough were this the only such EA^(Mt-Lk) to be explained away, but it is not. Moreover, as Goulder observes, this is hardly a conjectural emendation that has commended itself to text critics.[13] Neither will it do to suggest that a common oral tradition might be responsible for this EA^(Mt-Lk), since it is hard to see how it could be brought about by an oral tradition that would have to preserve the precise wording of a brief phrase of no obvious poetic merit for insertion at precisely the same point in a longer narrative.[14]

Goulder formerly argued that Matthew's seemingly awkward text could be due to Matthean clumsiness in redacting Mark of a type Matthew exhibits elsewhere.[15] He subsequently suggested that far from being clumsy, Matthew envisages two sets of mockers, one who spit in Jesus' face (requiring it not to be blindfolded) and another (οἱ δὲ – Mt. 26.67) who hit him from behind and tell him to prophesy who struck him.[16]

Downing has offered the ingenious suggestion that Luke and Matthew may have coincidentally hit upon the same wording here under the influence of Job 16.10-11,

---

[10] Streeter, *Four Gospels*, 295–8; Goulder, *Luke*, 48; M.D. Goulder, 'On Putting Q to the Test', *NTS* 24 (1978), 218–34, here 219; Goodacre, *Case*, 152–4.
[11] For a review of the discussion of this agreement, see Steve D. Black, 'One Really Striking Minor Agreement ΤΙΣ ΕΣΤΙΝ Ο ΠΑΙΣΑΣ ΣΕ in Matthew 26:68 and Luke 22:64', *NovT* 52 (2010), 313–33.
[12] Goodacre, *Case*, 159–60; Goulder, 'Putting Q to the Test', 226–8, Goulder, *Luke*, 6–10.
[13] Goulder, *Luke*, 9–10; cf. David C. Parker, *The Living Text of the Gospels* (Cambridge: Cambridge University Press, 1997), 112–17, who concludes that a conjectural emendation to protect the 2DH is unjustified here and that the agreement should therefore be allowed to stand. Bruce Metzger, *A Textual Commentary on the Greek New Testament* (Stuttgart: United Bible Societies, 1975), 65 [p. 54 in the 2nd edn of 1994], does not even mention this putative conjectural emendation.
[14] Eric Eve, 'Memory, Orality and the Synoptic Problem', *EC* 6 (2015), 311–33, here 325–7. R.E. Brown, *The Death of the Messiah: From Gethsemane to the Grave* (London: Geoffrey Chapman, 1994), vol. 1, 579, argues that the question 'who is that struck you?' refers to a well-known game, but Black, 'Striking', 326–7, counters that there is insufficient evidence that this game would have been familiar to the audience of the gospels.
[15] Goulder, *Luke*, 9.
[16] M.D. Goulder, 'Two Significant Minor Agreements (Mat. 4:13 Par.; Mat. 26: 67–68Par.)', *NovT* 45 (2003), 365–73, here 371–3. Black, 'Striking', 327–30, is lukewarm towards both of Goulder's suggestions but does not rule them out.

which also uses the verb παίω to express someone striking a victim (on the cheek). That the evangelists were likely to have been influenced by this passage is suggested to Downing by the resemblance of the words Παρέδωκεν γάρ με ὁ κύριος εἰς χεῖρας ἀδίκου at Job 16.11 to the expressions used to describe Jesus being given over into the hands of his captors at Mk 14.41, Mt. 26.45 and Lk. 24.7. Moreover, Downing points out that the construction τίς ἐστιν ὁ is quite common in the gospels (citing Mt. 12.11, 22.28, 24.45, 26.68; Lk. 5.21, 7.49, 9.9, 12.42, 20.2; Jn 5.12, 12.34),[17] implying that it would not be too much of a stretch for both Matthew and Luke to employ it independently.[18]

This explanation is not impossible, but it still requires quite a coincidence. The appeal to Job 16.11 is weakened by the fact that the idiom παράδιδωμι + χείρ is extremely common in the LXX (a quick search turned up 133 instances, 50 of which use the precise form παρέδωκεν). To be sure, not of all of these are used in the negative sense shared by Job 16.11 and the gospels, but quite a few are (e.g. Lev. 26.25; Deut. 1.27; Judg. 2.14). This surely diminishes the case for taking Job 16.11 to be the source of the expression independently employed by the evangelists. Even quite improbable coincidences can sometimes occur and were this the only significant EA[Mt-Lk] threatening a 2DH supported by every other consideration it might be tempting to regard Downing's suggestion as a possible explanation – but it is not.

This agreement forms part of cluster with other nearby EA[Mt-Lk] in Luke, namely ἐξελθὼν ἔξω ἔκλαυσεν πικρῶς against Mark's ἐπιβαλὼν ἔκλαιεν at Mt. 26.75 ‖ Mk 14.72 ‖ Lk. 22.62 and τοῦ λαοῦ (added to Mark) together with ἀπήγαγον against Mark's ἀπήνεγκαν at Mt. 27.1 ‖ Mk 15.1 ‖ Lk. 22.66. The first of these is particularly significant given that πικρῶς occurs nowhere else in the NT. A handful of manuscripts omit Lk. 22.62, so it is possible to argue that it entered the text of Luke from Matthew later in the textual tradition, although Metzger reports that 'a majority of the [UBS] Committee regarded it as more probable that the words were accidentally omitted from several witnesses ... than added without variation ... in all other witnesses'.[19] On balance this EA[Mt-Lk] should also be allowed to stand.

These examples are not the only ones that could be cited, and it may in any case be argued that the sheer quantity of EA[Mt-Lk] threatens the mutual independence of Matthew and Luke. They occur in almost every triple tradition pericope and, depending on how they are counted, number at least 750 in total.[20] Richard Vinson has argued that the

---

[17] The precise phrase τίς ἐστιν ὁ occurs only at Mt. 26.28 (the EA[Mt-Lk] in question); Lk. 20.2 and Jn 5.12 in this list, although the wording at Mt. 24.45; Lk. 5.21, 7.49, 12.42 and Jn 12.34 is very close. In the last of these, however, the construction is used rather differently: 'Who is this "son of man"?'

[18] Downing, 'Plausibility', 317–19.

[19] Metzger, *Textual Commentary*, 178 [2nd edn 151]. Parker, *Living Text*, 160, supports the view that Lk 22.62 is a later intrusion from Matthew, although on p. 117, n. 18, he appears to argue the opposite. Goulder, 'Putting Q to the Test', 228–30, discusses both these agreements and argues for the originality of Lk. 22.62 in Luke's text on the grounds that Luke would not have omitted a notice of Peter's penitence, but this arguably presupposes he knew of a notice to omit. Goulder also points out, however, that the omission of Lk. 22.62 could have come about by homoioteleuton of ΣΚΑΙ at the beginning and end of the omitted line (τρίς καὶ ... πικρῶς καὶ).

[20] The most definitive list of minor agreements is that of Neirynk, *Minor Agreements*, which M.D. Goulder, 'On Putting Q to the Test', NTS 24 (1978), 218–34 (218), estimates contains 'more than 750' of them. Richard Vinson, 'How Minor? Assessing the Significance of the Minor Agreements as an Argument against the Two-Source Hypothesis' in Mark S. Goodacre and Nicholas Perrin (eds), *Questioning Q* (London: SPCK, 2004), 151–64, here 154, puts the number at 3,785.

number of minor agreements in the triple tradition (three thousand by his reckoning) is an order of magnitude too great to be explained as mere coincidence, although his results are questionable.[21] Werner Kahl develops a more cautious way of enumerating EAs, by ignoring agreements in omission and counting 'form-identical agreements of words in the same location and function' or 'syntagms which bring to expression more or less the same meaning' as one EA and identical words in variant forms or form-identical words in a different position or function as half an EA. He then computes the relative distance of Matthew and Luke in each triple tradition pericope according to the number of EAs between each pair of gospels, and on that basis finds that in 39 out of 99 pericopae Matthew and Luke are closer to each other than Luke is to Mark and that there are significant or numerous EA^{Mt-Lk} in 78 out of the 99 pericopae. Moreover, in 62 pericopae the EA^{Mt-Lk} occur in clusters, meaning either 'a syntactic sequence of identical or similar words' or 'the occurrence of a number of various agreements in a pericope'.[22] Although in several instances that meet Kahl's definition of a cluster the collocation of minimally impressive EA^{Mt-Lk} could plausibly be dismissed as coincidental,[23] many significant clusters nonetheless remain. This clustering of EA^{Mt-Lk} is acutely problematic for the mutual independence of Luke and Matthew since such clusters are less likely to arise from coincidence. While an individual cluster of EA^{Mt-Lk} that represent obvious improvements to Mark might sometimes come about coincidentally, the more such clusters there are, the more strained the coincidence becomes.

Kahl's results may arguably be skewed by the inclusion of too many insignificant EA^{Mt-Lk} in his count, and one may, of course, question the weighting he gives to different kinds of agreement or the objectivity with which they can be identified, but what he has shown is that, at least on the basis of counting EAs, Luke is closer to Matthew than to Mark rather more than is often supposed and not only in pericopae traditionally assigned to 'Mark-Q overlaps'.

Even a single-word EA^{Mt-Lk} may be significant if the word in question is sufficiently unusual or uncharacteristic of one of the evangelists. One example of this is the EA^{Mt-Lk} ὕστερον against Mark's ἔσχατον at Mt. 22.27 || Mk 12.22 || Lk. 20.32, since the word

---

[21] Vinson, 'How Minor?' 160–1. Against this, Timothy Friedrichsen, 'The Minor Agreements of Matthew and Luke Against Mark: Critical Observations on R.B. Vinson's Statistical Analysis' *ETL* 65 (1985), 395–408, questions whether the experiment on which Vinson relies adequately represents the compositional conditions of antiquity, while M. Eugene Boring, 'The "Minor Agreements" and Their Bearing on the Synoptic Problem' in Paul Foster, Andrew Gregory, John S. Kloppenborg and J. Verheyden (eds), *New Studies in the Synoptic Problem* (BETL, 139; Leuven: Leuven University Press, 2011), 227–51, argues how the difficulty of finding a generally agreed definition of what constitutes a minor agreement undermines the objectivity of counting them. Moreover, quite apart from the potential difficulty of including common omissions as minor agreements, the more trivial agreements reckoned in Vinson's total might be more noise than data. Again, if many such trivial agreements are largely the result of the two later writers making obvious improvements to their common source, they are arguably less likely to occur when the common source is Plato, Pindar or Euripides (some of the ancient sources Vinson used for comparison) than when the common source exhibits Mark's rough Greek. Vinson responds to some of these objections at 'How Minor', 162–3, but the problems remain.

[22] Kahl, 'Inclusive and Exclusive Agreements', 52–64.

[23] For example, at Mk 12.13-17 || Mt. 22.15-22 || Lk. 20.20-26; several other examples could be cited.

occurs nowhere else in Luke but six other times in Matthew.[24] Mark Goodacre finds six such EA[Mt-Lk] that are characteristic of Matthew but not of Luke, but also one or possibly two counter-examples of EA[Mt-Lk] that are characteristic of Luke but not of Matthew.[25] The clearer counter-example is the EA[Mt-Lk] ὡσεί before πεντακισχίλιοι at Mt. 14.21 || Mk 6.44 || Lk. 9.14, since it is characteristic of Luke, but not Matthew, to use ὡσεί with numbers (to mean 'about'). The more dubious one is the occurrence of the EA[Mt-Lk] νομικός against Mark at Mt. 22.35 || Mk 12.28 || Lk. 10.25. Luke uses νομικός six times while Matthew uses it only here – assuming that he uses it at all, since νομικός may not be part of the original text of Matthew.[26]

Relying on a handful of EA[Mt-Lk] that appear characteristic of Luke but not Matthew is not, however, the best indication of the mutual dependence of the two gospels, although it may help determine the likely direction of any dependence that is established on other grounds. While the six EA[Mt-Lk] Goodacre discusses are certainly significant, they are only a small proportion of the significant agreements, and it is this wider set of significant EA[Mt-Lk] that renders the mutual independence of Matthew and Luke implausible.

The existence of a large number of less significant EA[Mt-Lk] can, however, be made to appear problematic for the FH, for on, the face of it, they prompt the objection articulated by Christopher Tuckett:

The fact that the MAs are so minor makes it hard to believe that Luke has been both influenced positively by Matthew's text in such (substantively) trivial ways, but also totally uninfluenced by any of Matthew's substantive additions to Mark. Undoubtedly the MAs constitute a problem for the 2ST, but precisely their minor nature constitutes a problem for Goulder's theory as well.[27]

But Tuckett overstates his case here. It is not true that FH Luke is 'totally uninfluenced by any of Matthew's substantive additions to Mark', as the so-called Mark-Q overlap passages attest (and as will be further argued in Chapter 5). Moreover, as both Goulder and Goodacre point out, the issue is not the mass of EA[Mt-Lk] that can readily be dismissed as 'trivial' and 'so minor' but the smaller number of more

---

[24] Mark Goodacre, *Goulder and the Gospels: An Examination of a New Paradigm* (JSNTS, 133; Sheffield: Sheffield Academic Press, 1996), 115–16.

[25] Goodacre, *Goulder*, 107–22. The other five EA[Mt-Lk] Goodacre finds to be characteristically Matthean but unLukan occur at Mt. 12.15 || Mk 3.10 || Lk. 6.19 (πάντας), Mt. 8.27 || Mk 4.41 || Lk 8.25 (plural οἱ ἄνεμοι ... ὑπακούουσιν against Mark's singular ὁ ἄνεμος ... ὑπακούει), Mt. 13.54 || Mk 6.2 || Lk. 4.15-16 (αὐτῶν to denote Jewish synagogues), Mt. 14.13 || Mk 6.33 || Lk. 9.11 (οἱ ὄχλοι ἠκολούθησαν) and Mt. 26.47 || Mk 14.43 || Lk. 22.47 (ἰδοὺ following a genitive absolute, in this case αὐτοῦ λαλοῦντας). Goodacre is here evaluating and refining arguments made by Goulder, 'Putting Q to the Test' and Goulder, *Luke*, 47–51.

[26] Metzger, *Textual Commentary*, 59 [2nd edn 48–9], refers to 'an overwhelming preponderance of evidence supporting the word νομικὸς' but suggests that its absence from a number of witnesses 'takes on added significance when it is observed that, apart from this passage, Matthew nowhere else uses the word'. He thus regards it as 'not unlikely ... that copyists have introduced the word here from the parallel passage in Lk 10.25' but notes that given its strong manuscript support 'the Committee was reluctant to omit the word altogether'.

[27] Tuckett, *Q*, 28.

significant EA^(Mt-Lk).²⁸ Tuckett nevertheless has a point: even when EA^(Mt-Lk) occur together in significant clusters or involve significant words, it is far from obvious why Luke should bother, say, to use ὕστερον for ἔσχατον just because Matthew does. It hardly seems likely that he would carefully compare the Matthean and Markan versions of each pericope with a view to deliberately conflating them, as some earlier proponents of the FH appear to envisage.²⁹ It is far more plausible to assume that Luke was working primarily from memory, so that his recollection of Mark was often contaminated by his recollection of Matthew.

This is what Kirk calls the standard FH explanation of the minor agreements, which he goes on to criticize on two grounds. The first is that if the minor agreements are due to Luke's use of Mark being influenced by his memory of Matthew, one would expect a more uniform distribution of minor agreements, the cause being the same throughout. The second is that if Luke was more familiar with Mark than with Matthew, it is difficult to see why there should have been memory interference from Matthew.³⁰

Against the second objection, it may be observed that memory interference can be both retroactive and proactive (more recently and less recently acquired memories can interfere with each other).³¹ Moreover, we need not assume that Luke's memory of Mark was better than his memory command of Matthew; we may suppose that he had equally good memory command of both.

Against the first objection, it may be urged both that Kirk offers no reason for assuming that memory conflation would result in a uniform distribution, and that his objection would seem to apply to any proposed explanation of the minor agreements whatsoever. It could also be pointed out that the occurrence of EA^(Mk-Lk) is similarly uneven but this is not taken as an objection to Luke's memory use of Mark.

In any case, the distribution of EA^(Mt-Lk) is not solely dependent on the workings of Luke's memory. On any theory of Markan priority, Matthew and Luke both vary the extent to which they change Mark's wording from one pericope to the next. In pericopae where one or the other evangelist sticks particularly close to Mark's wording, there will be less scope for EA^(Mt-Lk) (the fewer disagreements there are between Matthew and Mark, the fewer opportunities there are for Luke and Matthew to agree against Mark). Conversely, in pericopae where either Luke or Matthew substantially reworks

---

²⁸ See n. 10 above.
²⁹ E.W. Lummis, *How Luke Was Written* (Cambridge: Cambridge University Press, 1915), 51–111, explicitly assumes such a model. Lummis should not be blamed for being of his time, but it is not always clear that subsequent twentieth-century defenders of the FH explicitly envisage something different.
³⁰ Kirk, 'Memory', 475–8; in Alan Kirk, *Memory and the Jesus Tradition* (London: Bloomsbury T&T Clark, 2018), 154, Kirk changes the wording of his first objection to refer to 'cognitive memory interference from Matthew being a neurobiological constant' which, in Kirk's view should have given rise in Luke to 'a more regular and evenly distributed pattern of these small-scale involuntary harmonizations to Matthew'. Yet as Kirk observes in a different context on p. 218, 'None of the neural activations of a specific memory is precisely identical to any other activation of that memory; because each is sensitive to immediate contextual cues and to other patterns of activation.' Kirk is admittedly talking about something different here (the discussion is about cognitive and cultural schemas), but his point nonetheless undermines confidence in the notion of a 'neurobiological constant' that can be expected to generate 'a regular and evenly distributed pattern' of memory interference.
³¹ *WTG*, 141–2.

Mark, the less chance there is that they will agree against Mark where the other evangelist's changes are more conservative. And in pericopae where either Matthew or Luke drastically abbreviates Mark, there will be less parallel text in which EA^{Mt-Lk} can occur. More generally, Matthew and Luke rewrite different parts of Mark in more or less divergent ways, which is *a priori* likely to lead to varying quantities of EA^{Mt-Lk}. One extreme of this variation is shown in the leftmost column of Kahl's table, which lists twenty-one pericopae in which EA^{Lk-Mk} is either totally absent or insignificant.[32] In seven of these cases there is only at best a partial or dubious Lukan parallel to the Markan pericope.[33] Luke very substantially rewrites or abbreviates another seven pericopae.[34] Another three lack a true Matthean parallel.[35] A further two pericope are much more drastically abbreviated in Matthew than in Luke.[36] In one other case, Matthew has substantially rewritten a Markan pericope he takes out of sequence.[37] This leaves only one pericope lacking significant EA^{Mt-Lk} (Mk 10.13-16 || Mt. 19.13-15 || Lk. 18.15-17) in which Luke and Matthew run sufficiently in parallel for EA^{Mt-Lk} to have much chance of occurring.

This is not quite the full story, however. Kahl's table of the relative proximities of Luke to Matthew and Mark shows a high clustering of EA^{Mt-Lk} (relative to the incidence of EA^{Mk-Lk}) in Luke 9 and 20, where one would expect FH Luke to be following Mark alone. The relatively high occurrence of EA^{Mt-Lk} (compared with EA^{Mk-Lk}) in Luke 22–23 is less problematic, since by the start of Luke 22 Luke's absolute position in Matthew (Mt. 26.1) corresponds to his position in Mark (Mk 14.1) and he could readily be following both sources in parallel (perhaps reading a portion of one, then a portion of the other, before composing his own version on the basis of his memory of both); the high incidence of EA^{Mt-Lk} especially at Lk. 22.54–23.1 suggests that this is what FH Luke may well have done. But although it would have been mechanically feasible for Luke to have (physically or mentally) jumped ahead to Matthew 14 so that he could follow both his sources in parallel when composing Luke 9, and to have resumed from his absolute position (Mt. 8.19-22) in Matthew on reaching the end of Luke 9, it is hard to see why he should have done so; and a similar point could be made about Luke 20 (where FH Luke would have to backtrack from his absolute position at Mt. 25.14-30 || Lk. 19.11-27 to Mt. 21.23 || Mk 11.27 || Lk. 20.1). That significant clusters of EA^{Mt-Lk} also occur in parallels to Markan pericopae that Matthew employs out of their Markan sequence makes it even less likely that they arise through Luke consulting a manuscript of Matthew.[38]

Many EA^{Mt-Lk} in Luke 9 and 20 are not particularly impressive and could be largely due to coincidence. But this is not always the case, a particularly salient example being

---

[32] Kahl, 'Inclusive and Exclusive Agreements', 59–61.
[33] Mk 1.1; 6.17-29; 10.1; 10.2-12; 11.11; 11.12-14; 14.3-9.
[34] Mk 1.14a; 1.39; 6.30-31; 11.15-17; 14.22-25; 15.27-32a; 15.32b.
[35] Mk 1.21-28; 1.35-38; 9.38-41.
[36] Mk 5.1-20; 6.14-16.
[37] Mk 1.32-34.
[38] For example, Sanders and Davies, *Studying*, 68–73, call attention to the cluster in the Healing of the Paralytic (Mt. 9.1-8 || Mk 2.1-12 || Lk. 5.17-26). Here the agreement of ἀπῆλθεν εἰς τὸν οἶκον αὐτοῦ against Mark's ἐξῆλθεν ἔμπροσθεν πάντων at Mt. 9.7 || Mk 2.12 || Lk. 5.25 is particularly striking, along with that of ἰδοὺ and ἐπὶ κλίνης at Mt. 9.2 || Mk 2.3 || Lk. 5.18 (although ἰδοὺ by itself would not be particularly noteworthy).

Table 4.1 Minor Agreements in the First Passion Prediction

Mt. 16.21	Mk 8.31	Lk. 9.22
Ἀπὸ τότε ἤρξατο ὁ Ἰησοῦς δεικνύειν τοῖς μαθηταῖς αὐτοῦ ὅτι δεῖ αὐτὸν εἰς Ἱεροσόλυμα ἀπελθεῖν καὶ πολλὰ παθεῖν <u>ἀπὸ</u> τῶν πρεσβυτέρων καὶ ἀρχιερέων καὶ γραμματέων καὶ ἀποκτανθῆναι καὶ <u>τῇ τρίτῃ ἡμέρᾳ ἐγερθῆναι</u>.	Καὶ ἤρξατο διδάσκειν αὐτοὺς ὅτι δεῖ τὸν υἱὸν τοῦ ἀνθρώπου πολλὰ παθεῖν καὶ ἀποδοκιμασθῆναι ὑπὸ τῶν πρεσβυτέρων καὶ <u>τῶν</u> ἀρχιερέων καὶ <u>τῶν</u> γραμματέων καὶ ἀποκτανθῆναι καὶ μετὰ τρεῖς ἡμέρας ἀναστῆναι·	εἰπὼν ὅτι Δεῖ τὸν υἱὸν τοῦ ἀνθρώπου πολλὰ παθεῖν καὶ ἀποδοκιμασθῆναι <u>ἀπὸ</u> τῶν πρεσβυτέρων καὶ ἀρχιερέων καὶ γραμματέων καὶ ἀποκτανθῆναι καὶ <u>τῇ τρίτῃ ἡμέρᾳ ἐγερθῆναι</u>.

the EA[Mt-Lk] Goulder considers most the striking, at Mt. 16.21 ‖ Mk 8.31 ‖ Lk. 9.22, where Goulder argued that the probability of all four minor agreements occurring by sheer chance is 3 in 100 (having originally proposed 1 in 334).[39]

Goulder argues that while Luke would certainly have changed Mark's μετὰ τρεῖς ἡμέρας ('after three days') to τῇ τρίτῃ ἡμέρᾳ ('on the third day') without any prompting from Matthew, he would have been much less likely to have changed ὑπὸ to ἀπὸ (to mean 'by') or ἀναστῆναι ('rise') to ἐγερθῆναι ('be raised') or to have omitted the repeated article τῶν before ἀρχιερέων ('chief priests') and γραμματέων ('scribes') on his own initiative, so that the occurrence of all three of these agreements together in so short a space is too improbable a coincidence to be down to chance.

Goulder's argument has provoked considerable debate, and while this cluster of EA[Mt-Lk] looks significant, it may be conceded that Goulder originally overestimated the odds of its occurring by chance.[40] But a potential difficulty for the FH here is to explain why Luke should be influenced by Matthew at all in this pericope, given that he is primarily following Mark at this point and has reached only as far at Matthew 11 in his absolute progress through Matthew (see Table 6.8). As Goulder notes, Luke hardly needs Matthew's help to change Mark's 'after three days' to 'on the third day' and the other EA[Mt-Lk] in this pericope look relatively trivial. That Luke had Mark's version rather than Matthew's primarily in mind would explain why he omits the Matthean addition about Peter being the rock on which the church will be built (Mt. 16.17-20). But why would Luke reject this passage only to incorporate minor details of wording from Mt. 16.21? Does this not once again raise Tuckett's spectre of a Luke who studiously takes over Matthew's minor alterations to Mark while avoiding his major additions?[41]

---

[39] Goulder, *Luke*, 48–50; Goulder, Review of F. Neirynck, *Evangelica. II. 1982–1991: Collected Essays* (ed. F. Van Segbroeck), *NovT* 35 (1993), 199–202, here 201.
[40] See Goodacre, *Goulder*, 96–7; F. Neirynck and Timothy A. Friedrichsen, 'Note on Luke 9.22: A Response to M.D. Goulder', *ETL* 65 (1989), 390–94; Robert H. Gundry, 'The Refusal of Matthean Foreign Bodies to Be Exorcised from Luke 9,22; 10,25-28', *ETL* 75 (1999), 104–22; F. Neirynck, 'Luke 9,22 and 10,25-28: The Case for Independent Redaction', *ETL* 75 (1999), 123–32.
[41] Tuckett, *Q*, 28, astutely observes this problem for this EA[Mt-Lk]. Against this one might tentatively suggest that in preferring to have Jesus predict that he would rise 'on the third day', Luke recalled the entirety of the Matthean phrasing.

Examples such as this virtually require the FH explanation of the EA^{Mt-Lk} to assume that FH Luke had good memory command of both sources. Where Matthew and Mark run closely in tandem, Luke could read both versions of a passage and then compose his own version immediately afterwards on the basis of his short-term memory of both, but this cannot account for the other examples given above. Thus, for the FH to account for the EA^{Mt-Lk} requires one of two things to be true. Either Luke is working almost entirely from memory, scarcely ever consulting a manuscript (at least, a manuscript of Mark) in the course of composition, or, if he is using a manuscript to refresh his memory of Mark, he must be doing so in substantial blocks rather than pericope by pericope, so that when he comes to compose his own version his immediate short-term memory of Mark's wording is not so strong as to overcome interference from his long-term memory of Matthew's. If FH Luke is largely relying on his memory of both sources to compose his own account, it is not so hard to see how he might (perhaps inadvertently) recall the wording of both where they deal with the same subject matter. This might also explain why he occasionally uses a Matthean word or construction that he would not normally choose on his own account; his attempt to compose his own version of a Markan passage might be influenced (perhaps unconsciously) by his memory of the Matthean parallel. A further factor that might affect Luke's memory of a passage is its previous oral cultivation in Luke's community (e.g. in preaching, debate or instruction).

That FH Luke is apparently capable of such mental conflation of Mark and Matthew is suggested by Lk. 14.34-35 (|| Mt. 5.13 || Mk 9.49-50), where he would be using material from both gospels out of sequence and presumably relying entirely on his memory of both to compose his own version. IA are shown in bold, EA^{Mt-Lk} underlined and EA^{Mk-Lk} italicized:

Καλὸν οὖν **τὸ ἅλας· ἐὰν δὲ** καὶ **τὸ ἅλας** μωρανθῇ, **ἐν τίνι** ἀρτυθήσεται; οὔτε εἰς γῆν οὔτε εἰς κοπρίαν εὔθετόν ἐστιν, ἔξω βάλλουσιν αὐτό.

To attempt to explain *how* this sort of thing came about in each case would be to go beyond what can possibly be known, insofar as it would require us to speculate how Luke's memory may have been shaped by, for example, the prior oral cultivation of the material he employed. The FH memory explanation nevertheless offers an explanation of many such Matthew-Luke agreements against Mark where the 2DH struggles to offer any explanation at all. Overall, the EA^{Mt-Lk} constitute a substantial set of similarities between Matthew and Luke that are far easier to explain on the FH than the 2DH, provided we allow for Luke's substantial reliance on memory.

Significant verbal similarities in the double tradition

One curious feature of the double tradition is the huge variation in its degree of verbal agreement, from virtually verbatim over extended passages such as the teaching of John the Baptist (Mt. 3.7b-10 || Lk. 3.7b-9) to virtually none in passages such as the Parable of the Talents/Pounds (Mt. 25.14-30 || Lk. 19.11-27). Moreover, a number of double tradition pericopae in which the overall degree of verbal agreement is not particularly high nevertheless contain substantial strings of words that are identical in Matthew and Luke. Mark Goodacre has observed that while such occurrences of high verbal agreement (HVA) are easy enough to explain on the assumption that Luke was directly copying Matthew, on the 2DH they require the strange coincidence that Matthew and Luke independently copied the precise wording of Q in just these cases (given that they seem far less inclined to do the same with Mark).[42]

Goodacre appeals to three kinds of data to make his case. The first is the greater verbal agreement between Matthew and Luke in the double tradition (71.0 per cent overall or 71.5 per cent in the sayings of Jesus) than in the triple tradition (56.0 per cent overall or 65.8 per cent in Jesus' sayings).[43] Here the percentages for the sayings material are likely to be a more meaningful comparator than the overall percentages, since one might expect different types of material to be treated differently, although, as Goodacre observes, the category 'sayings material' may in turn blur a distinction in form between narrative material (such as parables) and non-narrative sayings, with verbal disparities more apparent in the former. Nevertheless, as Goodacre notes, these figures suggest, though they do not prove, that there is a different (and more direct) relationship in the double tradition than in the triple tradition (where Matthew and Luke usually work independently on Mark).[44]

Goodacre's second kind of data is the occurrence of double tradition pericopae with an especially high degree of verbal agreement:

> If one were to express the agreements by means of percentages, there are passages with agreements of Matthew and Luke of 98% (Mt. 6.24//Lk. 16.13), 93% (Mt. 12.43-45//Lk. 11.24-26), 90% (Mt. 11.20-24//Lk. 10.13-15), 88% (Mt. 3.12//Lk. 3.17), 88% (Mt. 12.27-32//Lk. 11.19-23) and 85% (Mt. 23.37-39//Lk. 13.34-35).[45]

The incidence of these HVA passages is more significant than the differences in overall averages, since the average verbal agreement in double tradition material is pulled down by individual passages where it is very low. That Luke and Matthew should sometimes disagree in rendering double tradition is unsurprising; what is noteworthy is the extent to which, on occasion, they agree.[46]

---

[42] Mark Goodacre, 'Too Good to Be Q: High Verbatim Agreement in the Double Tradition' in John C. Poirier and Jeff Peterson (eds), *Marcan Priority without Q: Explorations in the Farrer Hypothesis* (LNTS, 455; London: Bloomsbury T&T Clark, 2015), 82–100. Cf. Wilhelm Wilkens, 'Zur Frage der literarischen Beziehung zwischen Matthäus und Lukas', *NovT* 8 (1966), 48–57, who additionally argues that six of the highly verbatim passages show evidence of Luke's taking over Matthean redaction.

[43] Goodacre, 'Too Good', 92, adapted from Charles E. Carlston and Dennis Norlin, 'Once More – Statistics and Q', *HTR* 1971 (2004), 59–78, here 71; cf. Sharon Lea Mattila, 'Negotiating the Clouds around Statistics and "Q"', *NovT* 46 (2004), 105–31.

[44] Goodacre, 'Too Good', 98.

[45] Goodacre, 'Too Good', 84, citing Kloppenborg *Excavating*, 56, in turn citing Robert Morgenthaler, *Statistische Synopse* (Zurich: Gotthelf, 1971), 258–61. Kloppenborg explains that the percentages express the number of common words as a proportion of the total number of Lukan words. See also Kloppenborg, 'Variation', 53.

[46] Goodacre, 'Too Good', 95; cf. Kloppenborg, 'Variation', 80: 'The real problem to be explained in the Synoptists' reproduction of Q is not their use of periphrastic technique, but the instances of high verbatim repetition.'

This leads into the third line of evidence, namely the occurrence of lengthy sequences of words where Matthew and Luke are in verbatim agreement, not only in passages where there is HVA overall but also in a number of parallels that exhibit a lower overall degree of verbal agreement; for example, Mt. 8.9-10a || Lk. 7.8-9a: καὶ γὰρ ἐγὼ ἄνθρωπός εἰμι ὑπὸ ἐξουσίαν [τασσόμενος], ἔχων ὑπ' ἐμαυτὸν στρατιώτας, καὶ λέγω τούτῳ· Πορεύθητι, καὶ πορεύεται, καὶ ἄλλῳ· Ἔρχου, καὶ ἔρχεται, καὶ τῷ δούλῳ μου· Ποίησον τοῦτο, καὶ ποιεῖ. ἀκούσας δὲ [ταῦτα] ὁ Ἰησοῦς ἐθαύμασεν ('for I also am a man [set] under authority, having under me soldiers, and I say to this one, "Go" and he goes, and to another, "come," and he comes, and to my slave "Do this" and he does it. And when he heard [these things] Jesus marvelled'). Here we would have a continuous string of thirty-six words in agreement, were it not for the two bracketed words that appear in Luke but not Matthew.[47] In any case there is an uninterrupted string of twenty-five words in agreement from ἔχων to δὲ, and it is debatable how far the two bracketed words should count against the longer string, given that the evangelists might be expected to introduce the occasional variation into material they were closely reproducing.

Goodacre goes on to point out that according to John Poirier's list of the thirty-eight most impressive verbatim sequences, sixteen occur in Matthew//Mark pairs, four in Mark//Luke pairs and eighteen in Matthew//Luke pairs, of which sixteen occur in the double tradition, the other two Matthew//Luke pairs only making the list by virtue of EA[Mt-Lk].[48] On the face of it, there is a substantially closer relationship between Matthew and Luke in the double tradition than in the triple tradition where they are making independent use of Mark. This suggests that in the double tradition Luke's use of Matthew looks more plausible than their common use of Q.

One might object that is it arbitrary to look only for sequences of sixteen words or more. Poirier's list of verbatim strings comes as part of his critique of McIver and Carroll's attempt to develop criteria for determining literary dependence. On the basis of experiments performed on Australian students, McIver and Carroll concluded that *'any sequence of exactly the same 16 or more words that is not an aphorism, poetry, or words to a song is almost certain to have been copied from a written document'*.[49] There are, however, any number of reasons why these experiments might fail to replicate the working practices of the evangelists, among which one might include different aims and different cultural experiences with reliance on memory.[50] Goodacre suggests differences in language as a further factor, pointing out that since English is an uninflected language with more restrictions on word order than koine Greek, it is easier to generate longer strings of verbatim agreement in English than in

---

[47] A number of manuscripts support the inclusion of τασσόμενος at Mt. 8.9, but Metzger, *Textual Commentary*, 20 [absent from 2nd edn], regards it as being clearly an interpolation from Luke since there would be no reason for so many witnesses to omit it were it original to Matthew.
[48] Goodacre, 'Too Good', 95, citing John C. Poirier, 'Memory, Written Sources, and the Synoptic Problem: A Response to Robert K. McIver and Marie Carroll', *JBL* 123 (2004), 315–22, here 320.
[49] Robert K. McIver and Marie Carroll, 'Experiments to Develop Criteria for Determining the Existence of Written Sources, and Their Potential Implications for the Synoptic Problem', *JBL* 121 (2002), 667–87, here 680; emphasis original.
[50] For more detailed criticism of McIver and Carroll, see Derico, *Oral Tradition*, 183–202.

Greek.⁵¹ It might then be questioned whether Poirier's table, listing sequential agreements of sixteen words or more, is the most appropriate dataset to use or whether one needs to look at a wider dataset that includes shorter strings as well. But in the absence of a compelling proposal for a dataset based on some other specific string length, such an objection fails to undermine the force of Poirier's data.

Poirier observes that many more sequences would have made it into his table but for the odd redactional word interrupting them.⁵² One of his examples is the set of parallels at Mt. 24.34-35 ‖ Mk 13.30-31 ‖ Lk. 21.32-33 (see Table 4.2).

Here we have what could very well be a sequence of twenty-eight words in Matthew-Luke agreement, and almost as many in triple agreement, apart from Luke's omission of ταῦτα, Mark's use of μέχρις οὗ in place of the EA^{Mt-Lk} ἕως ἂν and Matthew's

Table 4.2 Verbal Agreements in Mk 13.30-31 and par.

Mt. 24.34-35	Mk 13.30-31	Lk. 21.32-33
ἀμὴν λέγω ὑμῖν ὅτι οὐ μὴ παρέλθῃ ἡ γενεὰ αὕτη <u>ἕως ἂν</u> πάντα ταῦτα γένηται. ὁ οὐρανὸς καὶ ἡ γῆ παρελεύσεται, **οἱ δὲ λόγοι μου οὐ μὴ** παρέλθωσιν.	ἀμὴν λέγω ὑμῖν ὅτι οὐ μὴ παρέλθῃ ἡ γενεὰ αὕτη μέχρις οὗ ταῦτα **πάντα γένηται.** ὁ οὐρανὸς καὶ ἡ γῆ παρελεύσονται, **οἱ δὲ λόγοι μου οὐ μὴ** παρελεύσονται.	ἀμὴν λέγω ὑμῖν ὅτι οὐ μὴ παρέλθῃ ἡ γενεὰ αὕτη <u>ἕως ἂν</u> πάντα γένηται. ὁ οὐρανὸς καὶ ἡ γῆ παρελεύσονται, **οἱ δὲ λόγοι μου οὐ μὴ** παρελεύσονται.

Table 4.3 Verbal Agreement in Mk 8.34-36 and par.

Mt. 16.24-26	Mk 8.34-36	Lk. 9.23-25
Τότε ὁ Ἰησοῦς εἶπεν τοῖς μαθηταῖς αὐτοῦ· **Εἴ τις θέλει ὀπίσω μου ἐλθεῖν, ἀπαρνησάσθω ἑαυτὸν καὶ ἀράτω τὸν σταυρὸν αὐτοῦ καὶ ἀκολουθείτω μοι.** ὃς γὰρ ἐὰν θέλῃ τὴν ψυχὴν αὐτοῦ σῶσαι ἀπολέσει αὐτήν· ὃς δ' ἂν <u>ἀπολέσῃ</u> τὴν ψυχὴν αὐτοῦ **ἕνεκεν ἐμοῦ** εὑρήσει αὐτήν. 26 τί γὰρ ὠφεληθήσεται <u>ἄνθρωπος</u> ἐὰν **τὸν κόσμον ὅλον** κερδήσῃ τὴν δὲ ψυχὴν αὐτοῦ ζημιωθῇ; ἢ τί δώσει ἄνθρωπος ἀντάλλαγμα τῆς ψυχῆς αὐτοῦ;	Καὶ προσκαλεσάμενος τὸν ὄχλον σὺν τοῖς μαθηταῖς αὐτοῦ εἶπεν αὐτοῖς· **Εἴ τις θέλει ὀπίσω μου ἐλθεῖν, ἀπαρνησάσθω ἑαυτὸν καὶ ἀράτω τὸν σταυρὸν αὐτοῦ καὶ ἀκολουθείτω μοι.** 35 ὃς γὰρ ἐὰν θέλῃ τὴν ψυχὴν αὐτοῦ σῶσαι ἀπολέσει αὐτήν· ὃς δ' ἂν ἀπολέσει **τὴν ψυχὴν αὐτοῦ ἕνεκεν ἐμοῦ** καὶ τοῦ εὐαγγελίου σώσει **αὐτήν.** 36 τί γὰρ ὠφελεῖ ἄνθρωπον κερδῆσαι **τὸν κόσμον ὅλον** καὶ ζημιωθῆναι τὴν ψυχὴν αὐτοῦ;	Ἔλεγεν δὲ πρὸς πάντας· **Εἴ τις θέλει ὀπίσω μου** ἔρχεσθαι, ἀρνησάσθω **ἑαυτὸν καὶ ἀράτω τὸν σταυρὸν αὐτοῦ** καθ' ἡμέραν, **καὶ ἀκολουθείτω μοι.** 24 ὃς γὰρ ἂν θέλῃ τὴν ψυχὴν αὐτοῦ σῶσαι, ἀπολέσει αὐτήν· ὃς δ' ἂν <u>ἀπολέσῃ</u> τὴν ψυχὴν αὐτοῦ ἕνεκεν ἐμοῦ, οὗτος σώσει **αὐτήν.** 25 τί γὰρ ὠφελεῖται <u>ἄνθρωπος</u> κερδήσας **τὸν κόσμον ὅλον** ἑαυτὸν δὲ ἀπολέσας ἢ ζημιωθείς;

---

⁵¹ Mark Goodacre, 'A Flaw in McIver and Carroll's Experiments to Determine Written Sources in the Gospels' *JBL* 133 (2014), 667–87. Against this, Derico, *Oral Tradition*, 197, n. 73, objects that Goodacre's 'claim rests on a dubious view of the relevant mental processes', since persons relying on memory of an oral tradition might remember specific words and phrases rather than trying to generate an expression from its remembered gist. This objection finds partial support in Rubin, *Memory in Oral Traditions*, who argues that both surface features (of the sort to which Derico appeals here) and deeper meaning and imagery contribute to the stability of oral traditions.

⁵² Poirier, 'Memory', 321.

παρελεύσεται and παρέλθωσιν for the EA^{Mk-Lk} παρελεύσονται, differences that might easily disappear in English translation. Poirier goes on to say that 'this sort of thing can be observed throughout the Gospels' but gives no indication of its extent.

As Goodacre notes, two of Poirier's cases of extended sequential agreement occur in the triple tradition. One of these comes at Mt. 16.24-26 || Mk 8.34-36 || Lk. 9.23-25 (see Table 4.3). Here there is a verbatim Matthew-Luke agreement for sixteen words (θέλῃ to ἐμοῦ) that would be extended to thirty-seven words but for some trivial differences. It is strictly true that the sixteen-word verbatim sequence depends on the EA^{Mt-Lk} ἀπολέσῃ for Mark's ἀπολέσει, but that Matthew and Luke should independently correct Mark's indicative to the subjunctive here is hardly stretching coincidence, so this can still be taken as an example of Matthew and Luke independently generating a sixteen-word verbatim string in the triple tradition.

The other case is the eighteen-word sequential agreement between Matthew and Luke at Mt. 8.2-3 || Mk 1.40-42 || Lk 5.12-13, which once again occurs, thanks to a number of individually unimpressive EA^{Mt-Lk}.[53] But neither of these triple tradition cases is as impressive as the longest verbatim sequences Goodacre finds in the double tradition: twenty and twenty-four words at Mt. 3.7b-10 || Lk. 3.7b-9, twenty-six words at Mt. 6.24 || Lk. 16.13, twenty-seven words at Mt. 11.25-27 || Lk. 10.21-22 and twenty-five words at Mt. 8.9-10 || Lk. 7.8-9.[54] Most of these examples would be longer but for just the odd word that differs between Matthew and Luke (as in the Capernaum Centurion parallels above).

Unbroken sequences of precise verbatim agreement occur markedly more frequently in the double tradition than the triple tradition. This constitutes a species of significant similarity between Matthew and Luke that is potentially problematic for the 2DH, since it is easier to explain via Luke's direct use of Matthew than via their independent use of Q. By itself, this phenomenon is indicative rather than probative, both since the dataset in question is not all that large and because it could perhaps be adjusted in ways that might turn out to yield different results.[55] The phenomenon of close verbal agreement in the double tradition nevertheless constitutes further prima facie evidence of a direct connection between Matthew and Luke.

Significantly similar beginnings

The similarities between the first few chapters of Matthew and Luke are more extensive than is often recognized. They also afford a convenient opportunity both to examine

---

[53] Goodacre, 'Too Good', 99–100.
[54] Goodacre, 'Too Good', 83–7.
[55] See the comments in John S. Kloppenborg, 'The Farrer/Mark without Q Hypothesis: A Response' in John C. Poirier and Jeff Peterson (eds), *Marcan Priority without Q: Explorations in the Farrer Hypothesis* (LNTS, 455; London: Bloomsbury T&T Clark, 2015), 226–44, here 241–3. Kloppenborg suggests that 'a more balanced analysis' would require comparing the incidence of HVA in the double tradition with the comparable strings of sayings at Mk 4.3-9, 11-32; 13.5-37 and parallels. Poirier's examples of extended HVA at Mk 13.30-31 falls within this scope. But as Kloppenborg also observes, here we are confined to 'a data set that is perhaps too small to be meaningful statistically'. That being so, it is arguably preferable to extend the data set to all the triple tradition sayings material rather than restricting it to longer strings of sayings.

a number of verbal agreements in context and to draw out some further similarities between the two gospels.[56] In summary, Luke and Matthew agree against Mark in opening with infancy narratives that have many points in common. They also agree against Mark in restricting the quotation from Isaiah to what actually comes from Isaiah and placing it after the notice about the appearance of John the Baptist. Both Matthew and Luke (but not Mark) then go on to describe the preaching of John the Baptist (Mt. 3.7b-10, 11b-12 || Lk. 3.7b-9, 16b-17) in remarkably similar words before finally expanding Mark's brief Temptation Narrative (Mk 1.12-13) in substantially similar ways (Mt. 4.1-11 || Lk. 4.1-13). Finally, there are indications that the remainder of Matthew chapter 4 also influenced Luke.

On the 2DH, many of these similarities are explained by Mark-Q overlap. But this explanation risks either Q becoming so extensive that it is effectively identical to Matthew or else has Q presuppose elements of Matthew's account of John the Baptist that it does not narrate, such as the Baptist's ascetic lifestyle (Mt. 3.4; Q 7.24-27, 33).[57] These may be points that 2DH Matthew could in principle have picked up and developed from Q, but it is more straightforward to see them as features FH Luke has derived from Matthew.

Luke's opening appears to be largely dependent on Matthew (with just the occasional Luke-Mark agreements against Matthew). Since, however, it is not commonly seen as such, it will be necessary to examine the parallels in more detail. To this end we shall proceed in three stages: first, we shall argue that Matthew's Temptation Narrative fits so well into its Matthean context that it would be strange if it had come about by conflating Mark and Q; next we shall compare the two infancy narratives; and finally we shall examine the Matthew-Luke parallels in the Baptism and Temptation narratives and the remainder of Matthew chapter 4.

Matthew's opening

Matthew constructed the opening of his gospel (i.e. Mt. 1.1–4.11) around the combination of an Israel typology and a Moses typology.[58] The Israel typology is strongly signalled by the quotation from Hos. 11.1 at Mt. 2.15, 'Out of Egypt I have called my son'. In Matthew, this fulfilment formula quotation makes the infant Jesus the ostensible reference of 'my son', whereas in Hosea 11 the reference is clearly to Israel. Matthew is not outrageously misapplying a scriptural text here but instead using it to signal a hermeneutical key to his opening section.[59] The ostensible function of the genealogy with which the gospels open (Mt. 1.1-17) is to establish Jesus' Davidic descent and hence his messianic credentials, but it serves the additional function of recapitulating the story of Israel from Abraham, through the monarchy

---

[56] See also the discussion in Watson, *Gospel Writing*, 131–48.
[57] Goulder, *Luke*, 52–4.
[58] See especially, Dale C. Allison, *The New Moses: A Matthean Typology* (Edinburgh: T&T Clark, 1993), 140–72.
[59] Allison, *New Moses*, 140–2; Davies and Allison, *Matthew*, I, 263; Daniel J. Harrington, *The Gospel of Matthew* (SP, 1; Collegeville, MN: Liturgical, 1991), 44.

and exile, and down to the birth of Jesus, who is thus presented as its culmination and fulfilment.[60]

Jesus' supposed father Joseph shares several features with his patriarchal namesake. Both have fathers named Jacob (Mt. 1.16); both learn from dreams; the patriarch Joseph is responsible for Israel's descent into Egypt to escape famine (Gen. 45-47) while Jesus' father takes the infant Jesus down into Egypt to escape Herod (Mt. 2.13-14).[61]

Thereafter most parallels are with the exodus narrative. As in Exod. 1.8 so in Mt. 2.19-21 the return from Egypt is set in motion by a change of king, although there is also a close parallel with the description of Moses' return to Egypt at Exod. 4.19-20.[62] Both Jesus and Israel subsequently enter the wilderness via a passage through water, the baptism (Mt. 3.13-17) and the Red Sea (Exod. 14), a typological link also made by Paul (1 Cor. 10.1-2).[63] Once in the wilderness, both Israel and Jesus are tested, with the difference that Jesus passes the tests while Israel fails them, so that Jesus is shown to be the obedient Son of God that rebellious Israel fails to be (Mt. 4.1-11).[64] Moreover, Jesus' first temptation is to command stones to become bread (Mt. 4.3) just as Israel's first complaint after crossing the Red Sea concerns lack of food (Exod. 16.1-3).[65] Whether the stones that Jesus is urged to turn into bread are meant to echo the rock from which Moses subsequently drew water (Exod. 17.1-7) is less clear, although Paul makes Christological play with that same rock (1 Cor. 10.4). The temptation to worship Satan (Mt. 4.8-10) may in part be intended to echo Israel's worship of the Golden Calf (Exod. 32.1-6), which is also alluded to by Paul at 1 Cor. 10.6-7.[66]

The second and third temptations also foreshadow what is yet to come in Matthew's narrative.[67] In the second temptation the devil takes Jesus to Jerusalem, sets him on the pinnacle of the Temple and declares, 'If you are the Son of God, throw yourself down' (Εἰ υἱὸς εἶ τοῦ θεοῦ, βάλε σεαυτὸν κάτω – Mt. 4.6); later those mocking Jesus as he hangs on a cross say, 'If you are the Son of God, come down from the cross' (εἰ υἱὸς εἶ τοῦ θεοῦ, κατάβηθι ἀπὸ τοῦ σταυροῦ – Mt. 27.40), a taunt promptly repeated in

---

[60] Davies and Allison, *Matthew*, I, 186-8; Harrington, *Matthew*, 30-3; Karl-Heinrich Ostmeyer, 'Der Stammbaum des Verheißenen: Theologische Implikationen der Namen und Zahlen in Mt 1.1-17', *NTS* 46 (2000), 175-92; Brown, *Birth*, 66-84; Francis Watson, *The Fourfold Gospel: A Theological Reading of the New Testament Portraits of Jesus* (Grand Rapids, MI: Baker Academic, 2016), 30-3.
[61] Goulder, *Midrash*, 236.
[62] Allison, *New Moses*, 142-4. Davies and Allison, *Matthew*, I, 271.
[63] Davies and Allison, *Matthew*, I, 328, 344-5.
[64] Goulder, *Midrash*, 245; Harrington, *Matthew*, 69.
[65] Goulder, *Midrash*, 245-6; Harrington, *Matthew*, 66. Allison, *New Moses*, 166, argues that here Matthew has glossed Q's Israel typology with his own Moses typology on the grounds that 'and forty nights' in Mt. 4.2 applies to the latter but not the former. But Allison also believes that in Matthew 2 'the evangelist glossed the traditional Moses typology with an Israel typology'. One might then suppose that the combination of Israel and Moses typologies was Matthew's throughout; at the very least, the Moses typology can hardly have been absent from the putative Q version, since this would also would have had Jesus quote from Deuteronomy and survey kingdoms from a mountain as Moses was said to survey the land from Mount Pisgah (Num. 27.12-14; Deut. 3.27, 32.48-52; 34.1-4), for which see Allison, *New Moses*, 169-70.
[66] Goulder, *Midrash*, 246-7.
[67] Harrington, *Matthew*, 69-70, proposes a link between all three temptations and events later in the gospel: the miraculous feedings, the Transfiguration and the final commissioning scene. The first of these is plausible and the third agrees with the proposal made below.

slightly different words by the chief priests, scribes and elders at Mt. 27.41-43, where it is made explicit that Jesus is being ironically invited to prove his claims by saving himself and descending from the cross, just as the devil is presumably inviting Jesus to make a public demonstration of his divine sonship by casting himself down from a prominent public place so that angels can arrest his fall.[68] The effect is to show Jesus' mockers in the role of Satan and the crucified Jesus in the role of obedient son. In the third temptation the devil takes Jesus to a high mountain and offers him all the kingdoms of the world in return for his worship, whereupon Jesus retorts that worship is due to God alone (Mt. 4.8-10). In the final scene of the gospel, Jesus appears to the eleven disciples on a mountain, receives worship from them and declares that all authority in heaven and on earth has been given to him, the implication being that by resisting the devil's temptation and remaining steadfastly obedient to his Father's will, Jesus has received even more than that devil offered him (Mt. 28.16-20), rather as Philo (*Vit. Mos.* 1.148-9, 155-6) saw Moses' renunciation of earthly wealth and power as leading to God's granting him a superior authority.[69]

The Temptation Narrative also serves to clarify Matthew's understanding of the title 'Son of God' immediately after God's voice has declared Jesus to be God's son at the baptism (Mt. 3.17). The devil's repeated 'if you are the Son of God' tests what kind of Son of God Jesus will be.[70] As we have seen, Jesus is a totally obedient son, but the devil's temptations would be meaningless if Jesus were not able to perform the feats the devil invites him to; the narrator thus shares the devil's assumption that the title 'Son of God' implies the possession of power and authority even while rejecting the devil's view on how that power and authority should be used.[71]

Matthew's Moses typology is also apparent throughout this opening section. Like the infant Moses, the infant Jesus' life is threatened by a hostile king whose determination to kill him he nonetheless escapes.[72] This and other parallels between Moses and Jesus become even more apparent in Josephus' account of Moses' birth and early life at *Ant.* 2.205-34 (and other Jewish midrashic traditions).[73] In the Temptation Narrative, just as Moses fasted for forty days and forty nights on the mountain (Exod.

---

[68] So also Wilhelm Wilkens, 'Die Versuchung Jesu nach Matthäus', *NTS* 28 (1982), 479–89, here 484–5. Davies and Allison, *Matthew*, I, 366–7, note but reject this interpretation of the second temptation on the grounds that no spectators are mentioned and there is no evidence that the Messiah was expected to perform such a demonstration; they suggest instead that Jesus is being tempted to compel God's response for self-assurance. But this ignores the verbal link with Mt. 27.40 and fails to explain why Jesus should have been transported to Jerusalem rather than hurling himself off a convenient cliff in the wilderness.

[69] Wilkens, 'Versuchung', 485–6; and Allison, *New Moses*, 171–2; the link between the third temptation and the final scene in Matthew's Gospel is further strengthened by the Moses typology that Allison, *New Moses*, 262–6, sees lying behind the latter. So also Davies and Allison, *Matthew*, I, 369–70.

[70] Harrington, *Matthew*, 66.

[71] Wilkens, 'Versuchung', similarly regards the Temptation Narrative as a Matthaean composition (taken over by Luke) that reflects Matthean concerns.

[72] Harrington, *Matthew*, 46–50, sees the Moses-Jesus typology as constituting the theological and narrative unity of Matthew chapter 2.

[73] Brown, *Birth*, 107–16; Allison, *New Moses*, 140–65; Davies and Allison, *Matthew*, I, 192–3; see also Harrington, *Matthew*, 38, 48, for possible parallels with *LAB* 9.10 as well as *Ant.* 2.205-37. Whether Matthew can be said to be *imitating* this material is less clear; the typological correspondences he creates lie in the fuzzy borderland between imitation and allusion.

34.28) so Jesus fasts for forty days and forty nights in the wilderness (Mt. 4.2). Each time the devil tries to tempt him, Jesus responds by citing a text from Deuteronomy 6-8, which is supposedly part of a speech given by Moses on the eve of Israel's entry into the Promised Land.[74] The notice at Mt. 4.11 that angels ministered to Jesus after the devil's departure may be intended to echo a tradition that Moses was fed by angels (seemingly implied by *Ant.* 3.99).[75]

Among the other functions it performs (such as presenting Jesus as descended from David and as fulfilling prophecy), the opening of Matthew's Gospel at Mt. 1.1-4.11 sets out Matthew's Christological stall and foreshadows what will happen at the end of his gospel. It is skilfully done, with Moses typology and Israel typology blended together, and Jesus thus shown to be both new Moses and true Israel, the obedient son that Israel should have been but failed to be. This opening also introduces other facets of Matthean Christology such as the Son of David title and the fulfilment of scripture (both of which will feature distinctively in the body of his gospel) and the Emmanuel, 'God with us', title that will be echoed right at the end (Mt. 28.20). This is an impressive construction, however it was arrived at; for Matthew to have managed it by simply combining Mark, Q and whatever sources may have lain behind his Infancy Narrative would be quite remarkable.[76]

To be sure, 'quite remarkable' does not equate to 'impossible'. The partial parallels between Mt. 3.13-4.10 and 1 Cor. 10.1-7 alluded to above could be taken as indicating a common tradition of Moses typology. Moreover, Matthew may have been extraordinarily lucky in finding a document Q that fitted his purpose so neatly, providing not only a Temptation Narrative that chimed with Matthew's Israel typology, Moses typology and Son of God Christology but also sayings of John the Baptist that neatly fitted into the Markan opening and expressed Matthean sentiments about the coming judgement. Coincidences sometimes happen and perhaps this one did; or perhaps Matthew found Q's ideas so congenial he adopted them all as his own. But the more natural conclusion to draw is that both the Matthean Infancy Narrative and the double tradition material in Mt. 3.1-4.11 are essentially of Matthean origin (even if he composed some of it on the basis of earlier material). There is certainly little in the vocabulary of these passages that demands a non-Matthean origin.[77] Thus, on the basis of Matthew alone, there would be little to suggest at this point that Matthew was combining Mark with a second source Q as opposed to expanding Mark in his own

---

[74] Harrington, *Matthew*, 68.
[75] Allison, *New Moses*, 169.
[76] For the possible sources behind Matthew's Infancy Narrative and Matthew's own contribution, see Brown, *Birth*, 99-119. Brown nevertheless finds that 'no matter what the prehistory of his material, Matthew had made the narrative an effective vehicle of *his* theology and message' (p. 119) and that 'the skill of the evangelist is admirable. He has woven disparate pre-Matthean material into a remarkable preface to his Gospel' (p. 231).
[77] Goulder, *Midrash*, 235, 241, 244-5, 247, 238-9. On the other hand, Davies and Allison, *Matthew*, I, 190-5, argue that Matthew's Infancy Narrative represents Matthew's minimal redaction of a source. In their view the narrative contains too many inconcinnities to be the work of a single author, but too much unity to have been stitched together by a final redactor from disparate traditions. One might suppose these arguments to be mutually cancelling, but in any case, no denial is intended here that Matthew may have worked with some antecedent traditions.

way (which might include adapting traditions available to him but seems far less likely to involve closely copying a second written source).

It might nevertheless be argued that Matthew has rewritten his sources so thoroughly as to disguise their existence, so the next step is to see how Luke's version compares.[78]

The infancy narratives in Luke and Matthew

At first sight, Luke's Infancy Narrative looks so different from Matthew's that it is often assumed that Luke could not possibly have used Matthew in composing it. In brief, Matthew begins with a genealogy, then has Jesus born in Bethlehem (apparently his parents' home), flee to Egypt to escape death at the hands of King Herod and subsequently move to Nazareth, while Luke has Mary and Joseph domiciled in Nazareth, sent to Bethlehem for an imperial census and then return home to Nazareth after encountering nothing more threatening than a group of inquisitive shepherds.[79] A further major difference between the Lukan and Matthean infancy narratives is that Luke includes parallel annunciation and birth narratives for John the Baptist and Jesus, while Matthew deals with Jesus' birth alone.[80]

Yet despite these differences, the two accounts contain many significant similarities. In both accounts, Jesus' ostensible father is named Joseph and his mother Mary, and he is descended from David through Joseph. In both, Jesus is raised in Nazareth having previously been born in Bethlehem during the reign of Herod the Great (ἐν Βηθλέεμ τῆς Ἰουδαίας ἐν ἡμέραις Ἡρῴδου τοῦ Βασιλέως, Mt. 2.1; ἐν ταῖς ἡμέραις Ἡρῴδου Βασιλέως τῆς Ἰουδαίας, Lk. 1.5).[81] In both, an angel announces to one of Jesus' parents that Mary, who at that point is betrothed but not married to Joseph, will conceive a son by the power of the Holy Spirit despite being an unmarried virgin. In both the angel tells the future parent that Mary will conceive and commands him or her in precisely the same words, 'you shall call his name Jesus' (καὶ καλέσεις τὸ ὄνομα αὐτοῦ Ἰησοῦν – Mt. 1.21 ∥ Lk. 1.31). In both the infant Jesus is subsequently visited by a group of people who have been guided to him by means of a celestial revelation resulting in great joy (χαρὰν μεγάλην in both Mt. 2.10 and Lk. 2.10), and in both he is said to be a saviour (Mt. 1.21; Lk. 2.11).[82]

---

[78] McAdon, *Rhetorical Mimesis*, 74–119, argues that Matthew's Infancy Narratives derive entirely from mimesis of various OT passages and themes (such as genealogies and birth annunciation) and are aimed at constructing an apologetic response to the charge that Jesus was conceived out of wedlock (although this hardly seems to be the *sole* point of Matthew's Infancy Narratives).

[79] For a convenient summary of the differences between the two infancy narratives, see Brown, *Birth*, 35–6.

[80] For why Luke may have done this, see Karl A. Kuhn, 'The Point of the Step-Parallelism in Luke 1–2', *NTS* 47 (2001), 38–49; cf. Brown, *Birth*, 282–5.

[81] Goulder, *Luke*, 216–17, argues that Luke has borrowed this phrasing from Matthew, since ἐν ἡμέραις is characteristically Matthean and Herod has no place in Luke's story, which takes place ten years later when Quirinius was governor of Syria. These points may not be decisive in themselves, but in conjunction with other similarities between the Lukan and Matthean infancy narratives the similarity in wording here may well be a further indication of Luke's use of Matthew.

[82] Cf. the list of similarities at Brown, *Birth*, 34–5, and the discussion of resemblances in Barbara Shellard, *New Light on Luke: Its Purpose, Sources and Literary Context* (London: T&T Clark, 2002), 79–81; Watson, *Gospel Writing*, 131–6; and Goodacre, *Case*, 55–8.

Some of these resemblances are more significant than others. That Jesus' mother was called Mary would have been known to both Matthew and Luke from Mk 6.3. That he came from Nazareth would be apparent from Mk 1.9, 24; 16.6. That he was of Davidic descent was known to Paul (Rom. 1.3). That he was born in Bethlehem might conceivably be something Matthew and Luke independently deduced from his Davidic descent (cf. Jn 7.42). The angelic annunciation of an unlikely birth might be independently based on OT models (e.g. Gen. 16.7-15, 17.15-19). The words 'you shall call his name Jesus' are based on an OT formula applied, for example, to the birth of Isaac at Gen. 17.19 and are similar to those used of the Immanuel child at Isa. 7.14 (which Matthew explicitly quotes).[83]

Nevertheless, it was by no means inevitable that both evangelists should choose to employ this formula. It fits the Matthean context well enough since Matthew goes on to cite the similar formula from Isa. 7.14 at Mt. 1.22-23. Moreover, in Matthew the words 'you [singular] shall call his name Jesus' are appropriately addressed to Joseph, who as the ostensible father would normally be expected to name his son. In Luke, the same words are addressed rather less appropriately to Mary, the mother, who would not have the sole responsibility for naming the child, as Luke is well aware (Lk. 1.59-63). Luke could have avoided this problem by using the alternative formula 'and his name shall be called Jesus'. That Jesus was conceived by the Holy Spirit of the Virgin Mary

Table 4.4 The Annunciation in Luke and Matthew

Lk. 1.26-35	Mt. 1.20-25a
Ἐν δὲ τῷ μηνὶ τῷ ἕκτῳ ἀπεστάλη ὁ ἄγγελος Γαβριὴλ ἀπὸ τοῦ θεοῦ εἰς πόλιν τῆς Γαλιλαίας ᾗ ὄνομα Ναζαρὲθ πρὸς παρθένον ἐμνηστευμένην ἀνδρὶ ᾧ ὄνομα Ἰωσὴφ ἐξ οἴκου Δαυὶδ, καὶ τὸ ὄνομα τῆς παρθένου Μαριάμ. καὶ εἰσελθὼν πρὸς αὐτὴν εἶπεν· Χαῖρε, κεχαριτωμένη, ὁ κύριος μετὰ σοῦ. ἡ δὲ ἐπὶ τῷ λόγῳ διεταράχθη καὶ διελογίζετο ποταπὸς εἴη ὁ ἀσπασμὸς οὗτος. καὶ εἶπεν ὁ ἄγγελος αὐτῇ· Μὴ φοβοῦ, Μαριάμ, εὗρες γὰρ χάριν παρὰ τῷ θεῷ· καὶ ἰδοὺ συλλήμψῃ ἐν γαστρὶ καὶ τέξῃ υἱόν, καὶ καλέσεις τὸ ὄνομα αὐτοῦ Ἰησοῦν. οὗτος ἔσται μέγας καὶ υἱὸς Ὑψίστου κληθήσεται, καὶ δώσει αὐτῷ κύριος ὁ θεὸς τὸν θρόνον Δαυὶδ τοῦ πατρὸς αὐτοῦ, καὶ βασιλεύσει ἐπὶ τὸν οἶκον Ἰακὼβ εἰς τοὺς αἰῶνας, καὶ τῆς βασιλείας αὐτοῦ οὐκ ἔσται τέλος. εἶπεν δὲ Μαριὰμ πρὸς τὸν ἄγγελον· Πῶς ἔσται τοῦτο, ἐπεὶ ἄνδρα οὐ γινώσκω; καὶ ἀποκριθεὶς ὁ ἄγγελος εἶπεν αὐτῇ· Πνεῦμα ἅγιον ἐπελεύσεται ἐπὶ σέ, καὶ δύναμις Ὑψίστου ἐπισκιάσει σοι· διὸ καὶ τὸ γεννώμενον ἅγιον κληθήσεται, υἱὸς θεοῦ·	ταῦτα δὲ αὐτοῦ ἐνθυμηθέντος ἰδοὺ ἄγγελος κυρίου κατ' ὄναρ ἐφάνη αὐτῷ λέγων· Ἰωσὴφ υἱὸς Δαυίδ, μὴ φοβηθῇς παραλαβεῖν Μαρίαν τὴν γυναῖκά σου, τὸ γὰρ ἐν αὐτῇ γεννηθὲν ἐκ πνεύματός ἐστιν ἁγίου· τέξεται δὲ υἱὸν καὶ καλέσεις τὸ ὄνομα αὐτοῦ Ἰησοῦν, αὐτὸς γὰρ σώσει τὸν λαὸν αὐτοῦ ἀπὸ τῶν ἁμαρτιῶν αὐτῶν. τοῦτο δὲ ὅλον γέγονεν ἵνα πληρωθῇ τὸ ῥηθὲν ὑπὸ κυρίου διὰ τοῦ προφήτου λέγοντος· Ἰδοὺ ἡ παρθένος ἐν γαστρὶ ἕξει καὶ τέξεται υἱόν, καὶ καλέσουσιν τὸ ὄνομα αὐτοῦ Ἐμμανουήλ· ὅ ἐστιν μεθερμηνευόμενον Μεθ' ἡμῶν ὁ θεός. ἐγερθεὶς δὲ ὁ Ἰωσὴφ ἀπὸ τοῦ ὕπνου ἐποίησεν ὡς προσέταξεν αὐτῷ ὁ ἄγγελος κυρίου καὶ παρέλαβεν τὴν γυναῖκα αὐτοῦ· καὶ οὐκ ἐγίνωσκεν αὐτὴν ἕως οὗ ἔτεκεν υἱόν

---

[83] Kloppenborg, 'On Dispensing with Q?', 223.

in both gospels is even more striking, given that this virginal conception is mentioned nowhere else in the New Testament.[84]

Many of the more striking similarities occur within a relatively short section of Luke and Matthew (the Annunciation—see Table 4.4).

It will be observed that the angel, the names Joseph, Mary and David and the phrase 'bear a son, and you shall call his name Jesus' occur in the same order in both texts, while both texts additionally state or imply Mary is a virgin, attribute the conception to the Holy Spirit, speak of Mary and Joseph not 'knowing' (i.e. having sexual intercourse with) each other and have the angel issue a command not to be afraid. Moreover, at the point where Matthew explicitly claims fulfilment of Isa. 7.14, Luke implicitly claims fulfilment of 2 Sam. 7.13-14 (καὶ ἀνορθώσω τὸν θρόνον αὐτοῦ ἕως εἰς τὸν αἰῶνα. ἐγὼ ἔσομαι αὐτῷ εἰς πατέρα, καὶ αὐτὸς ἔσται μοι εἰς υἱόν; cf. 2 Sam. 7.16).[85] Given that Luke generally avoids formula quotations (preferring, as here, a subtler method of signalling scriptural fulfilment)[86] and that the Lukan angel is addressing Mary rather than Joseph, the material Lk. 1.26-35 shares with Mt. 1.20-25a is substantial. One might reasonably suppose Luke was imitating Matthew here.

How are these similarities to be explained if Matthew and Luke are mutually independent? There would seem to be two possibilities. Either both evangelists were independently adapting an earlier source (let us call it INS – Infancy Narrative Source) that contained all these common elements, or they each independently combined a number of scattered traditions in broadly similar ways.

The problem with the INS proposal is that it is difficult to imagine what the INS could have looked like. If it simply contained the material common to Matthew and Luke, it would have to be something like:

> In the days of Herod the king, Joseph, who was of the house of David, was betrothed to a virgin named Mary who was found to be with child. An angel appeared to Joseph and said, 'Joseph, son of David, that which is conceived in Mary is of the Holy Spirit, for she will bear a son and you will call his name Jesus'. And Mary gave birth to the child in Bethlehem. Visitors came to pay homage to the saviour child there. Then Joseph and Mary took the child to Galilee and lived in a town called Nazareth.[87]

---

[84] Franklin, *Luke*, 358–60. Gudrun Nassauer, 'Göttersöhne: Lk 1.26-38 als Kontrasterzählung zu einem römischen Gründungsmythos', *NTS* 61 (2015), 144–64, argues that Luke based his account on the story of Mars impregnating Rhea Silvia, the mother of Romulus and Remus, to create a myth of origins countering Roman claims. It is conceivable that Luke may have had some such secondary motive in mind, but Luke's annunciation story resembles Matthew's far more closely than it does the Rhea Silvia story and seems clearly to be referencing OT rather than Roman motifs. It is also surprising that an NT author referencing the Rhea Silvia myth made no attempt to exploit the obvious Mosaic parallel to the servant setting Rhea Silvia's children afloat on the Tiber to save them from their uncle, the usurping king Amulius.

[85] Goulder, *Luke*, 222–3, points out that Luke has also echoed Isa. 7.14 in the words spoken by the angel at Lk. 1.31 and goes on to suggest other parallels with Isa. 7.17, 8.14 and 9.5-7; Luke may also have had these in mind, but they are more dispersed than the 2 Samuel passage.

[86] John Drury, *Tradition and Design in Luke's Gospel: A Study in Early Christian Historiography* (London: Darton, Longman and Todd, 1976), 53, 126.

[87] For the sake of argument, I have assumed the address to Joseph to be original on account of the words 'you will call his name Jesus' common to both gospels.

This seems a strangely sparse story. It might conceivably come about as a summary of earlier traditions, and Matthew and Luke could conceivably have independently obtained copies of such a summary, but if so, they have both been highly creative with it; so much so, in fact, that little is gained by suggesting Matthew's and Luke's common use of INS over Luke's use of Matthew. One might instead postulate that INS contained a rather fuller account than this, but this then raises the question, did this fuller account resemble Matthew or Luke or something unlike both of them? Whichever answer is given the problem of Luke's apparent freedom in using Matthew is simply pushed back a stage to one or other evangelist's equal freedom in using INS.

The alternative is that Matthew and Luke independently assembled a number of individual traditions into broadly similar narrative patterns. We have already seen that the name Mary, Jesus' Davidic descent and Nazareth domicile were already present in either Mark or Paul, and that Bethlehem as the birthplace might conceivably have been a common deduction from messianic prophecy and Davidic ancestry. It is also conceivable that the name Joseph could have been passed on in collective semantic memory independently of any stories about Mary's husband. Moreover, broadly similar narrative patterns could result from the logic of the events described together with the use of common cultural schemata derived from OT prototypes. The main difficulty comes with the annunciation, which would seem to require a larger narrative context to make sense as opposed to being handed on as an isolated unit of tradition.[88]

The question nonetheless remains, could Luke have created his Infancy Narrative out of Matthew's? Downing, for one, is quite sure that he could not:

> IF Luke was following redactional conventions similar to those adopted by Josephus, he could have produced from his own pen a great deal of the incidental matter of the Infancy Narrative ('righteous', 'blameless', 'old', 'fearful', the angelic messages, etc.; compare *Ant.* II. 205–238, Moses' birth and childhood), but not the whole framework of the story. That is not to say that the Infancy Narrative could not have grown from very small beginnings before reaching Luke; but we would not expect him, if he were following the conventions accepted by Josephus, simply to make it up, even from scriptural meditation, or haggadic legends attached to other figures. But neither would we expect a source shared by Matthew and Luke to have emerged so differently from each: so, they had no common infancy tradition.[89]

But as we saw in the previous chapter, Josephus is not the only possible model for Luke's working methods.[90] As a counter-example one might cite Pseudo-Philo's expansion of the bare mention of Kenaz at Judg. 3.9, 11 into an extended account of

---

[88] So also Watson, *Gospel Writing*, 133.
[89] Downing, 'Redaction Criticism II', 33–4.
[90] Moreover, as Drury, *Tradition*, 47, points out, Josephus 'shows a marked tendency to embroider the details of those [stories concerning birth and childhood] which he finds in the scriptures'. On the following page Drury draws attention to similar elaborations found in *1 Enoch* 106 (birth of Noah) and *Jubilees* 2 (Abraham's childhood). To this one might add the account of the birth of Moses at *LAB* 9, which greatly magnifies the role of Moses' father Amram.

his deeds at *LAB* 25–28, in part through imitation of other biblical material.[91] Luke's adaptation of Matthew would be modest by comparison; his Infancy Narrative makes perfectly good sense as an emulation (i.e. a competitive imitation) of Matthew along with an imitation of the OT (in particular, though not exclusively, the opening chapters of 1 Samuel).[92]

An imitation is not a copy, so Luke is free to transform what he imitates. That Luke might be imitating Matthew becomes apparent not only from the Annunciation scenes in both gospels but from a comparison of Luke chapter 2 and Matthew chapter 2, which shows both post-natal narratives following a similar structure.[93]

This set of parallels satisfies virtually all the criteria for imitative dependence set out at the end of Chapter 3, with the exception of clear verbal similarities (unless one counts χαρὰν μεγάλην at Mt. 2.10 ‖ Lk. 2.10).[94] The parallels clearly satisfy the criterion of Thematic Congruence (both are concerned with events concerning Mary, Joseph and the birth of Jesus). They share a number of distinctive features (e.g. a movement from birth in Bethlehem to settlement in Nazareth and the guiding of persons to the infant Messiah by celestial phenomena). There are also clear similarities in narrative structure, details and actions which occur with considerable density.

Moreover, the transformations in narrative details from Matthew to Luke lie within the range of imitative techniques set out towards the end of Chapter 3. From Luke's perspective one of the chief ones employed would be positivization. The bloodthirsty account surrounding the tyrant Herod is transformed into a more celebratory story concerning the pious poor waiting for the redemption of Israel.[95] Matthew's magi (items D–G in Table 4.5) become Luke's shepherds. For Luke, this avoids both introducing Gentile worshippers of Jesus too early and association with pagan magic practices (which the magi might all too easily be seen as exemplifying, particularly if their interest in the star is understood to be astrological; compare the negative

---

[91] See, e.g., Frederick J. Murphy, *Pseudo-Philo: Rewriting the Bible* (Oxford: Oxford University Press, 1993), 116–33. Murphy does not use the terminology of imitation, but he does point to the numerous biblical influences that go into Pseudo-Philo's account, not least the modelling of Kenaz's victory on that of Gideon in Judges 6, in which Kenaz is portrayed rather more positively than the biblical Gideon.

[92] Goulder, *Luke*, 208–13, perceives a number of OT influences, notably 'the application of the Abraham-Sarah-Isaac type to John'. At *Luke*, 224–8, he goes on to identify Hannah as the clearest type for Mary, with 1 Samuel (or 1 Kgdms) 1–3 as 'the most important passage Luke draws on'. Luke could be imitating more than one model and influences from Genesis are by no means to be excluded, not least the Abraham typology Goulder perceives for Luke's John. In common with the present chapter, McAdon, *Rhetorical Mimesis*, 120–60, also argues that Luke's Infancy Narrative is a mimetic transformation of Matthew's. My argument was nevertheless written before I encountered McAdon's work and was thus developed quite independently, although it naturally has several points of similarity.

[93] Brown, *Birth*, 247, finds that 'the core of the Lucan post-birth narrative has some deep (not surface) resemblances to the post-birth narrative in Matt 2'. Since Brown effectively assumes the validity of the 2DH on the basis of majority scholarly opinion (p. 34), he does not even consider the possibility of mutual dependence here but instead proposes 'a common underlying association of the Bethlehem and Migdal Eder motifs in Micah 4–5 and Gen 35:19-20' (p. 247).

[94] Elsewhere in the NT the precise phrase χαρὰν μεγάλην occurs only at Acts 15.3, although Mt. 28.8 has the virtually identical χαρᾶς μεγάλης.

[95] Cf. Watson, *Fourfold Gospel*, 74–9.

Table 4.5 Parallel Structure in Matthew 2 and Luke 2

	Matthew 2	Luke 2
A.	1. In the time of King Herod.	1. A decree went out from Caesar Augustus.
B.	2. Jesus is born in Bethlehem.	4-7. Jesus is born in Bethlehem.
C.	5-6. Bethlehem is the city prophesied to be the birthplace of the Messiah.	4. Bethlehem is the City of David.
D.	2, 9. The Magi are guided to the infant Messiah by a star.	8. The Shepherds are guided to the infant Messiah by an angel.
E.	11. The Magi see the child with Mary his mother.	16. The Shepherds find Mary and Joseph with their child.
F.	11. The Magi pay homage to the child and offer him gifts from their treasury.	17-19. The Shepherds tell Mary and Joseph what the angel said and Mary keeps their words.
G.	12. The Magi return to their own country.	20. The Shepherds return (to their fields).
H.	14. Joseph takes Mary and Jesus to Egypt.	22. Joseph and Mary take Jesus to the Temple in Jerusalem.
I.	16. Herod kills all the infants up to two years old in and around Bethlehem, but Jesus escapes.	23-24. Two pigeons are sacrificed (killed) in the Temple to redeem the firstborn Jesus (Exod. 13.2, 13).
J.	17-18. Jeremiah prophesied Rachel weeping for her children. 3-4. Herod and all Jerusalem are troubled by birth of the new king.	34. Simeon prophesies that the child is destined for the falling and rising of many in Israel and that a sword will pierce Mary's soul.
K.	22-23. Joseph takes his wife and child to Galilee and settles in Nazareth.	39. Joseph and Mary return with their child to Galilee, to their own town of Nazareth.

portrayal in Acts of the Simon who practised magic – μαγεύων, Acts 8.9).[96] More positively, shepherds might commend themselves to Luke as poor outsiders on the margins of society, to whom, therefore, the good news was especially destined and by whom it would especially be received (cf. Lk. 4.18; 6.20; 7.22; 14.21; 16.22). Moreover, the young David was a shepherd when Samuel first anointed him king (1 Sam. 16.11-13), as was Moses when God first called him (Exod. 3.1-2).

Item F could be seen as an example of internalization: the magi's physical gifts become the shepherd's words which Mary stores up in her heart. Item H may arguably have more to do with Luke's imitation of the Samuel narrative (for which see below) than of Matthew, but he could be imitating both here. Although Luke has dropped the journey to Egypt, he retains the motif of Jesus being taken somewhere by his parents. If Item I is intended to be part of Luke's imitation, it is admittedly quite subtle: it would constitute a further instance of positivization in which the negative image of Herod

---

[96] Goodacre, *Case*, 56; Drury, *Tradition*, 126; for Luke's objection to magical practices more generally, see Susan R. Garrett, *The Demise of the Devil: Magic and the Demonic in Luke's Writings* (Minneapolis: Fortress Press, 1989). Brown, *Birth*, 190–6, plausibly suggests that Matthew's magi are based on the Balaam story of Numbers 22–24; if Luke thought the same, this might have strengthened their pagan magical associations for him.

slaughtering the holy innocents was transformed into the positive one of the law-observant sacrifice of two pigeons, with Jesus being rescued from death in the first case and redeemed from sacrifice in the latter (if that is how Luke understands Exod. 13.2, 13, to which he alludes). The parallel in Item J may not be precise, but it represents the fact that both Matthew and Luke see the coming of Jesus as provoking opposition in Israel (with Mt. 2.16-18 forming the culmination of the opposition noted at Mt. 2.3-4).[97]

Overall, the sequence and density of parallels make it highly plausible that Luke was imitating Matthew here, but this was not all he was imitating. Luke's Infancy Narrative also imitates several parts of the OT. This is suggested by his use of Septuagintal style, which he probably adopted in order to signal the fulfilment of the scriptures alluded to.[98] Several details point to 1 Samuel as his principal (though not sole) model.[99] Elizabeth, like Hannah, is barren (Lk. 1.7; 1 Sam 1.5), although since Luke adds that Elizabeth was 'advanced in years' there is contamination from the story of Sarah (Gen. 18.9-15), as well as that of the birth of Samson (Judg. 13) in relation to that of John.[100] Elizabeth is married to a priest who is serving in the temple when events start to unfold whereas Hannah's story is closely associated with a priest serving in the temple; he is not her husband but the splitting and combination of roles is, as we have seen, a common enough imitative technique. This splitting of roles continues into the annunciation, where the promise of a son to Mary and the declaration of his name are similar in language to 1 Sam. 1.20; other OT parallels (notably Gen. 16.7-15, 17.15-19 and Isa. 7.14) are closer in wording to the formula Luke takes over from Matthew, but there is still enough general similarity for an imitation of 1 Samuel to have been suggested to Luke here (along with these other models).

Like Hannah (1 Kgdms 1.11), Mary identifies herself as God's δούλη (Lk. 1.38). The Song of Mary (Lk. 1.46-55) is clearly modelled (at least in part) on the Song of Hannah (1 Sam. 2.1-10).[101] At Lk. 2.12 the phrase 'and this will be a sign for you' (καὶ τοῦτο ὑμῖν τὸ σημεῖον) is very similar to that in 1 Kgdms/1 Sam. 2.34 (καὶ τοῦτο σοι τὸ σημεῖον), although beyond the fact that both signs concern male offspring, they

---

[97] Brown, *Birth*, 444–5.
[98] Franklin, *Luke*, 353.
[99] So also Drury, *Tradition*, 58; cf. Brown, *Birth*, 302, 446, 469.
[100] Goulder, *Luke*, 209, 213; Drury, *Tradition*, 56–7; Brown, *Birth*, 375.
[101] See Goulder, *Luke*, 225–8, for a fuller exposition of the parallels; see also Franklin, *Luke*, 354–5. As both authors observe, the militant language of Mary's song celebrates the culmination of the whole of God's saving work for Israel. Cf. the discussion in Brown, *Birth*, 358–63, which sees Hannah's song as the principal model for the Magnificat but finds the latter to be a cento of other OT passages in addition. Robert Simons, 'The Magnificat: Cento, Psalm or Imitatio?', *TynBul* 60 (2009), 25–46, argues that the Magnificat is a speech in character composed by Luke by imitation of Old Testament models including the Song of Hannah. Brown, *Birth*, 346–55, argues that the canticles in Luke 1–2 were pre-Lukan (in terms of both their style and content), apart from a few lines Luke added to make them fit their new context. He suggests that Luke added the canticles to a second version of his completed Infancy Narrative but does not explain why he should have seen fit to do so. Against Brown, Simons, 'Magnificat', argues that the Magnificat fits its context well, not least through introducing the theme of reversal that will be worked out as the consequence of Jesus' ministry throughout Luke-Acts, thereby showing, by echoing themes and phrases from the OT, that Jesus' activity is in continuity with God's. Simons suggests that Luke, like Thucydides, may have left the composition of speeches (such as the canticles) to the end of his writing process, to ensure that they fit the larger work.

are so different in import as to cast doubt on the significance of the allusion, unless, perhaps, Luke is subtly calling attention to the contrast between God's obedient son and Eli's wicked ones. Jesus' unscheduled stay in the Temple as a boy (Lk. 2.41-50) may have been in part inspired by Samuel's service in the temple as a boy (1 Sam. 3.1-18), with both Samuel and Jesus outperforming their supposed elders and betters, and also, perhaps, by Samuel's being left behind in the Temple in the context of his parents' visits there (1 Sam. 1.21-28).[102] Luke's notice that 'Jesus increased in wisdom and in stature, and in favour with God and man' (Lk. 2.52) looks closely modelled on the very similar statement about Samuel at 1 Sam. 2.26 (cf. also Lk. 2.40 and 1 Sam. 2.21b). The presentation of Jesus in the Temple (Lk. 2.22-40) may have been inspired by the presentation of Samuel to the Temple (1 Sam. 1.22-28), since it does not reflect Jewish custom.[103] It also contributes to the Lukan emphasis on Jerusalem and the Temple at the opening of his gospel, which will emerge again at the end of Luke's Gospel and the beginning of Acts.[104] It is less clear whether Luke intended the baptism of Jesus (followed by the descent of the Spirit) to recall the anointing of David (followed by the Spirit coming upon David) at 1 Sam. 16.13.[105] It is more likely that Luke was simply following Matthew and Mark here.

Luke's imitation of 1 Samuel also operates at a more thematic level. The story in 1 Samuel leads through the birth of Samuel, who is quickly recognized as a reliable prophet (1 Sam. 3.20), through oppression by the Philistines, the promise and hope of restoration if Israel repents (1 Sam. 7.3) via the chequered career of Saul to the hope for deliverance by the anointed king David. John is presented as a prophet of repentance by Luke, not only by the way he acts and preaches at Lk. 3.7-18 but by what is prophesied of him at Lk. 1.14-17 (where the notice that John will refrain from alcohol perhaps echoes the Nazirite lifestyle Hannah vows for her son Samuel at 1 Sam. 1.11) and Lk. 1.68-79. The expectation of a Davidic deliverer (a prominent theme in 1 Samuel) is expressed by the angel at Lk. 1.32-33 and by Zechariah at 1.68-75 (expanding on what Mary says at 1.54-55). Luke's imitation of 1 Samuel thus extends beyond particular phrases, incidents and characters to hopes of deliverance for Israel.

None of this, however, entirely explains *why* Luke should have chosen to transform Matthew's Infancy Narrative in this way (the final criterion for assessing dependency). Some partial explanations have already been offered in terms of Luke's positivization of Matthew's narrative, but this does not address what is arguably the principal effect of Luke's changes, namely to largely dismantle Matthew's carefully constructed Moses and Israel typologies. FH Luke has replaced a story based on the stories of Joseph and Moses (and Israel) in Genesis and Exodus with one based principally on the story of Samuel along with echoes of other figures such as Abraham, Sarah and the birth of Samson.

The transposition of the genealogy from the beginning of the gospel removes the recapitulation of Israel's story that introduces Matthew's Israel typology. Its relocation

---

[102] Goulder, *Luke*, 265.
[103] Goulder, *Luke*, 255.
[104] Drury, *Tradition*, 52–3.
[105] Drury, *Tradition*, 58, notes that Samuel's mission reaches its climax with his anointing of David, after which he largely drops out of the narrative, rather as John does in Luke. The fact that Luke removes John from the scene before the baptism, however, tends to undermine the parallel.

to a place between the Baptism and the Temptation interrupts the link between baptism (typologically related to the Red Sea crossing) and the entry into the wilderness. The reversal of the order of the genealogy together with the extension of Jesus' ancestry all the way back to 'Adam, the son of God' (Lk. 3.38) not only universalizes Jesus' origin (to humanity as a whole rather than the Jewish patriarch Abraham) but means that Luke's audience hears the Temptation Narrative immediately preceded by the words 'son of Adam, son of God', therefore priming them to hear the Temptation Story against the background of the fall story (Genesis 3) rather than (or as well as) the exodus story, as in Matthew. The removal of any explicit mention of a mountain from Luke's second temptation (Matthew's third) further downplays the allusion to Moses on Mount Nebo/Pisgah.[106] Instead of being son of God by virtue of being true Israel or New Moses, Luke's Jesus is son of God by virtue of being true Adam (i.e. true humanity).

Yet Luke has no aversion to Moses or exodus typology. On the contrary, he is keen to present Jesus as the prophet like Moses (Acts 3.22) and hints at exodus typology in his account of the Transfiguration (Lk. 9.30-31). But FH Luke appears reluctant to introduce either typology prior to the Transfiguration. Matthew's Sermon on the Mount is moved to the plain (Lk. 6.17) and stripped of its explicit engagement with the Torah. Luke relocates the Feeding of the Five Thousand from a wilderness to an urban setting (Lk. 9.10) – albeit not very consistently (Lk. 9.12) – and suppresses the sea-crossing miracle that follows at Mk 6.45-52 || Mt. 14.22-33. These changes loosen the association of the feeding story with the exodus events, allowing it instead to be seen more as an imitation of the Elisha miracle at 2 Kgs 4.42-44. Luke also omits the second feeding miracle, whereas the doublet in Mark and Matthew might be seen as reflecting the doublet of feeding miracle accounts in the Pentateuch (Exod. 16 and Num. 11).[107] Luke wishes to present Jesus as a *prophet* like Moses rather than a *lawgiver* like Moses and so diminishes any Mosaic associations until he has securely established Jesus as a *prophet* like Elijah and Elisha (Lk. 4.24–27; 7.11-17; 9.19).[108] While Luke regards the law as having ongoing validity for pious Israelites, he does not see it as binding on the Gentile church (Acts 15) and so does not want to model Jesus on Moses the lawgiver. Luke's Gentile orientation would also lead him to suppress Matthew's Israel typology in favour of a more universalistic Jesus.

A final point is whether Luke could have felt justified in transforming Matthew in this way, given the expectations of his chosen genre (a *bios* within a two-volume history). Biographers might be more inventive when it came to filling in details of their subject's birth and childhood when reliable information was in short supply, and there was an expectation that the birth of significant figures should be accompanied by strange events, which might perhaps be invented.[109] But Luke already had a ready-made

---

[106] Allison, *New Moses*, 171.
[107] Allison, *New Moses*, 239.
[108] Cf. J. Severino Croatto, 'Jesus, Prophet Like Elijah, and Prophet-Teacher Like Moses in Luke-Acts', *JBL* 124 (2005), 452–65, who argues that Luke presents Jesus as a prophet like Elijah in his gospel and a prophet-teacher like Moses in Acts.
[109] Keener, *Christobiography*, 169–70, 320.

account in Matthew. For Luke to transform it so radically suggests that he had reason to doubt its historical veracity. One such reason could be alternative traditions available to Luke. These need not be particularly detailed; it may have sufficed, for example, for Luke to be convinced that Mary and Joseph were natives of Nazareth and that Jesus had spent his entire childhood there, in which case the Matthean construction suggesting that Mary and Joseph originally lived in Bethlehem and only moved to Nazareth after a stay in Egypt would strike Luke as factually suspect. It may be that Luke was led to such a view by Mk 6.1-4; 16.6 in conjunction with traditions firmly linking Jesus' family with Nazareth all along. Luke's imitation of Matthew's Infancy Narrative would have been a way of retrieving what he could from it while transforming it in the direction of what Luke considered historical verisimilitude.[110]

In assessing whether one text might be an imitation of another, provided sufficient similarities can be found between the two texts, we should 'be clear that differences between texts do not rule out the possibility of dependency'.[111] Imitation is not a slavishly wooden procedure. Once that is accepted, it becomes highly plausible that Luke's Infancy Narrative is an imitation of Matthew's. The similarities between them are much harder to account for on the assumption that they were independent. While many of these similarities may seem individually coincidental, in combination they add up to strong prima facie evidence of Luke's knowledge of Matthew.

John the Baptist

Following the infancy narratives, Matthew and Luke move broadly in concert with Mark's account of John the Baptist, while sometimes making remarkably similar changes to that account. Luke 3.1 contains a dating of events in relation to the reign of the Emperor Tiberias and the roles of Pilate, Herod, Philip, and Annas and Caiaphas, before continuing broadly in parallel with Matthew and Mark (see Table 4.6).

In this section, the triple agreements are limited to the quotation from Isaiah, the phrase ἐν τῇ ἐρήμῳ ('in the wilderness') and the word κηρύσσων ('preaching'), which, however, appears in a slightly different place in Luke and Mark than in Matthew. The clause κηρύσσων βάπτισμα μετανοίας εἰς ἄφεσιν ἁμαρτιῶν ('preaching a baptism of repentance for the forgiveness of sins') is a major EA^{Mk-Lk}. In addition, all three evangelists mention the prophet Isaiah but use slightly different constructions to refer to him (although Luke is closer to Mark).

The agreements of Matthew and Luke against Mark are mainly structural, although they also agree in mentioning 'all the region about the Jordan' (πᾶσα ἡ περίχωρος τοῦ Ἰορδάνου, Mt. 3.5; πᾶσαν τὴν περίχωρον τοῦ Ἰορδάνου, Lk. 3.3) and in opening their

---

[110] McAdon, *Rhetorical Mimesis*, 9, 154–60, suggests rather different reasons for Luke's transformation here: first that Luke rejected Matthew's implication that Mary became prematurely pregnant (causing Luke to not only exculpate but elevate Mary's role) and second that Luke was polemically countering Marcion's distancing of Jesus from his Jewish roots. McAdon's first suggestion could well be complementary to those offered above, but the possible relationship between Luke and Marcion is too big a topic to be discussed here.
[111] O'Leary, *Matthew's Judaization*, 23.

Table 4.6 The Ministry of John the Baptist

Mk 1.2-6	Mt. 3.1-6	Lk. 3.1-6
2 Καθὼς γέγραπται ἐν τῷ **Ἠσαΐᾳ τῷ προφήτῃ**· Ἰδοὺ ἀποστέλλω τὸν ἄγγελόν μου πρὸ προσώπου σου, ὃς κατασκευάσει τὴν ὁδόν σου· 3 **φωνὴ βοῶντος ἐν τῇ ἐρήμῳ· Ἑτοιμάσατε τὴν ὁδὸν κυρίου, εὐθείας ποιεῖτε τὰς τρίβους αὐτοῦ,** 4 ἐγένετο Ἰωάννης ὁ βαπτίζων **ἐν τῇ ἐρήμῳ** κηρύσσων βάπτισμα μετανοίας εἰς ἄφεσιν ἁμαρτιῶν. 5 καὶ ἐξεπορεύετο πρὸς αὐτὸν πᾶσα ἡ Ἰουδαία χώρα καὶ οἱ Ἱεροσολυμῖται πάντες, καὶ ἐβαπτίζοντο ὑπ' αὐτοῦ ἐν τῷ Ἰορδάνῃ ποταμῷ ἐξομολογούμενοι τὰς ἁμαρτίας αὐτῶν. 6 καὶ ἦν ὁ Ἰωάννης ἐνδεδυμένος τρίχας καμήλου καὶ ζώνην δερματίνην περὶ τὴν ὀσφὺν αὐτοῦ, καὶ ἔσθων ἀκρίδας καὶ μέλι ἄγριον.	1 Ἐν δὲ ταῖς ἡμέραις ἐκείναις παραγίνεται Ἰωάννης ὁ βαπτιστὴς **κηρύσσων** κηρύσσων τῆς Ἰουδαίας 2 καὶ λέγων· Μετανοεῖτε, ἤγγικεν γὰρ ἡ βασιλεία τῶν οὐρανῶν. 3 οὗτος γάρ ἐστιν ὁ ῥηθεὶς διὰ **Ἠσαΐου τοῦ προφήτου** λέγοντος· **Φωνὴ βοῶντος ἐν τῇ ἐρήμῳ· Ἑτοιμάσατε τὴν ὁδὸν κυρίου, εὐθείας ποιεῖτε τὰς τρίβους αὐτοῦ.** 4 αὐτὸς δὲ ὁ Ἰωάννης εἶχεν τὸ ἔνδυμα αὐτοῦ ἀπὸ τριχῶν καμήλου καὶ ζώνην δερματίνην περὶ τὴν ὀσφὺν αὐτοῦ, ἡ δὲ τροφὴ ἦν αὐτοῦ ἀκρίδες καὶ μέλι ἄγριον. 5 τότε ἐξεπορεύετο πρὸς αὐτὸν Ἱεροσόλυμα καὶ πᾶσα ἡ Ἰουδαία καὶ πᾶσα ἡ περίχωρος τοῦ Ἰορδάνου, 6 καὶ ἐβαπτίζοντο ἐν τῷ Ἰορδάνῃ α ποταμῷ ὑπ' αὐτοῦ ἐξομολογούμενοι τὰς ἁμαρτίας αὐτῶν.	1 Ἐν δὲ πεντεκαιδεκάτῳ ἔτει τῆς ἡγεμονίας Τιβερίου Καίσαρος, κτλ. 2 ἐπὶ ἀρχιερέως Ἄννα καὶ Καϊάφα, ἐγένετο ῥῆμα θεοῦ ἐπὶ Ἰωάννην τὸν Ζαχαρίου υἱὸν **ἐν τῇ ἐρήμῳ.** 3 καὶ ἦλθεν εἰς πᾶσαν περίχωρον τοῦ Ἰορδάνου κηρύσσων βάπτισμα μετανοίας εἰς ἄφεσιν ἁμαρτιῶν, 4 ὡς γέγραπται ἐν βίβλῳ λόγων **Ἠσαΐου τοῦ προφήτου· Φωνὴ βοῶντος ἐν τῇ ἐρήμῳ· Ἑτοιμάσατε τὴν ὁδὸν κυρίου, εὐθείας ποιεῖτε τὰς τρίβους αὐτοῦ.** 5 πᾶσα φάραγξ πληρωθήσεται καὶ πᾶν ὄρος καὶ βουνὸς ταπεινωθήσεται, καὶ ἔσται τὰ σκολιὰ εἰς α εὐθείαν καὶ αἱ τραχεῖαι εἰς ὁδοὺς λείας· 6 καὶ ὄψεται πᾶσα σὰρξ τὸ σωτήριον τοῦ θεοῦ.

accounts with the construction Ἐν δὲ to introduce a temporal reference.[112] Matthew and Luke agree against Mark in placing the quotation from Isaiah after mentioning John's presence in the wilderness and in omitting the words 'Behold, I send my messenger before thy face, who shall prepare thy way' from the quotation attributed to Isaiah, presumably because they do not come from him.[113]

The coincidence of Matthew and Luke both making the same structural changes to Mark has to be weighed against the major agreement of Mk 1.4b ‖ Lk. 3.3b against Mt. 3.2 (which retains the substance of Mark in different words). This Luke-Mark agreement could be the result of Luke's memory of Mark if he is employing Matthew as his main source here, but it would not be unreasonable to suppose that here, where Matthew and Mark run in tandem for the first time and Luke is near the start of his

---

[112] Werner Kahl, 'The Gospel of Luke as Narratological Improvement of Synoptic Pre-Texts: The Narrative Introduction to the Jesus Story (Mark 1.1-8 Parr.)' in Mogens Müller and Heike Omerzu (eds), *Gospel Interpretation and the Q-Hypothesis* (LNTS, 573; London: Bloomsbury T&T Clark, 2018), 223–44, here 241–2, suggests that here Luke is improving on Matthew by including 'a detailed list of *historical* references' (emphasis original) at this point, while 'in those days' at Mt. 3.1 appears literally to refer to the point in time at which the boy Jesus was first taken to Nazareth (Mt. 2.22-23).
[113] Cf. Kahl, 'Narratological Improvement', 237.

own work, Luke might read both his sources before proceeding to compose his own version.[114] It is not impossible that Matthew and Luke could independently decide to transpose the order of the quotation and the notice about John the Baptist and to correct the mistaken quotation from Isaiah, but Matthew and Luke later use the omitted portion at Mt. 11.10 || Lk. 7.27, which on 2DH creates the oddity that Q incorporates a Matthean-style formula quotation of Mal. 3.1 mixed with Exodus 23 that Luke and Matthew independently omit from their parallels to Mk 1.2-3.[115]

Whether Luke is following Mark or Matthew here he has reworked his source with considerable freedom, first fixing the date of John's appearance in relation to the people mentioned in Lk. 3.1-2a, then employing the biblical (OT) formula 'the word of God came to John the son of Zechariah', presumably to align John with the prophets of old, perhaps Samuel in particular (1 Sam. 15.10), or as Goulder suggests, the biblical Zechariah (Zech. 1.1).[116] Luke then extends the Isaiah quotation up until 'and all flesh shall see the salvation of God' (which suits Luke's universalist agenda), while omitting the entire substance of Mk 1.5-6 || Mt. 3.4-6 concerning John's appearance and the notice about everyone coming to him to be baptized (to which we shall return below).

Immediately following this, Lk. 3.7-9 agrees with Mt. 3.7-10 in incorporating a section of John the Baptist's teaching, aimed in Matthew against the Pharisees and Sadducees in particular and in Luke against the expectant crowd in general. The warning to repent or face judgement is then expressed in virtually identical words in Matthew and Luke, a string of sixty-three Greek words in Matthew, with Luke differing only in having the plural καρποὺς ἀξίους for Matthew's singular καρπὸν ἄξιον (to express 'fruit worthy'), ἄρξησθε ('begin') for Matthew's δόξητε ('presume') and an extra καὶ ('even') between Matthew's ἤδη δὲ and ἡ ἀξίνη ('even now the axe'). If Matthew and Luke are independently copying Q here then they have independently decided to copy it almost verbatim and insert it at exactly the same place. While this is not impossible, it is simpler to suppose that Luke is following Matthew.

That Luke is secondary to Matthew is suggested by at least two points. The first that Luke's change to the plural 'fruits worthy' at Lk. 3.8 is not carried through consistently in Luke's conclusion at Lk. 3.9, where Luke retains the singular 'every tree that does not bear good fruit is cut down' as in Matthew (although some manuscripts have the singular at Lk. 3.8 as well). Of more note is that the address 'You brood of vipers!' at Mt. 3.7b || Lk. 3.7b fits the Matthean context (where it is addressed to the Pharisees and Sadducees) far better than the Lukan one, where it is addressed to a multitude

---

[114] Kahl, 'Narratological Improvement', 236-7, notes that in relation to the numbers of exclusive agreements between each pair of gospels over Mk 1.1-8 parr. 'the Gospel of Matthew and the Gospel of Luke by far have most of the material in common, with Luke sharing more with Mark than Matthew with Mark' although elsewhere 'Matthew *in general* is closer to Mark than is Luke' (emphasis original). This would seem to be consistent with Luke primarily using Matthew here while also relying on, or refreshing, his memory of Mark.

[115] Wilhelm Wilkens, 'Die Täuferüberlieferung des Matthäus und ihre Verarbeitung durch Lukas', NTS 40 (1994), 542-57, here 546, points to Luke's knowledge of Matthean redaction at Mt. 11.10, not least since Luke employs Matthew's typical introduction to a biblical quotation.

[116] Goulder, *Luke*, 270. Kahl, 'Narratological Improvement', 227, observes that by introducing John the Baptist into his birth narrative, Luke better prepares for his appearance here than does Matthew. Such an improvement would be consistent with an author emulating his source.

whose only offence is to respond to John by coming out to be baptized by him.[117] One could argue that this is due to Lukan editorial clumsiness with respect to Q rather than Lukan editorial clumsiness with respect to Matthew, but employing Pharisees as stock enemies of the gospel is certainly not uncharacteristic of Matthew, who has Jesus address the Pharisees as 'you brood of vipers' again at Mt. 12.34 and 23.33, making it a characteristically Matthean insult. One could argue that Matthew found the insult in Q and liked it so much he used it elsewhere, but while this is clearly not impossible, once again the simpler explanation is that Luke has followed Matthew.

Luke then inserts a further piece of John the Baptist's teaching at Luke 3.10-14 in which John recommends sharing, honest tax-collecting and decently behaved soldiering, before Matthew and Luke both more or less return to the Markan narrative at Mk 1.7-8 || Mt. 3.11-12 || Lk. 3.15-17 (see Table 4.7).

Once again, IA are indicated in bold, EA$^{Mt\text{-}Lk}$ underlined and EA$^{Mk\text{-}Lk}$ in italics. Luke and Matthew agree against Mark in changing ἐβάπτισα ('I have baptized') into the present tense, βαπτίζω ('I baptize'), and more strikingly in adding καὶ πυρί ('and with fire') after 'he will baptize you with the Holy Spirit' and then extending the Baptist's words with the eschatological warning about the winnowing fork and the threshing floor, again in near identical words. There is also a structural agreement in placing the saying 'I baptize you with water' before the material about the stronger one who is to come. On the other hand, Luke agrees with Mark against Matthew about what John is unworthy to do with the mightier one's sandals.

Once again, the most natural explanation is that Luke primarily followed Matthew here but has used the Markan version of the saying about sandals from memory. On

Table 4.7 John and the Coming One.

Mk 1.7-8	Mt. 3.11-12	Lk. 3.15-17
καὶ ἐκήρυσσεν λέγων· Ἔρχεται ὁ **ἰσχυρότερός μου** ὀπίσω μου, **οὗ οὐκ εἰμὶ ἱκανὸς** κύψας λῦσαι τὸν ἱμάντα τῶν ὑποδημάτων αὐτοῦ·		Προσδοκῶντος δὲ τοῦ λαοῦ καὶ διαλογιζομένων πάντων ἐν ταῖς καρδίαις αὐτῶν περὶ τοῦ Ἰωάννου, μήποτε αὐτὸς εἴη ὁ χριστός, ἀπεκρίνατο λέγων πᾶσιν ὁ Ἰωάννης·
ἐγὼ ἐβάπτισα ὑμᾶς ὕδατι,	Ἐγὼ μὲν ὑμᾶς βαπτίζω ἐν ὕδατι εἰς μετάνοιαν· ὁ δὲ ὀπίσω μου ἐρχόμενος **ἰσχυρότερός μού** ἐστιν, **οὗ οὐκ εἰμὶ ἱκανὸς** τὰ **ὑποδήματα** βαστάσαι	Ἐγὼ μὲν ὕδατι βαπτίζω ὑμᾶς· ἔρχεται δὲ ὁ **ἰσχυρότερός μου**, **οὗ οὐκ εἰμὶ ἱκανὸς** λῦσαι τὸν ἱμάντα τῶν ὑποδημάτων αὐτοῦ·
αὐτὸς δὲ βαπτίσει ὑμᾶς ἐν πνεύματι ἁγίῳ.	αὐτὸς ὑμᾶς βαπτίσει ἐν πνεύματι ἁγίῳ καὶ πυρί· οὗ τὸ πτύον ἐν τῇ χειρὶ αὐτοῦ, καὶ διακαθαριεῖ τὴν ἅλωνα αὐτοῦ καὶ συνάξει τὸν σῖτον αὐτοῦ εἰς τὴν ἀποθήκην, τὸ δὲ ἄχυρον κατακαύσει πυρὶ ἀσβέστῳ.	αὐτὸς ὑμᾶς βαπτίσει ἐν πνεύματι ἁγίῳ καὶ πυρί· οὗ τὸ πτύον ἐν τῇ χειρὶ αὐτοῦ διακαθᾶραι τὴν ἅλωνα αὐτοῦ καὶ συναγαγεῖν τὸν σῖτον εἰς τὴν ἀποθήκην αὐτοῦ, τὸ δὲ ἄχυρον κατακαύσει πυρὶ ἀσβέστῳ.

[117] Goulder, *Luke*, 273; Wilkens, 'Täuferüberlieferung', 554–5.

the 2DH it is necessary to postulate a Mark-Q overlap with Q containing the substance, and much of the wording, of Mt. 3.11-12 || Lk. 3.16-17 and thus coinciding with much of Mk 1.7-8 (not least because Luke's source for καὶ πυρί must have contained something appropriate before the conjunction καὶ). Presumably this would immediately follow Q 3.7-9 (the speech about the winnowing fork and the threshing floor), before which would be some mention of people coming to John to or from all the region about the Jordan (Q 3.3a).[118] Q is in some danger of becoming rather too much like Matthew here, but if one can live with that one still has the coincidence of Matthew and Luke independently combining Mark and Q in very similar ways, including the decision to copy the wording of Q (both at Mt. 3.7b-10 || Lk. 3.7b-9 and at Mt. 3.11b-12 || Lk. 3.16c-17) rather more closely than the wording of Mark. On either the 2DH or the FH there has been some conflation of sources by at least one evangelist, so that does not strongly select between the two theories. Overall, though, Luke's use of Matthew is once again the more obvious theory than Luke's and Matthew's independent use of Q.

Luke again inserts his own material, this time at Lk. 3.18-20, which rounds off the preaching of John the Baptist with a summary and reports that Herod the Tetrarch shut him up in prison. Luke then avoids any explicit mention of John in his account of Jesus' baptism (Lk. 3.21-22). In the baptism scene (Mk 1.9-11 || Mt. 3.13-17 || Lk. 3.21-22) Matthew and Luke agree against Mark in asserting that the purpose of coming to John was to be baptized (βαπτισθῆναι), although in Matthew this is Jesus' purpose while in Luke it's the purpose of people in general. They also concur that the heaven was 'opened' rather than 'torn' (ἠνεῴχθησαν/ἀνεῳχθῆναι as against σχιζομένους) and that the spirit descended 'upon' (ἐπ') rather than 'into' (εἰς) Jesus. They also agree in employing a participle construction (βαπτισθείς/βαπτισθέντος) against Mark's finite verb ἐβαπτίσθη and in explicitly supplying Jesus' name in narrating the fact of Jesus' baptism. Conversely, Luke and Mark agree against Matthew in having the voice from heaven address Jesus in the second person ('Thou art my beloved son') rather than the third ('This is my beloved son') and in lacking the conversation between Jesus and John that Matthew inserts at Mt. 3.14-15. Here Luke's account looks pared down to the bare essentials and it is not immediately obvious whether, on the FH, to suppose that Luke primarily used Mark (with the odd reminiscence of Matthew) or Matthew (with the odd reminiscence of Mark) or simply composed his own version on the basis of his memory of both.

The EA^{Mt-Lk} are not individually compelling here. Mark's 'into' could easily have looked odd to both Matthew and Luke, with a suggestion of spirit-possession neither was keen to follow. Substituting an open heaven for a torn one could be accounted for on the basis of apocalyptic language used elsewhere (cf. Rev. 4.1; 19.11). Again, changing a main verb into a participle is a stylistic choice that could plausibly have occurred to two independent redactors, and one could argue the reason for coming to John was sufficiently obvious for both Luke and Matthew to hit upon the same way of describing it. These agreements do not compel the 2DH to postulate a Mark-Q overlap here,[119] but cumulatively they begin to stretch coincidence and in combination with

---

[118] *CEQ*, 6–17.
[119] On Streeter's reasons for doing so, see n. 131 below. Contrast *CEQ*, 18–21.

the other Luke-Matthew agreements in Mt. 3.1-17 || Lk. 3.1-22 they could be taken as a further indication of Luke's knowledge of Matthew.

The main effect of Luke's changes in 3.1-22 is to emphasize John's prophetic activity at the expense of his baptizing. The latter is not suppressed altogether, but Luke first introduces John not as 'the Baptist' or 'the baptizer' but as 'the son of Zechariah', and removes him from the scene before Jesus is baptized, as well as suppressing the notice about people going out to him to be baptized (Mk 1.5 || Mt.3.5). Indeed, Luke never describes John actually doing any baptizing as opposed to just talking about it (Lk. 3.3 || Mk 1.4; Lk. 3.16 || Mt. 3.11 || Mk 1.8). The material Luke adds, along with most of what he retains, largely concerns what John says (Lk. 3.7-18), much (though not quite all) of it in close agreement with Matthew.[120]

Luke's omission of the description of John the Baptist at Mk 1.6 || Mt. 3.4 is consistent with this tendency to focus on what John said. One possible reason for it may have been to move as swiftly as possible from the mention of John's preaching at Lk. 3.3b to its content at Lk. 3.7-14 after the extended quotation from Isaiah that intervenes, which might also explain moving the echo of Mt. 3.5 to Lk.3.3a. Another possible reason is that Luke wished to avoid portraying John as Elijah.[121] Downing objects (a) that this would represent a change of mind from Lk. 1.17, where John is prophesied to go before the Lord 'in the spirit and power of Elijah'; (b) that if Luke had nevertheless wished to suppress the Elijah connection he need only have rewritten or omitted the description of John's clothing; and (c) that Lk. 3.3a nevertheless conflates Mk 1.4b and Mt. 3.5b, thereby preserving John's preaching of repentance, which is 'a clear back reference to John's assumption of Elijah's mission to elicit such repentance'.[122]

Apart from the point about conflation, however, all these objections could be made against the 2DH Luke, who would have (a) undergone the same change of mind from Lk. 1.17, (b) failed simply to delete the description of the Baptist's clothing and (c) retained a notice of John's preaching of repentance. *Pace* Downing, the fact that the material Luke omitted from Mk 1.6 was supported by Mt. 3.4 is irrelevant; if Luke had reason to omit it, that reason would apply whether or not Matthew agreed with Mark at that point; if Luke had no reason to omit this material, then 2DH Luke's omission is as puzzling as FH Luke's. Moreover, Lk. 1.17 does not *identify* John with Elijah and could be taken as a way of avoiding doing so while retaining the forerunner motif. Luke's John is an ordinary human being born of first-century parents, not Elijah returned from heaven.[123] Moreover, repentance is one of Luke's favourite themes, so it is hardly

---

[120] Kahl, 'Narratological Improvement', 243, suggests: 'Luke glosses over Mark 1.5-6 and Matt 3.4-6, probably because he wants to de-focus John (cf. also 3.19-20 where he moves forward and sharply shortens the reference to John's imprisonment and death as compared to the accounts in Mark 6 and Matt 14).' But his perception of John's role in Luke's narrative needs nuancing in light of the additions Luke makes to John's preaching.

[121] Goulder, *Luke*, 271.

[122] Downing, 'Disagreements', 465. But F. Gerald Downing, 'Imitation and Emulation, Josephus and Luke: Plot and Psycholinguistics' in John S. Kloppenborg and Joseph Verheyden (eds), *The Elijah-Elisha Narrative in the Composition of Luke* (London: Bloomsbury T&T Clark, 2014), 113–29, here 117, appears to accept that John's coming 'in the spirit and power of Elijah' could be part of Luke's reluctance to identify the two, consonant with Luke's omission of the description of John's clothing.

[123] Goulder, *Luke*, 210.

surprising that he should take it over from Mk 1.4b, without thereby implying any connection with Elijah.

The extensive agreements of Matthew and Luke against Mark in this section constitute further prima facie evidence of Luke's use of Matthew. While independent use of Mark and Q by both later evangelists is not demonstrably impossible, it would involve an uncomfortably large number of coincidences.

The temptation and beyond

Mark's temptation story is tantalizingly brief (Mk 1.12-13). Both Luke and Matthew expand it in very similar ways by describing three temptations. These are the same in each case, except that the order of the last two differs between Matthew and Luke, with Matthew preferring to end with the temptation on a mountain and Luke with the temptation set in Jerusalem, preferences which are reflected in the endings of their respective gospels (on a high mountain in Matthew and in the temple in Jerusalem in Luke).[124]

Luke's and Matthew's wording is not particularly close in this pericope, except where both are citing scripture or, to a lesser extent, the words attributed to the devil. Luke and Matthew agree against Mark in explicitly naming Jesus at the start of the pericope, in referring to Jesus' hunger (ἐπείνασεν), and in calling the tempter 'the devil' rather than 'Satan' (Mk 1.13 || Mt. 4.1 || Lk. 4.1-2), although Matthew subsequently retains 'Satan' in Jesus' direct address to the devil (Mt. 4.10), possibly as a deliberate foreshadowing of Jesus' rebuke to Peter at Mt. 16.23 (to which Luke has no parallel). Matthew, but not Luke, retains the ministering angels at the conclusion of the pericope (Mk 1.13b || Mt. 4.11b), with Matthew retaining nearly all of Mark's words verbatim while inserting some additional ones of his own: 'and *behold*, [the] angels *came and* ministered to him' (Matthew adds 'behold' and 'came and' but drops the article before 'angels'). Luke and Matthew agree against Mark in dropping any mention of wild beasts while adding the fact that Jesus was fasting, in stating that the temptations came at the end of the period of forty days (rather than extending over them, as Mark suggests) and in using ἡμέρας τεσσεράκοντα rather than τεσσεράκοντα ἡμέρας to express 'forty days'.[125] The double tradition Temptation Narrative is thus not merely an expansion of the Markan one; it tells a somewhat different story even where there is a degree of overlap.

---

[124] N.H. Taylor, 'The Temptation of Jesus on the Mountain: A Palestinian Christian Polemic against Agrippa I', *JSNT* 83 (2001), 27–49, here 33. Goulder, *Luke*, 294, prefers the explanation that Luke's concluding the dialogue with 'you shall not tempt the Lord your God' creates an *inclusio*.

[125] C.F. Evans, *Saint Luke* (TPINTC; London: SCM, 1990), 256, argues that Luke cannot be dependent on Matthew here, since Luke creates a muddle, not found in Matthew, by combining Mark's temptations lasting throughout Jesus' time in the wilderness with Matthew's temptations occurring at the end of the forty-day period. But Luke can be read as meaning that Jesus was tempted throughout the forty-day period, which was capped off with the three specific temptations Luke then narrates, or else that those three temptations are representative of what took place over the forty-day period; no muddle need be involved.

Provided one can accept the presence of a Temptation Narrative in Q,[126] these parallels present no insuperable difficulty for the 2DH. If Q existed, it is hardly surprising that Luke and Matthew should prefer its Temptation Story to Mark's and insert it at the same point. That said, Goulder observes that the identical citation of Deut. 6.13 at Mt. 4.10 ‖ Lk. 4.8 departs from the wording of the LXX in characteristically Matthean ways, with the characteristically Matthean προσκυνήσεις for LXX φοβηθήνῃ and the insertion of the characteristically Matthean clarifying μόνῳ.[127]

Against Wilhelm Wilkens' argument that Luke followed a Temptation Narrative composed by Matthew, Davies and Allison suggest that 'Luke sometimes represents a more primitive or original wording'.[128] The detailed commentary that follows, however, often turns out to make bare assertions of Matthean redaction: for example that 'and forty nights' at Mt. 4.2 'is a Matthean addition, no doubt primarily prompted by Exod. 34.28 and Deut. 9.9'.[129] No reason is offered here why it could not equally well be part of Matthew's composition prompted by the same texts or why Luke could not have omitted the words in question in the course of substantially recasting Matthew's sentence. Davies and Allison often appear to argue in a circle by tacitly assuming the existence of Q and then attributing anything distinctively Matthean to Matthew's redaction of Q.[130]

As we have seen, the Matthean version of the Temptation Story fits the Matthean context particularly well, not least because much of the point of the story resides in the contrast of Israel and Jesus in the wilderness, which continues the typology Matthew has already initiated.[131] Moreover, there is little in this pericope that is obviously unMatthean in style or vocabulary, and the order of temptations in Matthew is usually

---

[126] That John S. Kloppenborg, *The Formation of Q: Trajectories in Ancient Wisdom Collections* (SAC; Harrisburg, PA: Trinity Press International, 1999), 247–8, perceives the Temptation Story as a late interpolation into Q because its form and motifs are 'quite unparalleled in Q' surely raises suspicion on this point.

[127] Goulder, *Luke*, 294–5, comparing κύριον τον θεόν σου φοβηθήσῃ καὶ αὐτῷ λατρεύσεις at Deut. 6.13 with κύριον τον θεόν σου προσκυνήσεις καὶ αὐτῷ μόνῳ λατρεύσεις at Mt. 4.10 ‖ Lk. 4.8; cf. Taylor, 'Temptation', 37–8.

[128] Davies and Allison, *Matthew*, vol. 1, 350.

[129] Davies and Allison, *Matthew*, vol. 1, 358.

[130] Cf. Goulder, *Luke*, 15–17.

[131] Goulder, *Luke*, 296; cf. Harrington, *Matthew*, 69, 'If we grant that Matthew took over his version of the "Testing of God's Son" from Q, it was an especially congenial text for him and his audience.' Harrington (p. 68) recognizes that the Temptation Narrative is something of an outlier in Q and is open to the suggestion that the story may go back to Jewish-Christian scribes, but does not go on to draw the conclusion that the scribe in question might as well be Matthew. I. Howard Marshall, *The Gospel of Luke: A Commentary on the Greek Text* (NIGTC; Grand Rapids: Eerdmans, 1978), 165, notes that 'the twin themes in the story of the baptism of Jesus are taken up in the story of his temptation, so that there is no doubt that this narrative was derived from a source in which the baptism and temptation stood together'. Marshall takes that source to be Q, but if the presence of a baptism narrative in Q is doubted, that source can only be Matthew. The main reason Streeter, 'Four Gospels', 188, gives for including the Baptism in Q is that 'John's Preaching, the Baptism, and the Temptation obviously form a single section, and a source which contains the first and third must have contained the second'. One's suspicion mounts that the only reason to suppose the presence of a baptism narrative in Q is to save the 2DH. On the connection of the Temptation Story with the preceding baptism account in Matthew, see also Wilkens, 'Versuchung', 481.

taken to be the original one.¹³² Conversely, while Luke has no aversion either to Moses typology in general or to Deuteronomy in particular (or, indeed, to portraying a pious Jew as faithful to the Torah), Israel typology has played no role in his gospel up until now, and the Moses typology of the Temptation Story is at some odds with the Adam typology set up by what immediately precedes it in Luke ('the son of Adam, the son of God'). While none of this precludes Luke's use of Q, it would make Matthew's use of Luke unlikely here.

On balance, then, the evidence of this pericope favours the FH over against the 2DH (and the MPH). At the very least, even though the Mark-Q overlap theory may be available to the 2DH here, this set of parallels represents another striking similarity between Luke and Matthew insofar as both evangelists have expanded Mark at the same point in very similar ways. Given the other considerations noted above, this is further prima facie evidence of Luke's use of Matthew. The principal counterargument would be to cast doubt on the likelihood of Matthew's elaborating Mark to the extent that he would needed to have done here. But given that the double tradition version of the Temptation Story must have come from somewhere, someone has to have created it, and that someone may as well have been Matthew, even if he did so out of earlier traditions which he further elaborated.¹³³ As argued above, Matthew would have been particularly fortunate to find in Q a ready-made narrative that fit his own concerns so well.

Immediately following the Temptation all three evangelists agree that Jesus went to Galilee, although they express this in different ways, agreeing only on the phrase εἰς τὴν Γαλαίαν ('into Galilee'). At this point it is not immediately obvious whether FH Luke has switched to following Mark or is still following Matthew, since at Mt. 4.12 || Mk 1.14 || Lk. 4.14-15 Matthew and Mark resemble each other far more than either resembles Luke. It will nevertheless be argued here that FH Luke continues to follow Matthew until switching to the Markan story of the Capernaum Demoniac (Lk. 4.31 || Mk 1.21).

Luke's summary of the start of Jesus' public ministry (Lk. 4.14-15) is his own, loosely based on reminiscence of his sources, most probably Mt. 4.23-24, with which it shares the spread of Jesus' fame and the phrase διδάσκων/ἐδίδασκεν ἐν ταῖς συναγωγαῖς αὐτῶν ('their synagogues' being characteristic of Matthew but used nowhere else in Luke).¹³⁴

Luke's account of Jesus' inaugural sermon at Nazareth (Lk. 4.16-30) appears to be his own reworking of the Rejection at Nazareth at Mt. 13.53-58 || Mk 6.1-6a and could in principle be based on either Matthew or Mark (or a reminiscence of both).¹³⁵ It

---

¹³² On the order, see Wilkens, 'Versuchung', 486–7, Marshal, *Luke*, 167, and Taylor, 'Temptation', 33. On the wording, see Wilkens, 'Versuchung', 479–80, and Goulder, *Luke*, 297–8, but contrast Evans, *Luke*, 256.

¹³³ For example, Taylor, 'Temptation', 35–49, argues that Matthew's third temptation derives from Palestinian Christian polemic against Agrippa I.

¹³⁴ Goulder, *Luke*, 300. Admittedly 'their synagogues' also occurs at Mk 1.39, but there the complete expression is κηρύσσων εἰς τὰς συναγωγὰς αὐτῶν, which is more remote from Lk. 4.15 and is paralleled at Lk. 4.44, where αὐτῶν is dropped.

¹³⁵ Goulder, *Luke*, 301, further suggests that the theme of the sermon in Luke was suggested by Mk 1.15. This may be so, but it may be that Luke simply chose a theme that would be programmatic for his own narrative. Jean-René Moret, '"Aucun prophète n'est propice dans sa propre patrie": la péricope de Nazareth', *NTS* 60 (2014), 466–74, however, cautions against reading Lk. 4.16-30 through the lens of Mt. 13.53-58 || Mk 6.1-6a. While Matthew and Mark depict Jesus as being dishonoured in his hometown because his familiarity there prompts lack of faith, in Luke 4 Jesus alienates an initially friendly audience by refusing to do them any special favours.

nevertheless has a number of intriguing points of contact with Mt. 4.13-16.[136] Both passages mention Capernaum (Mt. 4.13; Lk. 4.23), albeit in very different ways; oddly, Lk. 4.23 refers to deeds performed in Capernaum that Luke is yet to narrate. Both passages cite prophecies from Isaiah (Mt. 4.15-16 || Isa. 9.1-2; Lk. 4.18-19 || Isa. 61.1-2a) which are said to be fulfilled (Mt. 4.14 πληρωθῇ; Lk. 4.21 πεπλήρωται) and which are followed by Jesus' preaching (Mt. 4.17; Lk. 4.21). Both passages hint that Jesus' mission is to extend to Gentiles (Mt. 4.15-16; Lk. 4.25-27). But most strikingly of all, both use the hapax Ναζαρά to refer to Nazareth (Mt. 4.13; Lk. 4.16), a coincidence that seems hard to explain on the thesis of the mutual independence of Luke and Matthew.[137] Admittedly Mt. 4.13 speaks of Jesus leaving Ναζαρά, while Lk. 4.16 speaks of his going there, but Jesus' departure is strongly implied at Lk. 4.30, while his prior arrival there is clearly presupposed by Mt. 4.13 (while not at all suggested by Mark). Luke thus agrees with Matthew against Mark in having Jesus travel from Nazareth to Capernaum following the Temptation (Lk. 4.30-31; Mt. 4.13). Luke may also be thereby filling in an apparent lacuna in the Matthean narrative by explaining why Jesus did so, based on his hostile reception at Nazareth.[138]

Taken together, these points of contact suggest that Luke is continuing to use Matthew here (they occur where FH Luke would still be following Matthew in Matthew's sequence, would stretch coincidence and would be hard to explain on the basis of Mark-Q overlap).[139] If so, the way Luke uses Matthew here is significant for another reason, namely that it would be quite different from a copy-and-redact mode of source utilization. It is rather closer to an imitation of Mt. 4.13-17 along with Mt. 13.53-58 or Mk 6.1-6a, perhaps on the basis of other Jewish and Christian traditions.[140] If so then it provides a partial parallel to the kind of imitation FH Luke employed in composing his Infancy Narrative from Matthew's. As with the Infancy Narrative, so in Jesus' inaugural sermon, Luke is setting out material that is programmatic for his entire composition and on which he might therefore be particularly expected to place his own stamp.

Matthew swiftly moves on to his programmatic statement of Jesus' preaching, the Sermon on the Mount, while Luke switches to following Mark. We have now progressed beyond the beginnings of all three Synoptic Gospels, and to pursue the discussion much further would take us into territory covered in Chapter 6, but there is one more point that may conveniently be discussed here. Proponents of the 2DH

---

[136] Erik Aurelius, 'Gottesvolk und Außenseiter: Eine geheime Beziehung Lukas – Matthäus', *NTS* 47 (2001), 428–41, argues for a connection between Matthew and Luke (with Matthew dependent on Luke) via Lk. 4.25-27 and Mt. 8.5-13; 15.21-8. This will be addressed when we come to Luke's use of Matthew 8 in Chapter 6 below; it may, however, be noted in anticipation that I am not convinced that Aurelius has demonstrated a connection here in either direction, although he may be pointing to some interesting connections within Luke.

[137] Goulder, 'Two Significant Minor Agreements', 366–70, suggests that Matthew also wrote Ναζαρά in the similarly worded passage at Mt. 2.23 in order to bring the place name in closer conformity to his scriptural citation Ναζωραῖος κληθήσεται in the same verse.

[138] Watson, *Gospel Writing*, 145–8.

[139] What could Q possibly look like here? *CEQ*, 42, can get only as far as assigning the single word Ναζαρά to Q 4.16.

[140] For the creative use of traditions in this passage, see Rafael Rodríguez, *Structuring Early Christian Memory: Jesus in Tradition*, Performance *and Text* (LNTS, 407; London: T&T Clark, 2010), 138–73.

generally maintain that following the Temptation, Luke and Matthew fail to agree on their placement of any double tradition material relative to Mark. A standard FH rejoinder is that Matthew and Luke agree in placing the Sermon on the Mount/Plain immediately after Mk 3.7-13.[141] This would appear to be supported by the way in which Matthew and Luke introduce their respective sermons (see Table 4.8).

One can, however, make an equally strong case for Matthew having inserted his Sermon at Mk 1.21.[142] Here Mark states that Jesus taught but fails to say what he taught. Whatever it was, it nevertheless sufficed to cause an amazed response (Mk 1.22), which Matthew picks it up at the conclusion of his Sermon (see Table 4.9).

In addition to the high degree of verbal agreement that suggests Mt. 7.28-29 corresponds to Mk 1.22, the insertion of the Sermon on the Mount between Mk 1.21 and 1.22 avoids the need to suppose Matthew skipped forward to Mk 3.7-13 and then went back to Mk 1.29 to start picking up the material he used in chapters 8 and 9. On

Table 4.8 The Setting of the Sermon.

Mt. 4.24–5.3	Mk 3.7-13	Lk. 6.17-20
24 καὶ ἀπῆλθεν ἡ ἀκοὴ αὐτοῦ εἰς ὅλην τὴν Συρίαν· καὶ προσήνεγκαν αὐτῷ πάντας τοὺς κακῶς ἔχοντας ποικίλαις νόσοις καὶ βασάνοις συνεχομένους, δαιμονιζομένους καὶ σεληνιαζομένους καὶ παραλυτικούς, καὶ ἐθεράπευσεν αὐτούς. 25 καὶ ἠκολούθησαν αὐτῷ ὄχλοι πολλοὶ ἀπὸ τῆς Γαλιλαίας καὶ Δεκαπόλεως καὶ Ἱεροσολύμων καὶ Ἰουδαίας καὶ πέραν τοῦ Ἰορδάνου. 5.1 Ἰδὼν δὲ τοὺς ὄχλους ἀνέβη εἰς τὸ ὄρος· καὶ καθίσαντος αὐτοῦ προσῆλθαν αὐτῷ οἱ μαθηταὶ αὐτοῦ· 2 καὶ ἀνοίξας τὸ στόμα αὐτοῦ ἐδίδασκεν αὐτοὺς λέγων· 3 Μακάριοι οἱ πτωχοὶ τῷ πνεύματι, ὅτι αὐτῶν ἐστιν ἡ βασιλεία τῶν οὐρανῶν.	7 Καὶ ὁ Ἰησοῦς μετὰ τῶν μαθητῶν αὐτοῦ ἀνεχώρησεν πρὸς τὴν θάλασσαν· καὶ πολὺ πλῆθος ἀπὸ τῆς Γαλιλαίας ἠκολούθησεν, καὶ ἀπὸ τῆς Ἰουδαίας 8 καὶ ἀπὸ Ἱεροσολύμων καὶ ἀπὸ τῆς Ἰδουμαίας καὶ πέραν τοῦ Ἰορδάνου καὶ περὶ Τύρον καὶ Σιδῶνα, πλῆθος πολύ, ἀκούοντες ὅσα ἐποίει ἦλθον πρὸς αὐτόν. 9 καὶ εἶπεν τοῖς μαθηταῖς αὐτοῦ ἵνα πλοιάριον προσκαρτερῇ αὐτῷ διὰ τὸν ὄχλον ἵνα μὴ θλίβωσιν αὐτόν· 10 πολλοὺς γὰρ ἐθεράπευσεν, ὥστε ἐπιπίπτειν αὐτῷ ἵνα αὐτοῦ ἅψωνται ὅσοι εἶχον μάστιγας. 11 καὶ τὰ πνεύματα τὰ ἀκάθαρτα, ὅταν αὐτὸν ἐθεώρουν, προσέπιπτον αὐτῷ καὶ a ἔκραζον λέγοντα ὅτι Σὺ εἶ ὁ υἱὸς τοῦ θεοῦ. 12 καὶ πολλὰ ἐπετίμα αὐτοῖς ἵνα μὴ αὐτὸν φανερὸν ποιήσωσιν. 13 Καὶ ἀναβαίνει εἰς τὸ ὄρος καὶ προσκαλεῖται οὓς ἤθελεν αὐτός, καὶ ἀπῆλθον πρὸς αὐτόν.	17 Καὶ καταβὰς μετ᾽ αὐτῶν ἔστη ἐπὶ τόπου πεδινοῦ, καὶ ὄχλος a πολὺς μαθητῶν αὐτοῦ, καὶ πλῆθος πολὺ τοῦ λαοῦ ἀπὸ πάσης τῆς Ἰουδαίας καὶ Ἰερουσαλὴμ καὶ τῆς παραλίου Τύρου καὶ Σιδῶνος, 18 οἳ ἦλθον ἀκοῦσαι αὐτοῦ καὶ ἰαθῆναι ἀπὸ τῶν νόσων αὐτῶν· καὶ οἱ ἐνοχλούμενοι ἀπὸ πνευμάτων ἀκαθάρτων ἐθεραπεύοντο· 19 καὶ πᾶς ὁ ὄχλος ἐζήτουν ἅπτεσθαι αὐτοῦ, ὅτι δύναμις παρ᾽ αὐτοῦ ἐξήρχετο καὶ ἰᾶτο πάντας. 20 Καὶ αὐτὸς ἐπάρας τοὺς ὀφθαλμοὺς αὐτοῦ εἰς τοὺς μαθητὰς αὐτοῦ ἔλεγεν· Μακάριοι οἱ πτωχοί, ὅτι ὑμετέρα ἐστὶν ἡ βασιλεία τοῦ θεοῦ.

---

[141] Goulder, *Luke*, 340–1; Watson, *Gospel Writing*, 148–55.
[142] *QiM*, 231–5.

Table 4.9 The Reaction to Jesus' Preaching.

Mt. 7.28-29	Mk 1.22
Καὶ ἐγένετο ὅτε a ἐτέλεσεν ὁ Ἰησοῦς τοὺς λόγους τούτους, **ἐξεπλήσσοντο** οἱ ὄχλοι **ἐπὶ τῇ διδαχῇ αὐτοῦ· ἦν γὰρ διδάσκων αὐτοὺς ὡς ἐξουσίαν ἔχων καὶ οὐχ ὡς οἱ γραμματεῖς** αὐτῶν.	καὶ **ἐξεπλήσσοντο ἐπὶ τῇ διδαχῇ αὐτοῦ, ἦν γὰρ διδάσκων αὐτοὺς ὡς ἐξουσίαν ἔχων καὶ οὐχ ὡς οἱ γραμματεῖς**.

this understanding, Mt. 4.23–5.1 is not a direct parallel to Mk 3.7-13 but rather, as Kirk argues, a pastiche of various Markan passages, composed on the basis of Matthew's memory competence in the language of Markan summaries.[143]

There is merit in both positions. Kirk may well be correct from the perspective of Matthew's composition; it does indeed seem more likely that Matthew understood himself to be inserting his Sermon between Mk 1.21 and Mk 1.22, in the process tidying up what he saw as a Markan muddle of teaching and exorcism by suppressing the exorcism (apart from a vestigial mention of demoniacs at Mt. 4.24) and supplying the missing teaching. Goulder and Watson may nevertheless be right about what FH Luke intended. Apart from supplying his own version of the Call of the Disciples at Lk. 5.1-11, Luke more or less follows Mark throughout Lk. 4.33–6.16 || Mk 1.29–3.19a. At some point FH Luke needs to switch back to Matthew to incorporate his version of the Sermon. From FH Luke's perspective, Mt. 4.24–5.1 could well appear to be Matthew's parallel to Mk 3.7-8, 13. If he was working forwards through Matthew while possessing good knowledge of Mark, Mt. 4.24–5.1 would almost inevitably appear in this light, since in working forwards through Matthew up to this point Luke will have seen nothing to contradict such a perception, and even if FH Luke knows what is coming in Matthew 8–9, there is no reason to suppose that he will be particularly exercised by how Matthew arrived at his arrangement of material from earlier in Mark. That FH Luke saw Mt. 4.24–5.1 as parallel to Mk 3.7-13 is further suggested by his transposition of Mk 3.7-10 || Lk. 6.17-19 to after Mk 3.13-19a || Lk. 6.12-16 so that it leads directly into the Sermon, as it appears to do in Matthew. To frame the matter another way, on arriving at Mt. 4.24–5.1 FH Luke perceives Matthew as having skipped from Mk 1.15 to Mk 3.7 and so, doing his best to reconcile the order of his two principal sources, FH Luke inserts his version of the intervening Markan material before returning to Matthew at Lk. 6.20 || Mt. 5.2. FH Luke thus does his best to place his version of the Sermon at the same point in the Markan framework as Matthew.[144]

Conclusion

This chapter has presented a substantial body of evidence suggesting a direct connection between Luke and Matthew. This consists, first, of the extensive verbal agreements of

---

[143] *QiM*, 237–41.
[144] See also the discussion of this point in Christopher M. Tuckett, 'Watson, Q and "L/M"' in Müller, *Gospel Interpretation*, 115–38 (125–8), and Francis Watson, 'Seven Theses on the Synoptic Problem, in Disagreement with Christopher Tuckett' in Müller, *Gospel Interpretation*, 139–47, here 142–3.

Matthew and Luke against Mark, which are hard to account for if each were making independent use of Mark; second, the instances of close verbatim agreement in double tradition material, which would be oddly coincidental if Matthew and Luke were making independent use of Q (given that we do not find the same degree of agreement when they are both using Mark); and, third, significant similarities between Matthew and Luke over the first four chapters of their gospels, which are particularly compelling when taken in aggregate. In the absence of good reasons to the contrary, the most natural conclusion to draw is that Luke has used Matthew (along with Mark).

Since Luke is a different author with a different agenda, his gospel is bound to differ from Matthew's (otherwise there would be no point in Luke's writing it). Similarities between Matthew and Luke are therefore more significant in assessing their mutual dependence than differences, especially when there are so many similarities. 2DH advocates nevertheless argue that various differences between Matthew and Luke make it unlikely that the latter could have known the former. We shall address these over the course of the next two chapters and, in so doing, uncover further potentially significant similarities between Luke and Matthew.

5

Difficult differences

Infancy and resurrection narratives

Defenders of the 2DH may acknowledge many of the similarities between Matthew and Luke identified in the previous chapter, but still maintain that key differences between these two gospels render the dependence of either upon the other unlikely. One such difference is the way the two gospels begin and end: Luke's similarity with Matthew extends only as far as their common use of Mark, starting where Mark starts, with the ministry of John the Baptist, and ending where Mark ends, with the Empty Tomb. In their infancy and resurrection narratives, Matthew and Luke each goes his separate way. On the face of it, this seems odd if Luke knew Matthew.[1]

Since FH Luke cannot have been wholly satisfied with Matthew (else he would not bother to write a gospel of his own) he would have wanted to put his own stamp on the material. The places where it might be most effective to do so would be at the beginning and end, first where he sets out his own stall in contrast with Matthew's and second where he leaves his audience with a final impression. But while this observation may suggest a general motive for being more radical in his use of Matthew at the beginning and end of his gospel, it does not fully explain why Luke looks so different there. The previous chapter nevertheless argued that far from posing a problem for Luke's use of Matthew, the similarities between their openings, not least the infancy narratives, in fact support the FH. That leaves only the resurrection accounts to be discussed here.

It is not hard to see why Luke would have departed from Matthew's resurrection account. Matthew's principal resurrection appearance takes place in Galilee (Mt. 28.16-20), presumably picking up on the hint provided by Mk 16.7. Luke, however, needs to keep the disciples in Jerusalem. Luke's account both opens and ends in the Temple (Lk. 1.5-22; 24.53). Luke's second volume requires the disciples to remain in Jerusalem for Pentecost, which is central to Acts' project of describing the spread of the gospel 'in Jerusalem and in all Judea and Samaria and to the end of the earth' (Acts 1.8). This follows on from Jesus' command at the end of Luke's Gospel to preach in

---

[1] Kloppenborg, *Excavating*, 41.

Christ's name 'to all nations, beginning in Jerusalem' but to 'stay in the city, until you are clothed with power from on high' (Lk. 24.47, 49).[2] That Jerusalem is the hinge on which Luke's two volumes turn makes his drastic transformation of Matthew's Galilean appearance story virtually inevitable.[3] Moreover, the traditions available to Luke for the period from Easter to Pentecost may well have persuaded him that the disciples must have remained in Jerusalem throughout this time, so that he would have seen himself as correcting a Matthean error (perhaps, in Luke's view, Matthew's mistaken inference from Mk 16.7 leading Matthew to mislocate the mountain of the commissioning appearance in Galilee).

There are nevertheless several points of contact between the Lukan and Matthean resurrection accounts that suggest that Luke drastically transformed rather than totally rejected Matthew's conclusion, and that he was doing so under the twin constraints of needing everything to take place around Jerusalem and adapting the material to his own theological agenda. It may or may not be pertinent that at Mt. 28.9 the women who meet Jesus near the tomb hold his feet, while at Lk. 24.39 the risen Jesus shows his hands and feet to his disciples and invites them to handle him. Both scenes demonstrate the physicality of Jesus' resurrection body, but only Luke emphasizes the point.[4] More importantly, Luke's resurrection appearances contain a number of features that have parallels at Mt. 28.16-20:

Table 5.1 Common Features in Matthew's and Luke's Resurrection Appearances.

Matthew Commissioning Appearance	Luke Resurrection Appearances
Occurs on a mountain (28.16)	Final one occurs on a mountain (Lk. 24.50 locates it at Bethany, which Lk. 19.29 locates on the Mount of Olives; cf. Acts 1.12)
Gives rise to doubt among some of the eleven (28.17)	Some disciples in Luke express disbelief (Lk. 24.11, 24, 41)
Jesus declares that all earthly and heavenly authority has been given to him (28.18)	Jesus is taken up into heaven, from where he will exercise authority at God's right hand (Lk. 24.51; 22.69; Acts 7.56)[5]

---

[2] See Odette Mainville, 'De Jésus à l'Église: Étude rédactionnelle de Luc 24', NTS 51 (2005), 192–211, for a fuller discussion of how Luke chapter 24 is carefully constructed to form a bridge from the ministry of Jesus to the church's mission in Acts.

[3] Cf. the transformation of Mk 16.7 into Lk. 24.6-7 for the same end.

[4] Goulder, Luke, 791. On how Luke presents Jesus' resurrected body as something beyond conventional expectations, see further Deborah Thompson Prince, 'The "Ghost" of Jesus: Luke 24 in Light of Ancient Narratives of Post-Mortem Apparitions', JSNT 29 (2007), 287–301, and Israel Muñoz Gallarte, 'Luke 24 Reconsidered: The Figure of the Ghost in Post-Classical Greek Literature', NovT 59 (2017), 131–46. Prince calls attention to an intriguing parallel between Luke's and Homer's description of a shade lacking flesh and bones: οὐ γὰρ ἔτι σάρκας τε καὶ ὀστέα ἶνες ἔχουσιν (Od. 11.219) || ὅτι πνεῦμα σάρκα καὶ ὀστέα οὐκ ἔχει καθὼς ἐμὲ θεωπεῖτε ἔχοντα (Lk. 24.39b).

[5] Parker, Living Text, 170–1, points out that the phrase 'and was carried up into heaven' is a Western non-interpolation and argues that it was probably added to the text of Luke's Gospel to harmonize it with the beginning of Acts. This does not substantially affect the point being made, however, since Parker suggests that if Acts directly followed Luke the force of 'he parted from them' remains much the same.

Jesus commands the eleven to go and make disciples of all nations (πάντα τὰ ἔθνη) baptizing them in the name (εἰς τὸ ὄνομα) of the Father, Son and Holy Spirit (28.19)	Repentance and forgiveness of sins are to be preached in Jesus' name (ἐπὶ τῷ ὀνόματι αὐτοῦ) to all nations (πάντα τὰ ἔθνη; Lk. 24.47)
Concludes with the promise, introduced with the words καὶ ἰδοὺ ἐγώ, that Jesus will remain with his disciples until the end of the age (28.20)	Jesus makes his disciples a promise, introduced with the words καὶ ἰδοὺ ἐγώ,[6] that they will be clothed with power from on high, in other words the Holy Spirit, who substitutes for Jesus' ongoing personal presence in Acts (Lk. 24.49)
The disciples worship Jesus (αὐτὸν ποσσεκύνησαν) (28.17)	The disciples worship Jesus (προσκυνήσαντες αὐτόν; Lk. 24.52)[7]

There are also several EA$^{Mt\text{-}Lk}$ (or near EA$^{Mt\text{-}Lk}$) in the Empty Tomb story that could further point to Luke's knowledge of Matthew's ending:

Table 5.2 The Empty Tomb

Mt. 28.3-6	Mk 16.5-6	Lk. 24.4-6
ἦν δὲ ἡ εἰδέα αὐτοῦ ὡς <u>ἀστραπὴ</u> καὶ τὸ ἔνδυμα αὐτοῦ λευκὸν ὡς χιών. ἀπὸ δὲ τοῦ φόβου αὐτοῦ ἐσείσθησαν οἱ τηροῦντες καὶ ἐγενήθησαν ὡς νεκροί. ἀποκριθεὶς δὲ ὁ ἄγγελος <u>εἶπεν</u> ταῖς γυναιξίν· Μὴ φοβεῖσθε ὑμεῖς, οἶδα γὰρ ὅτι Ἰησοῦν τὸν ἐσταυρωμένον ζητεῖτε· <u>οὐκ ἔστιν ὧδε</u>, <u>ἠγέρθη</u> γὰρ καθὼς εἶπεν· δεῦτε ἴδετε τὸν τόπον ὅπου ἔκειτο·	καὶ εἰσελθοῦσαι εἰς τὸ μνημεῖον εἶδον νεανίσκον καθήμενον ἐν τοῖς δεξιοῖς περιβεβλημένον στολὴν λευκήν, καὶ ἐξεθαμβήθησαν. ὁ δὲ λέγει αὐταῖς· Μὴ ἐκθαμβεῖσθε· Ἰησοῦν ζητεῖτε τὸν Ναζαρηνὸν τὸν ἐσταυρωμένον· <u>ἠγέρθη, οὐκ ἔστιν ὧδε</u>· ἴδε ὁ τόπος ὅπου ἔθηκαν αὐτόν·	καὶ ἐγένετο ἐν τῷ ἀπορεῖσθαι αὐτὰς περὶ τούτου καὶ ἰδοὺ ἄνδρες δύο ἐπέστησαν αὐταῖς ἐν ἐσθῆτι <u>ἀστραπ</u>τούσῃ. ἐμφόβων δὲ γενομένων αὐτῶν καὶ κλινουσῶν τὰ πρόσωπα εἰς τὴν γῆν <u>εἶ</u>παν πρὸς αὐτάς· Τί ζητεῖτε τὸν ζῶντα μετὰ τῶν νεκρῶν; <u>οὐκ ἔστιν ὧδε</u>, ἀλλὰ <u>ἠγέρθη</u>. μνήσθητε ὡς ἐλάλησεν ὑμῖν ἔτι ὢν ἐν τῇ Γαλιλαίᾳ,

In Mark, the young man is described as dressed in a white robe, whereas in Matthew and Luke his appearance is compared to lightning; in Mark this provokes amazement, whereas in Matthew and Luke it provokes fear. Moreover, Matthew and Luke agree against Mark in placing οὐκ ἔστιν ὧδε before ἠγέρθη. Finally, whereas Mark ends with the women fleeing and saying nothing to anyone, in Mt. 28.8 and Lk. 24.9 they report (ἀπαγγεῖλαι/ἀπήγγειλαν) what they have seen to the eleven disciples.[8] As ever, the clustering of EA$^{Mt\text{-}Lk}$ makes them more significant in aggregate than any of them might appear in isolation.

---

[6] Some MSS omit ἰδοὺ at Lk. 24.49. The expression καὶ ἰδοὺ ἐγώ occurs also at Lk 23.14 but nowhere else in Matthew; καὶ ἰδοὺ occurs multiple times in Matthew and Luke-Acts; ἰδοὺ ἐγώ occurs in three other places in Matthew and three in Acts.

[7] Although some MSS omit προσκυνήσαντες αὐτὸν from Lk 24.52. Metzger, *Textual Commentary*, 190 [2nd edn 163], suggests that the words were probably omitted by a copyist. On the other hand, Parker, *Living Text*, 171–2, regards this as another Western non-interpolation added by a later scribe.

[8] Goulder, *Luke*, 774–5.

Sceptics may feel these parallels are not sufficiently compelling to prove Luke's use of Matthew's ending, but in combination they suffice to undermine the assumption that Luke could not have known it. They suggest rather that Luke adapted it to his own interests.[9]

Alternating primitivity

Another common objection to Luke's use of Matthew is that it is (allegedly) sometimes Luke and sometimes Matthew that contains the more primitive form of a tradition, so that neither can have used the other but each must instead have employed an earlier source.[10]

There are two potential counters to this objection. One is to suggest that in cases where Luke's version of a double tradition parallel such as the Lord's Prayer or the Beatitudes appears more primitive, Luke obtained his version not from Matthew but from oral tradition. This may well be the case, but it is open to the counter-objection that while this appeal to oral tradition is perfectly plausible in principle, the more it is appealed to, the weaker the FH starts to appear.[11]

The second way of meeting this objection is to deny that there is any case in which Luke's form of the double tradition is demonstrably more primitive that Matthew's. This is essentially the argument offered in outline by Austin Farrer, who maintained that judgements of the primitivity of a tradition are too subjective to bear the weight placed upon them by defenders of the 2DH.[12] It is also the position taken by Michael Goulder, who argues in some detail for the derivation of the Lukan wording from the Matthean in his commentary on Luke.[13]

This is straightforward to argue in the case of one of the most common examples, namely that Matthew's 'Blessed are the poor in spirit' (Mt. 5.3) must be secondary in relation to Luke's 'Blessed are you poor' (Lk. 6.20) since (it is claimed) Matthew has clearly spiritualized the more primitive beatitude found in Luke.[14] Yet Luke's Gospel displays a consistent interest in the literally poor. Moreover, Luke's beatitudes are matched with corresponding woes, with Lk. 6.24, 'But woe to your who are rich', matching Luke 6.20, 'Blessed are you poor'. Had Luke simply taken over Matthew's 'poor in spirit' it is hard to see how the corresponding woe could have been constructed. Furthermore, Matthew's more poetically balanced version of the beatitudes is arguably better fitted to survive in oral tradition, thus making it *more* likely to be the earlier version. If Luke's version happens to be closer to something uttered by the historical

---

[9] Cf. Drury, *Tradition*, 127–8; Goulder, *Luke*, 792–7; Franklin, *Luke*, 364–6; and Goodacre, *Case*, 58–9.
[10] Streeter, *Four Gospels*, 183; Davies and Allison, *Matthew*, I, 116; Kloppenborg, *Excavating*, 42; Tuckett, Q, 10, 13–14.
[11] Kloppenborg, *Excavating*, 43.
[12] A.M. Farrer, 'On Dispensing with Q' in D.E. Nineham (ed.), *Studies in the Gospels: Essays in Memory of R. H. Lightfoot* (Oxford: Blackwell, 1955), 55–88, here 63–5.
[13] Goulder, *Luke*, 45–6 *et passim*.
[14] Tuckett, Q, 10.

Jesus, that might simply mean that Luke is more convincing to modern historians in the way he presents what Jesus said; it does not necessitate that he had access to a more primitive tradition.[15]

At first sight the other parade example, the Lord's Prayer (Mt. 6.9-13 || Lk. 11.2-4), may look harder to explain as Luke's reworking of Matthew, since so many scholars have regarded it as self-evident that Matthew's more elaborate version is the result of liturgical additions to a simpler original.[16] To be sure, one can argue that the Lord's Prayer is precisely the kind of material that might be handed on in primitive Christian worship so that Luke would have known a version of it independently of Matthew.[17] But while this is plausible, the FH has no need of this hypothesis, since Matthew's more poetically elaborate version is better fitted to survive in oral transmission, and is in that sense more likely to be more primitive than Luke's, which has more of the character of a literary abbreviation. David Rubin argues that a major factor that lends stability to oral tradition is *serial cueing*, whereby one line of a song or poem prompts the next, and that the effectiveness of serial cueing is greatly enhanced by the use of multiple cues. Such cues can include the meaning and imagery of a text, but they also include such surface features as rhyme, rhythm, assonance and alliteration.[18] The Matthean version of the Lord's Prayer employs such features far more abundantly than the Lukan one. Thus what scholars have often identified as Matthew's liturgical elaborations should instead be understood as the kind of poetic structuring that makes a piece of tradition more memorable and hence better fitted to survive in oral transmission.[19] The assumption that the Lukan version must be more primitive because it is shorter and less elaborate is unfounded; one might equally well argue that the Lukan version betrays the kind of stripped-down economy that is more characteristic of a literary text than an oral tradition.[20]

A further pair of common examples are those suggested by Craig Evans.[21] The first of these is the well-known difference between Matthew and Luke at Mt. 12.28 || Lk. 11.20, 'if it is by the Spirit/finger of God that I cast out demons, then the kingdom of God has come upon you'. Here Matthew has 'Spirit' while Luke has 'finger' and Evans confidently asserts that 'Spirit' must be the more primitive, in part because Luke, who shows great interest in the Spirit elsewhere, would have had no reason to change 'Spirit' to 'finger'.

---

[15] Goodacre, *Case*, 133–51; Mark A. Matson, 'Luke's Rewriting of the Sermon on the Mount' in Mark S. Goodacre and Nicholas Perrin (eds), *Questioning Q* (London: SPCK, 2004), 43–70, here 65–7; Watson, *Gospel Writing*, 160–3; Eve, 'Memory, Orality', 329–30.
[16] Marshall, *Luke*, 454; Tuckett, *Q*, 10; Kloppenborg, *Excavating*, 42.
[17] Evans, *Luke*, 476; Goodacre, *Case*, 64–5.
[18] Rubin, *Memory in Oral Traditions*, 39–193; Eve, 'Memory, Orality', 320–3; Eve, *Behind*, 100–2.
[19] Eve, 'Memory, Orality', 327–31. See also Michael Wade Martin, 'The Poetry of the Lord's Prayer: A Study in Poetic Device', *JBL* 134 (2015), 347–72.
[20] See also Ken Olson, 'Luke 11.2–4: The Lord's Prayer (Abridged Edition)' in Poirier and Peterson, *Marcan Priority*, 101–18. Kloppenborg, 'Farrer/Mark without Q', 240–1, accepts the general validity of Olson's arguments but counters that Olson has shown only the possibility, not the probability, of the derivation of the Lukan Lord's Prayer from Matthew's version. But in order to defeat the alternating primitivity objection, a demonstration of reasonable plausibility is all that is needed.
[21] Evans, 'Two Source Hypothesis', 43.

But several scholars who accept the 2DH take 'Spirit' rather than 'finger' to be at least possibly more original.[22] The priority of the Lukan version is therefore not as clear-cut as Evans supposes. After Luke 4, Luke is sparing with his allusions to the Spirit until Pentecost and does not explicitly associate Jesus' wonder-working abilities with the Spirit, while 'finger of God' is similar to OT expressions such as 'the power of the Lord' (Lk. 5.17) or 'the hand of the Lord' (Acts 13.11) that Luke uses elsewhere.[23] The phrase 'finger of God' at Lk. 11.20 may well have been chosen to create an allusion to Exod. 8.19 (8.15 LXX), where Pharaoh's magicians, who have been duplicating the signs performed through Moses and Aaron up to that point, are unable to replicate the plague of gnats, so that they are forced to acknowledge that this has been brought about by 'the finger of God'. Luke's point is to cast the other Jewish exorcists ('your sons') of the previous verse in the role of magicians, rather like the sons of Sceva at Acts 19.11-20, thereby clarifying why Jesus' exorcisms are signs of the coming of the kingdom while the other Jewish ones are not.[24]

John Kloppenborg has responded to this argument with two objections.[25] The first is that creating an allusion to Exod. 8.19 'seems rather at odds with the general consensus that Luke is at pains to distance Jesus from magical practices'.[26] Here Kloppenborg appears to have misunderstood my argument, which is that the allusion to Exod. 8.19 creates a *contrast* between the magical exorcisms of the Jewish exorcists ('your sons') and the eschatological exorcisms of Jesus. In the parallel at Mt. 12.27-28 it is not entirely clear why (or even whether) Jesus' exorcisms are superior to those of 'your sons'. By suggesting that the other Jewish exorcisms are magical, as Luke does with the sons of Sceva at Acts 19.13-20,[27] Luke clarifies the distinction between the two types of exorcism.

This leads into Kloppenborg's second complaint, namely that the allusion to Exod. 8.19 would be too subtle for Luke's (Gentile) target audience. Kloppenborg cites Heather Gorman as holding 'that Luke *eliminated* Aramaic terms and matters pertaining to the Torah because its content "is steeped in traditions that may have been unfamiliar to the Gentiles in Luke's audience"'.[28] But 'the finger of God' at Exod. 8.19 (8.15 LXX) is neither an Aramaic term nor something pertaining to some obscure part of the Torah, but an allusion to a well-known story related to a key event in Israel's past. That the phrase might have served as a mnemonic trigger to this story is suggested by Philo's account of the plagues in his *Life of Moses*. Whereas Philo usually paraphrases the biblical account, he chooses to quote it at precisely this point: 'For what is slighter than a gnat? Yet so great was its power that all Egypt lost heart, and was forced to cry

---

[22] Eve, 'Devil', 38, n. 52, citing Evans, *Luke*, 492; John Nolland, *Luke 9: 21–18:34* (WBC, 35B; Dallas, TX: Word Books, 1993), 639–40; and David R. Catchpole, *The Quest for Q* (Edinburgh: T&T Clark, 1993), 12 n.27.

[23] Evans, *Luke*, 492

[24] Eve, 'Devil', 35–6; Luke Timothy Johnson, *The Gospel of Luke* (SP, 3; Collegeville, MN: Liturgical, 1991), 204; Goulder, *Midrash*, 333 n.66; Goulder, *Luke*, 504; C.S. Rodd, 'Spirit or Finger', *ExpT* 72 (1961), 157–8. See also p. 178, where the Beelzebul Controversy is considered in its wider context.

[25] Kloppenborg, 'Farrer/Mark', 229–30.

[26] Kloppenborg, 'Farrer/Mark', 229.

[27] Eve, *Jewish Context*, 334–9.

[28] Kloppenborg, 'Farrer/Mark', 230, citing Gorman, 'Crank', 74–5.

aloud: "This is the finger of God" (δάκτυλος θεοῦ τοῦτ' ἐστί)' (Philo, *Vit. Mos.* 1.112). Along with other parts of the *Exposition*, the *Life of Moses* was most likely aimed at a non-Jewish audience familiar with the conventions of Roman historiography.[29] Whereas Philo may have been introducing his audience to the significance of 'finger of God', it would appear that Luke (in common with the other evangelists) presupposes an audience with a good knowledge of the OT throughout, so it is not too much of a stretch to suppose that they could have recognized the 'finger of God' allusion.

The next example cited by Evans is the parallel at Mt. 23.34-36 || Lk. 11.49-50, where Luke, but not Matthew, has 'the Wisdom of God' as the speaker of the saying about sending prophets and various other people who will be persecuted:

Table 5.3 The Sender of Persecuted Prophets.

Mt. 23.34-36	Lk. 11.49-50
Therefore I send you prophets and wise men and scribes, some of whom you will kill and crucify, and some you will scourge in your synagogues and persecute from town to town, that upon you may come all the righteous blood shed on earth, from the blood of innocent Abel to the blood of Zechariah the son of Barachiah, whom you murdered between the sanctuary and the altar. Truly, I say to you, all this will come upon this generation.	Therefore also the Wisdom of God said, 'I will send them prophets and apostles, some of whom they will kill and persecute,' so that the blood of all the prophets, shed from the foundation of the world, may be required of this generation, from the blood of Abel to the blood of Zechariah, who perished between the altar and the sanctuary. Yes, I tell you, it shall be required of this generation.

This is part of a complex parallel between Lk. 11.39-52 and Mt. 23.25-26, 23, 6-7, 27-28, 4, 29-32, 34-36, 13 (listing the Matthean verses in Luke's order). Either FH Luke has substantially selected from and rearranged the material he has taken from Matthew or 2DH Matthew had substantially rearranged and supplemented the material he has taken from Q. Either way, a full discussion of this passage would require too much space to be entered into here.

On the specific point about the Wisdom of God, Craig Evans does not say why he supposes the Lukan version to be more primitive; he simply states that it is.[30] He may have in mind the kind of argument offered by C.F. Evans, who states that 'the Wisdom of God said' in Lk. 11.49 'is likely to have been reproduced from Q. Luke will hardly have substituted it for "I send" (Matt. 23[34]), whereas Matthew (or his source) could have identified Wisdom with Jesus, and applied the whole saying to the Christian mission'.[31] But this still leaves unclear (since it is never argued but merely asserted) why Luke could not have added 'the Wisdom of God said' to his source (*pace* C.F. Evans he does not in fact *substitute* it for 'I send').

At Lk. 11.39-52 FH Luke appears not so much to be editing Mt. 23.6-36 as composing his own discourse based on Matthew's. This is indicated both by the

---

[29] Niehoff, *Philo*, 109–30. Philo also lays particular emphasis on the phrase 'finger of God' at *Migr.* 85.
[30] Evans, 'Two Source Hypothesis', 43.
[31] C.F. Evans, *Luke*, 508; See Tuckett, *Q*, 24–5, 166–73, for further discussion of this example from the 2DH perspective.

relative freedom with which Luke reproduces the substance of Matthew's discourse and by the fact that he uses the material selectively and out of its Matthean order. The Matthean parallel has the scribes and Pharisees condemn themselves out of their own mouths by disowning their ancestors who killed the prophets. It then goes on to have Jesus prophesy that in the future he will send prophets and wise men whom they will also persecute, so that the blood of all the righteous will be requited upon the present generation. Luke transforms this into a sequence that better fits the Lukan context, given Luke's theme that Jesus is the prophet like Moses who is destined to meet the rejection that Israel's prophets have always met. In Luke, the lawyers have just been castigated for building the tombs of the prophets killed by their fathers (Lk. 11.47-48). Lk. 11.49 continues this litany of misdeeds by citing a supposedly former prophecy that the people would be sent prophets (killed and persecuted in the past, as in Lk. 11.49) and apostles (presumably meaning Christian missionaries in the present) who will be treated in the same way. Jesus' prophecy of the future mistreatment of Christian 'prophets and wise men and scribes' at Mt. 23.34-36 is thus turned by Luke into an earlier prophecy emphasizing the Jewish leadership's consistent rejection of God's messengers (the prophets of old and the apostles of the Church). For Luke, this prophecy needs to have been uttered in the past by someone other than Jesus, who is now quoting this prior prophecy.

Tuckett is aware of arguments similar to these propounded by Goulder, but asks why Luke should have interpreted Matthew's prophets as OT figures or employed 'the highly unusual periphrasis' 'Wisdom of God' for the sender of these prophets, whom Goulder takes to be God.[32] Tuckett's first question has just been answered: Luke reinterprets Matthew's prophets to fit his own scheme of Israel's consistent rejection of prophets up to and including Jesus. It is in this context that Luke chooses the Wisdom of God as his spokesperson. Moreover, the expression is not quite such a Lukan outlier as Tuckett supposes. It is similar in kind to others that Luke uses elsewhere, as we have just seen in relation to 'the finger of God' (Luke 11.20). 'Mouth and wisdom' assume the function of the Holy Spirit at Lk. 21.15 || Mk 13.11. At Lk. 11.49 'Wisdom of God' may thus be a periphrasis not so much for God as for the Holy Spirit as the speaker (cf. Acts 28.25). As Goulder suggests, the particular expression ἡ σοφία τοῦ θεοῦ (the Wisdom of God) may additionally have been suggested by Matthew's σοφοὺς (wise men) at Mt. 23.34.[33]

In each of the examples just discussed, a plausible case can be made for Luke's derivation of his version from Matthew's, and in none of them is the Lukan version *demonstrably* (or even probably) more primitive. These four examples are among those often regarded as the most compelling, but many others have been suggested, and they cannot all be discussed here. So rather than multiply examples it may be more helpful to probe the principles involved.

The term 'alternating primitivity' conflates two related but conceptually distinct notions: primitivity proper and redactional (im)plausibility. The first of these presupposes that there is some more primitive form of a saying to be identified and

---

[32] Tuckett, *Q*, 25; Goulder, *Luke*, 523.
[33] So Goulder, *Luke*, 523.

attributed to an earlier source (such as Q). Behind 'primitivity' in this sense lurks the quest for the *ipsissima verba* of the historical Jesus. This is problematic at a number of levels, not least because it assumes that it is meaningful to look for the one original form of a saying that has undergone oral transmission (and translation from Aramaic to Greek) and that this one original form is recoverable from the later oral or written context in which it became embedded. Such assumptions are questionable and are being increasingly abandoned.[34] There is no guarantee that sayings that had been cultivated in the church for forty or fifty years would generally survive in pristine, primitive form for either Matthew or Luke to use; it is far more likely that many sayings transmitted over such a period would have undergone at least some (oral and written) performance variations, and that many of them existed in multiple forms right from the start (it is surely more plausible than not that Jesus would have repeated his teaching in different words on different occasions). It is also possible that some of them were coined later or brought into the Jesus tradition from another source. The argument from alternating primitivity proper thus *presupposes* the existence of something like Q as a stable deposit of sayings material from a much earlier stage in the tradition; it is thus effectively circular.

That said, most modern defenders of Q probably do not think of 'alternating primitivity' in quite these terms. Mostly, what is meant by 'alternating primitivity' is in reality 'alternating relative priority' or 'redactional implausibility', the argument that there are a number of cases where Matthew has written X^M where Luke has written X^L and it looks more plausible that X^M would have been derived from X^L than vice versa. The problem with this argument is the difficulty of avoiding subjectivity. As John Kloppenborg observes:

> It is abundantly clear, however, that such 'plausibility arguments' have been adduced for several mutually contradictory directions of borrowing and just as clear that the canons of plausibility differ from critic to critic. This is the level at which most of the SP argument in fact goes on; yet it is also one of the most subjective and reversible parts of the entire enterprise.[35]

Kloppenborg goes on to outline three types of arguments that have been employed in such cases: (1) renaming the problem (e.g. Luke changed X^M to X^L because he liked X^L or disliked X^M), (2) coherence arguments (e.g. Luke's change of X^M to X^L is analogous to other changes Luke makes elsewhere) and (3) externally buttressed arguments (e.g. Luke's change of X^M to X^L either is or is not in line with the compositional methods of other ancient authors). Kloppenborg goes on to suggest that type 1 arguments are probably unavoidable but are not compelling, that type 2 arguments are more plausible but can be invoked in support of mutually contradictory theories and that while they do not settle the issue, type 3 arguments offer the best hope of escaping subjectivity.[36]

---

[34] Eve, *Behind*, 181–3.
[35] John S. Kloppenborg, 'Conceptual Stakes in the Synoptic Problem' in Mogens Müller and Heike Omerzu (eds), *Gospel Interpretation and the Q-Hypothesis* (LNTS, 573; London: Bloomsbury T&T Clark, 2018), 13–42 (22).
[36] Kloppenborg, 'Conceptual Stakes', 22–9.

The alleged examples of alternating primitivity discussed above largely involve arguments of the first two types, which may explain why they continue to be debated even though both sides appear to believe that they have settled these cases in their own favour. It is unclear how far type 3 arguments would help in these particular instances, since expansion, compression and paraphrase (including the substitution of one term for another) are all within the range of transformational techniques ancient authors use (and which either 2DH Matthew or FH Luke will have used here).[37] Moreover, on the thesis that FH Luke is often employing his sources from memory, one does not have to suppose that every single transformation of Matthew's X^M to Luke's X^L is the result of deliberate calculation. One is then thrown back on arguments about what kinds of transformations ancient authors might have wished to make, say for the purpose of rhetorical effectiveness.[38] The difficulty for the redactional implausibility argument is then establishing a sufficient number of cases where Luke's transformation of Matthew is clearly less rhetorically effective than their different transformations of Q, without being certain of the precise wording of Q and without once again resorting to subjective judgement.[39]

For the alternating primitivity argument to succeed as an objection to the FH it must be able to demonstrate a number of cases where Luke's transformation of Matthew would be positively implausible. To defeat this argument, it is not necessary for the FH to demonstrate that Luke's transformation of Matthew is compelling in each case, but merely that it is not positively implausible. As matters stand, the argument from alternating primitivity does not bear the weight placed on it as an objection to Luke's use of Matthew.

Luke's non-use of Matthean additions to Mark

Another common objection against Luke's use of Matthew is that if Luke used Matthew one would have expected him to take over more of Matthew's changes, especially his additions to Mark.[40] It is generally recognized that FH Luke has taken over a number of these additions in the so-called Mark-Q overlap passages. This nevertheless needs to be emphasized since one is sometimes confronted with statements such as 'Luke never appears to know any of Matthew's additions to Mark's material'.[41] The real objection, however, is that FH Luke has not taken over as many of Matthew's changes to Mark as 2DH supporters think he should have done.

Mark Goodacre has responded to this objection by suggesting that many of Matthew's additions to Mark 'tend to have a strikingly Matthean stamp ... [and] appear to be

---

[37] So also Damm, *Ancient Rhetoric*, 167.
[38] Kloppenborg, 'Conceptual Stakes', 27–8, following Damm, *Ancient Rhetoric*, 168–70.
[39] Damm's examination of particular sets of parallels often tends to favour the 2DH slightly over the FH, but not to the extent that FH Luke is positively implausible.
[40] Kloppenborg, *Excavating*, 41.
[41] Tuckett, *Q*, 7–8. Tuckett at once goes on to acknowledge the existence of the Mark-Q overlap passages at n. 20 and goes on to discuss them as a problem for the FH (and 2GH) in connection with the 'unpicking' objection we shall discuss below.

uncongenial to what we know of Luke's interests'. Thus Luke takes only those features of Matthew that are 'Luke-pleasing'.[42] This is persuasive where 'Luke-pleasingness' can be shown to correspond to what are clearly Lukan compositional interests; for example, the Gentile-facing Luke would have had little reason to reproduce much of the Matthean Jesus' arguments over the interpretation of the Law or the practice of Jewish piety. But the 'Luke-pleasing' explanation should not be overworked, lest 'Luke-pleasing' end up as an effective synonym for 'material Luke took from Matthew' and the term thereby lose all explanatory power.

It is presumably awareness of both types of counter that has led Craig Evans to state the objection more carefully: 'Another problem for the Two Gospel and Farrer Hypotheses is having to account for Luke's omission of Matthean material that otherwise accords well with Luke's theology.'[43] He goes on to cite the Parables of the Labourers of the Field (Mt. 20.1-16) and of the Last Judgement (Mt. 25.31-46) as examples, although since these are examples of special M material rather than of Matthew's additions to Mark in Markan passages, they illustrate something slightly different from the particular argument we are now considering. Given that Luke had material of his own to add and presumably wished to keep his gospel to a manageable length, it should not be surprising if there were some M material he might decide to omit even if he found it quite congenial. In composing his own work Luke was hardly obliged to include everything useful he found in his sources. More directly relevant, then, are the examples adduced by Tuckett and Kloppenborg, such as Mt. 3.14-15; 12.5-7; 13.14-15; 14.28-31; 16.16-19; 27.19, 24.[44]

On the model of composition proposed here, Luke sometimes follows Mark, and sometimes Matthew, as his main source. In doing so, he accords with the procedure typically followed by other ancient authors, with the proviso that he may often have been working from memory rather than with a manuscript open 'before his eyes'.[45] All the cases where Luke does include a substantial Matthean addition to Mark (the so-called 'Mark-Q' overlap passages) occur where Luke is using Matthew as his main source. Conversely, nearly all the examples cited by Tuckett and Kloppenborg of Luke's non-use of Matthew's additions occur where Luke is following Mark (see Table 6.8). The vast proportion of Luke's omissions of Matthew's additions to Mark are therefore primarily to be explained not by what Luke found uncongenial but by which source he was following.[46]

Two of the Tuckett-Kloppenborg examples listed above lie outside the scope of this explanation. One of these, Mt. 14.28-31 (Peter's attempt to walk on water), is a trivial exception since it comes from a passage Luke omits altogether. The other, Mt. 3.14-15 (the conversation between Jesus and John the Baptist in the baptism scene), is more pertinent, since it lies in a section where FH Luke would most likely have been

---

[42] Goodacre, *Case*, 51.
[43] Evans, 'Two Source Hypothesis', 44.
[44] Kloppenborg, *Excavating*, 41; Tuckett, *Q*, 7–8.
[45] *WTG*, 55–8; Derrenbacker, *Ancient Compositional Practices*, 116–17; Downing 'Compositional Conventions', 71–82; Pelling, 'Plutarch's Method', 92.
[46] So also Goulder, *Luke*, 44.

following Matthew and might thus have been expected to pick up on this Matthean addition.

The exchange between Jesus and John, in which John questions whether he should be baptizing Jesus and Jesus replies that 'it is fitting for us to fulfil all righteousness', seems to have been occasioned by Matthew's embarrassment at the greater Jesus being baptized by the lesser John, with the apparent implication that Jesus might need to repent (Mt. 3.2, 6, 14). Luke deals with this problem differently by effectively removing John from the scene immediately prior to the baptism (Lk. 3.19-20). The exchange at Mt. 3.14-15 would have undermined Luke's attempt to de-emphasize John's role in the baptism. The saying about fulfilling all righteousness may also have struck Luke as too obscure to recycle.[47]

The omission of Mt. 12.5-7 (priests working in the temple are guiltless of profaning the Sabbath) and Mt. 13.14-15 (the extended quotation from Isa. 6.9-10) is hardly surprising if Luke is principally following Mark for these pericopae, although one might also suggest that Luke would have found no particular use for an argument over the niceties of the Law, that he consistently avoids Matthew's formula quotations (generally preferring either to place OT quotations in the mouth of his characters or to allude to the OT more subtly in his narrative) and that he goes on to quote Isa. 6.9-10 at Acts 28.26-27 and may not have wanted to use such an extensive quotation twice. It will nevertheless be argued in Chapter 6 that Luke picks up Mt. 12.5-7 at Lk. 10.25-37.

The omission of the commendation of Peter (Mt. 16.17-19) from Luke's account of Peter's Confession (Lk. 9.20-21) is more noteworthy, given the striking EA^{Mt-Lk} between Matthew and Luke at Mk 8.31 || Mt. 16.21 || Lk. 9.22, which were discussed in Chapter 4. It is doubtful that this has anything to do with 'Luke-pleasingness' or any supposed Lukan aversion to Peter. It has rather more to do with the fact that Luke is principally following Mark at this point. Moreover, Luke is substantially abbreviating Mark here, since he also omits Jesus' rebuke of Peter (Mk 8.32b-33 || Mt. 16.22-23). Indeed, Luke drastically abbreviates Mark throughout Luke 9, which begins with the mission of the Twelve (Mk 6.6b-13 || Lk. 9.1-6) and opinions about Jesus (Mk 6.14-16 || Lk. 9.7-9) before omitting the death of John the Baptist (Mk 6.17-29) and cutting to an abbreviated version of the return of the Twelve (Mk 6.30-31 || Lk. 9.10a) followed by the Feeding of the Five Thousand (Mk 6.32-44 || Lk. 9.10b-17). Luke then omits virtually the entirety of Mk 6.45–8.26 before arriving at Peter's Confession. Following Peter's Confession, Luke goes on to omit the discussion of the coming of Elijah in the descent from the mount of transfiguration (Mk 9.11-13) and drastically abbreviates Mark's account of the man with a possessed son (Mk 9.14-29 || Lk. 9.37-43a), while also abbreviating the argument among the disciples about which of them was the greatest and the strange exorcist (Mk 9.33-41 || Lk. 9.46-50) and omitting the warnings against temptation to sin (Mk 9.42-50; but see Lk. 17.1-2; 14.34-35).

At this point in his gospel, Luke is reworking Mark so extensively as virtually to produce a new composition of his own, perhaps, as Moessner suggests, to highlight a Deuteronomic prophet like Moses typology in preparation for his extended travel

---

[47] For the difficulties in interpreting this verse, see Davies and Allison, *Matthew*, vol. 1, 325–7.

narrative.⁴⁸ Luke notably omits the healing of the Blind Man of Bethsaida, which forms a hinge between Markan sections. Peter's Confession is not the great turning point in Luke's narrative that it is in Mark's;⁴⁹ Luke instead begins a major new section at Lk. 9.51. In a section of his gospel where Luke omits and compresses so much of Mark, it is hardly surprising if he does not always choose to add material from Matthew.

The final two Lukan omissions listed, Mt. 27.19, 24, both occur in the trial before Pilate. The first concerns the warning from Pilate's wife's dream and the second Pilate's subsequent handwashing, in a section where Matthew is otherwise substantially following Mark. Luke's version of this trial (Lk. 23.1-25) is notably different from both Matthew's and Mark's. Unlike the other two evangelists, Luke specifies the charges laid against Jesus (Lk. 23.2) in a way that lends greater verisimilitude to his account. Luke is also more specific about the 'many charges' against Jesus expressed at Mk 15.2-5 || Mt. 27.11-14 || Lk. 23.3-5. Unlike the other two evangelists, Luke inserts a hearing before Herod Antipas (Lk. 23.6-12). He further substantially rewrites the scene where the crowd is given the choice between Jesus and Barabbas (Mk 15.6-14 || Mt. 27.15-23 || Lk. 23.17-23) while (in common with John but not with Matthew or Mark) having Pilate three times declare Jesus innocent (Lk. 23.4, 13, 22; cf. Jn 18.38b; 19.4, 6). He also transfers the mockery of Jesus from Pilate's troops to Herod's (Lk. 23.11). Given such a major reworking of his source(s) Luke's failure to take over a couple of Matthean additions to Mark at a point where he is primarily following Mark is hardly noteworthy. That said, it is conceivable that Pilate's declaration of Jesus' innocence (e.g. at Lk. 23.13-16) reflects his wife's belief in Jesus' innocence and his washing his hands of responsibility for the verdict at Mt. 27.19, 24.

While Luke's omission of several of Matthew's additions to Mark turns out not to be so troublesome after all, there are also occasions where Luke may betray knowledge of Matthew's redaction of Mark beyond items noted as verbal EA^{Mt-Lk}. For example, at Mk 15.46 || Mt. 27.60 || Lk. 23.53 Matthew and Luke agree against Mark that the tomb in which Jesus was laid was one that had hitherto been unused, although they differ in how they express it. It may be that Matthew, writing for an audience familiar with Jewish burial customs, perceived a potential difficulty in Mark's account: normally, the burial of a condemned criminal would be in a communal tomb, so it is unlikely that the tomb would be discovered empty on Easter morning.⁵⁰ Matthew circumvents this by inserting the word 'new' into his account. Whether the point would have occurred independently to the more Gentile-inclined Luke is debatable, but he apparently clarifies it for his mainly Gentile audience by explaining that the tomb was one 'where no one had ever been laid'.

---

⁴⁸ David P. Moessner, 'Luke 9:1–50: Luke's Preview of the Journey of the Prophet like Moses of Deuteronomy', *JBL* 102 (1983), 575–605.

⁴⁹ For the significance of these pericopae in Mark, see Bas M.F. van Iersel, *Mark: A Reader-Response Commentary* (JSNTSup, 164; tr. W.H. Bisscheroux; Sheffield: Sheffield Academic Press, 1998), 270–86; John R. Donahue and Daniel J. Harrington, *The Gospel of Mark* (SP, 2; Collegeville: Michael Glazier, 2002), 257–8, 264–6.

⁵⁰ Byron R. McCane, *Roll Back the Stone: Death and Burial in the World of Jesus* (Harrisburg: Trinity Press International, 2003), 98–106.

Another possible example occurs at Lk. 14.1-6, the healing of a man with dropsy. On the face of it this is special L material, but the pericope resembles the Markan story of the healing of the man with a withered hand at Mk 3.1-6 || Mt. 12.9-14, which Luke has used at Lk. 6.6-11. In both cases the healing takes place on a Sabbath; in both Jesus is being watched by hostile Pharisees; in both Jesus challenges the onlookers with a question about what is lawful on the Sabbath; and in both Jesus proceeds to heal the man concerned. This suggests that Lk. 14.1-6 could be an imitation of Mt. 12.9-14 || Mk 3.1-6 || Lk. 6.6-11 created to provide another example of a Sabbath healing controversy in a section where Luke wants to show the Pharisees in a bad light. If so then Lk. 14.5, in which Jesus argues that his interlocutors would care for their animals on the Sabbath, betrays knowledge of the similar addition Matthew makes to Mark at Mt. 12.11, although the animal concerned has been changed from a sheep to an ox. As will be suggested in Chapter 6, the Lukan conclusion to the Widow's Son of Nain (Lk. 7.17) could similarly reflect the Matthean conclusion to the Raising of Jairus' Daughter (Mt. 9.26), and the exchange between Jesus and the Lawyer at Lk. 10.25-37 reflects some of the Matthean additions to the dispute over plucking corn at Mt. 12.3-7.

Five clearer examples of FH Luke's use of Matthean additions to Mark occur at Lk. 6.39 || Mt. 15.14 (Blind Leading the Blind), Lk. 12.54-56 || Mt. 16.2-3 (Signs of the Times), Lk. 13.28-29 || Mt. 8.11-12 (At Table with Abraham), Lk. 17.5 || Mt. 17.20 (Faith as a Mustard Seed) and Lk. 22.30 || Mt. 19.28 (Judging the Twelve Tribes). In each of these cases the Matthean addition is used in a different context, prompting proponents of the 2DH to argue that these additions must be Q material that Matthew has inserted into Markan contexts and to cite the alleged difficulty of FH Luke's separating such material from its Matthean contexts as an argument against the FH.[51] This point will be addressed in Chapter 6; for now we need only note that these constitute further counter-examples to the claim that FH Luke is ignorant of Matthew's redactional additions.

It is thus simply not true that the FH Luke fails to show knowledge of Matthew's additions to Mark. To assert this is to ignore all the major agreement ('Mark-Q overlap') passages along with all the other examples given above (and several more that will be suggested in Chapter 6). FH Luke has largely taken over Matthew's additions to Mark where he is principally following Matthew and has largely omitted them where he is principally following Mark. On either the FH or the 2DH, Luke has omitted a substantial amount of Markan material, so it is unsurprising that FH Luke should also omit a substantial amount of Matthean material. It would only appear surprising on the assumption that Luke felt obliged to include everything in his sources to which he did not positively object, but there is no warrant for assuming any such thing. Luke did not set out to produce an archive of source material but a composition of his own design, which he presumably wished to keep to a manageable length. To do this while including additional material of his own inevitably meant he could only use a selection of the material available in his sources, even if that required him to omit some material he might otherwise have liked to include. Luke's omission of Matthean material is thus

---

[51] So, e.g., Kirk, 'Memory', 477.

no argument against Luke's use of Matthew and can only appear so if one relentlessly focuses on what FH Luke did not take over from Matthew while resolutely ascribing everything he did to coincidence or Q.

Unpicking or 'minor disagreements'

Another influential objection to Luke's use of Matthew is that in many parallel passages where Matthew has added to or amended Mark, FH Luke allegedly takes over Matthew's additions more or less intact, adopts much of Matthew's amended version of Mark, but studiously avoids the sections where Matthew has followed Mark most closely, either omitting them altogether or totally rewording them. Thus, it is said, FH Luke must have carefully compared Matthew and Mark and then carefully unpicked the Matthean modifications from the Markan original to retain the former while discarding the latter. Such a procedure seems hard to envisage, both because it would be extremely difficult to carry out via a close comparison of uncial manuscripts and because it is hard to think of any reason why Luke should attempt it. This objection has been developed particularly in a series of closely argued articles by F. Gerald Downing[52] and subsequently taken up by other supporters of the 2DH.[53]

In his earliest article on the subject, Downing focuses on passages where Matthew substantially expands Mark, that is major agreement or 'Mark-Q overlap' passages. In a more recent article Downing extends the unpicking objection to a wider range of passages, including many in the triple tradition where no Q parallel is generally supposed to exist.

Downing also argues that since FH Luke has access to both Matthew and Mark, he might be expected to follow the common wording of both these sources where they agree, whereas no such expectation can apply to 2DH Luke working from Mark alone. Against this it should be pointed out that where FH Luke is principally following Mark, he has no need to consult Matthew and hence no reason to seek out the common wording of his sources. Indeed, to compare uncial manuscripts of Matthew and Mark to identify the common wording in order to follow it would be as much a difficult and eccentric exercise as doing so in order to avoid it. There is little to suggest that ancient authors went out of the way to incorporate the common witness of their sources, in terms of either wording or content.[54]

We are thus left with FH Luke's alleged tendency to avoid what Matthew has in common with Mark while adopting Matthew's additions or changes to Mark, or as Downing puts it:

---

[52] See especially Downing, 'Rehabilitation'; Downing, 'Disagreements'.
[53] E.g. Christopher M. Tuckett, 'The Current State of the Synoptic Problem' in Paul Foster, Andrew Gregory, John S. Kloppenborg and J. Verheyden (eds), *New Studies in the Synoptic Problem* (BETL, 139; Leuven: Leuven University Press, 2011), 9–50, here 44–5; Kirk, 'Memory', 476.
[54] Michael D. Goulder, 'Luke's Compositional Options', *NTS* 39 (1993), 150–2, here 150; Ken Olson, 'Unpicking on the Farrer Theory' in Mark Goodacre and Nicholas Perrin (eds), *Questioning Q* (London: SPCK, 2004), 127–50, here 131–8; Eve 'Synoptic Problem without Q', 566, n. 67.

It is possible, as has been said, to find piece-meal reasons for each change of Matthew's close quotation of Mark as it occurs. But it is still strange at the end to find that Luke ends up with 'pure Mark in Matthew' almost totally rejected; revised Mark in Matthew further revised; yet 'new' Matthew accepted, often as it stands.[55]

The passages where this objection is most likely to favour the 2DH are the so-called 'Mark-Q overlaps', which, on the FH, are where Luke would be following Matthew as his primary source. In these cases, Downing can argue that the pattern of agreements and disagreements has come about through Matthew conflating Mark and Q and Luke using Q alone; Luke's 'minor disagreements' with Matthew are thus to be explained by his agreement with a different source, namely Q.

Perhaps the most notable of these is the Beelzebul Controversy (Mt. 12.22-34 || Mk 3.22-30 || Lk. 11.14-24 – for which see Tables 5.4 and 5.5).[56] Here Downing divides the Matthean version into A material (where Matthew broadly copies Mark), B material (where Matthew has the same substance as Mark but in different words) and C material (where Matthew has material not found in Mark at all). After hinting that the B material might more naturally come from the same source as the C material rather than representing Matthew's redaction of Mark, Downing goes on to state that Luke takes over none of the A material, most of the B material (albeit in a different form) and virtually all the C material, thus indicating that Luke would have to have deliberately separated the Matthean material he chose to keep from the Markan substrate he chose to discard.

But as Ken Olson has observed, the amount of A material in this pericope is too small to establish Downing's case, and, moreover, since the parallel to Lk. 11.15 is not Mt. 12.24 but Mt. 9.34, Downing has omitted an A passage Luke does in fact takes over from Mark, τῷ ἄρξοντι τῶν δαίμονιων ἐκβαλλει τὰ δαιμόνια, 'He casts out demons by [Beelzebul], the prince of demons' (Mt. 9.34b || Mk 3.22b || Lk. 11.15b).[57] It is also

---

[55] Downing 'Redaction Criticism II', 44.
[56] Downing, 'Rehabilitation', 171–6; Olson, 'Unpicking', 139–42; Eve, 'Devil' 32–42.
[57] It is admittedly far from obvious why Luke should choose to follow Mt. 9.32-34 rather than Mt. 12.12-28 here; it is hard to see what Luke could achieve by employing Mt. 9.32-34 that he could not just as well have achieved by adapting Mt. 12.22-24. Perhaps the best one can suggest is that, for reasons now lost to us, this is how Luke's memory happened to work at this point. That Luke was reliant on memory is suggested by the inclusion of Βεελζεβοὺλ at Lk. 11.15b, indicating contamination from Mt. 12.24b (or possibly Mk 3.22b). One might hazard a guess that Luke (or his audience) was more familiar with the wording of the 'prince of demons' accusation at Mk 3.22 || Mt. 9.34, leading Luke to recall its immediate Matthean context along with this version of the saying, which in effect *retains* A material. In discussing this difficulty Kloppenborg, 'Farrer/Mark', 229, helpfully suggests that 'one might retort that the performative context in which Luke composed had already conflated Matthew 9 with Matthew 12 (inadvertently dropping the blind man)' but at once goes on to point out that it is just as plausible 'to suppose, as the 2DH does, that Mt. 9.32-34 is Matthew's abbreviated (and elaborated) version of Q 11.14-15'. The point is well made, but in turn invites the question why 2DH Matthew should have followed the wording of Q 11.14-15 when he was employing it out of sequence at Mt. 9.32-34 rather than when he was combining Mark and Q at Mt. 12.22-28; one might have expected Matthew to have adapted Q (or Mark) more freely at Mt. 9.32-34 than at Mt. 12.22-24. None of this, however, is germane to evaluating the unpicking argument, which must simply accept that FH Luke would be using Mt. 9.32–34 here.

not entirely accurate to say that Luke has omitted the other two A passages. One of them, Mk 3.27 || Mt. 12.29, concerns binding the strong man and plundering his goods. This is loosely paralleled by Lk. 11.21-22 which concerns the overcoming of a strong man by a stronger one who plunders his goods. The imagery and wording are different, but Luke's version is based on the same underlying idea. The other A passage is Mk 3.28-29 || Mt. 12.31-32, the Sin against the Holy Spirit, where the Matthean and Markan versions diverge quite a bit (so one might class this as a B passage). While Luke does not have a parallel to Mt. 12.31, he does have one to Mt. 12.32 at Lk. 12.10 (with wording that looks closer to Matthew than to Mark), and since Mt. 12.31 and 12.32 make essentially the same point, it is not especially surprising that Luke should choose to retain one version of the saying and not the other.

Downing also points out that although Luke takes over most of the B material, his changes to it make it look less like Mark, not more.[58] But if Luke were working from Matthew alone, this is precisely what one would expect. If Y reworks X's text and then Z comes along and reworks Y's, one would expect Z to be less like X than Y is, especially if Y and Z have any inclination to paraphrase and not just copy.[59] For Z's text to end up looking more like X when Z is neither using X nor has any reason to conform his version to X would be a strange coincidence indeed. The pattern of agreements in the body of the Beelzebul Controversy set out in Table 5.4 is thus compatible with what one might expect if Luke were using Matthew alone.

In Table 5.4, text in bold indicates where Luke has taken over words that Matthew shares with Mark (of which there are sixteen, if one counts close variants). Underlined text indicates words Matthew and Luke have in common that are not from Mark, of which there are twenty-four (or twenty-two if one discounts δὲ and εἶπον in Lk. 11.15) plus a further thirty-four where Matthew has added material not paralleled in Mark at all (Mt. 12.27-28 || Lk. 11.19-20).[60] Thus, where Matthew has reworked Mark, Luke is not all that much more inclined to take his changes to Mark than to accept what he has in common with Mark.

It is true that Luke is particularly close to Matthew in the material they share at Mt. 12.27-28 || Lk. 11.19-20, but this no more supports the 2DH than the FH. On the FH, Luke would have chosen to reproduce just this section of Matthew almost verbatim, while on the 2DH, Matthew and Luke must have both independently decided to copy just this section of Q almost verbatim, which requires a greater coincidence. Conversely, whatever explanation the 2DH might offer why the wording of the verses proved particularly attractive to both Matthew and Luke will apply equally well to FH Luke's use of Matthew.

---

[58] Downing, 'Rehabilitation', 172.
[59] Cf. Goodacre, 'Taking Our Leave', 217–18.
[60] These numbers become seventeen and twenty-one respectively if one takes Βεελζεβοὺλ at Mt. 12.24 || Lk. 11.15 as deriving from Βεελζεβοὺλ at Mk 3.22.

Table 5.4 The Beelzebul Controversy.

Mt. 12.22-28	Mt. 9.32-34	Mk 3.22-26	Lk. 11.14-20
Τότε προσηνέχθη αὐτῷ δαιμονιζόμενος τυφλὸς καὶ κωφός · καὶ ἐθεράπευσεν αὐτόν, ὥστε τὸν κωφὸν λαλεῖν καὶ βλέπειν. 23 καὶ ἐξίσταντο πάντες οἱ ὄχλοι καὶ ἔλεγον· Μήτι οὗτός ἐστιν ὁ υἱὸς Δαυίδ; 24 οἱ δὲ Φαρισαῖοι ἀκούσαντες εἶπον· Οὗτος οὐκ **ἐκβάλλει τὰ δαιμόνια** εἰ μὴ ἐν τῷ **Βεελζεβοὺλ ἄρχοντι τῶν δαιμονίων**. 25 εἰδὼς δὲ τὰς ἐνθυμήσεις αὐτῶν εἶπεν αὐτοῖς· Πᾶσα **βασιλεία μερισθεῖσα** καθ' **ἑαυτῆς ἐρημοῦται**, καὶ πᾶσα πόλις ἢ οἰκία μερισθεῖσα καθ' ἑαυτῆς οὐ σταθήσεται. 26 καὶ **εἰ ὁ Σατανᾶς** τὸν Σατανᾶν ἐκβάλλει, **ἐφ' ἑαυτὸν ἐμερίσθη**· πῶς οὖν σταθήσεται ἡ βασιλεία αὐτοῦ; 27 καὶ εἰ ἐγὼ ἐν Βεελζεβοὺλ ἐκβάλλω τὰ δαιμόνια, οἱ υἱοὶ ὑμῶν ἐν τίνι ἐκβάλλουσιν; διὰ τοῦτο αὐτοὶ κριταὶ ἔσονται ὑμῶν. 28 εἰ δὲ ἐν πνεύματι θεοῦ ἐγὼ ἐκβάλλω τὰ δαιμόνια, ἄρα ἔφθασεν ἐφ' ὑμᾶς ἡ βασιλεία τοῦ θεοῦ.	Αὐτῶν δὲ ἐξερχομένων ἰδοὺ προσήνεγκαν αὐτῷ ἄνθρωπον κωφὸν δαιμονιζόμενον· 33 καὶ ἐκβληθέντος τοῦ δαιμονίου ἐλάλησεν ὁ κωφός. καὶ ἐθαύμασαν οἱ ὄχλοι λέγοντες· Οὐδέποτε ἐφάνη οὕτως ἐν τῷ Ἰσραήλ. οἱ δὲ Φαρισαῖοι ἔλεγον· Ἐν τῷ ἄρχοντι τῶν δαιμονίων ἐκβάλλει τὰ δαιμόνια.	καὶ οἱ γραμματεῖς οἱ ἀπὸ Ἱεροσολύμων καταβάντες ἔλεγον ὅτι **Βεελζεβοὺλ** ἔχει καὶ ὅτι **ἐν τῷ ἄρχοντι τῶν δαιμονίων ἐκβάλλει τὰ δαιμόνια**. 23 καὶ προσκαλεσάμενος αὐτοὺς ἐν παραβολαῖς ἔλεγεν αὐτοῖς· Πῶς δύναται Σατανᾶς Σατανᾶν ἐκβάλλειν; 24 καὶ ἐὰν **βασιλεία ἐφ' ἑαυτὴν** μερισθῇ, οὐ δύναται σταθῆναι ἡ βασιλεία ἐκείνη· 25 καὶ ἐὰν οἰκία ἐφ' ἑαυτὴν μερισθῇ, οὐ δυνήσεται ἡ οἰκία ἐκείνη σταθῆναι· 26 **καὶ εἰ ὁ Σατανᾶς** ἀνέστη **ἐφ' ἑαυτὸν** καὶ **ἐμερίσθη**, οὐ δύναται στῆναι ἀλλὰ τέλος ἔχει.	Καὶ ἦν ἐκβάλλων δαιμόνιον κωφόν· ἐγένετο δὲ τοῦ δαιμονίου ἐξελθόντος ἐλάλησεν ὁ κωφός. καὶ ἐθαύμασαν οἱ ὄχλοι· 15 τινὲς δὲ ἐξ αὐτῶν εἶπον· Ἐν **Βεελζεβοὺλ τῷ ἄρχοντι τῶν δαιμονίων ἐκβάλλει τὰ δαιμόνια**· 16 ἕτεροι δὲ πειράζοντες σημεῖον ἐξ οὐρανοῦ ἐζήτουν παρ' αὐτοῦ. 17 αὐτὸς δὲ εἰδὼς αὐτῶν τὰ διανοήματα εἶπεν αὐτοῖς· Πᾶσα **βασιλεία ἐφ' ἑαυτὴν** διαμερισθεῖσα ἐρημοῦται, καὶ οἶκος ἐπὶ οἶκον πίπτει. 18 **εἰ δὲ καὶ ὁ Σατανᾶς ἐφ' ἑαυτὸν** διε**μερίσθη**, πῶς σταθήσεται ἡ βασιλεία αὐτοῦ; ὅτι λέγετε ἐν Βεελζεβοὺλ ἐκβάλλειν με τὰ δαιμόνια. 19 εἰ δὲ ἐγὼ ἐν Βεελζεβοὺλ ἐκβάλλω τὰ δαιμόνια, οἱ υἱοὶ ὑμῶν ἐν τίνι ἐκβάλλουσιν; διὰ τοῦτο αὐτοὶ ὑμῶν κριταὶ ἔσονται. 20 εἰ δὲ ἐν δακτύλῳ θεοῦ ἐκβάλλω τὰ δαιμόνια, ἄρα ἔφθασεν ἐφ' ὑμᾶς ἡ βασιλεία τοῦ θεοῦ.

The section concludes with the Binding of the Strong Man, and sayings about gathering and scattering and the Sin against the Holy Spirit, set out in Table 5.5:

Table 5.5 Overpowering the Strong Man and Blaspheming the Spirit.

Mt. 12.29-32	Mk 3.27-30	Lk. 11.21-24
ἢ πῶς δύναταί τις εἰσελθεῖν εἰς τὴν οἰκίαν τοῦ **ἰσχυροῦ** καὶ τὰ σκεύη αὐτοῦ ἁρπάσαι, ἐὰν μὴ πρῶτον δήσῃ τὸν ἰσχυρόν; καὶ τότε τὴν οἰκίαν αὐτοῦ διαρπάσει. 30 <u>ὁ μὴ ὢν μετ' ἐμοῦ κατ' ἐμοῦ ἐστιν, καὶ ὁ μὴ συνάγων μετ' ἐμοῦ σκορπίζει.</u> 31 διὰ τοῦτο λέγω ὑμῖν, πᾶσα ἁμαρτία καὶ βλασφημία **ἀφεθήσεται** τοῖς ἀνθρώποις, ἡ δὲ τοῦ πνεύματος **βλασφημ**ία οὐκ ἀφεθήσεται. 32 καὶ ὃς ἐὰν εἴπῃ <u>λόγον</u> κατὰ <u>τοῦ υἱοῦ τοῦ ἀνθρώπου,</u> <u>ἀφεθήσεται αὐτῷ·</u> ὃς δ' ἂν εἴπῃ κατὰ τοῦ πνεύματος τοῦ ἁγίου, <u>οὐκ ἀφεθήσεται</u> αὐτῷ οὔτε ἐν τούτῳ τῷ αἰῶνι οὔτε ἐν τῷ μέλλοντι.	27 ἀλλ' οὐδεὶς δύναται εἰς τὴν οἰκίαν τοῦ **ἰσχυροῦ** εἰσελθὼν τὰ σκεύη αὐτοῦ διαρπάσαι ἐὰν μὴ πρῶτον τὸν ἰσχυρὸν δήσῃ, καὶ τότε τὴν οἰκίαν αὐτοῦ διαρπάσει. 28 Ἀμὴν λέγω ὑμῖν ὅτι πάντα **ἀφεθήσεται** τοῖς υἱοῖς τῶν ἀνθρώπων, τὰ ἁμαρτήματα καὶ αἱ βλασφημίαι ὅσα ἐὰν βλασφημήσωσιν· 29 ὃς δ' ἂν **βλασφημ**ήσῃ <u>εἰς τὸ</u> <u>πνεῦμα τὸ ἅγιον,</u> οὐκ ἔχει ἄφεσιν εἰς τὸν αἰῶνα, ἀλλὰ ἔνοχός ἐστιν αἰωνίου ἁμαρτήματος. 30 ὅτι ἔλεγον· Πνεῦμα ἀκάθαρτον ἔχει.	21 ὅταν ὁ **ἰσχυρὸς** καθωπλισμένος φυλάσσῃ τὴν ἑαυτοῦ αὐλήν, ἐν εἰρήνῃ ἐστὶν τὰ ὑπάρχοντα αὐτοῦ· 22 ἐπὰν a δὲ ἰσχυρότερος αὐτοῦ ἐπελθὼν νικήσῃ αὐτόν, τὴν πανοπλίαν αὐτοῦ αἴρει ἐφ' ᾗ ἐπεποίθει, καὶ τὰ σκῦλα αὐτοῦ διαδίδωσιν. 23 <u>ὁ μὴ ὢν μετ' ἐμοῦ κατ' ἐμοῦ ἐστιν, καὶ ὁ μὴ συνάγων μετ' ἐμοῦ σκορπίζει.</u> {12.10 καὶ πᾶς ὃς ἐρεῖ <u>λόγον</u> εἰς <u>τὸν υἱὸν τοῦ</u> <u>ἀνθρώπου,</u> **ἀφεθήσεται** <u>αὐτῷ</u> τῷ δὲ <u>εἰς τὸ ἅγιον</u> <u>πνεῦμα **βλασφημ**ήσαντι <u>οὐκ</u> **ἀφεθήσεται**</u>.} 24 Ὅταν τὸ ἀκάθαρτον πνεῦμα ἐξέλθῃ ἀπὸ τοῦ ἀνθρώπου, διέρχεται δι' ἀνύδρων τόπων ζητοῦν ἀνάπαυσιν, καὶ μὴ a εὑρίσκον λέγει· Ὑποστρέψω εἰς τὸν οἶκόν μου ὅθεν ἐξῆλθον·

At first sight, this set of parallels appears to support Downing's case rather better. Luke refuses the common witness of Matthew and Mark in the Binding of the Strong Man, takes over verbatim the Matthean addition about gathering and scattering and lacks an immediate parallel to the Sin against the Holy Spirit (although he has a more distant one at Lk. 12.10). But closer examination dispels this initial appearance.

Matthew's version of the Binding of the Strong Man is very close to Mark's; so much so that there is nothing in the Matthean text to indicate any Mark-Q overlap. Luke has a parallel to this material that differs not only in wording but in imagery: the Mark/Matthew domestic burglary has become the invasion of a palace. Here FH Luke could have rewritten Matthew as easily as Mark; no 'unpicking' will have taken place. The 2DH alternative, that Luke has taken his version from Q, has little to commend it, not least because Luke's version looks so thoroughly Lukan.[61]

---

[61] Eve, 'Devil', 38–41; see also Goulder, *Luke*, 505; Evans, *Luke*, 492–3, H. Benedict Green, 'Matthew 12.22-50 and Parallels: An Alternative to Matthean Conflation' in Christopher M. Tuckett (ed.), *Synoptic Studies: The Ampleforth Conferences of 1982 and 1983* (JSNTSup, 7; Sheffield: JSOT Press, 1984), 157–76, here 162. For the view that Luke took the passage from Q, see Marshall, *Luke*, 476–7; Joseph A. Fitzmyer, *The Gospel according to Luke (X–XXIV): A New Translation with Introduction and Commentary* (AB, 28A; New York: Doubleday, 1985), 918, regards it as probably partially from Q. For arguments for and against its inclusion in Q, see John S. Kloppenborg, *Q Parallels: Synopsis, Critical Notes & Concordance* (Sonoma, CA: Polebridge, 1988), 92. *CEQ*, 234, regards the Binding of the Strong Man as being only probably in Q.

Luke and Matthew indeed share a sequence of fifteen identical words on gathering and scattering, but quite apart from the fact that on the 2DH, Luke and Matthew must have once again both independently decided to copy Q verbatim here, the saying fits Matthew's context rather better than Luke's. In Matthew, it leads into the saying about the Sin against the Holy Spirit and so helps reinforce the point that one must choose sides in the way one perceives Jesus' exorcisms; Matthew makes this connection clear with his διὰ τοῦτο at Mt. 12.31. In Luke, however, it is immediately followed by the Return of the Unclean Spirit, with which its connection is less clear (it disrupts the connection between the plundered palace and the vacated house, which are both images of exorcism).[62] On the 2DH one might make the case that Matthew's διὰ τοῦτο is his redactional means of joining Q 11.23 to the Blasphemy saying adapted from Mark. But then, either the Q 11.14-24 sequence is strangely disjointed or if Q 11.23 originally followed Q 11.14-20 as a comment on different types of exorcism, then the Binding of the Strong Man could not have stood at Q 11.21-22. The third possibility, that Q 11.23 was a floating saying that Luke and Matthew independently inserted at the same place, is too improbable to contemplate. That Luke took Lk. 11.23 from Mt. 12.30 would thus seem the least problematic explanation (or at least, no more problematic than anything that might be proposed on the 2DH).[63]

The parallels in the Blasphemy against the Holy Spirit are complex. Matthew has two versions of the saying against Mark's one, but neither of Matthew's versions looks especially close to Mark's; the division into A, B and C material is thus not so clear here as Downing suggests.[64] At best one might see B material at Mt. 12.31 and 12.32b, with C material at Mt. 12.32a, but the distinction is far from clean. While Lk. 12.10a bears some resemblance to the C material at Mt. 12.32a, it is far from verbatim, and Lk. 12.10b is closer in wording to Mk 3.29a. Luke's version can hardly be described as a rejection of A material, partial acceptance of B material and complete adoption of C material. *CEQ* reconstructs Q 12.10 more or less in accordance with Mt. 12.32 here (which avoids the need for 2DH Matthew to have conflated Mark and Q).[65] The Matthean doublet is thus formed by appending the Q version of the saying to Markan one. But then Lk. 12.10 may just as well be derived from a reminiscence of Matthew and Mark as of Q and Mark. Moreover, in creating his doublet from Mark and Q, 2DH Matthew must have started by adapting Mk 3.28 for the first version of the saying, then switched to Q 12.10 for the second and finally switched back to Mk 3.29b to append the detail that blaspheming against the Holy Spirit has eternal consequences. No doubt Matthew could have done this, but nothing in the wording of the parallels demands that he did. They could just as plausibly be interpreted as Matthew creating his double version of the saying out of Mark's single version, with echoes of Mark's wording occurring throughout (especially if Matthew's Christological τοῦ υἱοῦ τοῦ ἀνθρώπου was suggested by Mark's generic τοῖς υἱοῖς τῶν ἀνθρώπων). There is nothing

---

[62] For which see Farrer, 'Dispensing', 70–1. But one might make the case that the saying about gathering and scattering serves to introduce the danger of leaving the house empty; one must still choose sides.
[63] Eve, 'Devil', 41–2; R.T. Simpson, 'The Major Agreements of Matthew and Luke against Mark', *NTS* 12 (1966), 273–84, here 281–2; Goulder, *Luke*, 505–6.
[64] Downing, 'Rehabilitation', 173–4.
[65] *CEQ*, 310.

to indicate that Luke has strained out A material and swallowed C material or in any other way 'unpicked' Matthew from Mark.[66]

Two further examples Downing gives where the 2DH postulates a Mark-Q overlap are the mission discourses at Mt. 9.37-10.16 || Lk. 10.1-16 and the apocalyptic discourse at Mt. 24-25, in comparison with Luke's use of parallel material in Lk. 12, 17 and 19.[67] Both these differ from the Beelzebul Controversy in that while Luke has only a single version of the former, he has two mission discourses (Lk. 9.1-6 || Mk 6.b-16 and Lk. 10.1-12 || Mt. 9.37-38; 10.7-16) and two eschatological discourses (Lk. 17.20-37|| Mt. 24.17-41 and Lk. 21 || Mk 13), so that at first sight it looks plausible that in one case Luke follows the Markan version and in the other Q, while Matthew has conflated Mark and Q. But Olson has shown that in both these examples the situation is not quite as Downing describes. For example, the one A verse Luke omits from Matthew's version of the Mission Discourse (Mt. 9.36 || Mk 6.34) is omitted alongside the B/C verse Mt. 9.35 || Mk 6.6b, so Luke is not differentially rejecting A material here, but simply providing his own introduction in place of Matthew's.[68] Moreover, Luke also omits Mk 6.34b (the saying about sheep without a shepherd) in his parallel to the Markan pericope at Lk. 9.11, which hardly suggests that it was so congenial to Luke that he could not have omitted it had he encountered it in its Matthean context at Mt. 9.36.[69]

The eschatological discourses present a different kind of problem, since, as Downing observes, FH Luke has deployed material from Matthew 24–25 and Mark 13 across different contexts in Luke 12, 17, 19 and 21. The relevant material in Luke 12 is minimal (Mt. 10.19-20 || Mk 13.11 || Lk 12.11-12), comprising the promise that the Holy Spirit will teach people what to say when they are brought before the authorities. The wording is not particularly close to either Matthew or Mark, although it is slightly closer to Matthew, and is presumably a loose recollection of Mt. 10.19-20 incorporated by Luke immediately after his version of the saying about Blasphemy against the Holy Spirit. The rest of the Luke 12 material (Lk. 12.39-46 || Mt. 24.43-51) parallels a block of Matthean material readily separable from its context.

In Chapter 6 it will be argued that in Luke 17 and 19, Luke is following Matthew in Matthew's sequence, while in Luke 21 he is following Mark. The material in Luke 19 in any case presents no particular problems (neither does Downing suggest that it does), since it simply comprises the Lukan version of the Parable of the Pounds/Talents (Lk. 19.11-27 || Mt. 25.14-30), which clearly involves no unpicking of Matthew from Mark. We are left then with the Matthean material in Lk. 17.22-37 and the Markan in Luke 21.

Downing's complaint then largely boils down to Luke's avoiding Matthew's parallels to Mark when selectively employing material from Mt. 24.17-41 at Lk. 17.20-37. Downing nevertheless acknowledges that this is not entirely the case, since Lk. 17.23 parallels Mk 13.21. He takes the Matthean parallel to be Mt. 24.26, which enables him to claim that Luke has here followed Mark rather than Matthew (which would

---

[66] Eve, 'Devil', 29–31; Green, 'Matthew 12.22–50', 162–4.
[67] Downing, 'Rehabilitation', 177–80.
[68] There is a parallel to Mt. 9.35 || Mk 6.6b at Lk. 8.1, but this is in a different discourse; this B/C verse has still been replaced by Luke's own introduction to the Mission of the Seventy at Lk. 10.1.
[69] Olson, 'Unpicking', 143–4.

be equally odd if 2DH Luke were using Q), on the grounds that Luke's ἐκεῖ·Ἰδοὺ ὧδε echoes Mk 13.21 more closely than Mt. 24.26.⁷⁰ But the parallel to Mk 13.21 is Mt. 24.23:

Table 5.6 Mk 13.21 and parallels.

Mt. 24.23	Mk 13.21	Lk. 17.23
τότε ἐάν τις ὑμῖν εἴπῃ·Ἰδοὺ ὧδε ὁ χριστός, ἤ·Ὧδε, μὴ πιστεύσητε·	καὶ τότε ἐάν τις ὑμῖν εἴπῃ·Ἴδε ὧδε ὁ χριστός, Ἴδε ἐκεῖ, μὴ πιστεύετε·	καὶ ἐροῦσιν ὑμῖν·Ἰδοὺ ἐκεῖ· Ἰδοὺ ὧδε · μὴ ἀπέλθητε μηδὲ διώξητε.

There is also A material at Lk. 17.31:

Table 5.7 Mk 13.15-16 and parallels.

Mt. 24.17-18	Mk 13.15-16	Lk 17.31
ὁ ἐπὶ τοῦ δώματος μὴ καταβάτω ἆραι τὰ ἐκ τῆς οἰκίας αὐτοῦ, 18 καὶ ὁ ἐν τῷ ἀγρῷ μὴ ἐπιστρεψάτω ὀπίσω ἆραι τὸ ἱμάτιον αὐτοῦ.	ὁ ἐπὶ τοῦ δώματος μὴ καταβάτω μηδὲ εἰσελθάτω τι ἆραι ἐκ τῆς οἰκίας αὐτοῦ, 16 καὶ ὁ εἰς τὸν ἀγρὸν μὴ ἐπιστρεψάτω εἰς τὰ ὀπίσω ἆραι τὸ ἱμάτιον αὐτοῦ.	ἐν ἐκείνῃ τῇ ἡμέρᾳ ὃς ἔσται ἐπὶ τοῦ δώματος καὶ τὰ σκεύη αὐτοῦ ἐν τῇ οἰκίᾳ, μὴ καταβάτω ἆραι αὐτά, καὶ ὁ ἐν ἀγρῷ ὁμοίως μὴ ἐπιστρεψάτω εἰς τὰ ὀπίσω.

Here there are eleven words common to all three accounts, plus the near agreements of τῆς οἰκίας/τῇ οἰκίᾳ and ἐν τῷ ἀγρῷ/εἰς τὸν ἀγρὸν. It hardly looks as if Luke has unpicked Matthew from Mark here; instead Luke once again represents a third writer adapting a second writer's adaptation of the first, so that he ends up slightly further from Mark than does Matthew.⁷¹

The remainder of the Matthew 24 material employed in Luke 17 occurs in two Matthean blocks, Mt. 24.27-28 and Mt. 24.37-41. The second of these, about the days of Noah, stands out as a distinct addition to the Markan discourse and would be easily recognizable as such to someone who knows Mark as well as we are supposing FH Luke does. The sayings about lightning and eagles at Mt. 24.27-28 represent other easily separable Matthean additions. One might say there is unpicking of a sort here, but it would be of a sort that was easily accomplished (comparable, say, to Matthew's transfer of Mk 13.9-13 to Mt. 10.17-22). The 2DH alternative is that Matthew has assembled Mt. 24.23-51 by combining Mark and Q in the sequence Mk 13.21-23, Q 17.23-24, Q 17.37b, Mk 13.24-32, Q 17.26-36, Q 12.39-46. Matthew could presumably have done this, but 2DH Matthew's compilation of his discourse from Mark and Q is no more obviously compelling than FH Luke's compilation from various parts of Matthew.

A further major agreement that might seem to support Downing's case occurs in the Parable of the Mustard Seed.

---

⁷⁰ Downing, 'Rehabilitation', 178.
⁷¹ So also Olson, 'Unpicking', 144–5.

Table 5.8 The Mustard Seed.

Mt. 13.31-32	Mk 4.30-32	Lk. 13.18-19
Ἄλλην *παραβολὴν παρέθηκεν* αὐτοῖς λέγων· Ὁμοία ἐστὶν ἡ **βασιλεία** τῶν οὐρανῶν **κόκκῳ σινάπεως**, ὃν λαβὼν ἄνθρωπος ἔσπειρεν ἐν τῷ ἀγρῷ αὐτοῦ· 32 ὃ *μικρότερον μέν ἐστιν πάντων τῶν σπερμάτων, ὅταν δὲ* αὐξηθῇ *μεῖζον τῶν λαχάνων ἐστὶν* καὶ γίνεται δένδρον, ὥστε ἐλθεῖν **τὰ πετεινὰ τοῦ οὐρανοῦ** καὶ κατασκηνοῦν ἐν τοῖς κλάδοις αὐτοῦ.	Καὶ ἔλεγεν· Πῶς ὁμοιώσωμεν τὴν **βασιλείαν** τοῦ θεοῦ, ἢ ἐν τίνι αὐτὴν παραβολῇ θῶμεν; 31 ὡς **κόκκῳ σινάπεως**, ὃς ὅταν σπαρῇ ἐπὶ τῆς γῆς, *μικρότερον ὂν πάντων τῶν σπερμάτων τῶν* ἐπὶ τῆς γῆς— 32 καὶ ὅταν σπαρῇ, ἀναβαίνει καὶ γίνεται *μεῖζον πάντων τῶν λαχάνων* καὶ ποιεῖ κλάδους μεγάλους, ὥστε δύνασθαι ὑπὸ τὴν σκιὰν αὐτοῦ **τὰ πετεινὰ τοῦ οὐρανοῦ** κατασκηνοῦν.	Ἔλεγεν οὖν· Τίνι ὁμοία ἐστὶν ἡ **βασιλεία** τοῦ θεοῦ, καὶ τίνι ὁμοιώσω αὐτήν; 19 ὁμοία ἐστὶν **κόκκῳ σινάπεως**, ὃν λαβὼν ἄνθρωπος ἔβαλεν εἰς κῆπον ἑαυτοῦ, καὶ ηὔξησεν καὶ ἐγένετο εἰς δένδρον, καὶ **τὰ πετεινὰ τοῦ οὐρανοῦ** κατεσκήνωσεν ἐν τοῖς κλάδοις αὐτοῦ.

In Table 5.8, EA^Mk-Mt are shown in italics, EA^Mt-Lk underlined and IA in bold. Dotted underlining indicates partial agreement between Matthew and Luke, while wavy underlining indicates EA^Mk-Lk. The A material (matter taken over from Mark by Matthew but rejected by Luke) consists of the contrast between the smallest of seeds and the greatest of shrubs while the B material is mainly the way 'is like' is expressed, the fact that the seed becomes a tree rather than a shrub and that the birds make their nests in its branches rather than its shade. This would be consistent with Luke's use of Matthew alone but for two things. The first is that the double question with which Luke begins is closer to Mk 4.30 than to Mt. 13.31, suggesting that FH Luke must apparently have recalled the Markan formulation here, although this would equally be the case with 2DH Luke.[72] The second is Luke's non-use of the A material, which might be taken to suggest unpicking.[73]

In reply, Goulder argues, first, that Matthew's changes to Mark (which Luke mostly follows) are characteristic of Matthew and, second, that Luke's omission of the A material is entirely due to the different use to which he puts this parable in its Lukan context. While Matthew and Mark both draw attention to the contrast between the tiny seed and the large plant into which it grows, Luke focuses on the entry of the Gentiles (represented by the birds) into the kingdom (the immediate context being Jewish rejection) and so abbreviates the parable accordingly.[74]

---

[72] Zeba Antonin Crook, 'The Synoptic Parables of the Mustard Seed and the Leaven: A Test-Case for the Two-Document, Two-Gospel, and Farrer-Goulder Hypotheses', *JSNT* 78 (2000), 23–48, here 30–1, sees this as potentially problematic for the 2DH but proposes that the double question at Lk.13.18 is closer to Luke's own formulation at Lk. 7.31 'suggesting the possibility that Luke's similarity to Mark here is coincidental', although Crook goes on to say this is only a partial answer to the problem.

[73] Crook, 'Mustard Seed', 46. Crook introduces his discussion by talking about conflation but goes on to cite eleven words used by both Mark and Matthew and not Luke, the quite different phenomenon of alleged unpicking.

[74] Goulder, *Luke*, 41–3. See also Goodacre, 'Taking Our Leave', 216–17, who points to the extent of triple agreements in this passage, citing Sanders, 'Overlaps', 458. Crook, 'Mustard Seed', 26–9, is less sanguine that all of Matthew's changes to Mark are characteristic of Matthew, but the Matthean redactional inconsistencies he finds affect the 2DH as much as the FH.

Luke's introduction is closer to Mark's than to Matthew's; according to the *CEQ* reconstruction this is because Q's introduction resembles Mark.⁷⁵ Oddly, then, Q and Mark resemble each other more than either resembles Matthew at this point; 2DH Matthew has apparently refused the common witness of Mark and Q. In fact, however, Mt. 13.31a simply repeats the wording of Mt. 13.24a to fit a context where Jesus is delivering a number of parables in succession. In Luke, however, the Parable of the Mustard Seed follows directly after the Healing of the Crippled Woman on the Sabbath (Lk. 13.10-17), which would have made Matthew's introduction unsuitable and so may explain why Luke should resort to a recollection of Mark's. Luke's 'therefore' (οὖν) makes the parable a comment on what has just gone before, and so contrasts the inclusivity of the kingdom with the exclusivity exhibited by the synagogue ruler's carping at a healing on the Sabbath.⁷⁶

This seems a plausible enough explanation, but the important question is whether it seems more or less plausible than the 2DH alternative that Luke essentially followed Q while Matthew combined Q and Mark. 2DH Matthew would have to have taken μικρότερον ... πάντων τῶν σπερμάτων, ὅταν ... μεῖζον τῶν λαχάνων ... ὥστε ... [τὰ πετεινὰ τοῦ οὐρανοῦ καὶ κατασκηνοῦν?] from Mark, and Ὁμοία ἐστὶν ... [κόκκῳ σινάπεως?] ὃν λαβὼν ἄνθρωπος ... δένδρον ... ἐν τοῖς κλάδοις αὐτοῦ from Q, while apparently interleaving the Markan καὶ γίνεται ... ὥστε construction with the Q version of the text. Arguably, his awkward combination of Mark's large shrub with Q's big tree suggests that he may have done something of the sort, although this could equally well be explained as Matthew's clumsy reworking of Mark at the point he introduced the biblical image of the tree. Presumably 2DH Matthew will have preferred the Q version with its biblical echo while wanting to preserve the Markan contrast between small beginnings and impressive results. The main difficulty is that the close conflation that results would seem to be atypical of the way ancient authors are generally supposed to have worked, and that 2DH Matthew could have obtained his desired result more simply by following Mark for the bulk of the parable and replacing its conclusion with Q's. The 2DH explanation for this passage is thus not obviously more compelling than the FH one offered by Goulder, in which no deliberate unpicking has taken place.⁷⁷

---

⁷⁵ *CEQ*, 401–3, tentatively reconstructs Q here as looking broadly similar to Luke, with the apparent support of *G. Thom.* 20.

⁷⁶ Cf. David K. Bryan, 'Transformation of the Mustard Seed and Leaven in the Gospel of Luke', *NovT* 58 (2016), 115–34, who argues that Luke redeploys the Parable of the Mustard Seed to emphasize the choice demanded by the kingdom's assured coming, rather than the process of growth or the contrast with its beginnings.

⁷⁷ Crook, 'Mustard Seed', 44–5, points to the difficulty of FH Luke's changing Matthew's ἔσπειρεν to ἔβαλεν, when the former word is clearly more applicable to sowing a seed, and likewise ἀγρῷ to κῆπον, given that in a Jewish context a field is a more appropriate place to grow mustard than a garden, and that κῆπος is otherwise rare in the NT (occurring elsewhere only in John). That said, βάλλω is a word Luke uses eighteen times, so he is not obviously averse to it. He has just used it in a horticultural context at Lk. 13.8 to describe putting manure on the barren fig tree. Conversely, Lk. 8.12 (∥ Mk 4.15) suppresses Mark's σπείρεται in describing the seed 'sown' on the path and σπειρόμενοι at 8.13 (∥ Mk 4.16) of the seed on the rocky ground. Likewise Lk. 8.14 prefers to speak of the seed that fell (πεσόν) among thorns as against the seed sown among them as in Matthew and Mark. A Luke working from memory should not be thought of as deliberately considering every word that differs from Matthew and Mark, but maybe at 13.19 he envisages the man casually throwing the seed into the garden (instead of carefully sowing it where he should) and the mustard plant growing even so: Luke's Kingdom of God does not grow in the way Jesus' synagogue-based interlocutors believe it should, any more than Jesus' healings conform to their idea of Sabbath observance (Lk. 13.15-17).

Downing has also argued that FH Luke persistently refuses Mark-Matthew agreements in a substantial number of triple tradition passages where no Q parallel is thought to exist. On the face of it, this would be even stranger on the 2DH, where it would have to be down to pure coincidence (how could 2DH Luke contrive to consistently avoid Mark-Matthew agreements?), an explanation Downing is reluctant to allow FH Luke.[78] But rather than relying solely on this general point, it may be as well also to look at some of Downing's examples.[79]

The first of these, Mt. 3.1-4.11 || Mk 1.1-13 || Lk. 3.1-4.13, has already been discussed in Chapter 4.[80] The next is the call of the first disciples, Mk 1.16-20 || Mt. 4.18-22, but here Luke has chosen to substantially rework the Markan account by including a story of a miraculous catch of fish that resembles that in John 21. Given that FH Luke would here be primarily following Mark, this is no more a problem for FH Luke than it is for 2DH Luke. Downing's next example is the notice that Jesus taught with authority, not like the scribes, which is found at Mk 1.22 || Mt. 7.29 || Lk. 4.32, where Matthew and Mark are in verbatim agreement for thirteen words, while Luke partially rewrites his version in his own words, omitting any reference to the scribes. At first sight, this may look like A material rejected by Luke, but while in Luke and Mark this verse forms part of the introduction to the healing of the demoniac in the Capernaum Synagogue, Matthew does not have this pericope at all and has moved the notice about Jesus' teaching style to the conclusion of the Sermon on the Mount. This, then, is hardly a rejection by Luke of A material in its Markan context, and on the FH, Luke will have produced his version of the Capernaum demoniac without any reference to the ending of Matthew's Sermon on the Mount. No unpicking has taken place.

Downing's next example occurs at the call of Levi/Matthew at Mk 2.15b || Mt. 9.10b || Lk. 5.29, where there is near-verbatim agreement between Mark and Matthew while Luke goes his own way, but this should be seen in the context of the pericope as a whole:

Table 5.9 The Call of Levi/Matthew.

Mt. 9.9-13	Mk 2.13-17	Lk. 5.27-32
Καὶ παράγων ὁ Ἰησοῦς ἐκεῖθεν εἶδεν ἄνθρωπον **καθήμενον ἐπὶ τὸ τελώνιον**, Μαθθαῖον λεγόμενον, **καὶ** λέγει αὐτῷ· Ἀκολούθει μοι· καὶ ἀναστὰς ἠκολούθησεν αὐτῷ. Καὶ ἐγένετο αὐτοῦ ἀνακειμένου ἐν τῇ οἰκίᾳ, καὶ ἰδοὺ πολλοὶ τελῶναι καὶ ἁμαρτωλοὶ ἐλθόντες συνανέκειντο τῷ Ἰησοῦ καὶ τοῖς μαθηταῖς αὐτοῦ. καὶ ἰδόντες	Καὶ ἐξῆλθεν πάλιν παρὰ τὴν θάλασσαν· καὶ πᾶς ὁ ὄχλος ἤρχετο πρὸς αὐτόν, καὶ ἐδίδασκεν αὐτούς. καὶ παράγων εἶδεν Λευὶν τὸν τοῦ Ἁλφαίου **καθήμενον ἐπὶ τὸ τελώνιον**, καὶ λέγει αὐτῷ· Ἀκολούθει μοι. καὶ ἀναστὰς ἠκολούθησεν αὐτῷ. Καὶ γίνεται κατακεῖσθαι αὐτὸν ἐν τῇ οἰκίᾳ αὐτοῦ, καὶ πολλοὶ	Καὶ μετὰ ταῦτα ἐξῆλθεν καὶ ἐθεάσατο τελώνην ὀνόματι Λευὶν **καθήμενον ἐπὶ τὸ τελώνιον**, **καὶ** εἶπεν αὐτῷ· Ἀκολούθει **μοι. καὶ** καταλιπὼν πάντα ἀναστὰς ἠκολούθει αὐτῷ. Καὶ ἐποίησεν δοχὴν μεγάλην Λευὶς αὐτῷ ἐν τῇ οἰκίᾳ αὐτοῦ· καὶ ἦν ὄχλος πολὺς **τελωνῶν** καὶ ἄλλων οἳ ἦσαν μετ' αὐτῶν κατακείμενοι.

---

[78] Downing, 'Disagreements', 466.
[79] Listed at Downing, 'Disagreements', 464–5.
[80] Downing, 'Rehabilitation', 176–7.

οἱ Φαρισαῖοι ἔλεγον τοῖς μαθηταῖς αὐτοῦ· Διὰ τί **μετὰ τῶν τελωνῶν καὶ ἁμαρτωλῶν** ἐσθίει ὁ διδάσκαλος ὑμῶν; ὁ δὲ ἀκούσας εἶπεν·**Οὐ χρείαν ἔχουσιν οἱ** ἰσχύοντες **ἰατροῦ ἀλλὰ οἱ** κακῶς **ἔχοντες**. πορευθέντες δὲ μάθετε τί ἐστιν· Ἔλεος θέλω καὶ οὐ θυσίαν· **οὐ** γὰρ ἦλθον **καλέσαι δικαίους ἀλλὰ ἁμαρτωλούς**.	τελῶναι καὶ ἁμαρτωλοὶ συνανέκειντο τῷ Ἰησοῦ καὶ τοῖς μαθηταῖς αὐτοῦ, ἦσαν γὰρ πολλοὶ καὶ ἠκολούθουν αὐτῷ. καὶ οἱ γραμματεῖς τῶν **Φαρισαί**ων ἰδόντες ὅτι ἐσθίει μετὰ τῶν ἁμαρτωλῶν καὶ τελωνῶν ἔλεγον τοῖς μαθηταῖς αὐτοῦ·Ὅτι **μετὰτῶν τελωνῶν καὶ ἁμαρτωλῶν** ἐσθίει; καὶ ἀκούσας ὁ Ἰησοῦς λέγει αὐτοῖς ὅτι **Οὐ χρείαν ἔχουσιν οἱ** ἰσχύοντες **ἰατροῦ ἀλλ' οἱ** κακῶς **ἔχοντες**·οὐκ ἦλθον **καλέσαι δικαίους ἀλλὰ ἁμαρτωλούς**.	καὶ ἐγόγγυζον **οἱ Φαρισαῖ**οι καὶ οἱ γραμματεῖς αὐτῶν πρὸς τοὺς **μαθητὰς** αὐτοῦ λέγοντες· Διὰ τί **μετὰ τῶν τελωνῶν καὶ ἁμαρτωλῶν ἐσθίε**τε καὶ πίνετε; καὶ ἀποκριθεὶς ὁ Ἰησοῦς εἶπεν πρὸς αὐτούς· **Οὐ χρείαν ἔχουσιν οἱ** ὑγιαίνοντες **ἰατροῦ ἀλλὰ οἱ** κακῶς **ἔχοντες**·οὐκ ἐλήλυθα **καλέσαι δικαίους ἀλλὰ ἁμαρτωλούς** εἰς μετάνοιαν.

In Table 5.9, IA are marked in bold type, other EA[Mk-Mt] underlined and EA[Mk-Lk] agreements in italics (with the very occasional EA[Mt-Lk] shown as wavy underlines). Two things that stand out from this are, first, that there is a substantial amount of material in bold (A material that Luke has kept, thirty-seven whole words in Luke plus some parts of words), so it is hardly the case that Luke is systematically refusing Matthew-Mark agreements here; and second, that the extent of underlined material (A material that Luke has not retained, eighteen whole words in Matthew plus some odd parts of words) is less than this. The natural conclusion to draw is not that Luke is deliberately avoiding Mark-Matthew agreements (which would be even harder to explain on the 2DH) but that he is reworking Mark more extensively than Matthew does and so retains less of Mark's wording overall. That there should then be A material not employed by Luke is then simply the inevitable consequence.

There is insufficient space to examine Downing's other examples here, but those we have looked at fail to make his case. Where there is no likelihood of a Q parallel and both 2DH and FH Luke would be principally following Mark, the data to which Downing appeals cannot in any case select between the 2DH and the FH (since both would be working in much the same way). Elsewhere, the evidence still does not suggest any systematic attempt by Luke to avoid substantial Matthew-Mark agreements. Rather, as Olson points out, where two evangelists are reworking a third, there will inevitably be places where they disagree on what wording to retain from their source.[81] Moreover, if, as is often the case, Luke reworks Mark more freely than Matthew does, there will inevitably be some Mark-Matthew agreements he does not share. Moreover, there is absolutely no reason to suppose that FH Luke ought to have meticulously compared his manuscripts of Matthew and Mark to retain every passage (or even most passages) where they closely agreed, for this would be just as difficult as comparing them to avoid using such passages, which Downing rightly rejects as implausible.

---

[81] Olson, 'Unpicking', 131–2.

The evidence does not show that FH Luke consistently rejects the 'common witness' of Matthew and Mark while taking over Matthew's additions; a better interpretation of the evidence is that where FH Luke follows Matthew in preference to Mark, usually because Matthew supplies the fuller account in such passages, Luke unsurprisingly ends up further from Mark than does Matthew. The unpicking objection fails.

Conclusion

This chapter has examined four of the most common arguments against Luke's use of Matthew and found them unpersuasive. Each of the arguments discussed here has been countered by defenders of the FH before, yet they continue to be deployed. This chapter has therefore had to trample over some well-trodden ground yet again, adding little that is substantially new in order to emphasize just how inconclusive these common objections really are. Luke's infancy and resurrection narratives are not demonstrably independent of Matthew's. Luke does not have demonstrably more primitive versions of sayings he shares with Matthew. Luke does betray knowledge of many of Matthew's additions to Mark, while there is no reason why he should employ all the Matthean additions that supporters of the 2DH think he should. The objection that FH Luke must have carefully unpicked Matthew from Mark in some laborious and unprecedented fashion has itself been unpicked and shown to be threadbare. Even in combination, these four arguments do not constitute a convincing demonstration that Luke's use of Matthew is so improbable as to outweigh the evidence of significant similarities between Matthew and Luke identified in Chapter 4. On the contrary, closer examination of these arguments has revealed some further significant similarities.

Yet none of these four arguments is the main reason why Luke's use of Matthew is so often felt to be problematic. The main objection to Luke's use of Matthew is the difference between the context and order of so much of the double tradition in these two gospels. We shall address this objection in the next chapter.

6

The order objection

The problem

B.H. Streeter notoriously envisaged FH Luke tearing 'every little piece of non-Markan material he desired to use from the [exceedingly appropriate] context of Mark in which it appeared in Matthew ... in order to re-insert it into a different context of Mark having no special appropriateness', a procedure that is imaginable only 'if, on other grounds, we had reason to believe he was a crank'.[1] Streeter is clearly guilty of rhetorical excess here. His contention that the Markan contexts in which Matthew placed his double tradition material are always 'exceedingly appropriate' is a subjective value judgement, as is his complaint that the context Luke chooses for the same material is less appropriate; appropriateness is relative to the goal one is trying to pursue, and Luke's goals are different from Matthew's.[2] Moreover, Luke's rearrangement of Matthew's non-Markan material would not mainly consist of 'tearing' it (a needlessly pejorative image) from any Markan context but would mostly involve removing it from the context of one of Matthew's substantial discourses and redeploying it elsewhere, often not in any Markan context at all but in Luke's central section (hereafter CS).

Restated less stridently, however, the objection still appears cogent to opponents of Luke's use of Matthew, for whom it often constitutes the weightiest argument.[3] Matthew tends to arrange his sayings material in extended discourses. Luke often has his own versions of these discourses, but they tend to be shorter, and some (though not all) of the material omitted from these Lukan versions is found distributed elsewhere in Luke's Gospel, divorced from its Matthean context and out of its Matthean order. This invites two questions: first, why FH Luke should want to create such a rearrangement; and second, how he achieved it under the constraints of ancient writing technology. A Luke who has to keep scrolling back and forth through his copy of Matthew to find an odd verse here and an odd verse there to insert into his own composition seems implausible, especially when the rationale behind the resultant Lukan order appears less than immediately apparent. Assuming Luke's memory command of his sources eases the problem but does not instantly abolish it.

---

[1] Streeter, *Four Gospels*, 183.
[2] Matson, 'Luke's Rewriting', 46.
[3] Jeffrey Peterson, 'Order in the Double Tradition' in Mark Goodacre and Nicholas Perrin (eds), *Questioning Q* (London: SPCK, 2004), 25–42, here 28–30.

We should nevertheless enquire how the sauce for the FH gander differs from that on the 2DH goose. On the assumption that the order of Luke largely represents that of Q, all 2DH Luke needs to do is to alternate blocks of Mark and Q, inserting his own special (L) material into Q contexts as he sees fit. But whatever complicated reordering FH Luke would have to have performed on material taken from Matthew, 2DH Matthew would necessarily have to have performed in reverse on Q; one set of transpositions logically *must* be the mirror image of the other.[4] Defenders of the 2DH might propose that since Q is significantly shorter than Matthew, Matthew's rearrangement of the shorter Q would have been easier to perform than Luke's selection and rearrangement of material from the longer Matthew. But whereas FH Luke can be selective about what material he takes from Matthew, 2DH Matthew has to incorporate the whole of Q. It is not immediately apparent why FH Luke's task should be any more difficult than 2DH Matthew's.

Some defenders of the 2DH (notably Alan Kirk) have nevertheless argued that while Matthew would have found it reasonably easy to combine Mark and Q from memory, Luke would have had a much harder task combining Mark and Matthew, due to the way memory cueing would have aided recall of both texts. But this can be challenged.[5] As noted in Chapter 2, Philo's selective rearrangement of material from the Jewish Scriptures suggests that memory cueing may be less restricted than Kirk suggests. Moreover, as Kirk allows, Matthew's well-ordered text supplies every bit as helpful a set of memory cues for FH Luke to search as Q does for 2DH Matthew.

Arguing at this level of generality is, however, inevitably inconclusive. What is needed is a more detailed comparison of FH Luke's utilization of Mark and Matthew with 2DH Matthew's utilization of Mark and Q. We shall therefore begin by examining Kirk's proposals for the latter. We shall then apply what emerges to the explanation of FH Luke's order. This does not mean that we shall take FH Luke's working methods to be identical to those Kirk attributes to 2DH Matthew, but we shall attempt to explain and justify the differences, and we shall argue that in common with Kirk's 2DH Matthew, FH Luke primarily works forwards in his absolute movement through both his sources.

Matthew's order

Several advocates of the 2DH recognize 2DH Matthew's rearrangement of Q material (notably but not exclusively in the Sermon on the Mount) as a potential problem. Both Robert Derrenbacker and Alan Kirk have not only suggested how Matthew's memory of his sources might offer a solution but also argue that such a use of memory favours the 2DH against its main competitors, including the FH.[6] Kirk has presented his

---

[4] Admittedly, this is so only at a high level of abstraction counting the minimum set of transpositions that would be needed in each case, rather than the actual operations a writer might need to perform in practice, which may depend on a number of factors. The point nonetheless stands as a reasonable approximation.
[5] See *WTG*, 93–9, 133–9.
[6] Robert A. Derrenbacker, 'The "External and Psychological Conditions under Which the Synoptic Gospels Were Written": Ancient Compositional Practices and the Synoptic Problem' in Foster, *New Studies*, 435–57; Kirk, 'Memory'; cf. Gregory, 'Literary Dependence', 95–114, who does not claim that the use of memory favours the 2DH.

proposal for Matthew's use of Mark and Q in considerable detail, so it is this proposal we shall examine here.

Kirk proposes that Matthew had memory control of Q and was able to access it out of order by following cued sequences forward from various textual locations. Although Matthew often used Q sequences out of order, overall he moved forward through Q and through the shorter sequences he used from Q.[7] This forward movement is central to Kirk's understanding of Matthew's memory use of Q. He insists that Q is no more a ragbag of sayings material than Mark is a ragbag of deeds and sayings; both texts have an intelligible order that facilitates their use in memory. Memory access to both texts has to work with the narrative and topic sequences they provide, since it is these sequences that cue memory (of what comes next in either text) and enable an efficient indexing strategy for searching. For example, to retrieve a particular saying in Q one first identifies to which topos-sequence it belongs (such as the mission discourse) and then runs through that topos-sequence until one finds the item one wants.

Matthew 5–7

For Kirk, Q is a cultural text that is carefully arranged in argumentative topoi-sequences, whose recurrent argumentative patterns aid its appropriation via memory.[8]

> Matthew takes over the *topoi* sequence of the Q Sermon and makes it foundational for his Sermon while augmenting it with *topoi* of his own. These *topoi* activate and guide the appropriation of materials from elsewhere in Q. Each Matthean *topos* enables search and location operations in his Q source, itself a *topos*-organized work. Consistently with this search protocol, the Q deliberative sequences are reproduced in Matthew's *topoi* sequences mostly in their relative order. Moreover, with some exceptions Matthew does not alter order *within* these sequences of Q material.[9]

Matthew's rearrangement of Q indeed appears most problematic in the Sermon on the Mount (hereafter SM). 2DH Matthew uses Q 6.20-49 as the framework for Matthew 5–7, but then has to retrieve much of the other material he uses from later in Q. This can be seen from Table 6.1:

Table 6.1 2DH Matthew's use of Mark and Q in the Sermon on the Mount

5.1a	Introduction	(Mk 3.13a)
5.1-4,6	Common Beatitudes	Q6.20b-21
5.7-10	**Matthean Beatitudes**	
5.11-12	Blessed when reviled	Q6.22-23
5.13	Salt of the Earth	Q14.34-35

---

[7] Kirk, 'Memory', 471–3.
[8] *QiM*, 174–83.
[9] *QiM*, 189.

5.14-16	*Light of the World*	Q11.33 [Mk 4.21]
5.17	**Not abolish but fulfil**	
5.18	*Permanence of Law and Prophets*	Q16.17
5.19-20	**True Righteousness**	
5.21-24	**Murder and Wrath**	
5.25-26	*Settling with your Accuser*	Q12.58-59
5.27-28	**Adultery**	
5.29-30	*Excising offending body parts*	Mk 9.47, 43
5.31-32	*Divorce*	Q16.18? Mk 10.4, 11?
5.33-37	**Oaths**	
5.38	**Lex Talionis**	
5.39-42	*Non-Retaliation*	Q6.29-30
5.43-48	*Love of Enemies*	Q6.27-28, 35, 32-34, 36
6.1-4	**Almsgiving**	
6.5-8	**Pray in Secret and not like Gentiles**	
6.9-13	*The Lord's Prayer*	Q11.2b-4
6.14-15	*Forgiving Trespasses*	Mk 11.25
6.16-18	**Fasting**	
6.19-21	*Earthly and Heavenly Treasure*	Q12.33-34
6.22-23	*Sound and Unsound Eyes*	Q11.34-35
6.24	*Serving Two Masters*	Q16.13
6.25-34	*Don't be Anxious*	Q12.22-32
7.1-2	*The Measure of Judgment*	Q6.37-38
7.3-5	*Speck and Log in Eyes*	Q6.41-42
7.6	**Pearls before Swine**	
7.7-11	*Asking and Receiving*	Q11.9-13
7.12	*The Golden Rule*	Q6.31
7.13-14	*The Two Ways*	Q13.24
7.15	**Beware of False Prophets**	
7.16-18	*Good and Bad Fruit*	Q6.43-44
7.19-20	**Bad Trees are Cut Down**	
7.21	*Saying 'Lord, Lord'*	Q6.46
7.22-23	*'I never knew you'*	Q13.26-27
7.24-27	*Houses Built on Rock and Sand*	Q6.47-49
7.28	*End of the Sermon*	Q7.1
7.29	*Effect of the Sermon*	Mk 1.22

It appears from Table 6.1, however, that 2DH Matthew's use of Q (and Mark) in the SM is not precisely analogous to that of the scholarly writers Kirk appeals to. Those writers tended to rearrange their sources by moving related blocks of material around while retaining the relative order within such blocks. While 2DH Matthew largely retains the relative order of the Q 6 material he uses here, with only two items (Q 6.27-28 and Q 6.31) out of sequence, the Q material taken from elsewhere does not retain its overall relative order in Q. For example, the order of material between Q 6.23 and Q 6.29 in Matthew's sermon is Q 14.34-35, 11.33, 16.17, 12.58-59, 16.18.[10] Even more notable is the order of Q material employed at Mt. 6.19-34, where rather than preserving the relative sequence of Q, 2DH Matthew seems to have gone out of his way to disrupt it by splitting up Q 12.22-34, employing the separated segments in reverse order and interposing further out of sequence material in between, when one might have thought that the sequence Q 11.34-35, 12.22-34, 16.13 could have served just as well, absent any other constraints (although here *CEQ* reconstructs Q as following Matthew's order at Q 12.22-34). The point is not that 2DH Matthew could not have perfectly good reasons for doing what he would need to have done here (such as arranging his material in accordance with his previous section on prayer and piety),[11] but that he was not constrained to preserve Q's relative order.

Relative order is generally preserved in each miniblock: for example, the order of material in Q 12.58-59 is preserved at Mt. 5.25-26, although given the limited extent of this material, it is hard to see how it could be otherwise. As Kirk observes, 2DH Matthew usually deals in complete cognitive units and seldom attempts microconflation of Mark and Q.[12] A more significant example is the preservation of the Q 12.22-32 sequence at Mt. 6.25-34, although its length is exceptional (for Q material brought back into the Sermon). On the other hand, there is little sign of a consistent forward movement through Q for the material borrowed forward from beyond Q 6; the Matthean sequence of this material looks more like an alternating pattern of forward and backward steps through Q, although one could represent it as the result of two block-by-block (as opposed to pericope-by-pericope) forward sweeps, one gathering up material from Q 14 and 16 and the other from Q 11, 12 and 13.

One may also wonder why Matthew should go to the trouble of gathering all this material from dispersed Q contexts when it all made perfectly good sense in its original Q sequence. Kirk's answer is twofold: first, Matthew is expanding the Q 6 sermon with additional topoi-sequences of his own to express his own theological and redactional interests, and, second, he is at the same time taking the opportunity to gather together in one convenient place all the subsequent Q material that lacks any convenient peg in the ensuing Markan narrative (by 'pegs' Kirk means passages such as the mission discourse at Mk 6.7-11, which the Matthew 10 mission discourse combines with material taken from various parts of Q).[13]

---

[10] The reference to the Mosaic provision of divorce at Mt. 5.31 perhaps suggests Mk 10.4, 11, rather than Q as Matthew's source for the last of these.
[11] See *QiM*, 204–11.
[12] *QiM*, 189.
[13] *QiM*, 189, 223, 297.

This seems reasonable enough, but any devil will be in the detail, which Kirk goes on to supply in the form of a sustained analysis of Matthew's source utilization in the SM.[14] In the main Kirk's analysis looks plausible. Its immediate interest lies in the kinds of operation 2DH Matthew is made to perform. He is quite clearly capable of shaping the material at his disposal to suit his own compositional ends, for example by reshaping the Beatitudes to foreshadow the sequence of topoi his version of the Sermon will cover, and by finding and adapting material from quite scattered contexts in Q (and occasionally Mark) to fit the new topoi-sequences he constructs. He does this not by physically scrolling around in a manuscript but by associative cueing from the topos he is in the process of constructing (allowing him, for example, to discern and exploit thematic links between the exhortation to cut off offending body parts to escape being cast into hell at Mk 9.43, 47, and the themes of the lustful look at Mt. 5.28 and of being cast into prison at Mt. 5.25). In performing such operations, however, Matthew largely deals in complete cognitive units; he does not, for example, splice parts of two sayings or syntactic units together to form a third.

While Kirk (understandably) regards the tradition history of the M material as irrecoverable, in his view much of it may be due to 'Matthew's scribal competence in composing out of traditional motifs and materials'.[15] This may be so, but Kirk then goes a step further, claiming that the bulk of the M material in the Sermon represents Matthean mortar for binding the Q materials into the structure of his Sermon; it is not found in Luke because Luke has never seen Matthew.[16] This claim cannot be dissected in detail here, but it classifies too much material as 'mortar'. Such a description might apply to some of the introductory verses used to introduce a Matthean topos, such as the citation of the *lex talionis* at Mt. 5.38 to introduce the section on non-retaliation, but other M sections constitute complete (or virtually complete) topoi in themselves, such as those on true righteousness (Mt. 5.18-20), murder and wrath (Mt. 5.21-24), oaths (Mt. 5.33-37), almsgiving (Mt. 6.1-4) and fasting (Mt. 6.16-18). The distinctive body of M material in the Matthean prayer topos (Mt. 6.5-8) also looks rather more than mere mortar for the Q and Markan materials that follow. That the Gentile-facing Luke does not have any of this material may equally well reflect his lack of concern for arguments over Torah interpretation and Jewish forms of piety as his ignorance of Matthew.[17] On the FH, there may be material Matthew creates and material he inherits, but these categories do not map on to M and Q.

One may pose some further questions about how Kirk's proposals work out in practice. On Kirk's model, 2DH Matthew needs to employ his memory competence in Q to locate items that are both relevant to the topos-sequence he is currently constructing and unsuitable for subsequent attachment to a Markan peg. Moreover, he has to do this while composing a meaningful sequence of his own and ensuring that virtually the whole of Q is used up with minimal duplication; thus he has to keep track of what Q material he has already used or may intend to use later. Given that

---

[14] *QiM*, 190–224.
[15] *QiM*, 197.
[16] *QiM*, 204, 221–2.
[17] Matson, 'Luke's Rewriting', 48–50.

writing (in the sense of composing) is a particularly demanding cognitive task,[18] one wonders whether trying to manage all these tasks simultaneously in unaided memory would not exceed the working memory capacity of the human brain. To be sure, the task might be alleviated by the topical congruence between the material 2DH Matthew is gathering elsewhere from Q and the topical sequence he is constructing (e.g. both Mt. 6.5-15 and Q 11.2b-4, 9-13, contain sequences on prayer from which Matthew takes the Lord's Prayer), but one still wonders whether the index and search strategy proposed by Kirk can provide the whole picture.

For example, to compose Mt. 6.19-34 on the topical search model, 2DH Matthew has to mentally cue the Q 12.22b-34 sequence on treasure and anxiety (*CEQ* gives this in the Matthean order Q 12.33-34, 22b-31, which would slightly ease Matthew's task, though Kirk takes the Lukan order to be that of Q),[19] then the Q 11.33-35 lamp and eye topos for the Q 11.34-35 saying on the lamp of the body, then what Kirk calls the 'Q 16.13, 16-18 Law topos' to retrieve Q 16.13 on serving God and Mammon and then finally Q 12.22b-31 for the section on anxiety. Kirk points out that Matthew is constructing this section to elaborate on the previous discussion of true and false piety and hence orders his material at Mt. 6.19-24 to reflect that of Mt. 6.1-18; this may account for his order but then supplies a further compositional constraint Matthew has to keep in mind while performing his retrieval operations. The point is not that this is impossible but to question how much more Kirk's proposed indexing and sequential scanning of Q topoi-sequences explains than would the proposal that Matthew simply takes what material he needs from Q. Does Matthew really need to call up the Q 16.13, 16-18, sequence in order to retrieve its first item about serving God and Mammon? What work is the sequential scanning of topoi actually doing for locating material when Matthew retrieves Q 12.33-34, 22b-31, as complete blocks? Is indexing the entirety of Q 11.33-35 really of much help in retrieving Q 11.34-35? Or for that matter, does Matthew really need to call to mind the entire Q 11.2b-4, 9-13, sequence on prayer in order to be able to retrieve the Lord's Prayer? In these instances, it is hard to see how Kirk's proposed search algorithm differs much in practice from simply recalling what one needs.

In any case, there seems to be no clear cognitive reason why Matthew's use of a source should be restricted to the kind of locate and sequential scan algorithm Kirk suggests. This may indeed be one mnemonic strategy for retrieving material from different parts of a text, but there is no reason to suppose that is the only possible one. Sequential cueing is not the only way human memory retrieval works; memory cueing can also work in all sorts of other ways.[20] It can work by association of ideas or images without any need for sequencing (otherwise it would be hard to explain, for example, Philo's use of the Pentateuch).

---

[18] *WTG*, 92-3; Mark Torrance and Gaynor Jeffery, 'Writing Processes and Cognitive Demands' in Mark Torrance and Gaynor C. Jeffery (eds), *The Cognitive Demands of Writing* (Amsterdam: Amsterdam University Press, 1999), 1-11, here 1, 6; Michel Fayol, 'From On-line Management Problems to Strategies in Written Composition' in Torrance and Jeffery (eds), *Cognitive Demands*, 13-23, here 13; Ronald T. Kellogg, 'Components of Working Memory in Text Production' in Torrance and Jeffery (eds), *Cognitive Demands*, 43-61, here 49.

[19] *QiM*, 208.

[20] *WTG*, 94-9.

If Matthew is searching for Q material to fit his current topos construction, he would often have to know what he was looking for before he found it. For example, if he wants to insert the text of a prayer in his prayer topos at Mt. 6.9, then he presumably knows he is looking for the Lord's Prayer before he scans the Q 11 prayer topos, but if he already knows what he is looking for, he hardly needs to scan the entire Q topos to retrieve it. Such scanning may still have its uses. For example, sequential scanning may sometimes prompt greater verbal accuracy; or it may help where Matthew thinks 'I'm sure Q had something else on this topic but I can't quite recall what'; and it may be a useful strategy for ensuring that one has used up the whole of Q without missing anything, provided one has some means of keeping track of what one has already used (and, perhaps, of what one knows one will already have a place for in what is to come). It is a little hard to imagine how that could be achieved without some external aid, although perhaps someone adept in the use of mental *loci* might manage to devise some purely mental scheme to do it. Either way, it is unclear that Kirk's description of 2DH Matthew's procedure can be giving the complete picture or that 2DH Matthew would always need to follow a Q topos-sequence to retrieve some item he needed.

This is not to deny that 2DH Matthew's use of Q could be based on his scribal competence with Q as a mnemonically activated text, but rather to suggest that any such memory-based use of Q seems likely to have been both more flexible than Kirk supposes (including some direct access to Q items without the need for indexing and sequential scanning of Q topoi-sequences) and more complex, additionally requiring some means of keeping track of what Q material has been used or may be needed for later use in a discourse attached to a Markan peg. Such additional means might be an external physical aid such as a wax tablet or papyrus notebook, or it might be some further mnemonic technique.

This is not to object to the thesis that Matthew could have accessed Q through his scribally trained memory of the text, but rather to insist that the techniques and abilities needed by 2DH Matthew must also be allowed to FH Luke. From the foregoing discussion, it would seem that these would include not only the index and sequential searching strategy proposed by Kirk but also some facility for more general associative cueing and for the creative reworking and substantial reordering of material. It may also include some external aids to memory (such as ephemeral notes), though this is less certain.

Matthew 8–13

The utilization of Q in the SM is not the only order conundrum in the first part of Matthew. Scholars have long been puzzled by Matthew's reordering of Markan materials in Matthew chapters 8 and 9, so much so that after reviewing all the proposed solutions Delbert Burkett declares that Matthew cannot have used Mark at all, but rather that Matthew 8–9 constitutes further evidence for Matthew's and Mark's independent use of two different sources: Proto-Mark A and Proto-Mark B.[21] Kirk also finds previous explanations of Matthew's order wanting but proposes

---

[21] Burkett, *Rethinking*, 60–92.

a very different solution: the order of material in Matthew 8–12 is to be explained, and indeed can only be explained, by the compositional exigencies Matthew faced in combining his two sources Mark and Q while trying to respect the integrity of each source. If Kirk is right about this, then the order of this part of Matthew would constitute an argument for the existence of Q, and hence against the FH, but it may be that Matthew's reordering of Mark has a rather simpler explanation than either Kirk or Delbert supposes. A Matthew intent on reconciling the orders of Mark and Q could have gone about it with far fewer transpositions of Mark than our Matthew employed. If, as Kirk proposes, 2DH Matthew has incorporated into his SM all the Q material that lacks a suitable Markan peg, one might have expected him to proceed by simply attaching the remainder of the Q material to each Markan peg as he came to it in Mark's sequence, so that, for example, the Q11 Beelzebul material would be incorporated into an expanded Beelzebul Controversy in its Markan place, then the Q13 and M parables employed to expand the Mark 4 parable discourse and so on. According to Kirk, the reason Matthew does not adopt this solution is in part due to a desire to respect both the Q sequence (leading from instruction via the Capernaum Centurion through the John the Baptist material to commissioning the disciples for mission and then the Beelzebul Controversy) and the Markan sequence (call of disciples leading to various miracles and controversies culminating in the Beelzebul Controversy, followed by parables, more miracles and then the commissioning for mission) while integrating them into his own tightly integrated sequence (call of disciples, instruction on discipleships, various miracles, commissioning for mission), which emphasizes that discipleship leads swiftly to opposition and to mission: Jesus' Messianic mission is passed to his disciples.[22]

This is all well and good, except that, for the most part, when Kirk comes to detail how this results in Matthew's transposition of Mark (and Q, notably the Q 7.18-35 John the Baptist material to Matthew 11) most of the explanatory work appears to be done by Matthew's compositional aims rather than the order of Q. For example, as Kirk acknowledges, it might have been far simpler for Matthew to have resumed the Markan sequence at Mk 1.29 (the Healing of Peter's Mother-in-Law) after the Q Capernaum Centurion pericope and then continue to follow it. The reason Matthew did not do this, Kirk believes, is that his scribal competence led him to place the Healing of the Leper directly after the Sermon as an immediate illustration of the continuing validity of the Law (Mt. 8.4 || Mk 1.44). This in turn triggered a whole series of Matthean transpositions of Mark needed to co-ordinate Jesus' movements in and out of Capernaum.[23] This may be a perfectly reasonable explanation for Matthew's relocation of the healing of the leper, but it has nothing to do with the order of Q. Moreover, the odd redactional tweak to the opening of a pericopae or two (as Matthew has presumably done at Mt. 8.1) would have sufficed to preserve the narrative logic of Jesus' movements, without the need for a wholescale reordering of Mark to preserve Mark's narrative line.

---

[22] *QiM*, 263–4.
[23] *QiM*, 280–4.

Kirk offers a number of perfectly reasonable suggestions about Matthew's compositional constraints here. For example, he accepts the common suggestion that Matthew intends to compose a 'Messiah of Deed' section to complement and follow the 'Messiah of Word' section of Matthew 5–7, but points out the need for Matthew to include at least some controversy stories to prepare for the rejection of Jesus and John at Mt. 11.18-19 in addition to a set of miracles for the exchange between John and Jesus at Mt. 11.2-5 to refer back to.[24] But Matthew could have met these constraints with far fewer transpositions, while also respecting the order of Q, by moving Mk 3.20–4.34 (Beelzebul Controversy and Parable Discourse) after the Mission Discourse (in deference to the order of Q) and Mk 3.7-19 (Choosing the Disciples) to immediately before the Mission Discourse, thereby requiring only two transpositions in Mark. The only transposition that would then be required in Q would be of Q 13.18-21 (Parables) into the Markan parable sequence Mk 4.1-33. The resulting sequence (less any M material such a hypothetical Matthew might have added) would then run: Q 6.20-49, Mk 1.22, Q 7.1-10, Mk 1.29-3.6, Q 7.18-35, Q 9.57-60, Mk 4.35–6.6, <u>Mk 3.7-19</u>, Mk 6.7-13 + Q 10.2-24, <u>Mk 3.20-30</u> + Q 11.14-26, <u>Mk 3.31–Mk 4.33</u> + Q *13.18-21*, Mk 6.14–8.10, Mk 8.11-12 + Q 11.16, 29-32 (where underlining indicates transposed Markan blocks and italics the transposed Q block). If more miracles (including an example of raising the dead) were required as an antecedent to Q 7.18-35, this Q block could additionally be moved to just before Mk 8.11.

But this is not what Matthew did, so something else must have motivated him. We are then left with the strongest part of Kirk's case, namely that Matthew's reversal of the Markan order of the Beelzebul Accusation and the Mission Discourse (Mk 3.22-30; 6.7-13) is most plausibly explained by the order of these items in Q (Q 10.2-16 for the Mission Discourse and Q 11.14-32 for the Beelzebul Accusation).[25] It may be, though, that there is some other reason for Matthew's departure from Mark's sequence here and one that works just as well for FH Matthew.

It is commonly observed that Mt. 8.1–13.58 can be resolved into two forward movements through Mark, which finally come together with the death of John the Baptist at Mt. 14.1-12 ǁ Mk 6.14-29, after which Matthew more or less follows Mark's sequence (with additional material of his own) through to the end of both gospels.[26] This double movement is set out in Table 6.2, which shows the Matthean sequence from 8.1 to 14.12 with the Markan parallels set out in two columns headed Mark A and Mark B. A third column, Mark C, indicates items based on Markan material conforming to neither sequence. For the purposes of this table all other possible sources are ignored, and Mark is taken to be Matthew's source even where a Q parallel might be thought to exist. The task, then, is to explain why Matthew would have made these two passes through Mark, which overlap in their Matthean sequence (so it is not just a case of Matthew first making one pass through Mark 1–6 and then going back to make a second).

A possible answer lies in Matthew's concern for structure coupled with the most economical utilization of Mark consistent with that structure. Matthew's rearrangement

---

[24] *QiM*, 268.
[25] *QiM*, 278.
[26] *QiM*, 233; Watson, *Gospel Writing*, 150.

of Mark here results from meeting the constraints of his large-scale structuring of his gospel into five discourses interspersed with other material, his small-scale structuring of Matthew 8–9 into three groups of three miracle stories with intervening material and certain compositional goals he aims to meet with that intervening material.[27] It will be convenient to treat these in reverse order.

Table 6.2 Matthew's Utilization of Mark in Mt. 8.1–14.12

Slot	Matthew	Mark A	Mark B	Mark C	Mark D	Mark E
1	8.1-4 Leper		**1.40-45**		**1.40-45**	
2	8.5-13 Centurion					[~1.21-8]
3	8.14-17 Sick at Evening	1.29-34				1.29-34
α	8.18-22 On Following Jesus					
4	8.23-27 Stilling the Storm		**4.35-41**		**4.35-41**	
5	8.28-34 Gadarene Demoniac		5.1-20			5.1-20
6	9.1-8 Paralytic	**2.1-12**			**2.1-12**	
β	9.9-17 Controversies	**2.13-22**			**2.13-22**	
7	9.18-26 Two Sick Women		5.21-43			5.21-43
8	9.27-31 Two Blind Men			10.46-52		
9	9.32-34 Dumb Demoniac			1.23-27; 3.22		
γ	9.35-36 Preaching & Healing		6.6b	1.34-39		6.6b
				6.34		
	10.1 Commissioning the Twelve		6.7			6.7
	10.2-4 The Twelve Apostles			3.13-19		
	10.9-10 Prohibited Equipment		6.8-9			6.8-9

---

[27] Cf. Walter T. Wilson, *Healing in the Gospel of Matthew: Reflections on Method and Ministry* (Minneapolis: Fortress, 2014), 294–302.

10.11-14 Hospitality	6.10-11		6.10-11
10.17-18 Opposition		13.9	
10.19-20 Help of Holy Spirit		13.11	
10.21-22 Divisions & Hatred		13.12	
10.39 Gaining and Losing Life		8.35	
10.42 Cup of Cold Water		9.41	
12.1-8 Plucking Grain on Sabbath	2.23-28		2.23-28
12.9-14 Healing Withered Hand	3.1-6		3.1-6
12.15-16 Healing by the Sea	3.7-12		3.7-12
12.22-37 Beelzebul Accusation	3.22-30		3.22-30
12.46-50 Jesus' True Kindred	3.31-35		3.31-35
13.1-32 Parables	4.1-32		4.1-32
13.54-58 Rejection at Nazareth	6.1-6a		6.1-6a
14.1-12 Death of John the Baptist	6.14-29	6.14-29	6.14-29	6.14-29

As Kirk notes, not only is it politic to supply a series of miracles to prepare for the interchange between Jesus and John at Mt. 11.2-6, but it also makes better sense of the rejection of Jesus and John indicated by Mt. 11.16-24 if Matthew deploys at least some controversy stories beforehand. If no clashes between Jesus and the Jewish leadership had been narrated prior to Matthew 11, an audience unfamiliar with Mark might be left wondering what Jesus was complaining about. Furthermore, as Kirk has again noted, Matthew is keen to emphasize that discipleship leads quickly to mission; it therefore suits his purpose to emphasize following Jesus before he introduces the mission discourse at Matthew 10.

The reason why Matthew might want to introduce interludes into his 'Messiah of Deed' sequence is twofold. First, he may not wish to create the impression that Jesus' activity consisted merely of one damn miracle after another. Second, breaking up this section into three sets of three miracle stories makes its structure easier to grasp and remember.

Thus, on the one hand, Matthew needs material for the interludes between his triads of miracle stories while on the other, he has material he wants to deploy before he reaches his Mission Discourse. He deploys his Markan material to meet these twin constraints. Once he hit on the idea of turning the Stilling of the Storm miracle into an allegory of discipleship, the storm-stilling pericope had to be fitted in at slot 4, immediately following the first interlude (labelled α in Table 6.2), if this interlude were to contain the material on discipleship (in preparation for Matthew 10). Likewise, if Matthew wished to deploy some Markan controversy stories to prepare for Matthew 11, then interlude β would be the only place left to put them. Given that the Healing of the Paralytic is both a healing story and a controversy story, it would then be convenient to place it just before interlude β, namely at slot 6. Matthew thereby achieves a trio of controversy stories at Mt. 8.18-27 overlapping with a trio of miracle stories at Mt. 8.23-9.1, making for a serendipitously neat arrangement. Finally, as Kirk suggests, Matthew moves the Healing of the Leper to a position immediately following the SM in order to bring out the connection with observance of the Law.

The items thereby fixed in particular slots are shown in bold in Table 6.2. It will be observed that they straddle the Mark A and Mark B columns. The Mark D column shows these four items arranged in one sequence along with the Markan material employed in Mt. 12.1-14.12 with the remaining items taken from Mark placed in the Mark E column. It will then be seen that, with certain qualifications, Matthew has filled up the remaining slots in his trio of triads by using up the remaining Mark E material in Mark's sequence.

The first qualification is that Matthew replaces Mark's Capernaum demoniac with the story of the Capernaum Centurion. It would be hazardous to attempt to read Matthew's mind, but it may be that Matthew preferred the Centurion story for its insistence on the faith of a non-Israelite, thereby alerting his audience that the seeming prohibition of a mission to any Gentiles at Mt. 10.5-6 should not be taken as Matthew's (or Jesus') last word on the subject. It may also be that Matthew considered the centurion's faith a better lesson in potential discipleship than the antics of a demoniac.

The second qualification is that Matthew does not fill interlude β with the complete sequence of controversy stories available to him from Mk 2.1-3.6 but breaks off at Mk 2.22. One reason for this would be structural: to have included the entirety of Mk 2.1-3.6 at interlude β would have made the interlude too long, unbalancing the structure of Matthew 8-9. A triad of controversy stories (including the Paralytic) suffices at this point. It is then partly for this reason that Matthew skips the remainder of this Markan controversy sequence when he works forward through other unused Markan material to fill his remaining slots.

The third qualification is that Matthew runs out of available Markan miracle stories when he reaches slot 8. He therefore concocts his own out of Markan fragments (as Kirk also suggests).[28] The Healing of Two Blind Men at Mt. 9.27-31 both complements

---

[28] QiM, 269-71.

the healing/raising of a pair of woman at Mt. 9.18-26 and supplies a precedent needed at Mt. 11.5 ('the blind receive their sight'), while the deaf/dumb (κωφὸν) demoniac of Mt. 9.32-34 both supplies another missing precedent for Mt. 11.5 ('the deaf [κωφοὶ] hear') and anticipates the Beelzebul Accusation.

Matthew has now reached Mk 5.43 in his Mark E sequence. He then continues this sequence through Mk 6.6 to 6.11 at Mt. 9.35-10.14 (for his Mission Discourse) before going back to use up the remainder of Mark D (Mk 2.23-6.6a) at Mt. 12.1-13.58. This would seem to be a reasonably economical source-utilization strategy, using up the remainder of the Markan material in two forward movements (Mark E followed by Mark D), with the bulk of the out-of-sequence Mark C material being incorporated between the two.

Taken purely mechanically, it may seem odd that Mk 6.1-6a is omitted from its place in the Mark E sequence and left to be picked up in the Mark D sequence, but compositionally, it is not hard to see why Matthew might have felt the γ slot (occupied by Mt. 9.35-36) to be an inappropriate place for the Rejection at Nazareth, since it would introduce a new narrative turn at just the point Matthew is trying to wrap up his 'Messiah of Deed' section. Since Matthew presumably knew that he was going to make a second pass through Mark's material, it would have presented no particular difficulty to skip over this pericope in the first pass and leave it to be picked up later.

On this account, the transposition of the Beelzebul Accusation to a position after the Commissioning Discourse turns out to be a by-product of Matthew's twofold pass through Mark 1-6 prompted by the design of Matthew 8-9. But this same transposition could also be motivated by larger structural concerns. Matthew's Gospel is structured around five substantial discourses. The first of these, the SM, sets out Jesus' programme for discipleship. Given Matthew's concern to emphasize that discipleship leads to empowerment for mission, it is then appropriate that the second discourse should set out Jesus' programme for mission. This entails that the Parable Discourse, which Matthew in any case expands substantially, must be deferred to third place. To structure his narrative around five distinct discourses Matthew needs to find material to separate the discourses. The material on John the Baptist in Matthew 11 only partly fulfils this function, since it largely consists of Jesus speaking, with just a few minimal narrative asides. By deferring the hitherto unused material from Mk 2.23-3.35 until Matthew 12, Matthew creates a clearer interval between his second and third discourses while (more or less) preserving the contiguity of the material from Mk 3.20-35 and Mk 4.1-32. Reserving the controversy stories of Mk 2.23-3.6 until this point not only avoids overburdening interlude β in the 'Messiah of Deed' section but also provides a narrative lead-in to the Beelzebul Controversy by reminding the audience that Jesus' activity is proving controversial. Matthew's economical source utilization is thus opportunistically made to serve his compositional goals.

The foregoing explanation could apply as well to 2DH Matthew as to FH Matthew. 2DH Matthew has the added burden of also trying to accommodate the order of Q, but this is not demonstrably impossible; it is just a little harder to envisage than FH Matthew's working with Mark as his only substantial written source.

Luke's order

To address the questions of how and why FH Luke would have carried out his apparently radical reordering of Matthew we shall proceed in four stages. The first will argue that FH Luke's use of Matthew from memory raises no special problems in comparison with 2DH Matthew's use of Q. The second will give a brief overview of FH Luke's of Matthew throughout the non-Markan section Lk. 6.20–8.1. The third will explore the composition of CS on the assumption that FH Luke in fact continues to maintain a consistently forward movement in his absolute position in Matthew, much as Kirk's 2DH Matthew maintains a consistently forward movement in his absolute position in Q. The fourth will argue that the resulting picture of FH Luke's working methods falls within a credible model of ancient source utilization.

Luke's use of memory

In *Writing the Gospels*, I suggested that Luke could have used a notebook or wax tablet to record brief *aides memoire* to Matthean material that he proposed to use later in his gospel (notably but not exclusively material from the SM).[29] Kirk, however, believes that Matthew's and Luke's use of sources cannot be explained by excerpting, since excerpting was principally a copying process and 'Matthew and Luke clearly are not drafting up their compositions from an intermediary collection of excerpts from their sources'.[30] Kirk's reasoning is that Matthew's and Luke's use of the double tradition is unlike Varro's piecemeal use of his tradition, but that does not obviously exclude the use of notes as opposed to excerpts. The procedure I suggested for Luke was the noting of key words or phrases to act as later memory prompts, rather as Kirk states that the *incipit* (opening word or words) of a passage was used to cue recollection in the Middle Ages.[31] Thus, for example, on working through Matthew 6, FH Luke might inscribe ΠΑΤΕΡ ΗΜΩΝ on his wax tablet as a prompt for the Lord's Prayer. This proposal cannot be ruled out, but something like the memory utilization model Kirk develops for Matthew may provide a better model for how Luke worked. The advantage of the notebook model is that it allows Luke to keep track of what Matthean material he has used. But this model also has some disadvantages: first, Luke would need to know in advance what material he was later going to use from Matthew (or else note rather more of it just in case); second, the notebook would constitute one more physical document Luke would have to manipulate when composing his central section, in addition to Matthew and any written sources he had for L material; and third, Luke occasionally uses material he would not yet have encountered in his forward progress through Matthew; presumably he would then be relying on his memory of Matthew

---

[29] *WTG*, 144–5, developing an idea from Poirier, 'Roll', 19–24, in light of criticism from Robert A. Derrenbacker, 'Texts, Tables and Tablets: A Response to John C. Poirier', *JSNT* 25 (2013), 380–7, here 384–5, and Downing, F. Gerald, 'Waxing Careless: Poirier, Derrenbacker and Downing', *JSNT* 35 (2013), 388–93, here 391.
[30] *QiM*, 53–4.
[31] *QiM*, 139.

to access that material. It may be better, then, to assume that Luke's use of Matthean material outside its Matthean sequence is principally from memory.

What is source utilization for the 2DH goose should be source utilization for the FH gander, so the techniques ascribed to 2DH Matthew for the recycling of Q should also be available to FH Luke for the recycling of Matthew. Kirk, however, suggests that a memory-activated use of sources similar to that he proposes for 2DH Matthew would not have been so helpful to the FH Luke, first because Luke would have to have made too many backward movements through Matthew's text and second because it would have been far more difficult for the FH Luke to assemble the topoi-sequences in his travel narrative from material embedded in narrative Matthean contexts than for Matthew to have followed the topoi-sequences in Q.[32]

The first of these objections seems to be that FH Luke has to retrieve a substantial amount of material from earlier than his absolute position in Matthew, for example when he employs material from the SM in his central section, but it is not clear why this should be particularly problematic. If Luke knows Matthew's SM well, he can simply search through its topoi-sequences to retrieve what he needs, whatever his absolute position in Matthew. It is far from clear why backtracking from one's absolute position to retrieve earlier material should be any more difficult than backtracking to one's absolute position having moved forward to pull back later material. Kirk's point appears to be the absence of correlation between FH Luke's use of Matthew and 'memory competence in Matthew as an intelligibly performed script'.[33] The implication is that Luke's memory of Matthew should carry him predominantly forward through Matthew's Gospel, but it will be argued below that it does in fact do so. As already argued, this does not result in a restriction on other types of memory cueing.

Kirk concedes that 'one might propose that Luke has memory competence in Matthew's memorably arranged discourses and that he cycles these materials into memorable *topoi* sequences of his own devising, the Travel Narrative being the prominent example'.[34] But his second objection is that 'the sayings that Luke must retrieve from Matthew (on the FH), however, on a number of occasions are not embedded in a specific Matthean *topos* composition and *topoi* sequence, but isolated within narrative pericopes. This complicates memory-based search-and-location operations'.[35] Kirk then goes on to give a number of examples where FH Luke would need to retrieve sayings material from a Matthean narrative context: Lk. 6.39 || Mt. 15.14 (Blind Leading the Blind), Lk. 17.6 || Mt. 17.20 (Faith as a Mustard Seed) and Lk. 13.28-29 || Mt. 8.11-12 (At Table with Abraham). Kirk acknowledges that 'Luke of course is quite capable of recollecting these as uncontextualized sayings' but suggests that 'to argue along these lines is to weaken the case for Luke composing from systematic memory competence in Matthew'.[36]

---

[32] Kirk, 'Memory', 473-7; cf. *WTG*, 132-9.
[33] Kirk, 'Memory', 477.
[34] Kirk, 'Memory', 476.
[35] Kirk, 'Memory', 477.
[36] Kirk, 'Memory', 477.

The examples Kirk gives are very much in the minority, and there are only three more of just this kind: Lk. 12.1b || Mt. 16.6 || Mk 8.15 (Leaven of the Pharisees),[37] Lk. 12.54-56 || Mt. 16:2-3 (Signs of the Times) and Lk. 22.30 || Mt. 19.28 (Judging the Twelve Tribes). Against that are some twenty-seven cases where FH Luke recycles material from one of the major Matthean discourses and a further six cases where Luke takes over a complete Matthean unit (such as the Parable of the Great Supper) or else borrows from a lengthy speech in a narrative context. Thus what Kirk regards as the potentially difficult cases for Luke's use of Matthew represent only about 15 per cent of the whole or about 8 per cent in terms of the number of Matthean verses Luke redeploys.[38] Our discussion of Matthew's order suggested that in practice 2DH Matthew's memory use of Q often looks more like direct access to familiar material than strict use of any index and search algorithm; thus the relatively small number of cases in which FH Luke would need to have accessed Matthean material from memory without the benefit of a particular search strategy do not constitute a strong argument against Luke's use of Matthew.

It is nevertheless worth taking a closer look at individual cases. It will be argued below that in two out of Kirk's three examples, Luke's use of the Matthean saying taken out of sequence is prompted by one he finds in Matthean sequence. So, for example, Luke's deployment of the saying about faith like a mustard seed at Lk. 17.6 is prompted by the similar saying he finds at Mt. 21.21, which he encounters in his forward movement through Matthew, just as one saying about being cast out to wail and gnash one's teeth encountered in Matthean sequence at Mt. 13.47-50 prompts the use of another taken from Mt. 8.11-12. The same may also apply to Lk. 12.1 || Mt. 16.6 (prompted by the Parable of the Leaven at Mt. 13.33), although here FH Luke conceivably may, and 2DH Luke presumably must, be dependent on Mk 8.15.

The Lukan saying about Judging the Twelve Tribes (Lk. 22.30) is an interesting case, since the statement with which it is introduced ('You are those who have continued with me in my trials', Lk. 22.28) arguably better fits – or at least presupposes – the context of Mt. 19.27-28 (where Peter declares that the disciples have left all to follow Jesus) than that of Lk. 22.24-30, where it follows a dispute about precedence, which in turn might just as well be based on Mt. 20.24-28 out of sequence as on Mk 10.41-45 out of sequence.

The Blind Leading the Blind (Lk. 6.39 || Mt. 15.14) provides a striking example of Luke seemingly separating out a Matthean addition to a Markan pericope Luke otherwise omits (the handwashing dispute of Mk 7.1-23 || Mt. 15.1-20; but cf. Lk. 11.38). That said, the saying that FH Luke extracts here, about the blind leading the blind and both falling into the pit, is both memorable and easily detachable; it is a vivid image that can readily be deployed in multiple contexts (the phrase 'blind leading the blind' remains proverbial in modern English and the image was also proverbial in antiquity).[39] Along with Lk. 6.40 it appears intrusive in its Lukan context; the Matthean

---

[37] The EA^{Mt-Lk} προσέχετε tips the balance in favour of Luke having used Mt. 16.6 rather than Mk 8.15 here.
[38] Note that these figures exclude instances where FH Luke would be directly using Matthean material in Matthean sequence, since these are not relevant to the argument here.
[39] Marshal, *Luke*, 269.

sequence at Mt. 7.1-5, which lacks it, flows better. Its use may have been prompted by the saying about the speck and log at Lk. 6.41-42 || Mt. 7.3-5, since a guide with a plank in his eye may as well be blind. Presumably, it then in turn prompted the use of the saying about disciple and teacher at Lk. 6.40 on the basis that a teacher is a better-sighted guide, although the sequence remains a little clumsy. One might ask what would prompt 2DH Matthew to retrieve Q 6.39 at Mt. 15.14. It may be that he wished to characterize the Pharisees as blind guides, but it is hard to see how he could have thought to do so unless he already knew the saying about blind guides: why would he suddenly start a sequential scan of the Q 6 topoi-sequence on judgement on the off-chance of happening upon something appropriate, unless he already knew there was something appropriate to find? But if he already knew, he had no need to scan, and so it seems much more likely that 2DH Matthew's recall of this material would have been direct and unmediated by any need for any sequential search procedure. As for 2DH Matthew, so also for FH Luke.

The saying about Signs of the Times (Lk. 12.54-56 || Mt. 16.2-3) looks similarly proverbial (again, compare the common 'red sky at night' proverb in English), although the Lukan and Matthean versions of the weather signs are so different one might question how far one is dependent on the other. Each version fits its context well: in Mt. 16.1-4 the request for a sign and in Luke the eschatological discourse. There thus seems to be no particular difficulty for either the 2DH Matthew to retrieve the saying from Q or the FH Luke to retrieve it from Matthew, whether directly (through recollection of the proverb alone) or via sequential scanning of Matthew's Request for a Sign pericope, from which it could readily be detached.

Overall, then, it would seem to be as feasible for FH Luke to access Matthew out of sequence as it would be for 2DH Matthew to access Q in the same way, with the proviso that neither evangelist would be restricted to the index and search algorithm proposed by Kirk (although that may well be one memory strategy often employed).

Luke's use of Matthew in Luke 6.20–8.1

It is Luke's central section (aka Travel Narrative) that is often considered particularly troublesome for his use of Matthew, but before we tackle that it will be helpful to consider FH Luke's prior use of Matthew, picking up from where we left off in Chapter 4.

After Lk. 4.15, FH Luke next employs Matthew in Luke's Sermon on the Plain (henceforth SP), which is largely an abbreviation on Matthew's SM, with a small amount of material from elsewhere in Matthew. While the SM is the first set-piece speech attributed to Jesus in Matthew, the SP is the second such speech in Luke, the first being the Nazareth Sermon at Lk. 4.16-30. Lk. 6.20–7.17 pick up on the themes of the Nazareth Sermon by first having Jesus preach good news to the poor (Lk. 6.20-23; 4.18-21) and then heal a foreign military officer's slave and raise a widow's son (Lk. 7.1-17; 4.23-27).

FH Luke's drastic abbreviation of the SM is often seen as problematic for the Farrer Hypothesis. It is achieved by a combination of omission and redeployment; there are some parts of the SM that FH Luke does not use at all, and other parts he uses elsewhere, mainly in his long central section. Why he reuses this material where he does can be left to our discussion of the central section. The question to be addressed here is why FH Luke might have abbreviated the SM to such an extent. This turns on three distinct but related issues: whether Luke avoids long speeches,[40] how Luke typically treats discourse material from his sources[41] and whether FH Luke might have had good rhetorical reasons for abbreviating the SM.

The first of these (Luke's alleged dislike of long speeches) is hard to evaluate without quantifying what we mean by 'long'. Luke's SP runs to 568 words compared to 1,932 words for Matthew's SM.[42] No other speech in Luke-Acts is as long as the SM. The longest in Acts, Stephen's speech at Acts 7.2-53, contains 993 words. The next longest speeches in Acts are Peter's Pentecost Sermon at Acts 2.14b-36 (429 words), Paul's address in Pisidian Antioch at Acts 13.16b-41 (424 words) and Paul's defence before Agrippa at Acts 26.2-23 (419 words), all slightly shorter than the SP. Luke's trio of parables at Lk. 15.4-32 runs to 528 words, which is again shorter than the SP. Kloppenborg takes Lk. 12.1b–13.9 to be 'a single discursive event',[43] which would amount to 1,192 words, which is long for Luke but still substantially shorter than the SM. If one divides this speech up into sections delivered to different audiences, there is still a continuous section of 554 words at Lk. 12.22-53 addressed entirely to the disciples.[44] Most of the speeches in Luke-Acts are quite a bit shorter than this. The SM would thus constitute an exceptionally long speech for Luke.

The second issue concerns how Luke typically treats the discourse material he finds in his sources. Luke's Parable Discourse (Lk. 8.5-18) runs to 282 words compared to 494 words for the parallel section in Mk 4.3-32. Similarly, the series of sayings at Mk 9.35b-50 occupies 271 words which are reduced to 98 words (of which only 44 are spoken by Jesus) in the parallel passage at Lk 9.46-50. In both these cases some of the omitted Markan material is redeployed elsewhere in Luke, which is the procedure attributed to FH Luke's handling of the SM. The 66 words in Mark's mission instruction at Mk 6.8-11 are reduced to 51 at Lk. 9.3b-5, and at 449 words the Lukan eschatological discourse at Lk. 21.8-36 is also shorter than its Markan counterpart at Mk 13.5-37 (522 words). If Luke tends to abbreviate Matthean discourses, this is consistent with what he does to Markan ones.

It appears that FH Luke does consistently abbreviate Matthean discourses. The discussion about John the Baptist in at Lk. 7.22-35 runs to 230 words compared with 441 words at Mt. 11.4-30. Luke's second mission discourse at Lk. 10.2b-16 is 249 words long compared to 638 words in Mt. 10.5-42 (with Luke's version divided by a 32-word authorial aside at 7.29-30). The ecclesiastical discourse of Mt. 18.3-35 occupies 640 words. The fragmentary parallel at Lk. 17.1-4 runs to a mere 65 words, or 167 if one

---

[40] This argument is sometimes attributed to Goulder and Goodacre, and countered by Tuckett, Q, 27; Kloppenborg, *Excavating*, 16; and Kloppenborg, 'On Dispensing', 229–30.

[41] This is the argument Goulder, *Luke*, 39–41, and Goodacre, *Case*, 91–6, in fact make.

[42] This and the other word counts that follow were obtained by copying and pasting the relevant Greek passages into Microsoft Word and reading off the resulting word count from the first word uttered by the speaker to the last one inclusive of any narrative asides or interruptions that occur in the course of the speech. Since it is relative rather than absolute numbers that matter here, this should suffice for the purpose.

[43] Kloppenborg, 'On Dispensing', 229.

[44] This example of a long Lukan discourse is suggested by Tuckett, Q, 26–7.

takes this discourse as running on to Lk. 17.10, although if one instead takes Luke's parable discourse at Lk. 15.4-32 as his parallel to Mt. 18.12-14, then Luke's parable discourse (528 words) is still shorter than the full Matthew 18 discourse; but Luke's fragmentary use of Matthew 18 may make these comparisons meaningless. The woes on scribes at Mt. 23.2-39 takes up 644 words compared with 250 words for the comparable material at Lk. 11.39-52. The eschatological discourse at Lk. 17.20b-37 has 264 words compared with 746 at Mt. 24.4b-51, but since Luke here omits most of the Mark-based material he will use at Luke 21, this may not be a fair comparison. Luke 19.12-27 parallels only one of the parables of Mt. 25.1-46 and thus runs to 253 words compared with Matthew's 753. If one takes Matthew 24–25 to be one long discourse of 1,499 words, then we could take Luke as abbreviating part of it to 264 words at Lk. 17.20b-37 and redistributing another part to Lk. 19.12-27. While the 2DH could attribute each of these instances to Matthew's practice of constructing longer discourses out of material taken from various location in Q and/or expanding them with his own material, this does not negate the consistency with which FH Luke abbreviates Matthean discourses (and often redistributes parts of them) or the fact that he tends to treats Markan ones in the same way.

The third point is that Luke abbreviates the SM to focus it on fewer themes, thereby enhancing the conciseness and clarity of Jesus' keynote speech, in line with rhetorical aims common at the time.[45] Conciseness is not merely a matter of length; it is about including only what is relevant and appropriate while 'saying neither too much nor too little'.[46] In particular FH Luke would not regard either the interpretation of the Torah offered in Matthew chapter 5 or the polemical contrasts over pious practices in the first half of Matthew chapter 6 as relevant to his largely Gentile audience, since both passages primarily concerned intra-Jewish debate. The themes Luke focuses on are those of eschatological reversal (favouring the literally and not just spiritually poor)[47] and responding to persecution with love of enemies rather than demanding reciprocity,[48] which leads into the admonition to refrain from judging others and is then rounded off, as in the SM, with a peroration urging the listener to act on what has just been taught.[49] This focus leaves Luke free to reuse some of the omitted material in other contexts (particularly in his central section where he is keener to be polemical) while foregrounding aspects of Jesus' teaching that lead on from the final beatitude (about persecution) and that are of particular concern to Luke.

After the Sermon, Luke continues to follow Matthew with the story of the Capernaum Centurion (Lk. 7.1-10 || Mt. 8.5-13), passing over the healing of the Leper at Mt. 8.1-4

---

[45] Gorman, 'Crank', 73–80.
[46] Gorman, 'Crank', 79, citing Theon (Kennedy, *Progymnasmata*, 32) and Quintilian, *Inst.* 4.2.40-46.
[47] Luke's recasting of Matthew's Beatitudes echoes the Magnificat; cf. Lk. 6.21, 24-25a and 1.52-53.
[48] The Lukan transition here seemingly betrays knowledge of Matthew. At Mt. 8.44 ἐγὼ δὲ λέγω ὑμῖν· ἀγαπᾶτε τοὺς ἐχθροὺς ὑμῖν is clearly contrasted to what 'you have heard that it was said' at Mt. 8.43. The contrast at Lk. 6.27, Ἀλλὰ ὑμῖν λέγω τοῖς ἀκούουσιν· ἀγαπᾶτε κτλ., is less obviously appropriate following immediately after Lk. 6.26; Jesus' speech to the disciples can perhaps be contrasted with that of the ancestors to the false prophets, but 'speaking well of' does not so obviously contrast with 'love your enemy'. It may also be that Luke's τοῖς ἀκούουσιν was prompted by Ἠκούσατε at Mt. 5.43.
[49] Goodacre, *Case*, 96–103; Matson, 'Luke's Rewriting', 48–54; Franklin, *Luke*, 318–23.

since he has already used its Markan parallel at Lk. 5.12-16.⁵⁰ The rest of Matthew chapters 8–9 mostly consists of parallels to Markan material Luke has either already used or will use later in its Markan sequence, with the exception of Mt. 8.18-22; 9.37-38 which Luke will use for the introduction to the Mission of the Seventy, into which parts of Matthew 10 will also go. Luke will employ his version of Mark's Commissioning discourse in its Markan sequence at Lk. 9.1-6 and so largely reserves the Matthew 10 Commissioning discourse for the Mission of the Seventy. Meanwhile, in transitioning back from following Matthew to following Mark, Luke deploys special Lukan material (Lk. 7.11-17, 36-50; 8.1-3) either side of the section on John the Baptist he next takes from Matthew (Lk 7.18-35 || Mt. 11.2-11, 16-19). This section (not least in the L interpolation at Lk. 7.29-30) anticipates the theme of rejection that will be developed further in the central section but leaves until then material that can readily be detached from John the Baptist (Mt. 11.20-27 || Lk. 10.12-15, 21-22).⁵¹ If Luke wants to use Matthew's Baptist material, he has to do so before he mentions the Baptist's death in its Markan sequence at Lk. 9.7-9, and so inserts it in a Matthean sequence before he resumes following Mark for Lk. 8.4–9.50.

This raises a pair of interrelated questions. The first is whether Luke employs the John the Baptist material in its Matthean sequence, effectively skipping from Mt. 8.13 to Mt. 11.2 in his forward movement through Matthew, or whether he pulls it forward. The second is whether, despite initial appearances, Luke makes any further use of the material he apparently skips over in Matthew chapters 8 and 9. The questions are interrelated because if Luke has used Mt. 11.2-11, 16-19, in its Matthean sequence, any further use of Matthew 8 and 9 would then be out of sequence.

Although what actually went through Luke's mind is irrecoverable, it is more economical to assume that Luke pulled the Baptist material forward from its position

---

50 Aurelius, 'Gottesvolk', argues that the Matthean redaction of the stories of the Capernaum Centurion (Mt. 8.5-13) and the Canaanite woman (Mt. 15.21-28), who in Matthew are both commended for their faith, shows dependence on Jesus' reference to healings performed for Gentiles at Lk. 4.25-27, which Matthew omits because it went against his programme of 'go nowhere among the Gentiles'. Aurelius observes that Luke also has a pair of healing stories at Lk. 7.1-17 that look related to Lk. 4.25-27, but argues that Matthew illustrates Lk. 4.25-27 better than Luke does, because the story of the Widow of Nain does not concern a Gentile. Against that is the fact that Luke's story of the Widow of Nain more closely resembles the story of the Widow of Zarephath referenced at Lk. 4.26 than does anything in Matthew and that simultaneously illustrating and omitting Lk. 4.25-27 for the reasons Aurelius suggests looks suspiciously self-contradictory. The alleged connection Aurelius finds between Matthew and Luke here might equally well be explained by their common recognition of the imitation of 1 Kgs 17.7-16 at Mk 7.24-30, for which see Winn, *Mark*, 84–90. Aurelius has nevertheless pointed to a plausible connection between Lk. 4.25-27 and Lk. 7.1-17, since both concern a story about a foreign military officer and an allusion to the Widow of Zarephath. For the suggestion that Lk. 7.1-10 draws primarily on 2 Kgs 5.1-19 (which supports the connection with Lk. 4.25-27), see John Shelton, 'The Healing of Naaman (2 Kgs 5.1-19) as a Central Component for the Healing of the Centurion's Slave (Luke 1.7-10)' in John S. Kloppenborg and Joseph Verheyden (eds), *The Elijah-Elisha Narrative in the Composition of Luke* (LNTS, 493; London: Bloomsbury T&T Clark, 2014), 65–87, and the evaluation of Shelton's case by Alexander Damm, 'A Rhetorical-Critical Assessment of Luke's Use of the Elijah-Elisha Narrative' and Joseph Verheyden, 'By Way of Epilogue: Looking Back at the Healing of Naaman and the Healing of the Centurion's Slave – in Response to John Shelton' in Kloppenborg and Verheyden, *Elijah-Elisha Narrative*, 88–112 and 153–60 respectively. Overall it seems plausible, but by no means certain, that in producing his own version of the Capernaum Centurion pericope Luke may have adapted Matthew's version in light of the Naaman story.

51 For Luke's adaptation of the Baptist material in Mt. 11.2-19, see Wilkens, 'Täuferüberlieferung', 542–3.

in Matthew for the reasons stated: he had to use it before mentioning John's death at Lk. 9.7-9. Luke then used material from Matthew chapters 8, 9 and 10 roughly in Matthean sequence until arriving at Lk. 10.13-15 || Mt. 11.20-24.

An indication that Luke may be using Matthew 9 in the composition of the non-Markan section Lk. 6.20–8.3 comes in the report of Jesus' preaching tour at Lk. 8.1-2a, which is similar to that at Mt. 9.35 (see Table 6.3).

Table 6.3 Report of Jesus' Preaching Tour

Mt. 9.35	Lk. 8.1-2a
Καὶ περιῆγεν ὁ Ἰησοῦς τὰς **πόλεις** πάσας **καὶ** τὰς **κώμας**, διδάσκων ἐν ταῖς συναγωγαῖς αὐτῶν καὶ **κηρύσσων** τὸ **εὐαγγέλιον τῆς βασιλείας** καὶ **θεραπεύων** πᾶσαν νόσον καὶ πᾶσαν μαλακίαν.	Καὶ ἐγένετο ἐν τῷ καθεξῆς καὶ αὐτὸς διώδευεν κατὰ **πόλιν καὶ κώμην κηρύσσων** καὶ **εὐαγγελιζόμενος τὴν βασιλείαν** τοῦ θεοῦ, καὶ οἱ δώδεκα σὺν αὐτῷ, καὶ γυναῖκές τινες αἳ ἦσαν τε**θεραπευ**μέναι ἀπὸ πνευμάτων πονηρῶν καὶ ἀσθενειῶν,

While the verbal parallels are not that striking, Luke and Matthew agree in mentioning towns and villages, and in having Jesus preach the good news of the kingdom. They also agree in mentioning healing (albeit in different ways). Moreover, Luke's notice that Jesus was accompanied by the twelve plus some women may be loosely linked to the disciples and labourers Matthew goes on to mention at Mt. 9.37-38.

If Lk. 8.1-2a is indeed Luke's parallel to Mt. 9.35, then parts of Mt. 9.5-26 may be reflected in Lk. 7.11-17 and Lk. 9.36-50. The L story of the raising of the Widow's Son at Nain at Lk. 7.11-17 may in part have been prompted by the raising of the ruler's daughter at Mt. 9.18-19, 23-26, although it is more obviously inspired by the resuscitation performed by Elijah (1 Kgs 17.17-24).[52] One may wonder why of all the miracle and controversy stories Luke passes over in Matthew 8–9 he should choose just this one to reflect here. It may be that the raising of the widow's son was already available to him from a source, or it may be that Luke wanted to parallel a story about a man's daughter (which he will use at Lk. 8.40-56) with one about a woman's son, in line with his proclivity for such gender pairings.[53] Luke may also be picking up on Lk. 4.26 and preparing for the statement that 'the dead are raised' that follows as part of Jesus' reply to John the Baptist at Lk. 7.22.[54]

A particular point of contact between these Lukan and Matthean stories is that both end with similar notices (absent from the Markan parallel at Mk 5.35-43) that Jesus' action resulted in the spread of his fame over a wide area:

Table 6.4 The Spread of Jesus' Fame

Mt. 9.26	Lk. 7.17
καὶ **ἐξῆλθεν** ἡ φήμη <u>αὕτη</u> εἰς <u>ὅλην τὴν</u> γῆν ἐκείνην.	καὶ **ἐξῆλθεν** ὁ λόγος <u>οὗτος</u> ἐν <u>ὅλῃ τῇ</u> Ἰουδαίᾳ περὶ αὐτοῦ α καὶ πάσῃ τῇ περιχώρῳ.

---

[52] Evans, *Luke*, 346–7; Brodie, *Birthing*, 302–11.
[53] On such gender pairings in Luke, see, e.g., Robert C. Tannehill, *The Narrative Unity of Luke-Acts: A Literary Interpretation* 1: *The Gospel according to Luke* (Philadelphia: Fortress, 1986), 132–5.
[54] For the former, see n. 50 above.

Admittedly, the Lukan notice prepares for the messengers' report to John the Baptist at Lk. 7.18, and hence for John's question at Lk. 7.19, but the similarities remain. Given that FH Luke is going to redistribute the contents of Matthew 10 elsewhere, here he simply replicates the thrust of the Matthean sequence that leads from the miracles of Matthew 8–9 to the Baptist's question at Mt. 11.2-3, with the two non-Markan miracles Luke employs at Lk. 7.1-23 doing duty for the Markan miracles of Matthew 8–9 that Luke uses in their Markan sequence.[55]

There are also points of contact between Matthew chapter 9 and the L story of the sinful woman who washes Jesus' feet at Lk. 7.36-50. While this seems partly to be a Lukan version of Mark's anointing story at Mk 14.3-9, it shares with Mt. 9.2 an announcement of the forgiveness of sins (Lk. 7.48b Ἀφέωνταί σου αἱ ἁμαρτίαι = Mt. 9.2b), with Mt. 9.10-11 a Pharisaic complaint about Jesus consorting with sinners in the context of a meal and with Mt. 9.20-22 a woman who touches Jesus from behind (Lk. 7.38; Mt. 9.20) and is subsequently told that her faith has saved her (Lk. 7.50b Ἡ πίστις σου σέσωκέν σε = Mt. 9.22b).[56]

Luke has not yet finished with Matthew chapters 8 and 9, since he will return to them at the start of his central section, but after Lk. 8.4 he resumes following Mark until Lk. 9.51.

Luke's central section

Up to this point Luke has worked by alternating Markan and Matthean blocks, largely (though not exclusively) following the Markan narrative while mining Matthew for additional sayings material. On reaching his central section Luke once again switches back to Matthew while also bringing in material from elsewhere. Luke's task now becomes more complex because he is attempting to juggle a number of compositional aims and constraints. To identify what these are it will be convenient to review some previous attempts to explain the construction of the CS. C.F. Evans (followed, for example, by John Drury) proposed that the CS was structured as a Christian Deuteronomy. This suggestion founders on the tenuousness of many of the parallels needed to make Deuteronomy account for Luke's order,[57] but several of Evans' parallels nevertheless work quite well, and some of his insights are worth pursuing, including the recognition of Luke's presentation of Jesus as a prophet like Moses (made most explicit at Acts 3.22-23).[58] Not least, Evans calls attention to the portentous nature of Lk. 9.51, arguing that while Luke may not have got his Septuagintal idiom completely right, the notice that Jesus 'set his face to go to Jerusalem' is not simply a statement of

---

[55] So also Goulder, *Luke*, 381–7, who further suggests that Luke has also drawn on Mt. 9.2-8 for this story.
[56] Goulder, *Luke*, 397–402.
[57] C.F. Evans, 'The Central Section of St. Luke's Gospel' in D.E. Nineham (ed.), *Studies in the Gospels: Essays in Memory of R. H. Lightfoot* (Oxford: Blackwell, 1955), 37–53; Drury, *Tradition*, 138–64.
[58] For a sympathetic critique, including a list of the more plausible parallels with Deuteronomy, see Franklin, *Luke*, 335–6. Franklin also gives a helpful critique of the thesis that the central section is a chiasmus. Plausible parallels with material from Deuteronomy are shown in the L column of Table 6.8.

determination but implies that Jesus is going to confront Jerusalem.⁵⁹ Evans' discussion of ἀνάλημψις at Lk. 9.51 ('When the days drew near for him to be received up') points towards a Christological significance for the journey: Jesus' ἀνάλημψις will encompass not just his ascension but also all the events leading up to it, so that Jesus' journey is one leading through confrontation to his Passion and Resurrection.⁶⁰

David Moessner develops the notion that Luke portrays Jesus as the Prophet Like Moses setting out on a New Exodus (Lk. 9.31) to pronounce judgement on Jerusalem (the nation's centre) as a result of Israel's rejection of its Messiah and his offer of salvation. Luke thus presents Jesus as the latest in a long line of prophets whom Israel reject and kill.⁶¹ This reading finds support in Helmuth Egelkraut's earlier redaction-critical study of the CS, which argued, first, that Luke has tended to transfer controversy pericopae into his CS and to enhance their polemical aspect, and, second, that in the CS Jesus confronts Israel with the coming of the kingdom in his person, demanding a response Israel refuses to give, so that judgement comes upon Israel and a new community is formed in its place.⁶² Egelkraut nonetheless differs from Evans and Moessner in placing the emphasis almost exclusively on conflict.⁶³

More recently, Mark Goodacre has proposed that the CS should be understood as Luke's adoption of the Way of the Lord theme from Mark, which emphasizes Jesus' progress on the way towards his Passion, but also the Way as the path of discipleship (cf. Acts 9.2; 19.9, 23; 24.14). Whereas Mark's central section constitutes a substantial segment of Mark's Gospel, in Matthew the effect of this is lost through the expansion of Jesus' Galilean ministry with the inclusion of four substantial discourses. Luke's creation of an elongated central section, emphatically marked off by the notice at Lk. 9.51, restores both the Markan emphasis and the Markan proportion by incorporating much of Matthew's Galilean ministry.⁶⁴

Overall, then, Luke's CS serves a number of related purposes. One is to give instruction on discipleship, another is to chart the growing opposition to Jesus from the ancestral people of God in the course of forging a new people of God, which will lead to the tragedy of Israel's rejection of its Messiah. This in turn serves the Christological function of portraying Jesus on the way through suffering and death to resurrection and ascension, the soteriological function of pointing the way to the salvation and ultimate vindication of the faithful and the ecclesiological function of justifying the

---

⁵⁹ So also Robert Maddox, *The Purpose of Luke-Acts* (SNTW; Edinburgh: T&T Clark, 1982), 46–7.
⁶⁰ Brodie, *Birthing*, 351–82 (esp. 351–8), finds an imitation of 2 Kgs 1.1–2.15 in this section of Luke, not least of Elijah's journey to be taken up. While there is some merit in some of Brodie's suggestions, it seems more plausible to suppose that any imitation of the Elijah narrative here originated in Mark's imitation of 2 Kings, for which see Winn, *Mark*, 92–9, although it is conceivable that Luke built on this when he adapted Mark.
⁶¹ David P. Moessner, *Lord of the Banquet: The Literary and Theological Significance of the Lukan Travel Narrative* (Minneapolis: Augsburg Fortress, 1989), esp. 325.
⁶² Helmuth K. Egelkraut, *Jesus' Mission to Jerusalem: A Redaction Critical Study of the Travel Narrative in the Gospel of Luke, Lk 9: 51–19:48* (Frankfurt: Peter Lang, 1976), esp. 133, 189–96.
⁶³ Egelkraut, *Jesus' Mission*, 222–3.
⁶⁴ Mark Goodacre, 'Re-Walking the "Way of the Lord": Luke's Use of Mark and His Reaction to Matthew' in Mogens Müller and Jesper Tang Nielsen (eds), *Luke's Literary Creativity* (LNTS, 550; London: Bloomsbury T&T Clark, 2016), 26–43.

predominantly Gentile church whose growth will be charted in Acts.[65] All this is expressed typologically through portraying Jesus as the Prophet Like Moses who will suffer the fate of the prophets who came before, a typology in which Deuteronomy provides one possible hypotext but not a controlling one.[66]

Yet while the CS can be seen to exhibit reasonable thematic unity, questions might still be raised about its literary coherence, and in particular, the consistency of its travel motif. It has often been observed that Luke's Jesus sets out for Jerusalem at Lk. 9.51 and then spends many chapters going nowhere in particular. At Lk. 9.52-56, Jesus apparently prepares to strike south through Samaria, but on being rebuffed, moves on to another village whose location is unspecified. There are then occasional notices of Jesus and his disciples continuing on their way (Lk. 10.38; 13.22, 33; 14.25) but at Lk. 17.11 Jesus is still passing along between Samaria and Galilee. This has often been put down to Luke's hazy geography,[67] but it is better to assume that after Jesus' abortive foray into Samaria, Luke envisages him heading eastwards to continue his journey via Peraea (as in Mark). That Jesus is travelling through Jewish territory is in any case suggested by the Pharisees, lawyers and synagogues he encounters (or mentions) along the way. Luke thus combines Mark's important Way of the Lord theme with Matthew's extended Galilean ministry, much of which now takes place on a journey east to approach Jerusalem via Peraea and Jericho (Lk. 18.35).[68] The travel theme in Luke's CS is by no means limited to the notices of Jesus' movements but emerges also in a number of parables that involve a journey of some sort (Lk. 10.30-35; 11.5-6; 12.35-38; 15.3-7, 11-32; 19.11-27) and in the several meals, which can be understood as hospitality accorded to travellers on a mission (Lk. 10.7).[69]

Goodacre warns that proposals for how FH Luke's reordering of Matthew's material might be accounted for on some grand scheme such as a lectionary theory or sequential parallels with Deuteronomy serve only to undermine the case for Luke's use of Matthew by making it appear mysterious and implausible.[70] Nonetheless, some account needs to be given of FH Luke's method of working. A convenient jumping-off point for this is provided by an early suggestion of Michael Goulder that the CS is arranged chiastically.[71] The suggestion doesn't work all that well as it stands, since there is too much material it fails to account for and the chiasm is in any case far from exact. It nevertheless draws attention to two important features of the CS. The first is that the

---

[65] Cf. the summary at Franklin, *Luke*, 330.
[66] In addition to the Moses typology, and several plausible parallels to Lukan material, Deuteronomy also contains instructions for God's people set in the context of Israel's journey to the Promised Land (see, e.g., Deuteronomy 1-3, in which Moses recounts Israel's journey so far). Table 6.8 suggests possible secondary influence of passages from Deut. 1.22-8.30 for parts of Lk. 9.52-13.32 and Deut. 20.5-26.15 for parts of Lk. 14.15-18.14, in roughly corresponding order, but these are tangential to the argument below.
[67] E.g. by Fitzmyer, *Luke X-XXIV*, 1152-3.
[68] So also Goulder, *Luke*, 454-5, 644-5; and Moessner, *Lord of the Banquet*, 292-4, who suggests that the Lukan Jesus' route to Jerusalem might be even less direct.
[69] Goodacre, 'Re-Walking', 39-40.
[70] Goodacre, 'Re-Walking', 27-8; cf. Peterson, 'Order', 38.
[71] Michael Goulder, *Type and History in Acts* (London: SPCK, 1964), 138.

CS falls into two halves, with the mid-point of the journey occurring at Lk. 13.21-35 enclosed by the stories of the Bent Woman (Lk. 13.10-17) and the Man with Dropsy (Lk. 14.1-6). The second is that there is a section on each of three themes important to Luke that occur in both halves of the journey, with the order reversed in the second half: prayer (Lk. 11.1-13; 18.1-14), riches (Lk. 12.13-34; 16.1-31) and repentance (Lk. 12.57–13.9; 15.1-32). These are all themes that Luke will go on to present as occurring in the life and preaching of the church in Acts.[72] The two questions about what to do to inherit eternal life (Lk. 10.25-37; 18.18-30) also fit the chiasm. Thus, while Goulder's proposed chiasm fails to account for the CS as a whole, it does point to certain key themes Luke was keen to emphasize and appears to have done so by deploying them chiastically across the CS.

These are not the only themes found in the CS, however. As noted above, Luke also wishes to depict the gathering of a new people of God against the growing opposition of the Jewish establishment, another theme that will be further developed in Acts culminating in the Gentile mission against a background of growing Jewish intransigence (Acts 28.25-28). This opposition will lead to the suffering and death of Jesus (Lk. 9.22, 44; 13.33; 18.31-33; 23.32-46), just as it will lead to suffering and often martyrdom for many of his followers (e.g. Lk. 9.23; Acts 7.54-60; 9.16; 12.1-4; 14.19).

These themes require others to complete the picture Luke wants to paint. Repentance is for the purpose of salvation which the Lukan God is keen to offer to the lost. Failure to repent will lead to forfeiture of salvation, and so the need for repentance as a matter of urgency is pressed with reference to judgement and the end. Moreover, both the Lukan Jesus' stringent commands about the proper use of money and his warnings about potentially deadly opposition to the gospel imply a high cost of discipleship. These various themes are linked, so that they cannot always be neatly separated out into distinct blocks and are often intertwined (e.g. repentance should lead to proper use of one's wealth and may be motivated by signs of the approaching end).

Much of the material left over from the SM to be taken up in the CS is gathered under one or other of these themes: the cluster on Prayer (Lk. 11.1-13 ← Mt. 6.9-13; 7.7-11); the cluster on the Lamp on the Stand and the Sound Eye, taken as connoting generosity (Lk. 11.33-36 ← Mt. 5.15; 6.22-3); the cluster on Riches (Lk. 12.13-34 ← Mt. 6.25-34, 19-21); the cluster(s) on Preparedness for the End (Lk. 12.35–13.9, 13.23-35 ← Mt. 7.13-14, 22-23); and the cluster about Riches and the Law (Lk. 16.1-31 ← Mt. 6.24; 11.12-13; 5.17-20; 5.31-2).[73] That Luke intended to develop these themes in his CS further explains why he omitted this material from the SP to leave for later.

In sum, the composition of Luke's CS involves him in negotiating a number of constraints, chief among which are covering the themes he wishes to cover (not least

---

[72] Prayer: Acts 1.14; 2.42, 6.4; 7.59; 9.11; 10.2-4, 9, 30; 11.5; 12.12, 13.3, 14.23; 21.5; 22.17; Money: Acts 2.44-45; 4.32-35; 8.20; and possibly 20.35. Repentance: Acts 2.38; 3.19-26; 7.30-31; 8.22-24; 13.24; 19.4; 20.21; 26.20.

[73] See further, Matson, 'Luke's Rewriting', 50–62. See also the structural observations in Allan J. McNicol, David L. Dungan and David B. Peabody, *Beyond the Q Impasse: Luke's Use of Matthew* (Valley Forge: Trinity Press International, 1996), 152–3. Although McNicol et al. are writing from a 2GH rather than FH perspective, the scarcity of Markan material in CS means that many of their insights are equally applicable to either theory.

in anticipation of Acts) while continuing to follow Matthew as far as he can. Luke also aims to create a sense of both narrative and geographical movement within the framework of an extended Way of the Lord section (where 'way' refers to both the path to Jerusalem and the path of discipleship). The first two constraints pull both ways: sometimes the theme Luke wishes to present dictates the material he employs from Matthew and the use he makes of it, while sometimes what he encounters next in Matthew will influence which of his themes Luke takes up next.

The detailed discussion that follows will focus principally on exploring the extent to which Luke continues to follow Matthew, where following Matthew means continuing to work forward through Matthew's text, albeit often block by block rather than verse by verse or pericope by pericope. Some attention will be given to how this interacts with his other constraints, but to give a complete account of Luke's compositional procedure would require a detailed commentary on the entire CS, which would go well beyond what can be attempted here. The main point will be to demonstrate that Luke's order continues to be guided by Matthew's to a greater extent than is normally appreciated.

Luke's absolute position in Matthew has progressed steadily forward up until Lk. 8.1, with only one major departure from Matthew's order (bringing forward the John the Baptist material from Matthew 11). Luke proceeds block by block, rather than pericope by pericope, meaning that Luke reads or recalls several Matthean pericopae at a time before composing his next block and then sometimes rearranges the Matthean material within that block. For example, while Lk. 11.14-32 is derived from Mt. 12.22-50, the order of units within that block has been slightly rearranged (much as 2DH Matthew would have to have rearranged Q 11.14-32). Luke sometimes does this with Mark, for example, at Lk. 8.4-21 || Mk 3.21-4.25 where Luke repositions the pericope on Jesus' true family to after the parable section. Our proposal, then, is that this forward block-by-block movement through Matthew provides a framework around which Luke weaves the topical sequences he constructs out of Matthean material culled from elsewhere (such as Matthew's SM) and his own special material.[74] The principal Matthean framework for Luke's CS is set out in Table 6.5.

Table 6.5 Luke's Direct Movement through Matthew

D1	Lk. 9.57-62	|| Mt. 8.19-22?
D2	Lk. 10.2	|| Mt. 9.37-38
D3	Lk. 10.3-12	|| Mt. 10.7-16
D4	Lk. 10.13-15	|| Mt. 11.20-24
D5	Lk. 10.21-22	|| Mt. 11.25-27
D6	Lk. 11.14-32	|| Mt. 12.22-45, (50)
D7	Lk. 12.10	|| Mt. 12.31-32

---

[74] The presence of this framework by no means excludes the possible influence of others, such as one partly built on Deuteronomy (provided this is not taken to the extreme of making any such Deuteronomic frame the controlling one; see Franklin, *Luke*, 333–6).

D8	Lk. 13.18-21	‖ Mt. 13.31-33
D9	Lk. 15.3-7	‖ Mt. 18.12-14
D10	Lk. 17.1-4	‖ Mt. 18.6-7, 15, 21-22
D11	Lk. 17.20-37	‖ Mt. 24.17-41
D12	Lk. 19.11-27	‖ Mt. 25.14-30

The twelve items listed in Table 6.5 indicate a predominantly forward movement through Matthew. The extent of these parallels may not initially appear impressive, incorporating only 86 out of the 660 (13.0 per cent) Matthean verses in Mt. 8.19–25.30. But 379 (57.4 per cent) of these verses have parallels in Mark, which Luke (nearly always) employs either in their Markan sequence or not at all. A further 85 verses are M material that Luke does not (at least directly) employ. This leaves 196 double tradition Matthean verses from Mt. 8.19–25.30 which Luke employs in his central section, of which the 86 covered in Table 6.5 account for 43.9 per cent. Up until the end of Matthew 18 (D1–D10) this proportion rises to 53.3 per cent (56 out of 105 verses).[75]

Notable departures from this sequence occur in eight sections where Luke borrows forward from Matthew. These are listed in Table 6.6.

Table 6.6 Forward Borrowing from Matthew in Luke's Central Section

F1	Lk. 10.23-24	‖ Mt. 13.16-17
F2	Lk. 11.39-54	‖ Mt. 23.4, 6-7, 13, 23, 25-32, 34-36
F3	Lk. 12.1	‖ Mt. 16.6
F4	Lk. 12.35-38	‖ Mt. 25.1-13?
F5	Lk. 12.39-46	‖ Mt. 24.42-51
F6	Lk. 12.54-56	‖ Mt. 16.2-3
F7	Lk. 13.34-35	‖ Mt. 23.37-39
F8	Lk. 14.15-24	‖ Mt. 22.1-14

These eight forward borrowings constitute some 60 verses in Luke, of which 54 (90 per cent), or 56 out of 61 (92 per cent) Matthean verses, are taken from Matthew chapters 22–25. Possible reasons for these translocations will be suggested as we come to them below. Only two of these items (F5 and F7) exhibit a notably high degree of verbal agreement between Luke and Matthew, being about 85 per cent in each case.[76] It seems unlikely that Luke would scroll forwards from his absolute position in Matthew just to retrieve these ten verses, so it is better to assume that Luke had good memory command of these passages. The verbal agreement in the other passages is moderate to low, which is consistent with Luke having retrieved and adapted the material from memory (although, of course, it does not prove that he did so). The parallels at F4 are

---

[75] There is inevitably some element of subjectivity in judging a small number of instances where there may be more than one way of counting what should be taking as paralleling what.
[76] Calculated as a percentage of Luke's words, and excluding Peter's interruption at Lk. 12.41-42a, which lacks a parallel in Matthew.

sufficiently loose as to cast doubt on whether Luke was using the Matthean passage at all, although the contiguity of Lukan and Matthean material at F4 and F5 tips the balance in favour of Luke's having freely adapted Matthew here.

For D1–D5 (the first five items in Table 6.5), the Lukan sequence is tightly determined by the Matthean one: at Lk. 10.17-20 (the Return of the Seventy) Luke inserts a small amount of L material; otherwise he constructs this sequence almost entirely from Matthean material taken in its Matthean order, skipping over material where Matthew depends on Mark (Mt. 8.23–9.36; 10.1-4, 17-23), or which he has used previously (principally Mt. 11.2-19 on John the Baptist) or which he will keep for later (Mt. 10.26-42). Thereafter there are substantial gaps in the Lukan sequence shown in Table 6.5. In these gaps Luke deploys a combination of his own special material and Matthean material taken out of its Matthean sequence. These gaps correspond to substantial gaps in the Matthean sequence; for example, the gap between Lk. 10.23 and Lk. 11.14 (D5 and D6) corresponds to a gap between Mt. 11.27 and Mt. 12.22. Most of these gaps (the most substantial being Mt. 12.46–13.30; 13.34–18.10; and 18.23–24.16) occur where Matthew mainly has material he shares with Mark, which Luke either deploys in its Markan sequence or not at all. Luke will nevertheless encounter this Matthean gap material as he works steadily forwards through Matthew (whether he is reading from a manuscript or recalling Matthew from memory). This raises the possibility that this otherwise unused Matthean gap material may influence the choice of material Luke employs in the corresponding Lukan gaps. Such indirect use of Matthew would be at least partially analogous to that of Mt. 4.13-16 at Lk. 4.16-30 or Mt. 9.5-26 at Lk. 7.11-17 and Lk. 9.10-22.[77]

Table 6.7 lists the most plausible indirect parallels, the three shown in italics (I3, I10, I11) being the most tentative. Each of the thirteen will be discussed as it arises below.

Table 6.7 Indirect Uses of Matthew in Luke's Central Section

I1	Mt. 10.5	→ Lk. 9.52-56
I2	Mt. 12.1-7	→ Lk. 10.25-37
I3	*Mt. 12.33-37*	→ *Lk. 11.39-41*
I4	Mt. 13.1-50	→ Lk. 12.1–13.29
I5	Mt. 14.1-11	→ Lk. 13.31-33
I6	Mt. 14.1-21	→ Lk. 14.7-24
I7	Mt. 15.5-6; 16.24-26	→ Lk. 14.25-27
I8	Mt. 18.23-34	→ Lk. 16.1-12
I9	Mt. 19.1-26	→ Lk. 16.16-31
I10	*Mt. 20.1-16*	→ *Lk. 17.7-10*
I11	*Mt. 20.29-34*	→ *Lk. 17.11-19*
I12	Mt. 21.21	→ Lk. 17.6
I13	Mt. 24.29-31, 44-51	→ Lk. 18.1-8

---

[77] That Luke has already made indirect use of Mt. 9.10-26 may partially explain why he makes no attempt to make further use of this part of Matthew between D1 and D2.

If Luke's proposed indirect uses of Matthew are set alongside his direct uses, his consistent forward movement through Matthew becomes more apparent, as can be seen from Table 6.8 (at the end of this chapter). Together, the D and I sequences account for 265 (65.3 per cent) out of the 406 Lukan verses from Lk. 9.52 to 19.27, a further 29 (7.1 per cent) being accounted for by Luke following Mark at Lk. 18.15-43. This leaves 110 verses (27.1 per cent) in which Luke deploys material not accounted for in this way.[78] Some of this other material may also be due to the D+I sequence, as, for example, where Lk. 15.8-32 supplies two further parables of loss and restoration to follow the D Parable of the Lost Sheep at Lk. 15.3-7.

Table 6.7 is not intended to suggest that Luke consistently spins large amounts of material out of hints in the Matthean text. He may sometimes be creative in this way, but it seems unlikely that this accounts for all the L material. For one thing, in the CS Luke goes to some trouble to redeploy material taken from elsewhere in Matthew, which suggests a preference for using existing material. For another, much of the special Lukan material sits awkwardly in its Lukan context, so that, for example, the parables do not always obviously make the point Luke uses them to make. This suggests that he is more likely to be drawing the bulk of them from some (oral or written) source than creating them for the context in which he places them.[79]

While we cannot give a detailed commentary on every aspect of the CS here, it will be helpful to flesh out the bare bones set out above. In what follows we shall accordingly run through the CS to show how Luke is influenced by Matthew's order while at the same time pursuing his own compositional agenda. As stated above, sometimes the theme Luke wishes to present dictates the material he employs from Matthew and the use he makes of it, while sometimes what he encounters next in Matthew will influence which of his themes Luke takes up next.

The CS opens with the announcement of Jesus' imminent ἀνάλημψις together with his setting his face for Jerusalem. In keeping with this intention, Jesus first strikes south through Samaria, where he is at once rebuffed (Lk. 9.52-56). This pericope operates at several levels. Ostensibly Jesus shows mercy by refusing his disciples' inappropriate suggestion that he call down fire from heaven like Elijah in 2 Kgs 1.9-12.[80] But given the warning issued to unrepentant cities at Lk. 10.10-15, this may only be a temporary stay of execution. According to Lk. 10.12 it will be more tolerable for Sodom on the Day of Judgment than for towns that do not receive Jesus' mission, and according to Gen. 19.24 Sodom and Gomorrah were destroyed by fire from heaven.[81] It is too early for a Samaritan mission to succeed, since this is to be initiated after the Ascension (Acts 1.8; 8.4-25), but the abortive foray into Samaritan territory foreshadows what is to come.[82] The Samaritan rebuttal also allows Luke to have Jesus continue on his way

---

[78] Clearly the precise figures could be disputed; the point is to give a general sense of the proportions involved.
[79] Cf. Goodacre, *Goulder and the Gospels*, 132–291, esp. the conclusions at 281–91.
[80] Brodie, *Birthing*, 351–8, makes a reasonably plausible case for seeing Lk. 9.51-56 as (at least in part) a rhetorical imitation of 2 Kgs 1.1–2.6.
[81] McNicol et al., *Beyond*, 154–5, and Goulder, *Luke*, 458–9, similarly see links with Mt. 10.5 and the destruction of Sodom and Gomorrah here.
[82] Cf. Goulder, *Type*, 57–8.

through Galilee instead (see above). But the placement of this incident at the start of Jesus' journey could also result from Luke's first indirect use of Matthew in the CS:

I1 *Mt. 10.5 → Lk. 9.52-56*: With the rejection of Jesus by the Samaritans compare the command at Mt. 10.5 to 'enter no town of the Samaritans' εἰς πόλιν Σαμαριτῶν μὴ εἰσέλθητε; cf. Lk. 9.52 εἰσῆλθον εἰς κώμην Σαμαριτῶν. Luke partly reflects and partly corrects Matthew: it was not so much that Jesus rejected the Samaritans as that they rejected him.

The Mission of the Seventy, which forms Luke's next main unit, may in part be inspired by the appointment of the seventy elders at Num. 11.16-25 followed by the mission of the spies in Numbers 13;[83] it is given far greater emphasis than the Mission of the Twelve at Lk. 9.1-6 and evokes far more of a response. It may be intended to prefigure the Gentile mission in Acts, rather as the Mission of the Twelve at Lk. 9.1-6 might prefigure the Mission of the Twelve in Judaea at the start of Acts.[84] In constructing it, Luke gathers up hitherto unused material from Matthew 8–9 relevant to the sending out of the Seventy.[85] He first inserts material on following Jesus (D1: Lk. 9.57-62 || Mt. 8.19-22), which is appropriate to the start of a journey, not least since Lk. 9.57 adds the detail that the first would-be follower encounters Jesus ἐν τῇ ὁδῷ, in keeping with the 'Way of the Lord' theme taken over from Mark. Luke also adds a third would-be disciple to Matthew's two, the first of a number of instances in the CS displaying Luke's proclivity for patterns of three.[86] Coming near the start of the CS this pericope also gives Luke the opportunity to emphasize a theme that will recur throughout, namely that following Jesus in the way of discipleship comes with stringent demands for wholehearted commitment.

It is followed by instructions to missionaries preparing Jesus' further outreach to Israel (D2 & D3: Lk. 10.2-12 || Mt. 9.37-38; 10.7-16), which, as suggested above, may also be intended to prefigure the missionary endeavours in Acts. Paul, the main driver of the Gentile mission, will also embark on a fateful journey to Jerusalem resulting in a series of trials before a similar set of authorities to those that await Jesus.

---

[83] McNicol et al., *Beyond*, 160. Brodie, *Birthing*, 365–76, suggests Lk. 10.1-20 is an imitation of 2 Kgs 2.16–3.27, but here too many of the proposed parallels seem strained, and it is questionable whether the criterion of thematic congruence is adequately met.

[84] Cf. Goulder, *Type*, 57–61. Goulder has the Mission of the Seventy correspond to the Mission of the Seven in Acts, but the weight given to the Mission of the Seventy in Luke together with the possibility that seventy is intended to evoke the traditional number of the nations suggests that Luke has something more far-reaching in mind.

[85] It is admittedly awkward to incorporate both D1 and I1 into the forward sequence. If neither of them is included, then Luke neatly leaves Matthew behind at Lk. 8.1-2 || Mt. 9.35 and picks him up again at Lk. 10.2 || Mt. 9.37 having largely followed Mark in between. Including I1 is not that difficult, however, since it simply needs Luke to read (or recall) Mt. 9.37–10.16 before composing the block Lk. 9.52–10.12 (say). But incorporating D1 requires Luke to backtrack to Mt. 8.19-22 just to pick up that one pericope. If Luke is refreshing his memory from a manuscript of Matthew then D1 should perhaps instead be reckoned as an out-of-sequence recollection of material from earlier in Matthew; but if Luke is working purely from memory here, he still ends up recalling Mt. 8.19-22 followed by Mt. 9.37-38.

[86] Drury, *Tradition*, 145–6.

The connection of thought from D1 to D2 may be that Jesus needs committed followers to send out on mission. Since Luke is recounting Israel's rejection of Jesus, the next pericope from his direct Matthean sequence (woes on Galilean cities) is also relevant to his theme (D4: Lk. 10.13-15 || Mt. 11.20-24).[87] The L Return of the Seventy (Lk. 10.17-20) then rounds off the Mission of the Seventy, which can be conveniently capped by the next item in Matthew, Jesus' thanksgiving to the Father (D5: Lk. 10.21-22 || Mt. 11.25-27), after which Luke pulls in a couple of verses from later in Matthew (F1: Lk. 10.23-24 || Mt. 13.16-17) to round off the theme of privileged revelation.

The reasons why Luke should skip over the rest of Matthew 10 are not hard to discern: Mt. 10.17-22 is parallel to Mk 13.9-13, which Luke will use in its Markan sequence at Lk. 21.12-19, and the remainder of Matthew 10 is not especially relevant to the theme of commissioning, while the material Lk. 10.13-15 picks up from Mt. 11.20-24 continues the theme of judgement on unrepentant cities introduced at Lk. 10.10-12 || Mt. 10.14-15.[88]

At this point Luke has used up a substantial proportion of direct-sequence Matthean material and has seemingly exhausted the material directly relevant to the start of Jesus' journey. Luke makes no use of Mt. 11.28-30 ('come unto me') or Mt. 12.15-21 (the fulfilment of the servant prophecy), while Mt. 12.1-14 contains Markan material Luke has already used (at Lk. 6.1-11), so the next item Luke directly employs from his sequential use of Matthew will be the Beelzebul Controversy (D7: Lk. 11.14-23 || Mt. 12.22-30). Before he reaches it, he inserts three items of L material and two pieces from the SM. Together these concern three fundamental aspects of discipleship: love of neighbour, prayer and listening to the Lord, which would seem appropriate following the previous sequence on making disciples.

First comes the Lawyer's question and the Parable of the Good Samaritan. This picks up on the theme of loving not only neighbours but enemies which Luke foregrounds

---

[87] On Luke's redeployment of this material from Matthew 11, see also Wilkens, 'Täuferüberlieferung', 556–7. Alex Damm, 'Ancient Rhetoric and the Synoptic Problem' in Paul Foster, Andrew Gregory, John S. Kloppenborg and J. Verheyden (eds), *New Studies in the Synoptic Problem* (BETL, 139; Leuven: Leuven University Press, 2011), 483–508, here 494, sees Lk. 10.12 as the central maxim of the ring composition into which Luke has drawn Lk. 10.2-16.

[88] The Matthean material FH Luke passes over here would also not fit the ring construction identified by Damm, 'Ancient Rhetoric'. In the main Damm finds the changes FH Luke would have made to Matthew in this speech to be unproblematic in light of what would be expected from ancient rhetorical theory, but is less sanguine about some of the omissions FH Luke would have made from Matthew. Some of these may not be as troubling as Damm suggests, however. He points out, for example, that the mention of Jesus' compassion at Mt. 9.36 is not reflected at Lk. 10.1. But the context in Matthew is provided by Mt. 9.35, which explains the presence of the crowds on whom Jesus has compassion. Luke has already used Mt. 9.35 at Lk. 8.1, but at Lk. 10.1 he provides his own introduction to the Mission of the Seventy independently from Matthew and in a context from which the compassion-needing crowds are absent. Damm also points to the surprising omission of ἐξουσίαν (found in Mt. 10.1) from Lk. 10.1, when it might have helped strengthen a positive portrayal of Jesus' character. But Luke has already used Mt. 10.1 at Lk. 9.1, while at Lk. 10.1 he is composing his own introduction afresh (and as Damm notes, Luke subsequently does pick up on the missionaries' delegated authority at Lk. 10.19). Overall Damm (502) concludes that FH Luke's of Matthew would be reasonably plausible here, although 'there are cases where he seems to satisfy one rhetorical principle by attenuating another. This is not necessarily a problem, but it remains noteworthy'.

in the SP, but may also have been prompted by material Luke otherwise passes over in Matthew:

I2 *Mt. 12.1-7 → Lk. 10.25-37*: At first sight, the Lukan Parable of the Good Samaritan has little to do with the Matthean account of Plucking Grain on the Sabbath (which Luke has already used in its Markan sequence at Lk. 6.1-5). But Matthew's version includes a number of additions to Mark's. These include Matthew's citation of Hos. 6.6 'I desire mercy and not sacrifice' (Ἔλεος θέλω καὶ οὐ θυσίαν). Luke's parable could be read as a narrative illustration of the same point, given that it is a priest and a Levite who pass by on the other side (possibly so they can avoid the ritual defilement that might prevent their service in the temple, although they are travelling in the wrong direction for that to be an immediate concern). As Jesus' interlocutor is made to recognize, the person who acted as a neighbour was the Samaritan who showed mercy (ὁ ποιήσας τὸ ἔλεος μετ' αὐτοῦ). Moreover, while the Lukan introduction to the parable looks loosely based on the scribe's question at Mk 12.28-31, unlike Mark, Luke has Jesus initially respond with the counter-question 'What is written in the law, how do you read?' (Ἐν τῷ νόμῳ τί γέγραπται; πῶς ἀναγινώσκεις;). This echoes one of the questions Matthew adds to the grain-plucking pericope at Mt. 12.5, 'have you not read in the law ... ?' (ἢ οὐκ ἀνέγνωτε ἐν τῷ νόμῳ). Priests serving in the Temple are allowed to break the Sabbath (Mt. 12.5); could not the priest on the Jericho road (Lk. 10.31) have taken an equally flexible view about purity?[89] The suggestion is not that Luke has composed the entirety of Lk. 10.25-42 on the slender basis of these two verses in Matthew, but that coming upon this pericope in Matthew in the course of scrolling forwards from Matt 11.24 prompted the use of this material in Luke.[90]

Jesus' disciples have already been admonished to listen to him by the divine voice on the mount of Transfiguration (Lk. 9.35; cf. Acts 3.22 and Deut. 18.18-19). The next pericope in the CS, on Martha and Mary (Lk. 10.38-42), now emphasizes prioritizing listening to Jesus. Here Luke employs another of his common devices, pairing a story featuring a male protagonist with one featuring a female one.[91] Mary and the Lawyer represent contrasting ways of listening to Jesus (referred to as 'the Lord' throughout the Mary and Martha pericope), while Martha, the priest and the levite all exhibit forms of displacement activity falling short of true discipleship. Martha's criticism of Mary at Lk. 10.40 and Jesus' defence of her may also echo the contrasting reactions to the woman who showed devotion to Jesus at Mk 14.3-9.[92]

We have already seen that prayer is an important topic for Luke, so it comes as no great surprise that he should round off his teaching on the fundamentals of discipleship

---

[89] There could also be some influence from the following Matthean pericope, Mt. 12.9-14, which urges the appropriateness of doing good on the Sabbath.
[90] Goulder, *Luke*, 485–8, sees similar connections between Luke and Matthew here.
[91] McNicol et al., *Beyond*, 172, suggest Luke may be illustrating the blessing on those who see and hear at Lk. 10.23-24, balancing the preceding story about a man with one about a woman. See also n. 53.
[92] That John understood Luke this way is suggested by the fact that he made Mary the woman who anoints Jesus while Martha serves the meal (Jn 11.1-2; 12.1-8).

with a short section on prayer (Lk. 11.1-13). This is composed of the Lord's Prayer (Lk. 11.1-4 || Mt. 6.9-13), the Parable of the Importunate Friend at Midnight (Lk. 11.5-8) and the Encouragement to Pray (Lk. 11.9-13 || Mt. 7.7-11). With the end of this section Luke has covered three themes foundational to discipleship appropriately situated early in the journey ἐν τῇ ὁδῷ.[93]

Luke now moves on from the basics of discipleship to the opposition that the gospel provokes. He may have chosen to do this of his own accord in any case, since (as we have seen) it is clearly an issue he finds important, but he is also prompted to do so (at Lk. 11.14-32) by what he next comes across in his progress through Matthew, namely the Beelzebul Controversy and the material that follows it (D6: Lk. 11.14-23|| Mt. 12.22-45). Luke presents this material in a slightly different order from Matthew (Lk. 11.24-32 || Mt. 12.43-45, 50, 38-42), but by moving Mt. 12.43-45 to a position immediately following the Beelzebul Controversy, at Lk. 11.24-26, Luke makes it more clearly relate to the issue of exorcism rather than act as a metaphorical warning to the generation who fail to heed the sign of Jonah. Moreover, repositioning the vacated house pericope immediately after Luke's rendering of the strong man continues the metaphorical connection between invaded properties and the liberation of possessed persons.[94]

In Matthew it is the Pharisees who charge that Jesus is casting out demons by the power of Beelzebul; in Luke it is some of the crowd, perhaps because Luke wishes to make it clear that opposition to Jesus comes from Israel at large and not just the Pharisees (on whom, along with the lawyers, he will shortly concentrate his fire when he reaches the third of this trio of controversy units). This change also means that 'your sons' at Lk. 11.19 no longer refers speficially to Pharisaic exorcists; they will instead be exemplified by the sons of Scaeva whose failed attempt at exorcism is narrated at Acts 19.13-20. That their failure results in a bonfire of magical texts strongly suggests that Luke sees these Jewish exorcists as attempting magical practices.[95] The Egyptian magicians who similarly failed to replicate the plague of gnats were forced to declare 'this is the finger of God' (Exod. 8.19), an allusion which Luke creates here by changing Matthew's 'spirit' to 'finger' (see pp. 121-3 above).

The woman who calls out from the crowd at Lk. 11.27-28 looks like Luke's adaptation of the pericope about Jesus' true family at Mt. 12.46-50, which Luke has already employed in (more or less) its Markan sequence at Lk. 8.19-21 || Mk 3.31-35.[96]

Luke's rearrangement of the Matthean order now enables him to construct a second sequence around the sign of Jonah, which Luke adapts to make Jonah's preaching rather than his three days in the belly of a fish the sign in question. This fits Luke's

---

[93] Cf. the suggestion at Drury, *Tradition*, 144–5, that Luke's order follows the life of the church, starting with the call to discipleship and mission, and then such basic aspects of discipleship as love of neighbour and prayer. This will then lead through conflict and rejection (Israel's failure to respond to the crisis) to judgement. Goulder, *Luke*, 517, likewise sees Lk. 10.25–11.13 as a unit on 'Jesus' Yoke' or 'Christian Spirituality'.

[94] See Eve, 'Devil', for a fuller treatment of this section from an FH perspective.

[95] See Eve, *Jewish Context*, 334–9.

[96] Drury, *Tradition*, 151; Goulder, *Luke*, 509–11; Eve, 'Devil', 32.

presentation of Jesus as the rejected prophet like Moses:[97] the men of Nineveh repented at Jonah's preaching, but Israel will fail to repent in response to Jesus'.[98] Luke further pursues the theme of a sign that people ought to perceive by employing two more items from the SM, the Light on a Stand (Lk. 11.33 || Mt. 5.13) and the Sound Eye (Lk. 11.34-36 || Mt. 6.22-23), the first concerning the salience of the sign and the second one's ability to perceive it. Luke may also understand the sound and unsound eye as referring to generosity and meanness, which given that he will later attack the Pharisees' love of money would neatly prepare the way for Luke's next section.

While for Luke, Israel as a whole is responsible for rejecting its Messiah, the Jewish leadership are especially culpable for leading the nation astray, so the third of Luke's sequence of controversy units provides a climax with a fierce denunciation of the Pharisees and lawyers. This brings him to arguably his most notable departure from Matthew's sequence, the relocation of the woes against Pharisees and lawyers (F2: Lk. 11.39-52 || Mt. 23.4-36). Matson proposes that these people represent an example of the dark side of the contrast between light and darkness running through the cluster Lk. 11.29-54.[99]

This could well be another instance where a theme Luke is minded to pursue in any case is further prompted by what he encounters in Matthew, namely the harsh invective against the Pharisees at Mt. 12.33-37 (I3) which he has otherwise just passed over; Mt. 12.33-35 and Lk. 11.39-40 both contrast inner depravity and outward show.[100]

It is conceivable that Luke could have scrolled forward through Matthew to retrieve this material and then rewound to his previous position in Matthew, but it is more likely that he reworked Matthew from memory here. The Lukan version looks like a fairly free rendering of the Matthean (in terms of both order and wording). Luke's compositional hand is once again seen in his reworking of Matthew's seven woes into two sets of three each against the Pharisees and lawyers (exhibiting Luke's fondness for

---

[97] One might then wonder why Luke omits 'the prophet' from Mt. 12.39; it may be that he regarded it as superfluous for an audience who were assumed to know in what way Jonah was a sign to the Ninevites.

[98] Drury, *Tradition*, 151. Goulder, *Luke*, 511–12, argues that Luke was motivated to drop Matthew's allegorical reference to the resurrection since Matthew's Jesus illogically condemns his contemporaries for failing to respond to his resurrection, which is yet to occur. Matthew does not quite say this, however, although the whale/resurrection analogy at Mt. 12.40 does intrude into a sequence in which Jonah's preaching is the sign, as defenders of the 2DH will be quick to point out. That Luke removes a Matthean intrusion when the removal is in line with Luke's redactional interests does not, however, indicate that Luke had access to a pre-Matthean source. On the contrary, since Solomon and the queen of the South have no obvious connection with any sign of Jonah, it looks as if Matthew has combined a passage about Jonah and Solomon with the Markan refusal of a sign (Mk 8.11-12), adapting Mt. 12.39 || Mk 8.12 to form a link, in which case Lk. 11.29 clearly follows Matthew's redaction of Mark.

[99] Matson, 'Luke's Rewriting', 55–6.

[100] Damm, *Ancient Rhetoric*, 272–3, also notes this connection but finds it problematic that FH Luke failed to make use of 'this ready-made material [sc. Mt. 12.33–35] in Jesus' speech against the Pharisees'. However, Mt. 12.33-35 was not ready-made to fit the 'woe' form of the speech at Lk. 11.39-52. An adaptation along the lines of 'woe to you Pharisees, for you speak good things when your hearts are evil' might have seemed at best superfluous when Luke already had enough, more colourful, material ready-made at Matthew 23.

patterns of three yet again).[101] The setting (Lk. 11.38) appears to be borrowed from the otherwise unused dispute about handwashing at Mk 7.2-5 || Mt. 15.2. There is some similarity of theme between Mk 7.3-23 || Mt. 15.3-20 and the contrast of inner and outer purity at Lk. 11.39-41, while the washing of cups is mentioned at both Mk 7.4 and Lk. 11.39.

Luke caps this denunciation of Pharisees and lawyers with the saying about the leaven of the Pharisees at Lk. 12.1 (F3: Mk 8.14-15 || Mt. 16.5-6). Interestingly, it is Luke alone who interprets this as hypocrisy, while it is Matthew's Jesus, not Luke's, who explicitly addresses the scribes and Pharisees as hypocrites. Luke may thus be echoing a salient feature of Matthew 23 he used only implicitly when adapting Matthew 23; but he may also have been prompted by the incongruity of evil people speaking good things at Mt. 12.34. Be that as it may, Luke proceeds from the warning against Pharisaic hypocrisy to the warning that what is said in secret will be revealed (so one's hypocrisy will be uncovered), a reworking of what in Matthew is an exhortation to fearless confession (Lk. 12.2-9 || Mt. 10.26-33), which Luke turns into a threat for failing to confess Jesus. This could also have been prompted by another otherwise unused piece of material from Luke's absolute position in Matthew, namely the warning that one will be held to account for every careless word one utters (Mt. 12.36-37).

Luke then inserts another item not yet used from Matthew 12, the Sin against the Holy Spirit (D7: Lk. 12.10 || Mt. 12.31-32) which, in its new context, is now made to relate to failure to confess Jesus properly while also linking to the assistance of the Holy Spirit in making proper confession (Lk. 12.11-12 || Mt. 10.19-20).

There remain three themes of importance to Luke that he is yet to address in depth, namely riches, preparedness for the end and the consequent need for repentance. He now proceeds to deal with each of these in turn, leading up to the climax of the first half of the journey. He begins with two L items concerning riches (the Warning against Avarice, Lk. 12.13-15, followed by the Parable of the Rich Fool, Lk. 12.16-21) followed by two items from the SM: Anxieties about Earthly Things (Lk. 12.22-32 || Mt. 6.25-34) and Treasures in Heaven (Lk. 12.33-34 || Mt. 6.19-21), further expanded by Luke.

The notion of treasure in heaven (Lk. 12.33-34) leads to preparedness for the Lord's return and the possibility of judgement, and hence the need for repentance, which is the theme of the next Lukan sequence (Lk. 12.35–13.9), bracketed by a pair of parables, the Wakeful Servants (Lk. 12.35-38 || Mk 13.33-37 or F4: Lk. 12.35-38 || Mt. 25.1-13) and the Lukan Parable of the Fruitless Fig Tree (Lk. 13.6-9). Exhortations to watchfulness (Lk. 12.35-48) are here followed by images of judgement and division and the need to discern the signs of the times (Lk. 12.35-59) drawn from various parts of Matthew (F5: Lk. 12.39-46 || Mt. 24.42-51; F6: Lk. 12.54-56 || Mt. 16.2-3; Mt. 10.34-36, 5.25-26), with the fruitless fig tree parable perhaps suggested by Mt. 7.19. If Lk. 12.35-38 is taken from Mt. 25.1-13, Luke has very thoroughly reworked the Parable of the Wise and Foolish Virgins, reconfiguring the lamps, the wedding, the unpredictable arrival and the door into a master and servant parable more congruent with what follows at Lk.

---

[101] Drury, *Tradition*, 145.

12.42-48.[102] Whatever the origin of Lk. 12.35-38, the burglar of Lk. 12.39 intrudes not only into the master's house but into Luke's train of thought, looking rather as if he has inadvertently wandered in from Mt. 24.43 after Luke has used the mini-parable of Lk. 12.35-38 to illustrate rather than quote Mt. 24.42.

The L story of the healing of the crippled woman on the Sabbath (Lk. 13.10-17) looks like an imitation of Sabbath healing stories in Mark (notably Mk 3.1-6 || Mt. 12.9-14) and forms a pair with the healing of the man with dropsy (Lk. 14.1-6), another characteristic pairing of a story about a man with one about a woman. These two stories bracket the end of the first half of the journey, which climaxes in the lament over unrepentant Jerusalem (Lk. 13.34-35). This sequence continues the train of thought set in motion by the parable of the fig tree: the fig tree will not prove fruitful, Israel will not repent, the Gentiles will come in instead. In addition to providing a vivid incident in a section otherwise largely consisting of speech, the healing of the crippled woman suggests that the ruler of the synagogue (and through him, the Jewish leadership) is like the barren fruit tree. The comparison with care for animals on the Sabbath (Lk. 13.15) suggests familiarity with Matthew's similar addition to the Sabbath healing at Mt. 12.11-12 || Mk 3.4, although the parallel is closer at Lk. 14.5.

Luke then comes to his next direct sequential use of Matthew with the Parables of the Mustard Seed and the Leaven (D8: Lk. 13.18-21 || Mt. 13.31-33). Here Luke once again adapts Matthean material to his own purpose. In Matthew (as in Mark), the Parable of the Mustard Seed is one of a sequence of kingdom parables, in this case contrasting the tiny beginnings of the kingdom with its huge culmination. Luke repurposes the parable to fit its context in the CS: it is now made to emphasize the inclusiveness of the kingdom, in contrast to the synagogue ruler who wishes to exclude an infirm woman from salvation on the Sabbath (Lk. 13.14). The Parable of the Leaven may follow in Luke simply because it follows in Matthew and concerns the kingdom (Luke makes little effort to adapt it), although Goulder takes Luke to be using the leaven hidden in the flour as the spreading of the gospel to all nations.[103] Luke in any case continues to emphasize both the need to strive for salvation and the danger of exclusion at Lk. 13.22-30, which sweeps up material not yet employed from Mt. 7.13-14, 22-23; 8.11-12.

While Luke had good reasons of his own to treat these three themes (riches, the end and the need for repentance), he seems to have done so in dialogue with other material from Matthew 13:

I4 *Mt. 13.1-50→ Lk. 12.1–13.29*: The saying about leaven at Lk. 12.1 is perhaps cued by the parable of the leaven at Matt 13.33 (through the catchword 'leaven'). The saying 'Nothing is covered up that will not be revealed' at Lk. 12.2 is reminiscent

---

[102] Luke 12.35-38 also looks quite similar to Mk 13.34-37, but Mark lacks the wedding and the lamps; one might venture the suggestion that here Luke has reworked the Matthean passage in the light of the Markan one (or vice versa), although this is not something he does very often. Franklin, *Luke*, 345, suggests that the Markan passage formed the basis of the Matthean parallels and Luke did not take over Mk 13.32-37 in his chapter 21 discourse because that discourse is about hope, so he transferred the warnings to Luke 12.
[103] Goulder, *Luke*, 567.

of Mk 4.22. Matthew 13 lacks any parallel to this, but Luke's version of Mt. 10.26-33 at this point may have been cued by recalling this part of Mark via the use of Mark 4 at Mt. 13.1-23. The Parable of the Rich Fool at Lk. 12.16-20 contains echoes of the abundant harvest at Mt. 13.8, the plan to gather the harvest into barns at Mt. 13.30, and the danger of riches (choking by thorns) at Mt. 13.22, perhaps coupled with the blindness of those who fail to perceive God's word at Mt. 13.14-15. The admonition against anxiety at Lk. 12.22-30 shares with the Parable of the Wheat and Tares at Mt. 13.24-30 the motif of burning weeds or grass (Lk. 12.28; Mt. 13.30). The threat of eschatological judgment implied by Mt.13.30, 36-42 may have been the cue for Luke's sequence on preparing for eschatological judgment at Lk. 12.35-13.9, 13.22-30; here a link is suggested particularly by the uncharacteristic 'There you will weep and gnash your teeth' at Lk. 13.28 which echoes the characteristically Matthean 'weeping and gnashing of teeth' at Mt. 13.50 and arguably cues the use of the similar phrase from Mt. 8.11-12, which Luke more directly draws upon here. Luke thereby replaces the Matthean Parable of the Dragnet, which envisages the general eschatological division of the righteous and the wicked, with the Matthean saying about people coming from east and west to dine in the kingdom, which is more directly conducive to his themes of the impending judgment on Israel and the inclusion of Gentiles in its place. The Lukan weeping and gnashing of teeth is then an expression of deep regret at exclusion from the kingdom rather than the torment of Matthew's hell.[104]

Luke will not resume *direct* use of the Matthean sequence until the Parable of the Lost Sheep at Lk. 15.1-7 || Mt. 18.12-14.[105] While Luke continues to use Matthean material until the end of his CS, after Luke 13 his use tends to become more fragmentary; Goulder calculates that the proportion of words Luke has in common with Matthew drops from one in three (1,076 out of 3,302) in Lk. 9.51–13.21 to one in six (449 out of 2,861) in Lk. 13.22–18.14.[106] In common with Franklin, Goulder also sees Luke as arriving at the mid-point of Luke's journey section at around this point.[107] The material in Lk. 12.35-59 has warned of impending judgement. Lk. 13.1-5 employs violent deaths in Jerusalem as a warning to repent, while the material sandwiched between the two Sabbath healings at Lk. 13.10-17 and 14.1-6 focuses on Jesus' progress towards Jerusalem (13.22, 33-35) and the coming confrontation that awaits. This sequence could be seen as either rounding off the first half of the journey with an anticipation of Jesus' arrival at Jerusalem (signalled not least from the bringing forward of the Lament over Jerusalem from its Jerusalem temple setting at Mt. 23.37-39 to its journey setting at Lk. 13.34-35) or setting the second half in motion by emphasizing the goal of Jesus' travelling. It is probably best seen as a hinge passage connecting the two halves of the journey.

Although Luke has now used up most of his direct Matthean sequence, he still has the bulk of his indirect sequence (I5 to I13) to come. With the exception of the

---

[104] Goulder, *Luke*, 574–5.
[105] Franklin, *Luke*, 341–4, suggests that the first half of CS is controlled by Matthew's order.
[106] Goulder, *Luke*, 455.
[107] Goulder, *Luke*, 455–6, sees the first half of the journey ending at Lk. 13.21; Franklin, *Luke*, 337–8, sees it ending at 13.35.

discourses in Matthew chapters 18, 23, 24 and 25 (parts of which Luke employs), from now on Matthew is largely following Mark, which limits the direct use Luke can make of him. Luke's most substantial indirect use of Matthew thus corresponds to a stretch of Matthew paralleling Markan material Luke either omits altogether or uses elsewhere.

Jesus' sayings at Lk. 13.22-35 are eminently suitable for the mid-point of the journey, emphasizing, as they do, that Jesus is still bound for Jerusalem and expects to meet rejection there. The Pharisees' warning Jesus about Herod (Lk. 13.31) provides a perfectly reasonable occasion for these sayings, but hardly an inevitable one, let alone one that is obviously linked to what has gone before. Here again Luke has been prompted by his indirect use of Matthew:

I5 *Mt.14.1-13* → *Lk. 13.31-33*: Matthew describes Herod's execution of John the Baptist, while Luke has the Pharisees' warning to Jesus that Herod wants to kill him. John is described as a prophet at Mt. 14.5 and Jesus describes himself as a prophet at Lk. 13.33. In response to news of the Baptist's death, Jesus withdraws at Mt. 14.13, which is what the Pharisees are advising Jesus to do at Lk. 13.31.[108]

At first sight, the Pharisees' warning looks like it could have been friendly, but Luke probably intends to portray the Pharisees as trying to deter Jesus from his mission. That Jesus expects to be rejected in Jerusalem leads him to lament over the city (F7: Lk. 13.34-35 || Mt. 23.37-39) in terms that anticipate rejection ('but you would not'). Here, unusually, Luke not only borrows forward from Matthew but does so with a high degree of verbal agreement. This may perhaps indicate either that this was a Matthean passage Luke knew particularly well, or that it was one he later inserted into an earlier draft on subsequently coming upon it in its Matthean sequence.

Luke now continues with the theme of rejection by the Jewish establishment contrasted with the acceptance of the poor and the Gentiles, in yet another Lukan triad: the healing of the man with dropsy and a pair of parables set in the context of a meal. In addition to forming a pair with the Sabbath healing at Lk. 13.10-17, the healing of the man with dropsy (Lk. 14.1-6) dramatizes the conflict between Jesus and the Jewish leadership by narrating an incident in which the scribes and Pharisees appear hard-hearted and manifestly unreasonable (again modelled on the Sabbath healing of the man with a withered hand at Mk 3.1-6 || Mt. 12.9-14 with an echo of the Matthean addition at Mt. 12.11-12). It also introduces a sequence in which eating features prominently: Jesus is dining with a Pharisee at Lk. 14.1 and proceeds to utter a number of parables and admonitions about banquets at 14.7-24.

At one level, the first of these is about avoiding the social embarrassment that might result from trying to seat oneself too ambitiously and the second is about inviting the poor rather than friends and family when holding a banquet, which seemingly reflects Luke's concern for the disadvantaged, but when taken in conjunction with the parable of the marriage feast (F8: Lk. 14.15-24 || Mt. 22.1-14, a fairly loose parallel) the whole

---

[108] Goulder, *Luke*, 575–6, also sees a link between Mt. 14.1-14 and Lk. 13.31, but Goulder's Luke is now at Matthew 25 and about to start scrolling backwards, so this is out of sequence for him.

sequence takes on another meaning, namely that those who expect to be at the front of the queue when it comes to entering the kingdom of God may find themselves at the back, and they will only have themselves to blame for declining the invitation (i.e. for rejecting Jesus' message of salvation, which will instead be extended to the outcast and the Gentiles). Luke once again displays his liking for threes by introducing a trio of excuses into the second of these parables (Lk. 14.18-20). While this sequence makes perfectly good sense on its own terms, it may once again be influenced by Luke's indirect use of the same part of Matthew as before:

> I6 *Mt. 14.1-21* → *Lk. 14.7-24*: In Matthew, Herod hosts a banquet (to which he presumably invited his rich associates, as Mk 6.21 implies) which resulted in John's death, while Jesus hosted a feast for a great crowd (presumably of ordinary poor people and certainly of people currently lacking food), some of whom he healed. The meal setting, the healing, and the different kinds of guest are all themes picked up in the Lukan sequence. Luke has a parable about behaviour at feasts followed by an instruction to invite the poor and the sick (cf. Mt. 14.14) rather than friends and relatives when holding a feast, followed by a parable about a banquet.

There is a certain thematic coherence to Luke 14-17 in that these chapters tend to revolve around the themes of riches, repentance and meals in a house as a symbol of salvation, with the theme of repentance especially prominent in chapter 15 and the dangers of riches (still related to repentance) in chapter 16.[109] But there appears to be a sharp change of topic at Lk. 14.25-33, which deals with the cost of discipleship and the need to count that cost before committing oneself. There is a connection of sorts with what has just gone before, in that Jesus' offer of salvation is now portrayed as coming at a cost that some people might be unwilling to meet, so it is not so surprising that some of those invited to the marriage feast declined the invitation; but perhaps Luke's point here is that the cost of discipleship needs to be weighed against the promise of salvation (and that the proper response is to choose salvation despite the seemingly steep cost). This may then be the point of the otherwise puzzlingly placed saying about salt at Lk. 14.34-35; those who duck the challenge are as worthless as salt that has lost its saltiness. It could once again be Luke's indirect use of Matthew that has prompted the construction of this topical sequence:

> I7 *Mt. 15.5-6; 16.24-26* → *Lk. 14.25-27*: The Lukan pericope on hating family and bearing one's cross has its closest parallel at Mt. 10.37-38, but its use here could have been prompted by the passage on cross-bearing discipleship at Mt. 16.24-26, while the admonition to hate father and mother seems to reverse the law cited at Mt. 15.5-6. Luke apparently has no use for the intervening material in Matthew, which largely parallels material he has also omitted from Mark.[110]

---

[109] Hanna Roose, 'Umkehr und Ausgleich bei Lukas: Die Gleichnisse vom verlorenen Sohn (Lk 15.11-32) und vom reichen Mann und armen Lazarus (Lk 16.19-31) als Schwestergeschichten', *NTS* 56 (2009), 1–21, here 18–21. We shall return to Roose's treatments of the Parables of the Prodigal Son and of the Rich Man and Lazarus when we reach the latter of these below.

[110] Goulder, *Luke*, 596, suggests that Lk. 14.26-7 is composed from recollection of Mt. 10.37, 16.24 and 19.29, and points out that the 'if anyone comes to me' form of Lk. 14.26 is closest to Mt. 16.24.

For Luke, the cost of discipleship is manifested most notably in repentance leading to parting with possessions, which supply the themes of Luke 15–16. So when Luke resumes his direct sequential use of Matthew with the Parable of the Lost Sheep (D9: Lk. 15.3-7 || Mt. 18.12-14), to which he composes his own introduction (Lk. 15.1-2, perhaps loosely based on Mk 2.16 || Mt. 9.11), he gives the parable his own slant. In Matthew, the Parable of the Lost Sheep is used to make a point about rescuing church members who have gone astray; in Luke, it forms the first of a trio of parables (lost sheep, lost coin, lost son – yet another Lukan triad) whose thrust is that salvation comes to those one might least expect, provided they repent, a point made most clearly in the third parable where the straying younger son returns and is welcomed by his father while the fate of the hitherto obedient older son is left hanging in the balance. At Lk. 15.2 this sequence was set in motion by the carping of the scribes and Pharisees, so it is not unreasonable to see the scribes and Pharisees mirrored in the response of the older son at the end of the third parable. The sequence of parables thus serves the triple function of legitimating Jesus' ministry to the seemingly disreputable while both once again challenging the Jewish leadership's assumption that they can rely on their privileged position to gain entry to the kingdom and urging the need for repentance.[111] While the Parable of the Lost Coin is clearly modelled on that of the Lost Sheep, it is conceivable that a parable involving the finding of a coin was prompted by Mt. 17.27, which Luke will have recently encountered.

Luke 16 begins with a change of audience (to the disciples) to go with the ostensible change of subject to the characteristically Lukan theme of riches. But there is a continuity of thought in that for Luke it is the Pharisees' love of money that prevents their repentance and provokes their rejection of Jesus' message (Lk. 16.14).

The Parable of the Dishonest Steward (Lk. 16.1-7) is made to serve the moral that one cannot serve God and Mammon and that the sons of light had thus better make good use of any money they possess (Lk. 16.8-13). The warning against relying on riches is then graphically reinforced in the Lukan story of the Rich Man and Lazarus (Lk. 16.19-31). But Luke's train of thought is rather harder to discern in the sequence of sayings about the law and the prophets (Lk. 16.16-17 || Mt. 11.12-13; 5.18), divorce (Lk.

---

[111] See Drury, *Tradition*, 158–9, on this sequence and for plausible connections between the Parable of the Prodigal Son and Deut. 21.15–22.4. Goulder, *Luke*, 609–14, sees the Lukan Parable of the Prodigal Son as based on Matthew's Parable of the Two Sons at Mt. 21.28-32 with some help from the Genesis story of the lost son Joseph, who also goes to a far country and whose father also declares that he is alive (Gen. 45.28) and falls on his neck and weeps (Gen. 46.29). Marc Rastoin, 'Le génie littéraire et théologique de Luc en Lc 15.11-32 éclairé par le parallèle avec Mt 21.28-32', *NTS* 60 (2014), 1–19, argues in some detail for a connection between the Lukan and Matthean parables, on the basis of their strikingly similar openings and parallel structures, but believes that Luke and Matthew both adapted a parallel they found in Q. Rastoin complains that Goulder does not explain why Luke treats the parable so differently from Matthew, shifting it to a different location. But he partly goes on to answer his own question by showing how the parables function differently in their Matthean and Lukan contexts, without stopping to consider whether Matthew's relocating and repurposing of the putative Q original might not stand in equal need of explanation. If Luke has relocated Matthew's parable here – and Rastoin makes a good case for a link between the two – then this will be because he wishes to use it to cap his trio of parables of recovering the lost, the first of which comes in parallel to Mt. 18.10-14.

16.18 || Mt. 5.31-32; 19.9) and the Parable of the Rich Man and Lazarus. Admittedly the 2DH fares little better here, since either the sequence is equally puzzling in Q or the 2DH has exactly the same problem as the FH: if Luke represents the Q sequence then Q 16.16-17 immediately follows Q 16.13 on serving two masters which immediately follows Q 14.34-35 on salt; alternatively, if the original location of Q 16.16-17 was between Q 7.28 (|| Mt. 11.11) and Q 7.31 (|| Matt 11.16), that is in Matthew's order, then the 2DH is in no better position to explain Luke's relocation of it to Lk. 16.16-17 than is the FH.

This sequence may once again be informed by Luke's indirect use of Matthew:

18 *Mt. 18.23-34 → Lk. 16.1-12*: Both Matthew's Parable of the Two Debtors and Luke's Parable of the Dishonest Steward concern servants who are worried about settling accounts with their masters. In Luke, the dishonest steward forgives part of the debts owed to his master, as the lord in Matthew's parable forgives his slave's debt. Luke's parable is used to make a point about the use of wealth (a favourite Lukan theme), whereas Matthew's concerns forgiveness (a favourite Matthean theme).[112]

19 *Mt. 19.1-26 → Lk. 16.16-31*: Mt. 19.3-12 contains the question about divorce; Luke substitutes the shorter version from Mt. 5.32.[113] Mt. 19.16-26 contains the story of the so-called Rich Young Ruler which Luke will use in its Markan sequence at Lk. 18.18-25. At 16.19-31 Luke instead tells a parable about the dangers of riches, which concludes with a warning about not hearing Moses and the prophets; in Matthew, Jesus quotes Moses to the rich man at Mt. 19.17-19. The sequence divorce → riches is thus thematically similar to this section of Matthew.[114]

This still leaves Lk. 16.16-17 to be explained. At Lk. 16.14-15 Jesus has just switched back to addressing the Pharisees and accusing them of valuing the wrong things (which, in context, must certainly include money). Lk. 16.17 qualifies Lk. 16.16 to the extent of denying that the good news of the kingdom negates the law. The phrase 'the law and the prophets' is presumably intended by Luke to refer to scripture; Luke's only other use of the phrase occurs at Acts 13.15, where it refers to the reading of scripture in a synagogue. Elsewhere, Luke prefers the phrase 'Moses and the prophets', which he uses with much the same meaning (Lk. 16.29, 31; 24.27, 44). The thrust of the passage is then 'I have come now preaching the good news of the kingdom, but when it comes

---

[112] Goulder, *Luke*, 618–22, also sees a link between Luke's Parable of the Dishonest Steward and Matthew's Parable of the Two Debtors at Mt. 18.23-34. The difference is that his Luke is working backwards through Matthew at this point, while mine is working forwards.
[113] Cf. Wilkens, 'Täuferüberlieferung', 547–8.
[114] The connection between the pericopae of the rich ruler and the parable of the Rich Man and Lazarus seems also to have been made in the gospel according to the Hebrews in the passage cited by Ps. Origen, *Comm. Matt.* 15.14.4, where the encounter with the rich man appears to be interpreted through the lens of the parable; see Andrew F. Gregory, *The Gospel according to the Hebrews and the Gospel of the Ebionites* (OECGT; Oxford: Oxford University Press, 2017), 130–1, 137.

to the right use of your money, I'm not making some extraordinary new demand; it's already there in the scriptures you claim to follow – as the parable I'm about to tell you will make clear', hence the punchline at Lk. 16.31.

The interpretation of the puzzling καὶ πᾶς εἰς αὐτὴν βιάζεται then has to fit this context. Despite translations such as that of the RSV it is thus unlikely to involve violence: either perpetrated on the kingdom or as a means of entry into it, except perhaps in the attenuated sense that everyone who wishes to enter the kingdom must struggle to get in (which perhaps fits better with Lk. 13.24 and the warnings about the cost of discipleship at Lk. 14.25-35).[115] It may be Luke intends βιάζεται in a weakened sense: 'everyone is crowding in', in which case the point would be the success of the preaching of the kingdom.[116] Alternatively βιάζεται may be passive rather than middle, so that the meaning is 'everyone is forced into it' in the sense that God is trying to drive everyone into the kingdom. This has the merit of echoing the end of the parable of the banquet at 14.23 and of agreeing with a number of ancient translations, the use of βιάζομαι in the LXX and Greek literature and with the fact that βιάζεται is passive at Mt. 11.12. It also ties in with the theme of the three parables of Luke 15, which indicate God's concern to save the lost.[117] We do not need to choose between these possibilities because they all come down to the same idea: as a result of the preaching of the kingdom everyone is pressing (or being pressed) into it.

We do, however, need to determine who is meant by 'everyone', not least since Luke clearly doesn't depict everyone as crowding into the kingdom. One line of interpretation is that everyone (meaning the Pharisees and those like them) is trying (illegitimately) to force their way into the kingdom on the basis of their legalistic piety, wealth and status. The Parable of the Rich Man and Lazarus then stands as a warning to such people: had they really taken note of Moses and the prophets (which remain valid even with proclamation of the kingdom) they would have known better, but in fact, not even a resurrection will make them repent.[118] This interpretation fits reasonably well with what has just gone before at Lk. 16.14-15; the Pharisees, who are lovers of money, scoff at Jesus' teaching, but the very things they use to justify themselves before men are an abomination in the sight of God, as Luke proceeds to spell out. It also ties in nicely with Mt. 19.24, which warns that it is hard for a rich man to enter the kingdom of God, which might conceivably explain what prompted the inclusion of Lk. 16.16 at this point.[119] The problem is that Luke does not represent the Pharisees as making any effort to press into the kingdom.

---

[115] Goulder, *Luke*, 630, opts for a version of the former reading: the Pharisees are trying to force their way into the kingdom with their legalistic piety. Nolland, *Luke 9:21–18.34*, 821, and Marshall, *Luke*, 629–30, opt for the latter.

[116] So McNicol et al., *Beyond*, 224–6; and Evans, *Luke*, 607, who, however, refers the success to the time of Luke and the Gentile mission rather than the time of Jesus in Luke's narrative.

[117] Ilaria L.E. Ramelli, 'Luke 16:16: The Good News of God's Kingdom Is Proclaimed and Everyone Is Forced into It', *JBL* 127 (2008), 737–58.

[118] This is essentially the line taken by Wilkens, 'Täuferüberlieferung', 544, who sees Luke as transforming Matthew's βιάζεται from a negative to a more positive sense.

[119] One could also point to the extent of the teaching on the kingdom in this region of Matthew (e.g. Mt. 18.23; 19.12, 14, 24; 20.1) as prompting the Lukan summary 'the good news of the kingdom is preached', but preaching the kingdom is hardly distinctive to this part of Matthew.

It is far more likely that Luke means the precise opposite of this: 'everyone' is everyone *but* the Pharisees and those like them; everyone, that is, apart from unrepentant Israel; Luke's πᾶς thus partly anticipates the πάντα τὰ ἔθνη of Lk. 24.27. Luke 16.16b then means something like 'since then the good news of the kingdom of God is preached, pressing everyone to enter it (in accordance with God's wish to seek and save the lost and carry salvation to the ends of the earth) – but you stubborn Pharisees still refuse to respond'. The awkwardness of using βιάζεται to express this may result from Luke's attempt to repurpose the difficult saying at Mt. 11.12 to fit his own agenda.[120]

The isolated saying about divorce at Lk. 16.18 is often taken as exemplifying the continuing validity of the law, and it may be that it is intended as a critique of the Pharisaic teaching on divorce. But as it stands this saying is simply a pronouncement of Jesus about divorce, not an interpretation of what the Law teaches on the matter.[121] It only becomes explicitly related to the Mosaic Torah (and its Pharisaic interpretation) in the context of Mk 10.2-9 ‖ Mt. 19.1-9, and it is only in Matthew that it clearly exemplifies the continuing validity of the Torah. In Mark, Moses' permission of divorce is undermined by appeal to the creation ordinances of Gen. 1.27; 5.2; 2.24 (although that still presupposes the ongoing authority of scripture); it is only Matthew's redaction that turns the discussion into one about the interpretation, rather than the validity, of Moses' divorce legislation. Thus Luke's employment of the saying about divorce as an example of the continuing validity of the law presupposes the context of Mt. 19.1-9.[122]

Luke 16.18 would better fit the context if it related to the surrounding theme of riches, and it may be that Luke has the financial aspects of marriage and divorce in mind, since Palestinian marriage 'indirectly belongs to the topic of a man's possessions'.[123] Mikeal Parsons suggests that Jesus is here condemning divorce for the sake of obtaining a larger dowry from remarriage.[124] This is possible, but even if the connection were obvious to Luke's target audience, it is not the clearest example of avarice Luke could have chosen.

---

[120] *Pace* Ramelli, 'Luke 16:16', 757–8, who regards her interpretation as problematic for the FH because it would leave Luke's modification of Matthew unexplained unless we assumed Luke had access to a parallel oral tradition, but this seems to envisage a rather wooden Luke unable to adapt his source material on his own initiative. On Ramelli's own account, FH Luke would here have adapted Mt. 11.12 in light of Lk. 14.23 and Luke's emphasis on God's wishing all to enter the kingdom. Ramelli in any case undermines her own argument against the FH by suggesting that on the 2DH, Luke's different interpretation of the saying may go back to an oral L source. Fitzmyer, *Luke X–XXIV*, 1117–18, also understands βιάζεται as passive along the lines suggested here, while suggesting that Mt. 11.12 may be closer to the original form of a saying Luke has adapted (in Fitzmyer's view from Q) to better fit Luke's context.

[121] Marshall, *Luke*, 631, notes that 'Luke's saying goes against Jewish ideas' and remarks that 'the change of subject to divorce is strange'. Fitzmyer, *Luke X–XXIV*, 1119, is even clearer in stating, 'It is scarcely to be understood as an example of the "law," since it goes beyond it in imposing a prohibition not contained in it.'

[122] It may alternatively presuppose the context of Mt. 5.31-32, provided Luke interpreted the uncited Mt. 5.31 in light of Mt. 5.17-20, from which he has just used verse 18. But this doesn't explain why Luke fixed on divorce as an example of the ongoing validity of the law and would still imply Lukan awareness of a Matthean context.

[123] Fitzmyer, *Luke X–XXIV*, 1119.

[124] Mikeal C. Parsons, *Luke* (PCNT; Grand Rapids, MI: Baker Academic, 2015), 249.

Hanna Roose has argued that the Lazarus and Prodigal Son parables constitute 'sister stories' (*Schwestergeschichten*) that bring two core Lukan concepts into tension: repentance and compensation. The three parables of Luke 15 emphasize the salvation of the lost sinner who repents. The Lazarus parable, however, concerns a rich man who fails to repent in his lifetime and finds that it is too late to do so after death. The fates of the rich man and Lazarus are determined, however, not by their moral qualities but by the principle that each person has his allotted share of good and evil things, which must be balanced after death (Lk. 16.25; cf. 6.20-26). Roose finds a number of parallels between the Parables of the Prodigal Son and of Lazarus. The rich man and the younger son both squander their wealth in pleasure. Lazarus and the younger son both long to eat food (ἐπεθύμει/ἐπιθυμῶν χορτασθῆναι) not intended for them. The younger son returns to his father while Lazarus goes to Abraham's bosom. The ends of both stories concern the fate of brothers.[125]

The parallels Roose finds between these parables are instructive: the Prodigal Son and Dives (the Rich Man who neglects Lazarus) are indeed contrasting figures, but while Dives and Lazarus may indeed get their just reversals, the Lukan point is surely that Dives could have repented (as Lk. 16.19 and the story of Zacchaeus imply), and that the Pharisees are morally culpable for not doing so.

Roose's argument points to another possible influence of Matthew on Luke. One of the parallels she draws between the younger son and Lazarus is that both desired to eat food intended for impure animals (pigs or dogs), but Lk. 16.21 makes no explicit mention of dogs being fed; rather Lazarus 'longed to satisfy his hunger with what fell from the rich man's table; even the dogs would come and lick his sores'. That the dogs ate what fell from the rich man's table requires inference from the Syrophoenician Woman, Mt. 15.27 || Mk 7.28, which Luke does not reproduce but will have seen in his sources. Luke is closer to Matthew's wording than to Mark's here, which would seem to imply Luke's recollection of Matthean redaction:

Mk 7.28b καὶ τὰ κυνάρια ὑποκάτω *τῆς τραπέζης* ἐσθίουσιν ἀπὸ τῶν ψιχίων τῶν παιδίων.
Mt. 15.27b καὶ γὰρ τὰ κυνάρια ἐσθίει <u>ἀπὸ</u> τῶν ψιχίων <u>τῶν πιπτόντων ἀπὸ τῆς τραπέζης</u> τῶν κυρίων αὐτῶν.
Lk. 16:21 <u>ἀπὸ</u> <u>τῶν πιπτόντων ἀπὸ</u> <u>τῆς τραπέζης</u> τοῦ πλουσίου

The connection of thought between the Lazarus parable and temptations to sin and the other material that follow at Lk. 17.1-4 is unclear; one might propose that the rich man was tempted to sin by his wealth, which caused him and his brothers to ignore Moses and the prophets, but this is hardly a compelling link.[126] The connection is better explained by Luke's resuming his direct use of Matthew (D10: Lk. 17.1-4 || Mt. 18.6-7, 15, 21-22). Admittedly, we have just argued that Luke has already moved

---

[125] Roose, 'Umkehr und Ausgleich', 2–6; David Lyle Jeffrey, *Luke* (BTCB; Grand Rapids, MI: Brazos, 2012), 205, also sees links between these two parables.
[126] So also Marshall, *Luke*, 640. Fitzmyer, *Luke X–XXIV*, 1136, likewise sees the sayings at Lk. 17.1-10 as being totally unrelated either to one another or to what has just gone before.

on to Mt. 19.1-21 in his indirect use, but Luke could have held over the other material from Matthew 18 in memory, or it may be that he scrolls back a very short way to retrieve it, although in neither case is his motivation entirely clear. Goulder points to some possible links between the Parable of the Rich Man and Lazarus and material in Matthew 18 (the pitiless servant who is tormented at Mt. 18.34 and the threat of hell fire at Mt. 18.8-9),[127] and it is conceivable that Luke was prompted to revisit Matthew 18 by some such associations, but perhaps the most plausible explanation is that Luke has been focusing on the Pharisees' love of money throughout Luke 16 and so refrains from embarking on a new topic until he has finished with the previous one; when he has done so he takes the opportunity to retrieve any remaining usable material from Matthew 18, repurposing it from the topic of church discipline to teaching about relations between individual disciples. The phrase 'these little ones' at Lk. 17.2 has no clear referent and is more typically Matthean than Lukan, whereas at Mt. 18.6 it refers back to (literal or metaphorical) children; this suggests Luke's use of Matthew here.[128] The same phrase occurs in the same context at Mk 9.42, which is roughly the point Luke has reached in Mark, but the use of the non-Markan Mt. 18.15, 21-22, weighs in favour of Luke's use of Mt. 18.6-7 rather than Mk 9.42, as does the fact that Luke's wording is closer to Matthew's than to Mark's, especially since Lk. 17.1 || Mt. 18.7b lacks a Markan parallel.[129]

Luke's train of thought remains equally elusive over the next two pericopae, the request for increase of faith at Lk. 17.5-6 || Mt. 17.19-20 and the saying about being unworthy servants. The first of these could again be prompted by an indirect use of Matthew:

> I12 *Mt. 21.21 → Lk. 17.6*: Lk. 17.6 contains a saying on faith that more closely parallels Mt. 17.19-21, but if Luke is now advancing from Matthew 19 to Matthew 24 he would encounter a similar saying on faith at Mt 21.21 in a section which he does not otherwise use, which could cue the use of the one on faith in Luke. Mt. 17.21 speaks of faith moving mountains; Luke's otherwise curious sycamine tree (τῇ συκαμίνῳ ταύτῃ) seems to have been inspired by the withered fig tree (τῆς συκῆς) at Mt. 21.21, where faith is said to enable both afflicting a fig tree and casting a mountain into the sea (whereas the immediate Markan parallel at Mk 11.23 mentions only the mountain); 'you could say to this sycamine tree' suggests that Jesus has a particular tree in mind, but it is the Matthean context, not the Lukan one, that supplies one.[130] Perhaps Luke imagines Jesus passing a sycamine

---

[127] Goulder, *Luke*, 628.
[128] Fitzmyer, *Luke X–XXIV*, 1137, suggests a reference back to the 'babes' of Lk. 10.21, but this just underlines the problem since it is far from apparent why Luke's audience should make such a remote connection.
[129] Fitzmyer, *Luke X–XXIV*, 1136–7. Fitzmyer is obliged to postulate a Mark-Q overlap to account for this, as also in *CEQ*, 472–7.
[130] Goulder, *Luke*, 641–2, proposes that Luke reaches Mt. 17.20 at this point in the course of scrolling backwards through Matthew, but nevertheless notes the link with Mt. 21.21, as do McNicol et al., *Beyond*, 230. It is conceivable that 2DH Luke could have made the same connection via Mk 11.21-23 (which he does not otherwise use) under prompting from Q 17.6, but the link is more direct in Matthew (the saying in Mt. 21.21 explicitly refers to the fig tree, unlike that at Mk 11.23).

tree along a section of road (on the border between Galilee and Samaria, Lk. 17.11), where there is no obvious mountain to point to, and hits upon the miraculously transplanted tree as a conflated substitute for the miraculously moved mountain and the miraculously withered tree.[131]

It is tempting to suggest an indirect use of Mt. 20.1-16 at Lk. 17.7-10 (I10), on the basis that the Matthean and Lukan parables both concern workers who should expect no more than their due, despite the considerable extent of their labours. That Luke would have reversed the order of what he took from Matthew 20 and 21 is not an insuperable objection given his tendency to employ Matthew in blocks, and Matthew's Parable of the Labourers is otherwise unused by Luke. But the similarities between the Matthean and Lukan parables are far from compelling, and it is hard to see what might have prompted Luke to transform the one into the other. The connection becomes more plausible on the assumption that Lk. 17.7-10 was taken from a source;[132] Luke may then have substituted his source's brief parable for Matthew's longer one on a vaguely related point.

The Cleansing of the Ten Lepers at Lk. 17.11-19 acts as a bookend to the unwelcoming Samaritan village of Lk. 9.51-56, in that it is now a Samaritan (in contrast to the nine ungrateful Jews) who is presented in a good light, and we are once again informed that Jesus is travelling between Samaria and Galilee. The episode looks loosely based on Mk 1.40-45 or Mt. 8.1-4, with additional influence from the Naaman story of 2 Kings 5.[133] If there is an indirect link between the previous pericope and Mt. 20.1-16, one might also make a case for an indirect use of Mt. 20.29-33 in the present one (I11). In both cases the healing is requested while Jesus is proceeding on his way. Matthew's blind men and Luke's lepers address Jesus in similar terms: ἔκραξαν λέγοντες· ἐλέησον ἡμᾶς, κύριε (Mt. 20.30, 31); αὐτοὶ ἦραν φωνὴν λέγοντες· Ἰησοῦ ἐπιστάτα, ἐλέησον ἡμᾶς (Lk. 17.13). Moreover, Luke's conclusion to the story of the ten lepers is very similar to that of Mark's story of Blind Bartimaeus, to which Mt. 20.29-33 is parallel: καὶ ὁ Ἰησοῦς εἶπεν αὐτῷ· Ὕπαγε, ἡ πίστις σου σέσωκέν σε. (Mk 10.52); καὶ εἶπεν αὐτῷ· Ἀναστὰς πορεύου· ἡ πίστις σου σέσωκέν σε (Lk. 17.19).[134]

Luke now returns to the theme of judgement at Lk. 17.20-37 by advancing to Matthew 24 in his absolute progress through Matthew (D11: Lk. 17.20-37 ∥ Mt. 24.17-41). The intervening material Luke has skipped over in Matthew is largely parallel to the Markan material that Luke will use for Jesus' arrival and first few days in Jerusalem

---

[131] So also Drury, *Tradition*, 162. Fitzmyer, *Luke X–XXIV*, 1142, argues that Luke preserves the Q wording here (cf. *CEQ*, 492–3), on the grounds that he could have had no reason to change Matthew's mountain into a mulberry tree, but this ignores the contexts both of Lk. 17.6 and of Mt. 21.21. One may also wonder how we can be so confident that the grotesque image of an aquatically transplanted tree could not possibly have occurred to Luke when it was apparently quite acceptable to the compiler(s) of Q.

[132] As, for example, Nolland, *Luke 9:21–18.34*, 841, Fitzmyer, *Luke X–XXIV*, 1145, and McNicol et al., *Beyond*, 231, all suppose.

[133] For the possible influence of the Naaman story, see Goulder, *Luke*, 645–6 (cf. Lk. 4.27), and, more cautiously, Nolland, *Luke 9:21–18:34*, 845; for scepticism in this regard, see Fitzmyer, *Luke X–XXIV*, 1150–1.

[134] Drury, *Tradition*, 163, also notes these verbal links.

or has already been employed at Lk. 11.39-52, 14.15-24. In constructing his Luke 17 eschatological discourse, Luke picks out material that is relevant to his theme and which, for the most part, is not paralleled by the Mark 13 material he plans to use in its Markan sequence at Luke 21. He also references the Lot story (at Lk. 17.28-29) as a non-Matthean parallel to the Noah story referenced at Lk. 17.26-27 || Mt. 24.37-39. This recalls the threat of the fate of Sodom and Gomorrah explicitly mentioned at Lk. 10.12 and implicitly suggested at Luke 9.54, once again in a Samaritan context, so that as we near the end of Luke's travel narrative we are reminded of its beginning while at the same time being invited to reconsider the theme of eschatological judgement in the light of all that has gone in between.[135]

Most the material Luke takes from Matthew 24 here concerns the coming of the Son of Man while the material he uses in Lk. 21.5-24 mainly concerns the fall of Jerusalem and the events leading up to it, so that Luke's separation of Matthean additions from Mark's discourse is largely thematic. Coming near the end of the CS this discourse appears at an appropriate point along the way that began with discipleship and mission, continued through opposition, rejection, calls to repentance and warnings of judgement and now looks forward to the end.

The Parable of the Unjust Judge is the final instance of Luke's possible indirect use of Matthew in the CS:

I13 *Mt.24.29-31, 44-51* → *Lk. 18.1-8*: Luke's principal direct use of Matthew 24 has just come at Lk. 17.20-37. While the Parable of the Importunate Widow that immediately follows is ostensibly introduced as a parable about prayer, Lk. 18.8 indicates it is prayer for eschatological vindication that Luke specifically has in mind. The vindication of the elect in Lk. 18.7 together with the coming of the Son of Man in Lk. 18.8 echoes similar themes in Mt. 24.30-31 (which speaks of the coming of the Son of Man followed by the gathering of the elect). The word 'elect' (ἐκλεκτός) occurs only here in Luke, but three times in Mark and the parallel passages in Matthew (including Mt. 24.31). Luke could have obtained the same themes and the word 'elect' from Mt. 24.24-27, but the vindication of the elect in Luke seems closer in thought to the gathering of the elect at Mt. 24.31 than to the misleading of the elect at Mt. 24.24. Furthermore, both Lk. 18.8 and Mt. 24.44-51 are concerned with whether the Son of Man will find faithful service at his coming.[136]

---

[135] See McNicol et al., *Beyond*, 153, for further reappearances towards the end of Luke's CS of themes introduced near its beginning. Goulder, *Luke*, 648–54, proposed links with Matthew 16 at Lk. 17.20-37. While the proposed links have some plausibility, it is unclear why Luke would be using Matthew 16 here, absent Goulder's theory of reverse scrolling (which requires Luke to use Matthew 24 having arrived at Matthew 16 in the course of reversing through Matthew). That said, Matthew 16 does contain material that Luke has scattered across his CS.

[136] So also Goulder, *Luke*, 658–9, who suggests a verbal link between ὁ υἱὸς τοῦ ἀνθρώπου ἐλθὼν ἆρα εὑρήσει τὴν πίστιν at Lk. 18.8 and ὁ υἱὸς τοῦ ἀνθρώπου ἔρχεται ... πιστός ... ἐλθών ... εὑρήσει at Mt. 24.44-46. At first sight it may seem implausible that Luke would pick out individual words from Matthew to weave into his own text in such a way, but in favour of Goulder's suggestion is that fact that both Matthew and Luke are talking about what the Son of Man will find on his return. In addition to the link with Mt. 24.23-46, Goulder, *Luke*, 658–9, suggests Ecclus. 35.11-22 LXX as an influence behind this parable.

The Parable of the Unjust Judge picks up the theme of the eschatological discourse (since the end of the parable indicates that the prayer Jesus has in mind is for eschatological deliverance) and recalls the earlier Parable of the Importunate Friend at Midnight (Lk. 11.5-13), once again suggesting that as Luke reaches the end of the CS he recapitulates some of the themes from its beginning. Luke again exhibits his fondness for gender pairing by following his parable featuring a woman with one about a Pharisee and the publican at Lk. 18.9-14. This continues the theme of prayer from the previous parable but also encapsulates Luke's critique of the Pharisees and promises of salvation to the humble and outcast; the echo of Lk. 14.11 at Lk. 18.15 (the former having been uttered in the context of a meal with a Pharisee) is thus no accidental use of a floating saying tacked on the end of a parable to underline its moral but a reminder of what has gone before.

The commendation of humility in Lk. 18.9-14 segues nicely into the pericope about receiving children at Lk. 18.15-17, where Luke abandons Matthew to resume his use of Mark until the end of the Passion Narrative (although, as we shall see, further sequential uses of Matthew occasionally recur until the end of both gospels).[137]

After re-joining Mark at Lk. 18.15 || Mk 10.13, Luke continues to use Mark as his primary source up until the account of the Empty Tomb. Nevertheless, he also continues to make occasional use of Matthew (in Mathew's sequence) right up until the end of his gospel. The Parable of the Pounds is a Lukan adaptation of the Parable of the Talents (D12: Lk. 19.11-27 || Mt. 25.14-30). The relatively high incidence of EA^{Mt-Lk} at Lk. 22.39–23.1 || Mt. 26.36–27.1 may suggest that Luke is also working primarily from Matthew in this section. Although Luke's Empty Tomb story at Lk. 24.1-9 more closely resembles that at Mk 16.1-8 than the Matthean parallel at Mt. 28.1-8, as noted in Chapter 5 there are also a number of EA^{Mt-Lk} here: for example, the actions of the women leaving the tomb at Lk. 24.9 more closely resemble those at Mt. 28.8 (telling the disciples) than that narrated at Mk 16.8 (fleeing in terror and telling no one). Finally, as also noted in Chapter 5, the resurrection appearances at Lk. 24.11-53 look partly imitative of the closing resurrection appearance at Mt. 28.16-20.

Our canter through CS suggests that it is organized by playing variations on a limited set of interrelated themes: the cost of discipleship, the need to renounce riches or employ them for the kingdom, faith and persistence in prayer, the opposition of the scribes and Pharisees foreshadowing Israel's rejection of its would-be saviour, Jesus as the latest in the line of rejected prophets and the coming of judgement on Israel and vindication of the elect, all lying within the necessity of the divine plan. Many of the same themes can be found in Mark and Matthew, but in his CS Luke has chosen to foreground this particular set of themes, presenting them in the framework of a journey to Jerusalem which creates a sense of narrative movement and develops the Markan Way of the Lord. Although Luke is often content to make his Jesus speak for long stretches at a time, he avoids the appearance of long set-piece discourses by

---

[137] Goulder, *Luke*, 667–8, plausibly suggests that Luke deployed the Parable of the Publican and the Pharisee to lend weight to the brief pericope about the children, although it is another question whether Luke composed the parable especially for the context (as Goulder proposes) or adapted it from a (written or oral) source.

interposing questions and remarks from various interlocutors (usually disciples or Pharisees) with whom Jesus is then depicted as interacting (as opposed to simply lecturing), by including the occasional incident and by casting much of what Jesus says in the narrative form of story parables. Luke thereby produces a narrative that creates the appearance of ongoing action despite being largely composed of speech.

FH Luke has created his CS by weaving material from various parts of Matthew (not least material previously unused from the SM) together with his own special material into topical sequences onto a frame supplied by consistent forward movement through Mt. 8.19–25.30. Luke's agreement in order with his direct parallels from Matthew can equally well be explained on the FH (as above) or the 2DH (where it can be attributed to the order of Q). But since Luke's sequential indirect uses of Matthew (I1–I13) occur in either Matthew's Markan material or his special material, they cannot be accounted for by Q. That their occurrence in Luke broadly reflects Matthew's order (and often reflects Matthean redaction or special Matthean material) strongly suggests that Luke used Matthew.

The hypothesis that Luke made such indirect use of Matthew is both psychologically plausible and within the bounds of ancient scriptural interpretation. As we saw in Chapter 2, human memory can often work through associative cueing that may not be part of a deliberate search strategy and that can facilitate non-sequential access.[138] Moreover, FH Luke has not passively scanned his current location in Matthew's Gospel to see what associations it might trigger; for the most part he has actively engaged with Matthew in light of his own agenda so that his associations are cued both by what he comes across in Matthew and by the topical sequence he is in the course of constructing. Sometimes the theme Luke wishes to present dictates the material he employs from Matthew and the use he makes of it, while sometimes what he encounters in Matthew influences which of his themes Luke takes up next.

Two objections might nevertheless be raised against Luke's indirect use of Matthew. The first is that the particular instances proposed above are speculative. The second is that the procedure does not obviously conform to the way in which ancient authors typically employed their sources.

The proposals for Luke's indirect use of Matthew outlined above cannot be proved beyond all reasonable doubt, since they postulate what cannot strictly be known, namely what associations Matthew's text may have triggered in Luke's mind. But there are three considerations that, taken together, jointly suggest that the proposals are not just plausible but probable. The first is that several of the proposed indirect links either help explain what is otherwise puzzling in Luke's text, including the abrupt introduction of new topics (I5, I6, I8, I9), or else contain noteworthy verbal links (I2, I4, I13). The second is that the occurrence of as many as ten or even thirteen indirect links in Matthean sequence that help to explain features of Luke's composition becomes increasingly hard to ascribe to coincidence. The third is that indirect source utilization is consistent with what we have suggested Luke has been doing earlier in his gospel (e.g. in the Infancy Narrative and at Lk. 4.16-30; 7.11-17, 36-50).

---

[138] See pp. 13–14. Baddeley et al., *Memory*, 165–6.

That said, the force of the first objection derives from the second, namely the question whether Luke's proposed indirect use of Matthew represents a way in which an ancient author is likely to have worked. It is to this question that we shall now turn.

Luke as emulator

While Luke is part tradent, enacting the tradition he has received for his target audience, he is also part author, emulating his predecessors by choosing the best of each (roughly speaking Mark's narrative and Matthew's teaching material) and then seeking to improve on it. There is no fundamental conflict here: Luke's emulation is in service of his enactment of the tradition. At first sight, this may appear to involve a mixture of methods, since Luke largely composes via the assembling and close reworking of existing material rather than the imitative creation (or associative linking) of new material, but emulation can encompass both. In particular it can involve improving a model through paraphrase, as well as more adventurous transformations.[139] Emulation is competitive imitation, and there were no set rules on how to imitate. Luke's emulation of Matthew is an attempt to produce a gospel more suitable for his Gentile church. There is a loose analogy here with the way Virgil transforms Greek heroes into the proto-Roman Aeneas to appeal to a Roman audience. Luke does not transform Matthew's Jesus into someone else – that would not suit his purpose – but he does place his own emphasis on the issues and values Jesus is made to represent.[140] Matthew's Jesus is presented from the perspective of a Jewish sect that is primarily in conflict with other Jews. Luke's Jesus is required to legitimize, not a group within Israel that is competing with fellow Jews while evangelizing Gentiles but one that is now quite separate from Israel and needs to justify its separate existence. Luke's central section is partly designed to meet that need, by showing that Jesus' offer of salvation to Israel was tragically but unreasonably rejected, just as Israel had always rejected God's spokespeople (cf. Acts 7).

Luke's indirect use of Matthew in his CS is not imitation at the level of individual episodes or topoi-sequences that copy the structure of their Matthean hypotexts; at this level other forms of intertextuality (such as echo, allusion or catchword association) are at work. But we have also seen other forms of intertextuality at work in Virgilian imitation. For example, Luke's use of material taken from scattered contexts in Matthew to illuminate Luke's current theme has some analogy with Virgil's use of material from disparate parts of the *Iliad* and his own *Georgics* to provide the similes he employs in *Aen.* 2.469-99. Luke may also be seen as imitating Matthew

---

[139] Sandnes, '*Imitatio Homeri?*', 722–5.
[140] Once again, there may be a loose analogy with the different ways Josephus presents his own Galilean activities in *War* and *Life*. The order of events is sometimes changed between the two, and even where the two accounts run roughly in tandem, a brief summary in the *War* can be replaced with more substantial variant in the *Life* giving a different slant, for example on what Josephus was sent to Galilee for in the first place (cf. *War* 2.562-8; *Life* 28–9, 62–3), the function of the seventy local worthies he appointed to assist him (*War* 2.569-71; *Life* 79) or how Josephus dealt with the envoys from Jerusalem (*War* 2.626-31; *Life* 189–332).

at the macro level, where his broadly sequential use of Matthew resembles Tobit's sequential use of parts of Genesis and the *Odyssey* to create a narrative about the travels of Tobias.

Luke is less creative than Virgil, in part because he is more constrained by his tradition, but also because of his chosen genre. Scribal tradent and author are not binary opposites, but Luke needs to be more of a tradent than most Graeco-Roman authors employing imitation for literary ends. Luke's Gospel is a *bios* within a two-volume history, not a work of fiction; his chosen genre suits his aims but it also limits the liberties he can take. So while, as we have seen, Luke can be quite creative on occasion, his creativity in his CS appears relatively limited. Since we have no direct access to Luke's other sources, we cannot be certain where his L material comes from, but it is a reasonable guess that he patterned the healing stories in his central section on similar stories in Matthew or Mark, and that he probably created the frequent meal settings and many of the encounters with Jesus' interlocutors, but even here Luke may have been in part guided by the traditions available to him (e.g. these healing stories may reflect meagre information fleshed out by substantive imitation, rather like the Tacitus examples in Chapter 3). Otherwise Luke seems largely to have taken the words spoken by Jesus from various parts of Matthew or his own store of parables (although the creative reworking of some parabolic material by Luke cannot be ruled out).

Luke's Gospel satisfies all the criteria suggested in Chapter 3 for identifying imitation. In particular: (1) the proposed models, Matthew and Mark (and the OT), would have been readily accessible to Luke; (2) it is likely that the predecessor gospels were popular with his target audience; (3) it is plausible that Matthew and Mark were authoritative texts for Luke's audience;[141] (4) there is a broad similarity in structure and the order of events between Luke and Luke's sources; (5) there are a large number of similar narrative details and actions; (6) there are many instances of verbal similarities between Luke and Matthew; (7) there is a reasonable density of parallels; (8) several of the parallels are quite distinctive; (9) there is a general thematic congruence between all three Synoptic Gospels.

Luke clearly meets the criterion of thematic congruence in relation to Matthew and Mark as a whole, since all three texts concern the ministry of Jesus. But there is also congruence between the kind of material that appears in Luke 9–18 and that in Matthew 11–19. The corresponding segments in both gospels depict Jesus as wandering around, teaching in parables and discourses, responding to questions from his disciples and challenges from the Pharisees and performing the occasional miracle.

Luke can also be seen as a reputational entrepreneur constructing a Jesus to be the bearer of the community values Luke wishes to promote; to be effective, Luke must act within the constraints of the reputation Jesus already enjoys among Luke's target

---

[141] While it might be objected that Matthew and Mark would have been insufficiently classic texts to constitute fit objects of mimesis, Schippers, 'Dionysius and Quintilian', 187–249, argues that in the first century CE there was a tendency towards favouring the use of more recent (and practically useful) models over the more ancient ones favoured by older Greek mimetic practice.

audience, a reputation in part already shaped by Matthew's earlier gospel.[142] Imitating Matthew may be one way in which Luke tries to operate within those constraints.

FH Luke's *sequential* indirect use of Matthew will have been primarily a compositional convenience, arising from his sequential direct use and his other compositional aims. It seems unlikely that Luke could have intended his sequential use of Matthew to be recognized and appreciated as imitative by his audience. But his sequential indirect usage may nevertheless have served his imitative aim. The combined direct and indirect sequential use of Matthew set out in Table 6.8 shows Luke (more or less) sequentially employing material from every chapter of Matthew apart from 6, 15, 17, 22 and 23 (and using material from most of these chapters elsewhere). This suggests a desire to reflect as much of Matthew as possible given Luke's other compositional constraints. It may also represent an attempt to fulfil his promise to produce an orderly account by incorporating the order of both his main sources as far as possible while also imposing an order of his own. Many of the Matthean passages Luke employs indirectly occur in triple tradition material Luke directly employs elsewhere. If he wishes to reflect this Matthean material in Matthean sequence he must transform it in some way or another to avoid duplication. He often chooses not to use material directly because he thinks he can do better, for example, by entering into dialogue with a Matthean assertion (e.g. I1) or introducing a story parable to illustrate a Matthean theme (e.g. I2, I9), or replacing one of Matthew's parables with one he prefers (e.g. I8). Often Luke will then build on his sequential indirect (and direct) use of Matthew by taking Matthean material from elsewhere (such as the SM) to construct a topical sequence that serves both to advance his own agenda and to reuse valuable matter from Matthew. Luke goes part way towards emulating Seneca's bees, gathering nectar from a variety of Matthean plants in order to digest them into his own blend of honey.[143] He thereby endues his narrative with a dense Matthean substrate, even when the Matthean substrate is not instantly recognizable. What remains recognizable is the figure of a Jesus who ostensibly does and says much the same kinds of thing as Matthew's Jesus but transposed into a Lukan key.

It may be objected that the title it eventually acquired of 'the Gospel according to Luke' suggests rather that it was received not as an emulation of its predecessors but as a particular rendering of the Jesus tradition found also in the other canonical gospels. But this is not inconsistent with Luke emulating earlier gospels in the service of enacting the Jesus tradition for his Gentile target audience. According to Sandnes, 'In theory as well as in practice, emulation often implied copying and developing or

---

[142] For reputational entrepreneurship and the social construction of reputation, see Gary Alan Fine, 'Reputational Entrepreneurs and the Memory of Incompetence: Melting Supporters, Partisan Warriors and Images of President Harding', *AJS* 105 (1996), 1159–93; Lori J. Ducharme and Gary Alan Fine, 'The Construction of Nonpersonhood and Demonization: Commemorating the Traitorous Reputation of Benedict Arnold', *SF* 73 (1995), 1309–31; Barry Schwartz, 'The Social Context of Commemoration: A Study in Collective Memory', *SF* 61 (1982), 374–402; Barry Schwartz, 'Postmodernity and Historical Reputation: Abraham Lincoln in Late Twentieth-Century American Memory', *SF* 77 (1998), 63–103; for their application to the gospels, see Rodríguez, *Structuring*, 64–79; and *WTG*, 114–22.

[143] Cf. Sandnes, '*Imitatio Homeri?*' 725–7. I say 'part way' since the Matthean fragments are often such as to suggest only partial Lukan digestion.

improving an original, while still retaining traces of the first document.'[144] This is not a bad description of what Luke did with Matthew (and Mark). Luke may reasonably have expected that an audience familiar with Matthew would recognize the traces of that earlier gospel in his own work. Even if Luke's Gospel did not come to be seen as an improvement on Matthew's, that does not mean that it entirely failed as an emulation, that is, a competitive imitation, for it took its place in the fourfold gospel alongside Matthew; if Luke did not manage to surpass Matthew he at least managed to establish himself as his equal.

It may also be objected that Luke's emulation of Matthew would require him to use his two principal sources in very different ways, since, in the main, he simply copied and paraphrased Mark. But Luke's use of Mark also encompasses instances of more creative imitation. Goodacre's proposal that Luke takes over and develops Mark's 'Way of the Lord' theme illustrates this at the broad thematic level. There are also a number of instances where Luke's use of Mark resembles creative imitation rather than copying or close paraphrase, such as Jesus' inaugural sermon (Lk. 4.16-30 ← Mk 6.1-6); the call of the first disciples (Lk. 5.1-11 ← Mk 1.16-20, 4.1, 37b); the anointing of Jesus' feet (Lk. 7.36-50 ← Mk 14.3-9), the question about the greatest commandment (Lk. 10.25-28 ← Mk 12.13, 28-34; 10.17); the blessing on those who do the will of God (Lk. 11.27-28 ← Mk 3.31-5); washing hands before eating (Lk. 11.37-38 ← Mk 7.1-2, 5); healings on the Sabbath (Luke 13.10-17; 14.1-6; ← Mk 3.1-6); the healing of the ten lepers (Lk. 17.11-19 ← Mk 1.40-45; 10.46-52); and the hearing before Herod (Lk. 23.6-12 ← Mk 6.14; 15.3-5, 16-19).

Finally, Luke's imitation of his predecessors is consistent with his imitation of the Old Testament and with proposals for his imitation of Homer, Plato, Euripides and Galatians in Acts.[145] Once Luke is seen as an emulator of Matthew and Mark (albeit one strongly constrained by his fidelity to the tradition) rather than a mere compiler and editor of earlier material, his use of Matthew (including his reordering of Matthew) readily takes its place within the context of ancient compositional practices.

Conclusion

This chapter has attempted to show (1) that Luke's reordering of Matthew is plausible (given Luke's aims, ancient compositional practices and the reordering 2DH Matthew would have to have done); and (2) that given further apparent links that emerge between Luke and Matthew (in particular indications of Luke's indirect use of Matthean in roughly Matthean sequence), Luke's use of Matthew is not only plausible but probable. Achieving the first of these objectives defeats the argument that Luke's ordering of the double tradition makes his use of Matthew implausible. Achieving the second turns Luke's order into a further argument *for* his use of Matthew. Table 6.8 summarizes the proposals for Luke's use of his predecessors. The D Matt column lists Luke's direct use of Matthean (double tradition) material more or less in Matthean sequence. The OOS

---
[144] Sandnes, '*Imitatio Homeri*?' 725.
[145] See n. 167 on p. 72.

(out-of-sequence) Matt column lists Luke's direct use of Matthew out of Matthew's sequence. The I Matt column lists Luke's proposed indirect uses of Matthew's material; it is placed directly next to the D Matt column to facilitate seeing Luke's broad forward progress through Matthew in one or other mode. The Mark column lists Luke's direct use of Mark. Finally, the L column suggests possible hypotexts that may lie behind some of Luke's special material. Parentheses in any column indicate connections that are tentative.

Table 6.8 Luke's Use of Matthew and Mark

Luke		D Matt	I Matt	OOS Matt	Mark	L
1-2	Infancy Narratives		1–2			1 Sam.
3.1-18	John the Baptist	3.1-12				
3.19-20	Imprisonment of John				6.17-18	
3.21-22	Baptism of Jesus	3.13-17				
3.23-38	Genealogy of Jesus			(1.1-17)		
4.1-13	Temptation	4.1-11				
4.14-15	Start of Ministry	4.12, 23a-24				
4.16-30	Sermon at Nazareth		4.13-16			Mk 6.1-6
4.31-44	Galilean Ministry Part 1				1.21-39	
5.1-11	Miraculous Catch of Fish					Mk 4.1-2; 1.16-20
5.12–6.19	Galilean Ministry Part 2				1.40–3.19	
6.20-49	Sermon on the Plain	5, 7		15.14		
7.1-10	Capernaum Centurion	8.5-10				
7.11-17	Widow's Son at Nain		9.18-26			1 Kgs 17.17-24
7.18-35	Jesus and John			11.2-19		
7.36-50	Woman with Ointment		9.10-22			(Mk 14.3-9)
8.1	Preaching Tour	9.35				
8.2-3	Ministering Women					(Mk 16.9)
8.4-18	Parables				4.1-25	

Table 6.8 (*continued*)

Luke		D Matt	I Matt	OOS Matt	Mark	L
8.19-21	Jesus' True Kindred				3.31-35	
8.22-56	Galilean Ministry Part 2				4.35–5.43	
9.1-6	Mission Charge			(10.1-14)	6.6b-13	
9.7-9	Herod's Anxiety				6.14-16	
9.10-17	Feeding of 5,000				6.30-44	
9.18-36	Peter's Confession; Passion Prediction; Transfiguration				8.27–9.8	
9.37-50	Healing of Possessed Boy; Passion Prediction; True Greatness; Strange Exorcist				9.14-41	
9.51	Setting Out for Jerusalem				10.1, 32	
9.52-56	Rejection by Samaritans		10.5			Gen. 19.24;2 Kgs 1.9-12 (Deut. 2.26-30)
9.57-62	Following Jesus	8.19-22				
10.1-12	Commissioning the 70	9.37-38 10.7-15				Num. 11.24-25; Deut. 1.22-23
10.13-15	Woes on Galilean Cities	11.20-24				
10.16	Hearing and Rejecting			10.40		
10.17-20	Return of the 70					
10.21-24	Thanksgiving to the Father	11.25-27		13.16-17		
10.25-37	Lawyer's Question and Parable of Good Samaritan		12.5-7	22.34-40	12.28-34	Dt. 6.5
10.38-41	Martha and Mary					(Dt. 8.3)
11.1-4	The Lord's Prayer			6.9-13		(Mt. 11.25)

The Order Objection

Luke		D Matt	I Matt	OOS Matt	Mark	L
11.5-8	Importunate Friend		(12.3-4)			
11.9-13	Encouragement to Pray			7.7-11		
11.14-32	Beelzebul Accusation; Return of the Evil Spirit; True Blessedness; Sign of Jonah	12.22-45	12.50		8.11-12	
11.33-36	Light & the Sound Eye			5.15; 6.22-23		
11.37-38	Invitation to Dine					(Mt. 15.1-2)
11.39-52	Faults of Pharisees & Scribes		12.33-37	23.4-36		(Mt.15.3-20)
11.53-54	Pharisees lie in wait		(12.10)		3.2?	
12.1	Leaven of the Pharisees			16.6, 11-12	(8.15)	
12.2-9	Fearless Confession			10.26-33	(4.22)	
12.10	Sin against the Holy Spirit	12.31-32				
12.11-12	Assistance of the Spirit			10.19-20		
12.13-21	Against Avarice		13.1-30			(Deut. 8.11-20)
12.22-32	Against Worldly Anxiety		13.24-30	6.25-34		(Deut. 8.3-10)
12.33-34	Treasures in Heaven			6.19-21		
12.35-38	Watchfulness		13.30	(25.1-13)		Mk 13.33-37
12.39-48	Be Prepared for His Coming		13.36-42	24.42-51		
12.49-53	Division in Households			10.34-36		
12.54-56	Interpreting the Times			16.2-3		
12.57-59	Settling with Accuser			5.25-26		
13.1-9	Parable of Barren Fig Tree					(Mt. 7.19)

Table 6.8 (*continued*)

Luke		D Matt	I Matt	OOS Matt	Mark	L
13.10-17	Healing on Sabbath					Mt. 12.9-4
13.18-21	Mustard Seed & Leaven	13.31-33				
13.22-29	Exclusion from Kingdom		13.47-50	7.13-14, 22-23;8.11-12		
13.30	First and Last			19.30	10.31	
13.31-33	Warning against Herod		14.1-12			
13.34-35	Lament over Jerusalem			23.37-39		
14.1-6	Man with Dropsy		(14.13-21)			Mk 3.1-6/Mt. 12.9-14
14.7-14	Humility at Banquets					
14.15-24	Parable of Great Banquet		14.1-21	22.1-14		Deut. 20.5-7
14.25-33	Demands of Discipleship		15.5-6;16.24-26	10.37-38		
14.34-35	Worthless Salt			5.13		
15.1-7	Parable of the Lost Sheep	18.12-14				
15.8-10	Parable of the Lost Coin		(17.27)			
15.11-32	Parable of the Lost Son					Mt. 21.28-32; Deut. 21.15-21
16.1-12	The Dishonest Steward		18.23-34			
16.13	Serving two Masters			6.24		
16.14-15	Pharisees Reproved					
16.16	Law & Prophets till John			11.12-13		
16.17	Permanence of the Law			5.18		
16.18	Divorce		19.3-9	5.32		(Deut. 24.1-4)
16.19-31	Rich Man and Lazarus		19.16-26			(Deut. 24.10-15)

Luke		D Matt	I Matt	OOS Matt	Mark	L
17.1-4	Offences & Forgiveness			18.6-7, 15, 21-22		
17.5-6	Increase Our Faith!		21.21	17.19-20		
17.7-10	Unprofitable Servants		(20.1-16)			
17.11-19	Cleansing Ten Lepers		(20.29-33)			Mk 1.40-45; 10.52;Deut. 24.8
17.20-37	Coming of the Kingdom	24.17-41		10.39/16.25		
18.1-8	Parable of Unjust Judge		24.29-31			
18.9-14	Pharisee and Publican		(23.12)			(Deut. 26.12-15)
18.15-43	On the Road to Jerusalem				10.13-52	
19.1-10	Zacchaeus					Num. 5.6-7
19.11-27	Parable of the Pounds	25.14-30				
19.28-38	Entry into Jerusalem				11.1-10	
19.39-40	Rebuke Your Disciples					Mt. 21.14-16?
19.41-44	Lament over Jerusalem					Mt. 23.37-39?
19.45– 21.33	Jesus in Jerusalem				11.15-13.32	
21.34-36	Take Heed and Watch			(24.48-49)	13.33	
21.37-38	Olivet and Temple					Mk 12.35; 13.1-3;14.3
22.1-2	Priests' Plot				14.1-2	
22.3-6	Judas' Betrayal				14.10-11	
22.7-14	Preparations for Passover				14.12-17	
22.15-23	The Last Supper				14.18-25	1 Cor. 11.23-25
22.24-30	Rewards of Discipleship			20.24-28; 19.28	10.41-45	
22.31-24	Prediction of Peter's Denial				14.26-31	

Table 6.8 (*continued*)

Luke		D Matt	I Matt	OOS Matt	Mark	L
22.35-38	The Two Swords					Mt. 10.9-10; Isa. 53.12
22.39-46	Gethsemane				14.32-40	
22.47-53	Arrest of Jesus				14.43-52	
22.54–23.1	Jewish Hearing	26.57–27.2			14.53–15.1	
23.2-5	Jesus before Pilate				15.2-5	
23.6-12	Jesus before Herod		(27.12, 27-31)			Mk 15.3-4, 17-20
23.13-16	Jesus Declared Innocent		(27.19)			Mk 15.10, 14
23.17-25	Jesus Condemned				15.6-15	
23.26	Simon of Cyrene				15.22	
23.27-31	Daughters of Jerusalem					
23.32-48	Crucifixion and Death				15.23-39	
23.49	Women Who Followed	27.55			15.41	
23.50-56	The Burial	27.57-61			15.42-47	
24.1-9	The Empty Tomb	28.1-8			16.1-8	
24.10-11	The Women's Report		28.8, 17			
24.13-35	Road to Emmaus					
24.36-43	Appearance to the Eleven					Mk 6.49 (*Od.* 11.219)
24.44-53	Last Words & Ascension		28.16-20			Mt. 5.17-18; 16.21

7

Conclusion

Retrospect

There are ample significant similarities between the Gospels of Matthew and Luke to suggest that one must be dependent upon the other. The common objections to such dependence fail to discharge the burden of proof to the contrary. Closer examination of several of them has instead revealed further indications of a direct connection. Proponents of the 2DH have frequently questioned the plausibility of FH Luke's compositional practices, but once literary imitation is included among the available modes of source utilization, and FH Luke is allowed to use his memory as much any other ancient author, there is nothing untoward about the compositional methods that need to be ascribed to FH Luke.

Once Luke's use of Matthew is shown to be probable on other grounds, we may justly wield Occam's razor. If Luke knew Matthew there is no need for Q. This does not mean that all other (oral or written) sources are thereby precluded; it simply means that Q (in the form required by the 2DH) is not among them. Occam's razor may also lead us to prefer relatively simple source-utilization theories (such as the 2DH, FH, 2GH or MPH) over their more profligate rivals: the uncontrolled multiplication of hypothetical entities can be used to explain anything and thus ends up explaining nothing.

We should nevertheless distinguish between a source-utilization theory as an account of what actually happened and as a useful model. The FH is a model of how the Synoptic Gospels are related to one another; it is not a complete account of everything that went into their composition. The purpose of the FH (or any other such hypothesis) is to arrive at the most economical model that illuminates the data we have, not to account for the data we do not and can never have. It nevertheless seems likely that the FH (as defended here) will be a reasonable approximation to what took place, with the proviso that this must also have included many other factors we cannot reconstruct with any hope of precision, so that our best reasonable approximation will almost certainly involve a substantial simplification of a far messier historical reality.

Known unknowns

It may be worth reflecting briefly on what the complicating factors are and why it is unlikely that we shall ever be able fully to resolve them.

The first is that the texts of Mark used by Matthew and Luke will have differed both from each other and from our printed texts. Luke's autograph and Matthew's autograph and Luke's copy of Matthew will also have differed from our reconstructed texts. Indeed, recent approaches to text criticism have problematized the very notion of an autograph. For one thing, it is no longer believed possible to recover precisely what any of the evangelists originally wrote; the most we can achieve is to reconstruct the form of the text of any given book that logically stands as the ultimate ancestor of all the texts that survive. The earliest recoverable text of any gospel may stand at some remove from any putative autograph; there remains a stubborn gap between the first-century composition of the gospels and the, at best, second-century text form that textual criticism is able to recover. For another, we do not know nearly enough about the early stages of producing and disseminating the gospels to be sure that in each case a single author's autograph was the ultimate ancestor of all successive copies. For example, even allowing that there was a first time Mark's Gospel was committed to writing, it could be that Mark (or someone else) later produced a revised version in light of subsequent oral performance or that subsequent oral performance influenced the making of additional copies, so that multiple versions were circulated and copied, in a process somewhat analogous to the dissemination of the early texts of Shakespeare. This uncertainty grows further with Matthew and Luke, since the textual archetypes that proved most influential for the subsequent textual tradition of those gospels may well have differed from the text Matthew and Luke authored on the basis of their sources.[1]

The processes of producing, using and copying manuscripts will have resulted in considerable fluidity in the text of all the gospels, but we cannot pin down the effects of this with sufficient precision to factor them into a detailed account of how the texts we possess came about. As David Parker puts it:

> I am proposing a three-dimensional diagram, in which the third dimension represents a series of contacts between texts each of which may have changed since the previous contact. For example, Matthew copies bits out of Mark in reproducing a tradition; then a later copy of Mark is enriched by some of Matthew's alterations; and next a copy of Matthew (already different from the one we began with) is influenced by something from the also changed Mark. Add in Luke, and oral tradition, and any other sources that might have been available, at any points in the development that you please, and you have a process a good deal less recoverable than any documentary hypothesis.[2]

Parker does a good job of capturing the kind of complications that may have attended the actual processes that led to any text of the gospels we can now recover, but we should not exaggerate the difficulties this poses for the Synoptic Problem. The process of textual transmission has, after all, resulted in three distinct Synoptic Gospels and not in some undifferentiated Synoptic Soup. Arguments that turn on the precise wording of this or that gospel may be vulnerable to the vagaries of textual

---

[1] See Parker, *Living Text*, 1–7, 203–13.
[2] Parker, *Living Text*, 121.

transmission; a few of these have been noted in the preceding chapters. Nevertheless, the effect of known textual variants that merit serious consideration is not all that great and does not materially affect arguments that turn on the order, structure or literary and theological tendencies of the various gospels. While we should be aware of textual variants, we need not be paralysed by them, even though we must acknowledge them as contributing to a known unknown.

Chapter 2 emphasized the role of both individual and collective memory in the composition of the gospels. The use of individual memory of written sources has formed an important part of the argument of the preceding chapters, but little more has been made of collective memory. While it cannot be ruled out that individual eyewitness memory, even at one remove (someone else's recollection of an eyewitness report), played a role in the composition of the gospels, it cannot be demonstrated,[3] and for most members of the early church any knowledge of the earthly Jesus would most likely have taken the form of either collective semantic memory (general beliefs about Jesus) or collective episodic memory (stories of particular incidents), which in part will have been transmitted by oral tradition.[4]

But while it is always possible that one evangelist's use of another's material was influenced by the oral tradition available to him, this can never be demonstrated in any particular instance, so that appeal to oral tradition (or collective memory) as an explanation for any given set of Synoptic parallels is likely to be speculative. *Pace* James Dunn, one cannot assume any correlation between closeness or distance of wording in parallel passages and written or oral modes of appropriation, since on the one hand close verbatim agreement might result from accurate memory while differences in wording could be the consequence of deliberate compositional decisions.[5]

Overall, then, while oral tradition and collective memory may well have played a significant role in the composition of the Synoptic Gospels (and hence in the relationships between them), we cannot now reconstruct what their precise role was. While we can talk about them in general terms, neither the collective memory of the primitive church nor its oral tradition has survived to be examined, and we lack the means to reconstruct either with sufficient precision to enter usefully into the explanation of any particular set of Synoptic parallels. Oral tradition and collective memory thus constitute further known unknowns.[6]

These are far from trivial unknowns. Oral tradition and collective memory are not simply sources Luke and Matthew could employ alongside manuscripts but were part of the environment in which they worked. Neither were they wholly distinct from any written sources, which would have impacted on the oral tradition and collective memory, which may in turn have impacted on the manuscripts available to Matthew

---

[3] See Eve, *Behind*, 135–58; *WTG*, 44–6; for the opposite view, see especially Richard Bauckham, *Jesus and the Eyewitnesses: The Gospels as Eyewitness Testimony* (Grand Rapids: Eerdmans, 2006).
[4] For a fuller account, see *WTG*, 103–24.
[5] Dunn, 'Altering the Default Setting'; Kloppenborg, 'Variation', 63–74; Kirk, 'Memory', 469–70; *WTG*, 128–9; Eve, 'Memory, Orality', 323–5.
[6] See also Eve, 'Memory, Orality'. For a recent argument for the importance of oral tradition to the composition of the gospels, see David Wenham, *From Good News to Gospels: What Did the First Christians Say about Jesus?* (Grand Rapids, MI: Eerdmans, 2018).

and Luke. Matthew's and Luke's memory of their written sources will most likely have been affected by their re-oralization, their refraction in the collective memory of the communities in which the evangelists worked, and even, perhaps, by variant text forms already available within those communities.

A substantial proportion of the material in Matthew does not come from Mark, and a sizeable proportion of that in Luke does not come from Mark and either Matthew (on the FH) or Q (on the 2DH). We may wonder where this additional material came from (assuming the evangelists did not simply invent it). Some of it, perhaps even a good deal of it, could in principle be ascribed to oral tradition or some other form of collective memory, but we cannot automatically exclude the possibility of other written sources.

To object to Q is not to exclude hypothetical sources in general but simply to reject the mutual independence of Luke and Matthew on which Q is predicated. Other sources might still have existed, but they should not be confused with Q. The difficulty is then not the general plausibility of earlier written sources such as the sayings collections envisaged by Francis Watson[7] but our ability to identify and delimit any specific source. In the case of Q we have three extant texts (Mark, Matthew and Luke) to compare when venturing a reconstruction, with the first controlling what is probably not in Q and the other two controlling what probably is; but even then our ability to reconstruct Q with sufficient precision may be questioned.[8] It will be even more difficult to identify and reconstruct any other putative written source, be it an Infancy Narrative, a Passion Narrative or a sayings, parable or miracle story collection.[9] Suppose for the sake of argument that Matthew had been the only gospel to survive; one group of scholars searching for its sources might suggest the existence of a miracle story source, a sayings source, a parable source, a passion narrative source and so on, while another might confidently identify separate sapiential, apocalyptic and Judaizing layers, but it is far from certain whether anyone would postulate anything like our Gospel of Mark as Matthew's main source.

We can always attempt to identify the presence of a source by noting material that appears to be contrary to the given evangelist's style or interests, or which appears to reflect a primitive Palestinian situation better than that of the evangelist's own

---

[7] Watson, *Gospel Writing*, 249–85, but see the reservations expressed by Mark Goodacre, 'What Does *Thomas* Have to Do with Q? The Afterlife of a Sayings Gospel' in Catherine Sider Hamilton and Joel Willits (eds), *Writing the Gospels: A Dialogue with Francis Watson* (London: Bloomsbury T&T Clark, 2019), 81–9.

[8] See Eve, 'Reconstructing Mark'; Perrin, 'Limits'; and Mark Goodacre, 'When Is a Text Not a Text? The Quasi Text-Critical Approach of the International Q Project' in Goodacre and Perrin (eds), *Questioning Q*, 115–26.

[9] For example, the evidence that led Paul Achtemeier to propose a pre-Markan miracle catena might more plausibly be explained on the basis of Markan composition (and John's knowledge of Mark). Paul J. Achtemeier, 'Toward the Isolation of Pre-Markan Miracle Catenae', *JBL* 89 (1970), 265–91; Paul J. Achtemeier, 'The Origin and Function of the Pre-Marcan Miracle Catenae', *JBL* 91 (1972), 198–221; on Markan composition as providing the better explanation, see Robert M. Fowler, *Loaves and Fishes: The Function of the Feeding Stories in the Gospel of Mark* (Chico, California: Scholars Press, 1981); Norman R. Petersen, 'The Composition of Mark 4:1-8:26', *HTR* 73 (1980), 185–217; and Eric Eve, *The Healer from Nazareth: Jesus' Miracles in Historical Context* (London: SPCK, 2009), 92–101.

day. But while it is legitimate to make such attempts, it is hard for any of them to approach generally agreed certainty. Writers are seldom wholly uniform in their stylistic preferences and word choice, and Luke seems particularly prone to varying his style and employing hapaxes. We may question whether we know enough about the primitive church or first-century Judaism to be able to distinguish primitive Palestinian concerns from later ecclesiastical ones with sufficient confidence. Even if we believe we can, that would still not tell us whether some putative fossil was transmitted to the evangelist orally or in writing, or whether it was a piece of deliberate archaizing to lend colour or verisimilitude to the evangelist's tale.

So while an account of what actually happened in the composition of the gospels might well need to include other (oral and/or written) sources, we have no secure means of recovering what they were. Such putative sources can thus play no effective role in the FH *as model*, not because we can be sure they did not exist but because, absent our knowing what they contained, they have no explanatory power.

One other extant text that has been suggested as a possible source for Luke is the Gospel of John. The features shared by Luke and John but not the other two include the resurrection appearance in Jerusalem to the Eleven on Easter Day; Peter's visit to the Empty Tomb (arguably presupposed by Lk. 24.24 even if Lk. 24.12 is regarded as an interpolation); Pilate three times declaring Jesus to be innocent; the miraculous catch of fish; the idea of ascension and the focus on the Spirit; the anointing of Jesus' feet; the sisters Martha and Mary; and the name Lazarus. The case has been made that these indicate Luke's use of John.[10]

Attractive as this suggestion might seem at first sight, however, it quickly runs into a number of difficulties. Given the way FH Luke uses Matthew and Mark, one wonders why his use of John should be so limited. The likelihood that John used Luke rather than the other way around increases as one attends to certain points of detail, many of which were aptly noted by Streeter.[11] For example, at Jn 11.1 Lazarus of Bethany is introduced as the brother of Martha and Mary as if the two sisters should already be known to John's audience, although they have received no previous mention in John. The subsequent identification of Mary of Bethany as the woman who anointed Jesus' feet also appears to presuppose knowledge of an incident John is yet to narrate. Moreover, as Goodacre has remarked, John's account of this anointing (at Jn 12.1-8) looks like a muddled conflation of Luke and Mark.[12]

This is not the place to discuss the relationship between John and the Synoptics. Suffice to say that the incidence of verbal parallels between John and Mark or John and Luke together with indications that John is presupposing something like the Synoptic narrative (e.g. Jn 1.32 appears to presuppose a narrative of Jesus' baptism which it does not narrate, while Jn 3.24 similarly appears to presuppose a knowledge of John the Baptist's arrest), in conjunction with the kinds of arguments already noted above, make it likely that John knew both Mark and Luke (if not Matthew) and presupposed knowledge of both gospels in his target audience. Clearly, however, John did not use

---

[10] Notably by Shellard, *New Light*, 148–260.
[11] Streeter, *Four Gospels*, 401–8.
[12] In the Speaker's Lectures Goodacre delivered at Keble College, Oxford, in May 2017.

Mark and Luke in the way that Matthew and Luke used Mark. None of this precludes the possibility that John had access to other traditions which he also incorporated into his gospel. The point here is that John is unlikely to have been a source for Luke.

Thus, while it seems plausible that the evangelists used other written sources, none of these sources can be identified or reconstructed with any certainty. This is not to deny the value of attempting to probe the traditions and sources behind the gospels, but in the absence of further evidence or unforeseeable advances in critical method, such attempts seem unlikely to yield widely accepted results of sufficient precision to give more specific responses to the issues raised above. The extent of other written sources used by the evangelists is thus likely to remain yet another known unknown.

The existence of so many known unknowns should, finally, alert us to the fact that no theory of Synoptic relations will be able to account definitively for all the data, since there are too many irrecoverable factors involved, not least what exactly was going on in the evangelists' minds and what interactions they and their communities had had with their source material prior to the composition of their gospels.

Prospects

It goes without saying that not everyone will be convinced by the arguments set forth in this study (although hopefully some people may be persuaded). If it were that easy to settle the Synoptic Problem, it would have been settled long ago. No scholar, least of all the present author, can lay claim to any monopoly of wisdom; we all have our cognitive biases and our subjective preferences, however objective and honest we may strive to be in our scholarship, and there will inevitably be cases where what appears convincing or plausible to one person will seem quite unconvincing or implausible to another. And unless this book were made far longer than either author, publisher or reader could bear (Eccl. 12.12b!), there will inevitably be gaps in the case it makes. It has not been possible to deal with every single argument, objection and potentially problematic set of Synoptic parallels that anyone might raise. Debates over ancient compositional techniques will doubtless continue. More useful work could surely be done on the known unknowns. The list goes on.

The composition of the gospels was inevitably a messier and more complex process than any usable model of Synoptic relationships can capture. Whichever theory one adopts, there will be some data that stubbornly refuses to fit as neatly and convincingly as one would like. This book has argued that the Farrer Hypothesis supplies the most plausible model for the relationships between Mark, Matthew and Luke, but it cannot recapture everything that was going on in the minds of the evangelists or all the influences at play or all the vagaries of textual transmission; any attempt to do so in every single problematic case can only end up appearing speculative (however reasonable one's speculations can be made to appear). But assuming no mass conversion to the Farrer Hypothesis ensues, this book will nevertheless have fulfilled its purpose if it succeeds in advancing the debate.

Bibliography

Achtemeier, Paul J., 'Toward the Isolation of Pre-Markan Miracle Catenae', *JBL* 89 (1970), 265-91.
Achtemeier, Paul J., 'The Origin and Function of the Pre-Marcan Miracle Catenae', *JBL* 91 (1972), 198-221.
Adams, Sean A., 'Luke and *Progymnasmata*: Rhetorical Handbooks, Rhetorical Sophistication and Genre Selection', in Matthew Ryan Hauge and Andrew Pitts (eds), *Ancient Education and Early Christianity* (LNTS, 533; London: Bloomsbury T&T Clark, 2016), 137-54.
Alexander, Loveday, 'Luke's Preface in the Context of Greek Preface-Writing', *NovT* 28 (1986), 48-74.
Alexander, Loveday, *The Preface to Luke's Gospel: Literary Convention and Social Context in Luke 1.1-4 and Acts 1.1* (SNTSMS, 78; Cambridge: Cambridge University Press, repr. Paperback 2005 edn, 1993).
Alexander, Loveday, 'Memory and Tradition in the Hellenistic Schools', in Werner H. Kelber and Samuel Byrskog (eds), *Jesus in Memory: Traditions in Oral and Scribal Perspectives* (Waco: Baylor University Press, 2009), 113-53.
Alexander, Philip. S., 'Midrash and the Gospels', in Christopher M. Tuckett (ed.), *Synoptic Studies: The Ampleforth Conferences of 1982 and 1983* (JSNTSup, 7; Sheffield: JSOT Press, 1984), 1-18.
Allison, Dale C., *The New Moses: A Matthean Typology* (Edinburgh: T&T Clark, 1993).
Anonymous, 'The Aeneas-Legend from Homer to Virgil', *BICS*, BS 52: *Roman Myth and Mythography*, 34.S52 (July 1984), 12-24.
Assmann, Jan, *Religion and Cultural Memory* (tr. Rodney Livingstone; Stanford, CA: Stanford University Press, 2006).
Assmann, Jan, *Cultural Memory and Early Civilization: Writing, Remembrance, and Political Imagination* (tr. David Henry Wilson; Cambridge: Cambridge University Press, 2011).
Aurelius, Erik, 'Gottesvolk und Außenseiter: Eine geheime Beziehung Lukas – Matthäus', *NTS* 47 (2001), 428-41.
Baban, Octavian D., *On the Road Encounters in Luke-Acts: Hellenistic Mimesis and Luke's Theology of the Way* (PBM; Milton Keynes: Paternoster, 2006).
Baddeley, Alan, Michael W. Eysenck and Michael C. Anderson, *Memory* (Hove: Psychology Press, 2009).
Barker, James W., 'Ancient Compositional Practices and the Gospels: A Reassessment', *JBL* 135 (2016), 109-21.
Bauckham, Richard, *Jesus and the Eyewitnesses: The Gospels as Eyewitness Testimony* (Grand Rapids, MI: Eerdmans, 2006).
Beaton, Richard C., 'How Matthew Writes', in Markus Bockmuehl and Donald A. Hagner (eds), *The Written Gospel* (Cambridge: Cambridge University Press, 2005), 116-34.
Begg, Christopher, *Josephus' Account of the Early Divided Monarchy* (BETL, 108; Leuven: Leuven University Press, 1993).

Black, Steve D., 'One Really Striking Minor Agreement TIS ESTIN HO PAISAS SE in Matthew 26:68 and Luke 22:64', *NovT* 52 (2010), 313–33.
Bonz, Marianne Palmer, *The Past as Legacy: Luke-Acts and Ancient Epic* (Minneapolis: Fortress, 2000).
Borgen, Peder, *Philo of Alexandria: An Exegete for His Time* (NovTSup, 86; Leiden: Brill, 1997).
Boring, M. Eugene, 'The "Minor Agreements" and Their Bearing on the Synoptic Problem', in Paul Foster, Andrew Gregory, John S. Kloppenborg and J. Verheyden (eds), *New Studies in the Synoptic Problem* (BETL, 139; Leuven: Leuven University Press, 2011), 227–51.
Borman, Lukas, 'Rewritten Prophecy in Luke-Acts', in Mogens Müller and Jesper Tang Nielsen (eds), *Luke's Literary Creativity* (London: Bloomsbury T&T Clark, 2016), 122–43.
Botha, Pieter J. J., *Orality and Literacy in Early Christianity* (Biblical Performance Criticism 5; ed. Holly E. Hearon and Philip Ruge-Jones; Eugene, OR: Cascade, 2012).
Brodie, Louis T., 'A New Temple and a New Law', *JSNT* 5 (1979), 21–45.
Brodie, Thomas L., 'Luke 7,36-50 as an Internalization of 2 Kings 4,1-37: A Study in Luke's Use of Rhetorical Imitation', *Biblica* 64 (1983), 457–85.
Brodie, Thomas L., 'Towards Unraveling the Rhetorical Imitation of Sources in Acts: 2 Kgs 5 as One Component of Acts 8,9-40', *Biblica* 67 (1986a), 41–67.
Brodie, Thomas L., 'Towards Unravelling Luke's Use of the Old Testament: Luke 7.11-17 as an *Imitatio* of 1 Kings 17.17-24', *NTS* 32 (1986b), 247–67.
Brodie, Thomas L., 'Towards Tracing the Gospels' Literary Indebtedness to the Epistles', in Dennis R. MacDonald (ed.), *Mimesis and Intertextuality in Antiquity and Christianity* (Studies in Antiquity & Christianity; Harrisburg, PA: Trinity Press International, 2001), 104–16.
Brodie, Thomas L., *The Birthing of the New Testament: The Intertextual Development of the New Testament Writings* (NTM, 1; Sheffield: Sheffield Phoenix Press, 2004).
Brown, Raymond E., *The Birth of the Messiah: A Commentary on the Infancy Narratives in Matthew and Luke* (London: Geoffrey Chapman, 1977).
Brown, Raymond E., *The Death of the Messiah: From Gethsemane to the Grave*, vol. 1 (London: Geoffrey Chapman, 1994).
Bruce, F.F., *The Acts of the Apostles: The Greek Text with Introduction and Commentary* (London: Tyndale Press, 1951).
Bryan, David K., 'Transformation of the Mustard Seed and Leaven in the Gospel of Luke', *NovT* 58 (2016), 115–34.
Burkett, Delbert, *Rethinking the Gospel Sources: From Proto-Mark to Mark* (New York: T&T Clark, 2004).
Byrskog, Samuel, 'A New Quest for the Sitz im Leben: Social Memory, the Jesus Tradition and the Gospel of Matthew', *NTS* 52 (2006), 319–36.
Cairns, Francis, *Virgil's Augustan Epic* (Cambridge: Cambridge University Press, 1989).
Carlston, Charles E. and Dennis Norlin, 'Once More – Statistics and Q', *HTR* 1971 (2004), 59–78.
Carr, David M., *Writing on the Tablet of the Heart: Origins of Scripture and Literature* (Oxford: Oxford University Press, 2005).
Carruthers, Mary, *The Book of Memory: A Study of Memory in Medieval Culture* (CSML; Cambridge: Cambridge University Press, 2nd edn, 2008).

Casali, Sergio, 'The Development of the Aeneas Legend', in Joseph Farrell and Michael C.J. Putnam (eds), *A Companion to Vergil's Aeneid and Its Tradition* (Chichester: Wiley-Blackwell, 2010), 37–51.

Catchpole, David R., *The Quest for Q* (Edinburgh: T&T Clark, 1993).

Croatto, J. Severino, 'Jesus, Prophet Like Elijah, and Prophet-Teacher Like Moses in Luke-Acts', *JBL* 124 (2005), 452–65.

Crook, Zeba Antonin, 'The Synoptic Parables of the Mustard Seed and the Leaven: A Test-Case for the Two-Document, Two-Gospel, and Farrer-Goulder Hypotheses', *JSNT* 78 (2000), 23–48.

Damm, Alex, 'Ancient Rhetoric and the Synoptic Problem', in Paul Foster, Andrew Gregory, John S. Kloppenborg and J. Verheyden (eds), *New Studies in the Synoptic Problem* (BETL, 139; Leuven: Leuven University Press, 2011), 483–508.

Damm, Alex, *Ancient Rhetoric and the Synoptic Problem: Clarifying Markan Priority* (BETL, 252; Leuven: Peeters, 2013).

Damm, Alexander, 'A Rhetorical-Critical Assessment of Luke's Use of the Elijah-Elisha Narrative', in John S. Kloppenborg and Joseph Verheyden (eds), *The Elijah-Elisha Narrative in the Composition of Luke* (London: Bloomsbury T&T Clark, 2014), 88–112.

Davies, W.D. and Dale C. Allison, *A Critical and Exegetical Commentary on the Gospel according to Saint Matthew*, vol. 1 (ICC; Edinburgh: T&T Clark, 1988).

Dekel, Edan, *Virgil's Homeric Lens* (New York: Routledge, 2012).

Delling, Gerhard, 'Wunder-Allegorie-Mythus bei Philon von Alexandreia', in *Gottes ist der Orient* (Berlin: Evangelische Verlagsanstalt, 1959), 42–68.

Derico, T.M., *Oral Tradition and Synoptic Verbal Agreement: Evaluating the Empirical Evidence for Literary Dependence* (Cambridge: James Clarke, 2017).

Derrenbacker, R.A., *Ancient Compositional Practices and the Synoptic Problem* (BETL 186; Leuven: Peeters-Leuven, 2005).

Derrenbacker, Robert A., 'The "External and Psychological Conditions under Which the Synoptic Gospels Were Written": Ancient Compositional Practices and the Synoptic Problem', in Paul Foster, Andrew Gregory, John S. Kloppenborg and J. Verheyden (eds), *New Studies in the Synoptic Problem* (BETL, 139; Leuven: Leuven University Press, 2011), 435–57.

Derrenbacker, Robert A., 'Texts, Tables and Tablets: A Response to John C. Poirier', *JSNT* 25 (2013), 380–7.

Derrett, J. Duncan M., 'Homer in the New Testament', *ExpTim* 121 (2009), 66–9.

Dewey, Joanna, 'The Survival of Mark's Gospel: A Good Story?', *JBL* 123 (2004), 495–507.

Dewey, Joanna, 'The Gospel of Mark as Oral Hermeneutic', in Tom Thatcher (ed.), *Jesus, the Voice and the Text: Beyond the Oral and the Written Gospel* (Waco: Baylor University Press, 2008), 71–87.

Donahue, John R. and Daniel J. Harrington, *The Gospel of Mark* (SP, 2; Collegeville: Michael Glazier, 2002).

Downing, F. Gerald, 'Towards the Rehabilitation of Q', *NTS* 11 (1964), 169–81.

Downing, F. Gerald, 'Redaction Criticism: Josephus' Antiquities and the Synoptic Problem I', *JSNT* 8 (1980a), 46–65.

Downing, F. Gerald, 'Redaction Criticism: Josephus' Antiquities and the Synoptic Problem II', *JSNT* 9 (1980b), 29–48.

Downing, F. Gerald, 'Compositional Conventions and the Synoptic Problem', *JBL* 107 (1988), 69–85.

Downing, F. Gerald, 'Disagreements of Each Evangelist with the Minor Close Agreements of the Other Two', *ETL* 80 (2004), 445–69.

Downing, F. Gerald, 'Writers' Use or Abuse of Written Sources', in Paul Foster, Andrew Gregory, John S. Kloppenborg and J. Verheyden (eds), *New Studies in the Synoptic Problem* (BETL, 139; Leuven: Leuven University Press, 2011), 523-48.

Downing, F. Gerald, 'Waxing Careless: Poirier, Derrenbacker and Downing', *JSNT* 35 (2013), 388-93.

Downing, F. Gerald, 'Imitation and Emulation, Josephus and Luke: Plot and Psycholinguistics', in John S. Kloppenborg and Joseph Verheyden (eds), *The Elijah-Elisha Narrative in the Composition of Luke* (London: Bloomsbury T&T Clark, 2014), 113-29.

Downing, F. Gerald, 'Plausibility, Probability and Synoptic Hypotheses', *ETL* 93 (2017), 445-69.

Drury, John, *Tradition and Design in Luke's Gospel: A Study in Early Christian Historiography* (London: Darton, Longman and Todd, 1976).

Du Quesnay, Ian M. le M., 'From Polyphemus to Corydon: Virgil, Eclogue 2 and the Idylls of Theocritus', in David West and Tony Woodman (eds), *Creative Imitation and Latin Literature* (Cambridge: Cambridge University Press, 1979), 35-70.

Ducharme, Lori J. and Gary Alan Fine, 'The Construction of Nonpersonhood and Demonization: Commemorating the Traitorous Reputation of Benedict Arnold', *SF* 73 (1995), 1309-31.

Dunn, James D.G., 'Altering the Default Setting: Re-envisaging the Early Transmission of the Jesus Tradition', *NTS* 49 (2003a), 139-75.

Dunn, James D.G., *Jesus Remembered*, vol.1 of *Christianity in the Making* (Grand Rapids, MI: Eerdmans, 2003b).

Dupertuis, Rubén E., 'The Summaries of Acts 2, 4 and 5 and Plato's Republic', in Jo-Ann A. Brant, Charles W. Hedrick and Chris Shea (eds), *Ancient Fiction: The Matrix of Early Christian and Jewish Narrative* (Atlanta: SBL, 2005), 275-96.

Egelkraut, Helmuth K., *Jesus' Mission to Jerusalem: A Redaction Critical Study of the Travel Narrative in the Gospel of Luke, Lk 9: 51-19:48* (Frankfurt: Peter Lang, 1976).

Elder, Nicholas A., *The Media Matrix of Early Jewish and Christian Narrative* (LNTS 612; London: Bloomsbury T&T Clark, 2019).

Evans, C.F., 'The Central Section of St. Luke's Gospel', in D.E. Nineham (ed.), *Studies in the Gospels: Essays in Memory of R. H. Lightfoot* (Oxford: Blackwell, 1955), 37-53.

Evans, C.F., *Saint Luke* (TPINTC; London: SCM, 1990).

Evans, Craig A., 'The Two Source Hypothesis', in Stanley E. Porter and Bryan R. Dyer (eds), *The Synoptic Problem: Four Views* (Grand Rapids, MI: Baker Academic, 2016), 27-45.

Evans, Paul S., 'Creating a New "Great Divide": The Exoticization of Ancient Culture in Some Recent Applications of Orality Study to the Bible', *JBL* 136 (2017), 749-64.

Eve, Eric, *The Jewish Context of Jesus' Miracles* (JSNTSup, 231; Sheffield: Sheffield Academic Press, 2002).

Eve, Eric, 'Reconstructing Mark: A Thought Experiment', in Mark Goodacre and Nicholas Perrin (eds), *Questioning Q* (London: SPCK, 2004), 89-114.

Eve, Eric, *The Healer from Nazareth: Jesus' Miracles in Historical Context* (London: SPCK, 2009).

Eve, Eric, 'The Synoptic Problem without Q?' in Paul Foster, Andrew Gregory, John S. Kloppenborg and J. Verheyden (eds), *New Studies in the Synoptic Problem* (BETL, 139; Leuven: Leuven University Press, 2011), 551-70.

Eve, Eric, *Behind the Gospels: Understanding the Oral Tradition* (London: SPCK, 2013).

Eve, Eric, 'The Devil in the Detail: Exorcising Q from the Beelzebul Controversy', in John C. Poirier and Jeff Peterson (eds), *Marcan Priority without Q: Explorations in the Farrer Hypothesis* (LNTS, 455; London: Bloomsbury T&T Clark, 2015a), 16–43.

Eve, Eric, 'Memory, Orality and the Synoptic Problem', *EC* 6 (2015b), 311–33.

Eve, Eric, *Writing the Gospels: Composition and Memory* (London: SPCK, 2016).

Fantuzzi, Marco and Christos Tsagalis, 'Introduction: Kyklos, the Epic Cycle and Cyclic Poetry', in Marco Fantuzzi and Christos Tsagalis (eds), *The Greek Epic Cycle and Its Ancient Reception: A Companion* (Cambridge: Cambridge University Press, 2015), 1–40.

Farrer, A.M., 'On Dispensing with Q', in D.E. Nineham (ed.), *Studies in the Gospels: Essays in Memory of R. H. Lightfoot* (Oxford: Blackwell, 1955), 55–88.

Fayol, Michel, 'From On-line Management Problems to Strategies in Written Composition', in Mark Torrance and Gaynor C. Jeffery (eds), *The Cognitive Demands of Writing* (Amsterdam: Amsterdam University Press, 1999), 13–23.

Fine, Gary Alan, 'Reputational Entrepreneurs and the Memory of Incompetence: Melting Supporters, Partisan Warriors and Images of President Harding', *AJS* 105 (1996), 1159–93.

Finkelpearl, Ellen, 'Pagan Traditions of Intertextuality in the Greco-Roman World', in Dennis R. MacDonald (ed.), *Mimesis and Intertextuality in Antiquity and Christianity* (SAC; Harrisburg, PA: Trinity Press International, 2001), 78–90.

Fiske, George Converse, *Lucilius and Horace: A Study in the Classical Theory of Imitation* (UWSLL, 7; Madison: 1920).

Fitzmyer, Joseph A., *The Gospel according to Luke (X–XXIV): A New Translation with Introduction and Commentary* (AB 28A; New York: Doubleday, 1985).

Foster, P., A. Gregory, J.S. Kloppenborg and J. Verheyden (eds), *New Studies in the Synoptic Problem: Oxford Conference, April 2008: Essays in Honour of Christopher M. Tuckett* (BETL, 239; Leuven: Peeters, 2011).

Fowler, Robert M., *Loaves and Fishes: The Function of the Feeding Stories in the Gospel of Mark* (Chico, CA: Scholars Press, 1981).

Franklin, Eric, *Luke: Interpreter of Paul, Critic of Matthew* (JSNTS, 92; Sheffield: JSOT, 1994).

Friedrichsen, Timothy, 'The Minor Agreements of Matthew and Luke against Mark: Critical Observations on R.B. Vinson's Statistical Analysis', *ETL* 65 (1985), 395–408.

Friesen, Courtney, *Reading Dionysus: Euripides' Bacchae and the Cultural Contestations of Greeks, Jews, Romans, and Christians* (STAC, 95; Tübingen: Mohr Siebeck, 2015).

Frolov, Sergey and Allen Wright, 'Homeric and Ancient Near Eastern Intertextuality in 1 Samuel 17', *JBL* 130 (2011), 451–71.

Gallarte, Israel Muñoz, 'Luke 24 Reconsidered: The Figure of the Ghost in Post-Classical Greek Literature', *NovT* 59 (2017), 131–46.

Garrett, Susan R., *The Demise of the Devil: Magic and the Demonic in Luke's Writings* (Minneapolis: Fortress Press, 1989).

Gärtner, Ursula, 'Virgil and the Epic Cycle', in Marco Fantuzzi and Christos Tsagalis (eds), *The Greek Epic Cycle and Its Ancient Reception: A Companion* (Cambridge: Cambridge University Press, 2015), 543–64.

Goodacre, Mark, *Goulder and the Gospels: An Examination of a New Paradigm* (JSNTS, 133; Sheffield: Sheffield Academic Press, 1996).

Goodacre, Mark, 'Fatigue in the Synoptics', *NTS* 44 (1998), 45–58.

Goodacre, Mark, *The Case against Q: Studies in Markan Priority and the Synoptic Problem* (Harrisburg, PA: Trinity Press International, 2002).

Goodacre, Mark, 'On Choosing and Using Appropriate Analogies: A Response to F. Gerald Downing', *JSNT* 26 (2003), 237–40.

Goodacre, Mark, 'When Is a Text Not a Text? The Quasi Text-Critical Approach of the International Q Project', in Mark Goodacre and Nicholas Perrin (eds), *Questioning Q* (London: SPCK, 2004), 115–26.

Goodacre, Mark, 'A Flaw in McIver and Carroll's Experiments to Determine Written Sources in the Gospels', *JBL* 133 (2014), 793–800.

Goodacre, Mark, 'Too Good to Be Q: High Verbatim Agreement in the Double Tradition', in John C. Poirier and Jeff Peterson (eds), *Marcan Priority without Q: Explorations in the Farrer Hypothesis* (LNTS, 455; London: Bloomsbury T&T Clark, 2015), 82–100.

Goodacre, Mark, 'Re-Walking the "Way of the Lord": Luke's Use of Mark and His Reaction to Matthew', in Mogens Müller and Jesper Tang Nielsen (eds), *Luke's Literary Creativity* (LNTS, 550; London: Bloomsbury T&T Clark, 2016), 26–43.

Goodacre, Mark, 'Taking Our Leave of Mark-Q Overlaps: Major Agreements and the Farrer Theory', in Mogens Müller and Heike Omerzu (eds), *Gospel Interpretation and the Q-Hypothesis* (LNTS, 573; London: Bloomsbury T&T Clark, 2018), 201–22.

Goodacre, Mark, 'What Does *Thomas* Have to Do with Q? The Afterlife of a Sayings Gospel', in Catherine Sider Hamilton and Joel Willits (eds), *Writing the Gospels: A Dialogue with Francis Watson* (London: Bloomsbury T&T Clark, 2019), 81–9.

Goodenough, Erwin R., *By Light, Light: The Mystical Gospel of Hellenistic Judaism* (New Haven: Yale University Press, 1935).

Gorman, Heather M., 'Crank or Creative Genius? How Ancient Rhetoric Makes Sense of Luke's Order', in John C. Poirier and Jeff Peterson (eds), *Marcan Priority without Q: Explorations in the Farrer Hypothesis* (LNTS, 455; London: Bloomsbury T&T Clark, 2015), 62–81.

Goulder, Michael D., *Type and History in Acts* (London: SPCK, 1964).

Goulder, Michael D., 'On Putting Q to the Test', *NTS* 24 (1978), 218–34.

Goulder, Michael D., *Luke: A New Paradigm* (JSNTSup, 20; Sheffield: Sheffield Academic Press, 1989).

Goulder, Michael D., 'Review of F. Neirynck, Evangelica. II. 1982–1991: Collected Essays (ed. F. Van Segbroeck)', *NovT* 35 (1993a), 199–202.

Goulder, Michael D., 'Luke's Compositional Options', *NTS* 39 (1993b), 150–2.

Goulder, Michael D., 'Two Significant Minor Agreements (Mat. 4:13 Par.; Mat. 26: 67-68 Par.)', *NovT* 45 (2003), 365–73.

Goulder, Michael D., *Midrash and Lection in Matthew* (Eugene, OR: Wipf and Stock, 2004).

Green, H. Benedict, 'Matthew 12. 22-50 and Parallels: An Alternative to Matthean Conflation', in Christopher M. Tuckett (ed.), *Synoptic Studies: The Ampleforth Conferences of 1982 and 1983* (JSNTSup, 7; Sheffield: JSOT Press, 1984), 157–76.

Gregory, Andrew, 'What Is Literary Dependence?' in Paul Foster, Andrew Gregory, John S. Kloppenborg and J. Verheyden (eds), *New Studies in the Synoptic Problem* (BETL, 139; Leuven: Leuven University Press, 2011), 87–114.

Gregory, Andrew F., *The Gospel according to the Hebrews and the Gospel of the Ebionites* (OECGT; Oxford: Oxford University Press, 2017).

Gundry, Robert H., 'The Refusal of Matthean Foreign Bodies to Be Exorcised from Luke 9,22; 10,25-28', *ETL* 75 (1999), 104–22.

Güttgemanns, Erhardt, *Candid Questions Concerning Gospel Form Criticism: A Methodological Sketch of the Fundamental Problematics of Form and Redaction Criticism* (PTMS, 26; tr. William G. Doty; Pittsburgh, PA: Pickwick Press, 1979).

Harrington, Daniel J., *The Gospel of Matthew* (SP, 1; Collegeville, MN: Liturgical, 1991).
Harstine, Stan, 'Review of the New Testament Imitate Homer? Four Cases from the Acts of the Apostles, by Dennis R. MacDonald', *JBL* 124 (2005), 383–5.
Hauge, Matthew Ryan, 'Fabulous Parables: The Storytelling Tradition in the Synoptic Gospels', in Matthew Ryan Hauge and Andrew Pitts (eds), *Ancient Education and Early Christianity* (LNTS, 533; London: Bloomsbury T&T Clark, 2016), 89–105.
Hexter, Ralph, 'On First Looking into Vergil's Homer', in Joseph Farrell and Michael C.J. Putnam (eds), *A Companion to Vergil's Aeneid and Its Tradition* (Chichester: Wiley-Blackwell, 2010), 26–36.
Hock, Ronald F., 'Homer in Greco-Roman Education', in Dennis R. MacDonald (ed.), *Mimesis and Intertextuality in Antiquity and Christianity* (SAC; Harrisburg, PA: Trinity Press International, 2001), 56–77.
Holladay, Carl R., *Theios Aner in Hellenistic Judaism: A Critique of the Use of This Category in New Testament Christology* (Missoula, MT: Scholars Press, 1977).
Holmberg, Ingrid, 'The Creation of the Ancient Greek Epic Cycle', *OT* 13 (1998), 456–78.
Homer, *Iliad* (tr. A.T. Murray; LCL; 2 vols; London: Heinemann, 1924–25).
Homer, *Odyssey* (tr. A.T. Murray; LCL; 2 vols; Cambridge, MA: Harvard University Press, 1975).
Honoré, A.M., 'A Statistical Study of the Synoptic Problem', *NovT* 10 (1968), 95–147.
Horsley, Richard A., *Scribes, Visionaries and the Politics of Second Temple Judea* (Louisville: Westminster John Knox, 2007).
Hurtado, Larry W., 'Oral Fixation and New Testament Studies? "Orality", "Performance" and Reading Texts in Early Christianity', *NTS* 60 (2014), 321–40.
Jaffee, Martin S., *Torah in the Mouth: Writing and Oral Tradition in Palestinian Judaism, 200 BCE–400 CE* (Oxford: Oxford University Press, 2001).
Jeffrey, David Lyle, *Luke* (Brazos Theological Commentary on the Bible, Grand Rapids, MI: Brazos, 2012).
Johnson, Luke Timothy, *The Gospel of Luke* (SP, 3; Collegeville, MN: Liturgical, 1991).
Johnson, Luke Timothy, 'Review of the New Testament Imitate Homer? Four Cases from the Acts of the Apostles, by Dennis R. MacDonald', *TS* 66 (2005a), 489–90.
Johnson, Luke Timothy, 'Review of the New Testament Imitate Homer? Four Cases from the Acts of the Apostles, by Dennis R. MacDonald', *CL* 54 (2005b), 285–7.
Josephus, *Works* (tr. H. St. J. Thackeray et al.; LCL; 10 vols; London: Heinemann, 1926–65).
Kahl, Werner, 'Inclusive and Exclusive Agreements – Towards a Neutral Comparison of the Synoptic Gospels, Or: Minor Agreements as Misleading Category', in Mogens Müller and Jesper Tang Nielsen (eds), *Luke's Literary Creativity* (LNTS, 550; London: Bloomsbury T&T Clark, 2016), 44–78.
Kahl, Werner, 'The Gospel of Luke as Narratological Improvement of Synoptic Pre-Texts: The Narrative Introduction to the Jesus Story (Mark 1.1-8 Parr.)', in Mogens Müller and Heike Omerzu (eds), *Gospel Interpretation and the Q-Hypothesis* (LNTS, 573; London: Bloomsbury T&T Clark, 2018), 223–44.
Kartzow, Marianne Bjelland, 'Rewritten Stereotypes: Scripture and Cultural Echo in Luke's Parable of the Widow and the Judge', in Mogens Müller and Jesper Tang Nielsen (eds), *Luke's Literary Creativity* (LNTS, 573; London: Bloomsbury T&T Clark, 2016), 208–24.
Keener, Craig S., *Acts: An Exegetical Commentary*, vol. 1 (Grand Rapids, MI: BakerAcademic, 2012).
Keener, Craig S., *Acts: An Exegetical Commentary*, vol. 4 (Grand Rapids, MI: BakerAcademic, 2015).

Keener, Craig S., *Christobiography: Memory, History and the Reliability of the Gospels* (Grand Rapids, MI: Eerdmans, 2019).
Keith, Chris, 'Prolegomena on the Textualization of Mark's Gospel: Manuscript Culture, the Extended Situation, and the Emergence of the Written Gospel', in Tom Thatcher (ed.), *Memory and Identity in Ancient Judaism and Early Christianity: A Conversation with Barry Schwartz* (SS, 78; Atlanta: SBL, 2014), 161–86.
Keith, Chris, 'Social Memory Theory and Gospels Research: The First Decade (Part One)', *EC* 6 (2015a), 354–76.
Keith, Chris, 'Social Memory Theory and Gospels Research: The First Decade (Part Two)', *EC* 6 (2015b), 517–42.
Kelber, Werner H., *The Oral and the Written Gospel: The Hermeneutics of Speaking and Writing in the Synoptic Tradition, Mark, Paul and Q* (VPT; Bloomington: Indiana University Press, 1997).
Kelber, Werner H., 'The Works of Memory: Christian Origins as MnemoHistory – A Response', in Alan Kirk and Tom Thatcher (eds), *Memory, Tradition, and Text: Uses of the Past in Early Christianity* (SBL SS, 52; Leiden: Boston: Brill, 2005), 221–48.
Kelber, Werner H., *Imprints, Voiceprints & Footprints of Memory: Collected Essays of Werner Kelber* (RBS, 74; Atlanta: SBL, 2013).
Kellogg, Ronald T., 'Components of Working Memory in Text Production', in Mark Torrance and Gaynor C. Jeffery (eds), *The Cognitive Demands of Writing* (Amsterdam: Amsterdam University Press, 1999), 43–61.
Kennedy, George A., *Progymnasmata: Greek Textbooks of Prose Composition and Rhetoric* (tr. George A. Kennedy; Atlanta: SBL, 2003).
Kenney, E.J., 'Iudicium Transferendi: Virgil, Aeneid 2.469–505 and Its Antecedents', in T. West and D. Woodman (eds), *Creative Imitation and Latin Literature* (Cambridge: Cambridge University Press, 1979), 103–20.
King, Katherine Callen, 'Foil and Fusion: Homer's Achilles in Vergil's Aeneid', *MDLATC* 9 (1982), 31–57.
Kirk, Alan, 'Social and Cultural Memory', in Alan Kirk and Tom Thatcher (eds), *Memory, Tradition, and Text: Uses of the Past in Early Christianity* (SBL SS, 52; Leiden; Boston: Brill, 2005), 1–24.
Kirk, Alan, 'Memory, Scribal Media, and the Synoptic Problem', in Paul Foster, Andrew Gregory, John S. Kloppenborg and J. Verheyden (eds), *New Studies in the Synoptic Problem* (BETL, 139; Leuven: Leuven University Press, 2011), 459–82.
Kirk, Alan, 'Orality, Writing, and Phantom Sources: Appeals to Ancient Media in Some Recent Challenges to the Two Document Hypothesis', *NTS* 58 (2012), 1–22.
Kirk, Alan, *Q in Matthew: Ancient Media, Memory, and Early Scribal Transmission of the Jesus Tradition* (LNTS, 564; London: Bloomsbury T&T Clark, 2016).
Kirk, Alan, *Memory and the Jesus Tradition* (London: Bloomsbury T&T Clark, 2018).
Kirk, Alan and Tom Thatcher, 'Jesus Tradition as Social Memory', in Alan Kirk and Tom Thatcher (eds), *Memory, Tradition, and Text: Uses of the Past in Early Christianity* (SBL Semeia Studies, 52; ed. G. A. Yee; Leiden; Boston: Brill, 2005), 25–42.
Kloppenborg, John S., *Q Parallels: Synopsis, Critical Notes & Concordance* (Sonoma, CA: Polebridge, 1988).
Kloppenborg, John S., *The Formation of Q: Trajectories in Ancient Wisdom Collections* (SAC; Harrisburg, PA: Trinity Press International, 1999).
Kloppenborg, John S., 'On Dispensing with Q?: Goodacre on the Relation of Luke to Matthew', *NTS* 49 (2003), 210–36.

Kloppenborg, John S., 'Variation and Reproduction of the Double Tradition and an Oral Q?', *ETL* 83 (2007), 53–80.
Kloppenborg, John S., 'The Farrer/Mark without Q Hypothesis: A Response', in John C. Poirier and Jeff Peterson (eds), *Marcan Priority without Q: Explorations in the Farrer Hypothesis* (LNTS, 455; London: Bloomsbury T&T Clark, 2015), 226–44.
Kloppenborg, John S., 'Conceptual Stakes in the Synoptic Problem', in Mogens Müller and Heike Omerzu (eds), *Gospel Interpretation and the Q-Hypothesis* (LNTS, 573; London: Bloomsbury T & T Clark, 2018), 13–42.
Kloppenborg, John S., 'Macro-Conflation, Micro-Conflation, Harmonization and the Compositional Practices of the Synoptic Writers', *ETL* 95, 4 (2019), 629–43.
Kloppenborg Verbin, John S., *Excavating Q: The History and Setting of the Sayings Gospel* (Edinburgh: T&T Clark, 2000).
Knauer, Georg Nicolaus, 'Vergil's *Aeneid* and Homer', *GRBS* 5 (1964), 61–84.
Knoppers, Gary N., 'The Synoptic Problem? An Old Testament Perspective', *BBR* 19 (2009), 11–34.
Kochenash, Michael, 'You Can't Hear "Aeneas" without Thinking of Rome', *JBL* 136 (2017), 667–85.
Kochenash, Michael, 'The Scandal of Gentile Inclusion: Reading Acts 17 with Euripides' Bacchae', in Mark Glen Bilby, Margaret Froelich and Michael Kochenash (eds), *Classical Greek Models of the Gospels and Acts: Studies in Mimesis Criticism* (Claremont, CA: Claremont Press, 2018), 124–44.
Kuhn, Karl A., 'The Point of the Step-Parallelism in Luke 1–2', *NTS* 47 (2001), 38–49.
Landry, David, 'Reconsidering the Date of Luke in Light of the Farrer Hypothesis', in John C. Poirier and Jeffrey Peterson (eds), *Marcan Priority without Q: Explorations in the Farrer Hypothesis* (LNTS, 455; London: Bloomsbury T&T Clark, 2015), 160–90.
Larsen, Matthew D.C., *Gospels before the Book* (New York: Oxford University Press, 2018).
Last, Richard, 'Communities That Write: Christ-Groups, Associations, and Gospel Communities', *NTS* 58 (2012), 173–98.
Lear, Joseph M. Jr, 'Luke's Use of the Old Testament in the Sending of the Seventy(-Two): A Compositional Study', in Mogens Müller and Jesper Tang Nielsen (eds), *Luke's Literary Creativity* (LNTS, 550; London: Bloomsbury T&T Clark, 2016), 160–82.
Licona, Michael R., *Why Are There Differences in the Gospels? What We Can Learn from Ancient Biography* (New York: Oxford University Press, 2017).
Lord, Albert B., 'The Gospels as Oral Traditional Literature', in William O. Walker (ed.), *The Relationships Among the Gospels: An Interdisciplinary Dialogue* (TUMSR, 5; San Antonio: Trinity University Press, 1978), 33–91.
Lummis, E.W., *How Luke Was Written* (Cambridge: Cambridge University Press, 1915).
MacDonald, Dennis R., 'The Shipwrecks of Odysseus and Paul', *NTS* 45 (1999), 88–107.
MacDonald, Dennis R., 'Tobit and the *Odyssey*', in Dennis R. MacDonald (ed.), *Mimesis and Intertextuality in Antiquity and Christianity* (SAC; Harrisburg, PA: Trinity Press International, 2001a), 11–40.
MacDonald, Dennis R., 'Introduction', in Dennis R. MacDonald (ed.), *Mimesis and Intertextuality in Antiquity and Christianity* (SAC; Harrisburg, PA: Trinity Press International, 2001b), 1–9.
MacDonald, Dennis R., 'The Synoptic Problem and Literary Mimesis: The Case of the Frothing Demoniac', in Paul Foster, Andrew Gregory, John S. Kloppenborg and J. Verheyden (eds), *New Studies in the Synoptic Problem* (BETL, 139; Leuven: Leuven University Press, 2011), 509–21.

MacDonald, Dennis R., *Luke and Vergil: Imitations of Classical Greek Literature* 2 (NTGL, 2; Lanham, MD: Rowman & Littlefield, 2014).
MacDonald, Dennis R., *The Gospels and Homer: Imitation of Greek Epic in Mark and Luke-Acts* (NTGL, 1; Lanham, MD: Rowman & Littlefield, 2015).
MacEwen, Robert K., *Matthean Posteriority: An Exploration of Matthew's Use of Mark and Luke as a Solution to the Synoptic Problem* (LNTS, 501; London: Bloomsbury T&T Clark, 2015).
Mack, Burton L., *A Myth of Innocence: Mark and Christian Origins* (Philadelphia: Fortress, 1988).
MacKay, L.A., 'Achilles as Model for Aeneas', *TPAPA* 88 (1957), 11–16.
Maclean, Jennifer K. Berenson, 'Review of *Does the New Testament Imitate Homer? Four Cases from the Acts of the Apostles*, by Dennis R. MacDonald', *CBQ* 70 (2008), 381–2.
Maddox, Robert, *The Purpose of Luke-Acts* (SNTW; Edinburgh: T&T Clark, 1982).
Mainville, Odette, 'De Jésus à l'Église: Étude rédactionnelle de Luc 24', *NTS* 51 (2005), 192–211.
Marshall, I. Howard, *The Gospel of Luke: A Commentary on the Greek Text* (NIGTC; Grand Rapids: Eerdmans, 1978).
Martin, Michael W., 'Progymnastic Topic Lists: A Compositional Template for Luke and Other Bioi?' *NTS* 54 (2008), 18–41.
Martin, Michael Wade, 'The Poetry of the Lord's Prayer: A Study in Poetic Device', *JBL* 134 (2015), 347–72.
Matson, Mark A., 'Luke's Rewriting of the Sermon on the Mount', in Mark S. Goodacre and Nicholas Perrin (eds), *Questioning Q* (London: SPCK, 2004), 43–70.
Mattila, Sharon Lea, 'A Question Too Often Neglected', *NTS* 41 (1995), 199–217.
Mattila, Sharon Lea, 'Negotiating the Clouds around Statistics and "Q"', *NovT* 46 (2004), 105–31.
McAdon, Brad, *Rhetorical Mimesis and the Mitigation of Early Christian Conflicts: Examining the Influence That Greco-Roman Mimesis May Have in the Composition of Matthew, Luke, and Acts* (Eugene, OR: Pickwick, 2018).
McCane, Byron R., *Roll Back the Stone: Death and Burial in the World of Jesus* (Harrisburg: Trinity Press International, 2003).
McIver, Robert K. and Marie Carroll, 'Experiments to Develop Criteria for Determining the Existence of Written Sources, and Their Potential Implications for the Synoptic Problem', *JBL* 121 (2002), 667–87.
McNicol, Allan J., David L. Dungan and David B. Peabody, *Beyond the Q Impasse: Luke's Use of Matthew* (Valley Forge: Trinity Press International, 1996).
Metzger, Bruce M., *A Textual Commentary on the Greek New Testament* (Stuttgart: United Bible Societies, 1975) [2nd edn, 1994].
Mitchell, Margaret M., 'Homer in the New Testament?', *JR* 83 (2003), 244–60.
Moessner, David P., 'Luke 9: 1-50: Luke's Preview of the Journey of the Prophet like Moses of Deuteronomy', *JBL* 102 (1983), 575–605.
Moessner, David P., *Lord of the Banquet: The Literary and Theological Significance of the Lukan Travel Narrative* (Minneapolis: Augsburg Fortress, 1989).
Moessner, David P., 'Luke as Tradent and Hermeneut', *NovT* 58 (2016), 259–300.
Moles, John, 'Luke's Preface: The Greek Decree, Classical Historiography and Christian Redefinitions', *NTS* 57 (2011), 461–82.
Moret, Jean-René, '"Aucun prophète n'est propice dans sa propre patrie": la péricope de Nazareth', *NTS* 60 (2014), 466–74.

Morgan, Teresa, *Literate Education in the Hellenistic and Roman Worlds* (CCS; Cambridge: Cambridge University Press, 2007).
Morgenthaler, Robert, *Statistische Synopse* (Zurich: Gotthelf, 1971).
Moyise, Steve, *The Old Testament in the New: An Introduction* (CBSS; London: Continuum, 2001).
Müller, Mogens, 'The New Testament Gospels as Biblical Rewritings', *STNJT* 68 (2014), 21–40.
Müller, Mogens, 'Acts as Biblical Rewriting of the Gospels and Paul's Letters', in Mogens Müller and Jesper Tang Nielsen (eds), *Luke's Literary Creativity* (LNTS, 550; London: Bloomsbury T&T Clark, 2016), 96–117.
Murphy, Frederick J., *Pseudo-Philo: Rewriting the Bible* (Oxford: Oxford University Press, 1993).
Nassauer, Gudrun, 'Göttersöhne: Lk 1.26–38 als Kontrasterzählung zu einem römischen Gründungsmythos', *NTS* 61 (2015), 144–64.
Neirynck, Frans, *The Minor Agreements of Matthew and Luke against Mark with A Cumulative List* (BETL, 37; Leuven: Leuven University Press, 1974).
Neirynck, F., 'Luke 9,22 and 10,25-28: The Case for Independent Redaction', *ETL* 75 (1999), 123–32.
Neirynck, F. and Timothy A. Friedrichsen, 'Note on Luke 9.22: A Response to M.D. Goulder', *ETL* 65 (1989), 390–4.
Neville, David J., 'The Phantom Returns: Delbert Burkett's Rehabilitation of Proto-Mark', *ETL* 84 (2008), 135–73.
Nickelsburg, George W.E., 'Tobit, Genesis, and the *Odyssey*: A Complex Web of Intertextuality', in Dennis R. MacDonald (ed.), *Mimesis and Intertextuality in Antiquity and Christianity* (SAC; Harrisburg, PA: Trinity Press International, 2001), 41–55.
Niehoff, Maren R., *Philo of Alexandria: An Intellectual Biography* (New Haven: Yale University Press, 2018).
Nolland, John, *Luke 9:21-18:34* (WBC, 35B; Dallas, TX: Word Books, 1993).
O'Leary, Anne M., *Matthew's Judaization of Mark Examined in the Context of the Use of Sources in Greco-Roman Antiquity* (LNTS, 323; London: T&T Clark, 2006).
Olson, Ken, 'Unpicking on the Farrer Theory', in Mark Goodacre and Nicholas Perrin (eds), *Questioning Q* (London: SPCK, 2004), 127–50.
Olson, Ken, 'Luke 11.2-4: The Lord's Prayer (Abridged Version)', in John C. Poirier and Jeff Peterson (eds), *Marcan Priority without Q: Explorations in the Farrer Hypothesis* (LNTS, 455; London: Bloomsbury T&T Clark, 2015), 101–18.
Ostmeyer, Karl-Heinrich, 'Der Stammbaum des Verheißenen: Theologische Implikationen der Namen und Zahlen in Mt 1.1–17', *NTS* 46 (2000), 175–92.
Padilla, Osvaldo, 'Hellenistic paideia and Luke's Education: A Critique of Recent Approaches', *NTS* 55 (2009), 416–37.
Parker, David C., *The Living Text of the Gospels* (Cambridge: Cambridge University Press, 1997).
Parry, Adam, 'The Two Voices of Virgil's "Aeneid"', *Arion* 2 (1963), 66–80.
Parsons, Mikeal C., *Luke* (PCNT; Grand Rapids, MI: Baker Academic, 2015).
Parsons, Mikeal C. and Michael Wade Martin, *Ancient Rhetoric and the New Testament* (Waco, TX: Baylor University Press, 2018).
Pelling, C.B.R., 'Plutarch's Method of Work in the Roman Lives', *JHS* 99 (1979), 74–96.
Pelling, C.B.R., 'Plutarch's Adaptation of His Source-Material', *JHS* 100 (1980), 127–40.
Perrin, Nicholas, 'The Limits of a Reconstructed Q', in Mark Goodacre and Nicholas Perrin (eds), *Questioning Q* (London: SPCK, 2004), 71–88.

Petersen, Norman R., 'The Composition of Mark 4: 1-8:26', *HTR* 73 (1980), 185–217.
Peterson, Jeffrey, 'Order in the Double Tradition and the Existence of Q', in Mark S. Goodacre and Nicholas Perrin (eds), *Questioning Q* (London: SPCK, 2004), 28–42.
Philo, *Works* (tr. F.H. Colson et al.; LCL; 12 vols; London: Heinemann, 1929–71).
Pitts, Andrew W., 'The Origins of Greek Mimesis and the Gospel of Mark: Genre as a Potential Constraint in Assessing Markan Imitation', in Matthew Ryan Hauge and Andrew Pitts (eds), *Ancient Education and Early Christianity* (LNTS, 533; London: Bloomsbury T&T Clark, 2016), 107–36.
Poirier, John C., 'Memory, Written Sources, and the Synoptic Problem: A Response to Robert K. McIver and Marie Carroll', *JBL* 123 (2004), 315–22.
Poirier, John C., 'The Roll, the Codex, the Wax Tablet and the Synoptic Problem', *JSNT* 35 (2012), 3–30.
Poirier, John C., 'Delbert Burkett's Defence of Q', in John C. Poirier and Jeff Peterson (eds), *Marcan Priority without Q: Explorations in the Farrer Hypothesis* (LNTS, 455; London: Bloomsbury T&T Clark, 2015), 191–225.
Poirier, John C. and Jeffrey Peterson (eds), *Marcan Priority without Q: Explorations in the Farrer Hypothesis* (LNTS 455; London: Bloomsbury T&T Clark, 2015).
Praeder, Susan Marie, 'Acts 27: 1-28:16: Sea Voyages in Ancient Literature and the Theology of Luke-Acts', *CBQ* 46 (1984), 683–706.
Prince, Deborah Thompson, 'The "Ghost" of Jesus: Luke 24 in Light of Ancient Narratives of Post-Mortem Apparitions', *JSNT* 29 (2007), 287–301.
Rajak, Tessa, *Josephus: The Historian and His Society* (London: Duckworth, 1983).
Ramelli, Ilaria L.E., 'Luke 16:16: The Good News of God's Kingdom Is Proclaimed and Everyone Is Forced into It', *JBL* 127 (2008), 737–58.
Rastoin, Marc, 'Le génie littéraire et théologique de Luc en Lc 15.11–32 éclairé par le parallèle avec Mt 21.28–32', *NTS* 60 (2014), 1–19.
Reece, Steve, '"Aesop", "Q" and "Luke"', *NTS* 62 (2016), 357–77.
Robinson, James M., Paul Hoffmann and John S. Kloppenborg, *The Critical Edition of Q: Synopsis Including the Gospels of Matthew and Luke, Mark and Thomas with English, German and French Translations of Q and Thomas* (Hermeneia; Minneapolis: Fortress, 2000).
Rodd, C.S., 'Spirit or Finger', *ExpTim* 72 (1961), 157–8.
Rodríguez, Rafael, 'Reading and Hearing in Ancient Contexts', *JSNT* 32 (2009), 151–78.
Rodríguez, Rafael, *Structuring Early Christian Memory: Jesus in Tradition, Performance and Text* (LNTS, 407; London: T&T Clark, 2010).
Roose, Hanna, 'Umkehr und Ausgleich bei Lukas: Die Gleichnisse vom verlorenen Sohn (Lk 15.11–32) und vom reichen Mann und armen Lazarus (Lk 16.19–31) als Schwestergeschichten', *NTS* 56 (2009), 1–21.
Rubin, David C., *Memory in Oral Traditions: The Cognitive Psychology of Epic, Ballads, and Counting-out Rhymes* (Oxford: Oxford University Press, 1995).
Russell, D.A., 'De Imitatione', in David West and Tony Woodman (eds), *Creative Imitation and Latin Literature* (Cambridge: Cambridge University Press, 1979), 1–16.
Sabin, Marie Noonan, *Reopening the Word: Reading* Mark *as Theology in the Context of Early Judaism* (Oxford: Oxford University Press, 2002).
Sanday, William, 'The Conditions under Which the Gospels Were Written, in Their Bearing upon Some Difficulties of the Synoptic Problem', in William Sanday (ed.), *Oxford Studies in the Synoptic Problem* (Oxford: Clarendon, 1911), 3–26.
Sanders, E.P., 'The Overlaps of Mark and Q and the Synoptic Problem', *NTS* 19 (1972), 453–65.

Sanders, E.P. and Margaret Davies, *Studying the Synoptic Gospels* (London: SCM, 1989).
Sandnes, Karl Olav, '*Imitatio Homeri*? An Appraisal of Dennis R. MacDonald's "Mimesis Criticism"', *JBL* 124 (2005), 715–32.
Schacter, Daniel L., *Searching for Memory: The Brain, the Mind, and the Past* (New York: Basic Books, 1996).
Schippers, Adriana Maria, 'Dionysius and Quintilian: Imitation and Emulation in Greek and Latin Literary Criticism' (PhD Dissertation; Leiden, 2019).
Schwartz, Barry, 'The Social Context of Commemoration: A Study in Collective Memory', *Social Forces* 61 (1982), 374–402.
Schwartz, Barry, 'Postmodernity and Historical Reputation: Abraham Lincoln in Late Twentieth-Century American Memory', *SF* 77 (1998), 63–103.
Schwartz, Barry, 'Where There's Smoke, There's Fire: Memory and History', in Tom Thatcher (ed.), *Memory and Identity in Ancient Judaism and Early Christianity: A Conversation with Barry Schwartz* (SS, 78; Atlanta: SBL, 2014), 7–37.
Shea, Chris, 'Imitating Imitation: Vergil, Homer and Acts 10: 1-11:18', in Jo-Ann A. Brant, Charles W. Hedrick and Chris Shea (eds), *Ancient Fiction: The Matrix of Early Christian and Jewish Narrative* (Atlanta: SBL, 2005), 37–60.
Shellard, Barbara, *New Light on Luke: Its Purpose, Sources and Literary Context* (London: T&T Clark, 2002).
Shelton, John, 'The Healing of Naaman (2 Kgs 5.1-19) as a Central Component for the Healing of the Centurion's Slave (Luke 7.1-10)', in John S. Kloppenborg and Joseph Verheyden (eds), *The Elijah-Elisha Narrative in the Composition of Luke* (LNTS 493; London: Bloomsbury T&T Clark, 2014), 65–87.
Shuler, Philip L., 'Philo's Moses and Matthew's Jesus: A Comparative Study in Ancient Literature', in David T. Runia (ed.), *The Studia Philonica Annual*, vol. 2 (Atlanta: Scholars, 1990), 86–103.
Sim, David C., 'Matthew's Use of Mark: Did Matthew Intend to Supplement or to Replace His Primary Source?' *NTS* 57 (2011), 176–92.
Simons, Robert, 'The Magnificat: Cento, Psalm or Imitatio?', *TynBul* 60 (2009), 25–46.
Simpson, R.T., 'The Major Agreements of Matthew and Luke against Mark', *NTS* 12 (1966), 273–84.
Small, Jocelyn Penny, *Wax Tablets of the Mind: Cognitive Studies of Memory and Literacy in Classical Antiquity* (Abingdon: Routledge, 1997).
Spong, John Shelby, *Resurrection: Myth of Reality? A Bishop's Search for the Origins of Christianity* (San Francisco: HarperSanFrancisco, 1994).
Stemberger, Günter, *Introduction to the Talmud and Midrash* (tr. Markus Bockmuehl; Edinburgh: T&T Clark, 2nd edn, 1996).
Streeter, Burnett Hillman, *The Four Gospels: A Study of Origins Treating of the Manuscript Tradition, Sources, Authorship, & Dates* (London: Macmillan, 1926).
Styler, G.M., 'The Priority of Mark', in C.F.D. Moule, *The Birth of the New Testament* (London: A&C Black, 3rd edn, 1981), 285–316.
Tannehill, Robert C., *The Narrative Unity of Luke-Acts: A Literary Interpretation*, vol 1: *The Gospel according to Luke* (Philadelphia: Fortress, 1986).
Tannehill, Robert C., *The Narrative Unity of Luke-Acts: A Literary Interpretation*, vol. 2: *The Acts of the Apostles* (Philadelphia: Fortress, 1990).
Taylor, N.H., 'The Temptation of Jesus on the Mountain: A Palestinian Christian Polemic Against Agrippa I', *JSNT* 83 (2001), 27–49.

Torrance, Mark and Gaynor Jeffery, 'Writing Processes and Cognitive Demands', in Mark Torrance and Gaynor C. Jeffery (eds), *The Cognitive Demands of Writing* (Amsterdam: Amsterdam University Press, 1999), 1–11.
Troftgruben, Troy M., 'Slow Sailing in Acts: Suspense in the Final Sea Journey (Acts 27:1–28:15)', *JBL* 136 (2017), 949–68.
Tuckett, Christopher M., *Q and the History of Early Christianity* (Edinburgh: T&T Clark, 1997).
Tuckett, Christopher M., 'The Current State of the Synoptic Problem', in Paul Foster, Andrew Gregory, John S. Kloppenborg and J. Verheyden (eds), *New Studies in the Synoptic Problem* (BETL, 139; Leuven: Leuven University Press, 2011), 9–50.
Tuckett, Christopher M., 'Watson, Q and "L/M"', in Mogens Müller and Heike Omerzu (eds), *Gospel Interpretation and the Q-Hypothesis* (LNTS, 573; London: Bloomsbury T&T Clark, 2018), 115–38.
van Iersel, Bas M.F., *Mark: A Reader-Response Commentary* (JSNTS, 164; tr. W.H. Bisscheroux; Sheffield: Sheffield Academic Press, 1998).
Verheyden, Joseph, 'By Way of Epilogue: Looking Back at the Healing of Naaman and the Healing of the Centurion's Slave – in Response to John Shelton', in John S. Kloppenborg and Joseph Verheyden (eds), *The Elijah-Elisha Narrative in the Composition of Luke* (London: Bloomsbury T&T Clark, 2014), 153–60.
Vinson, Richard, 'How Minor? Assessing the Significance of the Minor Agreements as an Argument against the Two-Source Hypothesis', in Mark S. Goodacre and Nicholas Perrin (eds), *Questioning Q* (London: SPCK, 2004), 151–64.
Virgil, *Works* (tr. Henry Rushton; LCL; 2 vols; London: Heinemann, 1950).
Watson, Francis, *Gospel Writing: A Canonical Perspective* (Grand Rapids, MI; Cambridge: Eerdmans, 2013).
Watson, Francis, *The Fourfold Gospel: A Theological Reading of the New Testament Portraits of Jesus* (Grand Rapids, MI: Baker Academic, 2016).
Watson, Francis, 'Seven Theses on the Synoptic Problem, in Disagreement with Christopher Tuckett', in Mogens Müller and Heike Omerzu (eds), *Gospel Interpretation and the Q-Hypothesis* (LNTS, 573; ed. London: Bloomsbury T&T Clark, 2018), 139–47.
Wenham, David, *From Good News to Gospels: What Did the First Christians Say about Jesus?* (Grand Rapids, MI: Eerdmans, 2018).
West, David and Tony Woodman, 'Epilogue', in David West and Tony Woodman (eds), *Creative Imitation and Latin Literature* (Cambridge: Cambridge University Press, 1979), 195–200.
Whitmarsh, Tim, *Greek Literature and the Roman Empire: The Politics of Imitation* (Oxford: Oxford University Press, 2001).
Wilkens, Wilhelm, 'Zur Frage der literarischen Beziehung zwischen Matthäus und Lukas', *NovT* 8 (1966), 48–57.
Wilkens, Wilhelm, 'Die Versuchung Jesu nach Matthäus', *NTS* 28 (1982), 479–89.
Wilkens, Wilhelm, 'Die Täuferüberlieferung des Matthäus und ihre Verarbeitung durch Lukas', *NTS* 40 (1994), 542–57.
Wilson, Walter T., *Healing in the Gospel of Matthew: Reflections on Method and Ministry* (Minneapolis: Fortress, 2014).
Winn, Adam, *Mark and the Elijah-Elisha Narrative: Considering the Practice of Greco-Roman Imitation in the Search for Markan Source Material* (Eugene, OR: Pickwick, 2010).
Winsbury, Rex, *The Roman Book: Books, Publishing and Performance in Classical Rome* (London: Bristol Classical Press, 2009).

Wire, Antoinette Clark, *The Case for Mark Composed in Performance* (BPC, 3; Eugene, OR: Cascade, 2011).
Wolfson, Harry Austryn, *Philo: Foundations of Religious Philosophy in Judaism, Christianity and Islam*, 2 vols (Cambridge, MA: Harvard University Press, 1947, 1968).
Woodman, Tony, 'Self-Imitation and the Substance of History: Tacitus, *Annals* 1.61–5 and *Histories* 2.70, 5.14–15', in David West and Tony Woodman (eds), *Creative Imitation and Latin Literature* (Cambridge: Cambridge University Press, 1979), 143–56.
Yates, Frances A., *The Art of Memory* (London: Pimlico, 1992).

Index of References

HEBREW BIBLE/OLD TESTAMENT

Genesis
1.27	52, 188
1.31	53
2.9	53
2.24	188
3	102
3.14	53
3.19	53
4.1-8	53
5.2	188
6.5-7.24	48
6.12-9.1	48
12.1-3	52
12.1-3	53
12.1	53
12.2	54
12.12	53
13.9	53
15.6	53
16.7-15	95, 100
17.10-14	50
17.15-19	95, 100
17.19	95
18.9-15	100
19.1-23	48
19.24-29	48
19.24	174
24	59
25.5-6	54
26.2	53
27.42–35.29	59
28.17	53
30.13	54
31.3	53
35.19-20	98
39.7	53
39.8-9	53
39.12	53
40.8	53
40.15	53
41.41	53
42.18	53
45–47	91
45.7-18	53
45.28	53, 185
46.29	185
47	47
50.19	53
50.24	53
50.25	53

Exodus
1.8-14	47
1.8	91
1.9	53
1.15-16	47
1.22	47
2.10a	47
2.11-12	47
2.23	53
3.1-2	99
4.10	53
4.14	54
4.15-16	54
4.19-20	91
5.6-19	47
6.16-21	47
7.1	54
7.12	54
7.14–12.32	47
7.20-22	54
8.7	54
8.15 LXX	122
8.18	54
8.19	54, 122, 178
12.11	53
13.2	100
13.13	100
14	49, 50, 91
15.1-21	49, 50

15.5	49	*Leviticus*	
15.10	49	8	48
15.25	53	8.21	53
16	102	8.29	53
16.1-13	91	9	48
16.4-8	49, 50	10.8-11	52
16.13-31	47	11.42	53
16.13b-30	49, 50	12.3	50
17.1-7	91	16.4	52
17.2-7	47	19.4	51
20	47	19.28	51
20.8-11	48	19.34	51
20.18	50, 53	21.17-21	52
20.18 LXX	49	22.4	52
20.22	53	23.27-32	48
20.23	51	24.7 LXX	48
22.27 LXX	51	24.10-16	50
23	105	24.10-14	49
23.2 LXX	53	24.15-16	49
24.10-22	48	26.25	79
24.18	48		
25.23-30	48	*Numbers*	
25.31-40	48	9.1-14	49, 50
26.18-37	48	10	47
27.9-18	48	11	102
28.1	48	11.7-9	47
28.1-39	48	11.16-25	175
28.4-39	52	11.31-32	47
28.40-43	52	13	175
29.1-37	48	14.11-12	53
30.1-6	48	15-19	47
30.12-16	51	15.32-36	49, 50
31.14	50	16.1-4	49, 50
32	48, 49, 50	16.1-3	48
32.1-6	91	16.28-35	49, 50
32.16	54	17	48
32.25-29	52	17.8	48
33.13-23	51	20.2-13	47
34.12	53	21.30 LXX	54
34.14	49	23	47
34.28	48, 92–3, 110	25.1-13	51
35.2	49, 50	27.1-11	49, 50
35.3	49	27.12-14	91
35.22-23	54		
38.8	48	*Deuteronomy*	
38.26-27 LXX	48	1–3	169
38.26 LXX	54	1.22–8.30	169
40.6	48	1.27	79
40.29	48	3.27	91

4.4	51
4.6-7	53
4.12	53
4.19	51
6.13	110
6–8	93
7.7-8	53
9.9	48, 110
12.5-7	51
12.11-14	51
12.17-18	51
16.21	51
18.10-12	51
18.15-18	51
18.18-19	177
20.1	53
20.5–26.15	169
21.15–22.04	185
23.1-12	53
32.48-52	91
33–34	50
33	49
34	49
34.1-4	91
34.4	53

Judges
2.14	79
3.9	97
3.11	97
13	100

1 Samuel/1 Kingdoms
1–3	98
1.5	100
1.11	101
1.11 LXX	100
1.20	100
1.21-28	101
2.1-10	100
2.21b	101
2.26	101
2.34 LXX	100
3.1-18	101
3.20	101
7.3	101
9.9	53
15.10	105

16.11-13	99
16.13	101
17	57

2 Samuel/2 Kingdoms
7.13-14	96
7.16	96
7.18-29	38
23.8-39	38

1 Kings/3 Kingdoms
17.7-16	165
17.17-24	166

2 Kings/4 Kingdoms
1.1–2.15	168
1.1–2.6	174
1.9-12	174
2.16–3.27	175
4.42-44	102
5	191
5.1-19	165

1 Chronicles
11.10-47	38
17.16-27	38

Job
16.10-11	78
16.11	79

Psalms
32	13
107.23-32	67

Ecclesiastes
12.12b	210

Isaiah
6.9-10	128
7.14	95, 96, 100
7.17	96
8.14	96
9.1-2	112
9.5-7	96
9.6-10	41
61.1-2a	112

Hosea
6.6	177
11.1	90

Jonah
1.4-16	69
1.13-16	67

Micah
4–5	98

Zechariah
1.1	105

Malachi
3.1	105

NEW TESTAMENT
Q
3.3a	107
3.7-9	107
4.16	112
6	149
6.20-49	147, 154
6.23	149
6.27-28	149
6.29	149
6.31	149
6.39	162
7.1-10	154
7.18-35	153, 154
7.24-27	90
7.28	186
7.31	186
7.33	90
9.57-60	154
10.2-24	154
10.2-16	154
10.2-24	154
11	149, 152, 153
11.2b-4	151
11.9-13	151
11.14-32	154, 171
11.14-26	154
11.14-24	136
11.14-15	132
11.16	154
11.21-22	136
11.23	136
11.29-32	154
11.33-35	151
11.33	149
11.34-35	149, 151
12	149
12.10	136
12.22-34	149
12.22-32	149
12.22b-34	151
12.22b-31	151
12.33-34	151
12.39-46	138
12.58-59	149
13	149, 153
13.18-21	154
14	149
14.34-35	149, 186
16	149
16.13	149, 151, 186
16.16-18	151
16.16-17	186
16.17	149
16.18	149
17.6	190
17.23-24	138
17.26-36	138
17.37b	138

Matthew
1.1–4.11	90, 93
1.1-17	90
1.16	91
1.20-25a	95–6
1.21	94
1.22-23	95
2	98–9
2.1	94
2.3-4	100
2.10	94, 98
2.13-14	91
2.15	90
2.16-18	100
2.19-21	91
2.23	112
3.1	104
3.1–4.11	93, 141
3.1-17	108
3.1-6	104
3.2	104, 128

3.4-6	105, 108	5.25-26	149, 180
3.4	90, 108	5.28	150
3.5	103, 108	5.31-32	170, 186, 188
3.6	128	5.31	149, 188
3.7-10	77, 105	5.32	186
3.7b-10	26, 85, 89, 90, 107	5.33-37	150
3.7b	105	5.38	150
3.11-12	76, 106, 107	5.43	164
3.11	77, 108	5.47	18
3.11b-12	90, 107	6.1-18	18, 151
3.12	86	6.1-4	150
3.13–4.10	93	6.5-15	151
3.13-17	91, 107	6.5-8	150
3.14-15	107, 127, 128	6.7	18
3.14	128	6.9-13	121, 170, 178
3.17	92	6.9	152
4.1-11	76, 90, 91	6.16-18	150
4.1	109	6.19-34	149, 151
4.2	91, 93, 110	6.19-24	151
4.3	91	6.19-21	170, 180
4.6	91	6.22-23	170, 179
4.8-10	91, 92	6.24	86, 89, 170
4.10	110	6.25-34	149, 170, 180
4.11	93	6.32	18
4.12	111	7–8	158
4.13-17	112	7.1-5	162
4.13-16	112, 173	7.3-5	162
4.13	112	7.7-11	170, 178
4.14	112	7.13-14	181
4.15-16	112	7.19	180
4.17	112	7.22-23	181
4.18-22	141	7.28-29	113, 114
4.23–5.2	41	7.29	141
4.23–5.1	114	8–13	152–8
4.23-24	111	8–12	153
4.24–5.3	113	8–9	22, 114, 152, 155, 167
4.24–5.1	114	8.1–14.12	154–6
4.24	114	8.1-4	164, 191
5–9	42	8.1	153
5–7	147–52, 154	8.2-3	89
5.2	114	8.4	153
5.3	120	8.5-13	112, 164, 165
5.13	85, 179	8.9-10	89
5.15	170	8.9-10a	87
5.17-20	18, 170, 188	8.11-12	130, 160, 161, 181, 182
5.18-20	150	8.11	154
5.18	185	8.13	165
5.20	18	8.18-27	157
5.21-24	150	8.18-22	165

8.19–25.30	172, 194	10.34-36	180
8.19-22	83, 175	10.37-38	184
8.23–9.36	173	10.37	184
8.23–9.1	157	11–19	196
8.27	81	11	153, 158
8.43	164	11.2-19	165, 173
8.44	164	11.2-11	165
9.1-8	83	11.2-6	156
9.2-8	31	11.2-5	154
9.2	83, 167	11.2-3	167
9.5-26	166, 173	11.2	165
9.7	83	11.4-30	163
9.9-13	141–2	11.5	158
9.10-26	173	11.10	105
9.10-11	167	11.11	186
9.10b	141	11.12-13	170, 185
9.11	185	11.12	187, 188
9.18-26	157	11.16-24	156
9.18-19	166	11.16-19	165
9.20-22	167	11.16	186
9.20	167	11.18-19	154
9.22b	167	11.20-27	165
9.23-26	166	11.20-24	86, 166, 176
9.26	130, 166	11.24	177
9.27-31	157	11.25-27	89, 176
9.32-34	132, 134, 158	11.27	173
9.34	132	11.28-30	176
9.35–10.14	158	12.1–14.12	157
9.35-36	158	12.1–13.58	158
9.35	137, 166, 175, 176	12	158
9.36	137, 176	12.1-14	176
9.37–10.16	137, 175	12.1-7	177
9.37-38	165, 166, 175	12.3-7	130
9.37	175	12.5-7	127, 128
9.49-50	85	12.5	177
10	149, 156, 157	12.9-14	130, 177, 181, 183
10.1-4	173	12.11-12	181, 183
10.1	176	12.11	79, 130
10.5-42	163	12.15-21	176
10.5-16	76	12.15	81
10.5-6	18, 157	12.22-50	171
10.5	174, 175	12.22-45	178
10.7-16	175	12.22-34	132
10.14-15	176	12.22-32	24, 31, 76
10.17-23	173	12.22-28	132, 134
10.17-22	138, 176	12.22-24	132
10.19-20	137, 180	12.22	173
10.26-42	173	12.24	132, 133
10.26-33	180, 182	12.27-32	86

12.27-28	77, 122, 133	15.1-20	161
12.28	121	15.2	180
12.29-32	135	15.3-20	180
12.29	133	15.5-6	180, 184
12.30	136	15.6	161
12.31-32	133, 180	15.14	130, 160, 161, 162
12.31	133, 136	15.21-28	112, 165
12.32	133, 136	15.27	189
12.33-37	179	16–25	39
12.34	106, 180	16	192
12.38-42	178	16.1-4	162
12.39	179	16.2-3	130, 161, 162, 180
12.40	179	16.6	161
12.43-45	86, 178	16.12	31
12.46–13.30	173	16.16-19	127
12.46-50	178	16.17-20	84
12.50	178	16.17-19	31, 128
12.67-37	180	16.21	77, 84, 128
13.1-50	181	16.22-23	128
13.1-23	182	16.24-26	88–9, 184
13.8	182	16.24	184
13.13-14	41	17.19-21	190
13.14-15	127, 128, 182	17.19-20	190
13.16-17	176	17.20	130, 160
13.22	182	17.21	190
13.24-30	182	17.24-27	18
13.24a	140	17.27	185
13.30	182	18	183
13.31-33	181	18.3-35	163
13.31-32	76, 139	18.6-7	189, 190
13.31	77, 140	18.6	69, 190
13.33	181	18.7b	190
13.34–18.10	173	18.8-9	190
13.36-42	182	18.10-14	185
13.47-50	161	18.12-14	164, 185
13.50	182	18.15	189, 190
13.53-58	111, 112	18.17	18
13.54	81	18.21-22	189, 190
14	83, 108	18.23–24.16	173
14.1-21	184	18.23-34	186
14.1-14	183	18.23	187
14.1-13	183	18.34	190
14.1-12	154	19.1-26	186
14.5	183	19.1-21	190
14.13	81, 183	19.1-19	188
14.14	184	19.3-12	186
14.21	81	19.9	186
14.22-23	102	19.12	187
14.28-31	31, 127	19.13-15	83

19.14	187	24.42	181
19.16-26	186	24.43-51	137
19.17-19	186	24.43	181
19.24	187	24.44-51	192
19.27-28	161	24.45	79
19.28	130, 161	25.1-46	164
19.29	184	25.1-13	180
20.1-16	127, 191	25.14-30	26, 83, 85, 137, 193
20.1	187	25.31-46	127
20.20-21	21	26.01	83
20.22-23	21	26.28	79
20.24-28	161	26.36–27.01	193
20.29-33	191	26.45	79
20.30-31	191	26.47	81
21.21	161, 190, 191	26.67	78
21.23	83	26.68	77–9
21.28-32	185	26.75	79
22.1-14	183	27.1	79
22.15-22	80	27.11-14	129
22.27	77, 80	27.15-23	129
22.28	79	27.19	127, 129
22.35	81	27.24	127, 129
23–25	183	27.40	91
23	31, 180	27.41-43	92
23.2-39	164	27.60	129
23.4-36	179	28.1-8	193
23.6-36	123	28.3-6	119
23.33	106	28.8	98, 119, 193
23.34-36	123, 124	28.9	118
23.34	124	28.11-15	24
23.37-39	86, 183	28.16-20	92, 117, 118, 193
24–25	137, 164	28.16	118
24.4b-51	164	28.17	118
24.17-41	137, 191	28.18	118
24.17-18	138	28.19-20	18
24.23-51	138	28.20	93
24.23-46	192		
24.23	138	Mark	
24.24-27	192	1–6	158
24.24	192	1.1-13	141
24.26	137, 138	1.1-8	105
24.27-28	138	1.1	83
24.29-31	192	1.2-6	104
24.30-31	192	1.2-3	105
24.31	192	1.4	108
24.34-35	88–9	1.4b	104, 108, 109
24.37-41	138	1.5-6	105, 108
24.37-39	192	1.5	108
24.42-51	180	1.7-8	76, 106, 107

1.8	77, 108	3.22b	132
1.9-11	107	3.27-30	135
1.9	95	3.27	133
1.12-13	24, 76, 90, 109	3.28-29	133
1.13	109	3.29a	136
1.14	111	3.31–4.33	154
1.14a	83	3.31-35	178, 198
1.15	111, 114	4	153
1.16-20	141, 198	4.1-33	154
1.21	41, 111, 113, 114	4.1-32	158
1.21-28	83	4.1	198
1.22	113, 114, 141, 154	4.3-32	163
1.24	95	4.3-9	89
1.29–3.19a	114	4.11-13	89
1.29–3.6	154	4.15	140
1.29	153	4.16	140
1.32-34	41, 83	4.22	182
1.35-38	83	4.30-32	76, 139–40
1.39	41, 83, 111	4.30	140
1.40-42	89	4.31	77
1.40-45	191, 198	4.35–6.06	154
1.44	153	4.35-41	67
2.1–3.6	157	4.37b	198
2.1-12	31, 83	4.38	69
2.3	83	4.41	81
2.12	83	5.1-20	83
2.13-17	141–2	5.43	158
2.15b	141	6	108
2.16	185	6.1-6	111, 112, 198
2.23–6.6a	158	6.1-4	103
2.23–3.35	158	6.2	81
2.23–3.6	158	6.3	95
3.1-16	181, 198	6.6-11	158
3.1-6	130, 183	6.6-6a	158
3.4	181	6.6	41
3.7-19	154	6.6b-16	137
3.7-13	113, 114	6.6b-13	128
3.7-12	41	6.6b	137
3.7-10	114	6.7-13	76, 154
3.7	114	6.7-11	149
3.10	81	6.8-11	163
3.13-19a	114	6.14–8.10	154
3.20–4.34	154	6.14-29	154
3.20-35	158	6.14-16	83
3.20-30	154	6.14	198
3.21–4.25	171	6.17-29	83, 128
3.22-30	24, 31, 76, 132, 154	6.21	184
3.22-26	134	6.30-31	83, 128
3.22	132	6.32-34	128

6.33	81	12.13	198
6.34	137	12.13-17	80
6.44	81	12.22	77, 80
6.45–8.26	128	12.28-34	198
6.45-52	102	12.28-31	177
7.1-23	161	12.28	81
7.1-2	198	13	137, 192
7.2-5	180	13.5-37	89, 163
7.3-23	180	13.9-13	138, 176
7.4	180	13.11	124, 137
7.5	198	13.15-16	138
7.24-30	165	13.21	137, 138
7.28	189	13.21-23	138
8.1–13.58	154	13.24-32	138
8.11-12	154, 179	13.30-31	88–9
8.12	179	13.32-37	181
8.14-21	31	13.33-37	180
8.14-15	180	13.34-37	181
8.15	161	14.1	83
8.31	77, 84, 128	14.3-9	83, 167, 177, 198
8.32b-33	128	14.12	41
8.34-36	88–9	14.22-25	83
9.11-13	128	14.41	79
9.14-29	128	14.43	81
9.33-41	128	14.65	77, 78
9.35b-50	163	14.72	79
9.38-41	83	15.1	79
9.42-50	128	15.2-5	129
9.42	190	15.3-5	198
9.43	150	15.6-14	129
9.47	150	15.16-19	198
10.1	83	15.27-32a	83
10.2-12	32, 83	15.32b	83
10.2-9	188	15.46	129
10.4	149	16.1-8	193
10.11	149	16.5-6	119
10.13-16	83	16.6	95, 103
10.13	193	16.7	117, 118
10.17	198	16.8	18
10.35-40	21		
10.41-45	161	*Luke*	
10.46-52	198	1–2	32
10.52	191	1.1-4	11, 17, 35
11.11	83	1.3	10
11.12-14	83	1.4	19
11.15-17	83	1.5-22	117
11.21-23	190	1.5	94
11.23	190	1.7	100
11.27	83	1.14-17	101

1.17	108	4.15	111, 162
1.26-35	95–6	4.16-30	111, 162, 173, 194, 198
1.31	94, 96	4.16	112
1.32-33	101	4.18-21	162
1.38	100	4.18-19	112
1.46-55	100	4.18	99
1.52-53	164	4.21	112
1.54-55	101	4.23	112
1.59-63	95	4.24-27	102
1.68-79	101	4.25-27	112, 165
1.68-75	101	4.26	165, 166
2	98–9	4.30-31	112
2.10	94, 98	4.30	112
2.11	94	4.31	111
2.12	100	4.32	141
2.22-40	101	4.33–6.16	114
2.40	101	4.44	111
2.41-50	101	5.1-11	114, 198
2.52	101	5.12-16	164
3.1–4.13	141	5.12-13	89
3.1-22	108	5.17-26	31, 83
3.1-6	104	5.17	122
3.1-2a	105	5.18	83
3.1	103	5.21	79, 83
3.2-22	32	5.27-32	141–2
3.3	103, 108	5.29	141
3.3b	104, 108	5.33-39	32
3.7-18	101	6.1-11	176
3.7-14	108	6.1-5	177
3.7-9	77, 105	6.6-11	130
3.7b-9	26, 85, 89, 90, 107	6.12-16	114
3.7b	105	6.17-20	113
3.8	105	6.17-19	114
3.9	105	6.17	102
3.10-14	106	6.19	81
3.15-17	106	6.20–8.1	162–7
3.16-17	76, 107	6.20–7.17	162
3.16	77, 108	6.20-26	189
3.16b-17	90, 107	6.20-23	162
3.17-18	108	6.20	99, 114, 120
3.17	86	6.21	164
3.18-20	107	6.24-25a	164
3.19-20	108, 128	6.24	120
3.21-22	107	6.26	164
3.38	102	6.27	164
4.1-13	76, 90	6.39	130, 160, 161
4.1-2	109	6.40	161, 162
4.8	110	6.41-42	162
4.14-15	111	7.1-23	167

Index of References

7.1-17	164, 165	9.22	77, 84, 128, 170
7.1-10	164, 165	9.23-25	88-9
7.8-9	89	9.30-31	102
7.8-9a	87	9.31-32	31
7.11-17	102, 165, 166, 173, 194	9.31	168
7.17	130, 166	9.35	177
7.18-35	32, 165	9.36-50	166
7.18	167	9.37-43a	128
7.19	167	9.41	81
7.22-35	163	9.44	170
7.22	99, 166	9.46-50	128, 163
7.27	105	9.51-56	174, 191
7.29-30	163, 165	9.51	129, 167–9
7.31	139	9.52–19.27	174
7.36-50	165, 167, 194, 198	9.52–13.32	169
7.38	167	9.52–10.12	175
7.48b	167	9.52-56	169, 174, 175
7.49	79	9.52	175
7.50b	167	9.54	192
8.1-3	165	9.57-62	175
8.1-2	175	9.57	175
8.1-2a	166	10.1-20	175
8.1	137, 171, 176	10.1-16	137
8.4–9.50	165	10.1-12	76, 137
8.4-21	171	10.1	137, 176
8.4	167	10.2-16	176
8.5-18	163	10.2-12	175
8.12	140	10.2	175
8.13	140	10.2b-16	163
8.14	140	10.7	169
8.19-21	178	10.10-15	174
8.25	81	10.10-12	176
8.40-56	166	10.12-15	165
9–18	196	10.12	174, 176, 192
9	83	10.13-15	86, 166, 176
9.1-6	128, 137, 165, 175	10.17-20	173, 176
9.1	176	10.19	176
9.2-5	76	10.21-22	89, 165, 176
9.3b-5	163	10.21	190
9.7-9	128, 165, 166	10.23-24	176, 177
9.9	79	10.23	173
9.10-22	173	10.25–11.13	178
9.10	102	10.25-42	177
9.10a	128	10.25-37	128, 130, 177
9.10b-17	128	10.25-28	198
9.11	81, 137	10.25	81
9.12	102	10.30-35	169
9.19	102	10.31	177
9.20-21	128	10.38-42	177

10.38	169	12.13-15	180
10.40	177	12.16-21	180
11.1-13	170, 178	12.16-20	182
11.1-4	178	12.22-53	163
11.2-4	121	12.22-32	180
11.5-13	193	12.22-30	182
11.5-8	178	12.23	136
11.5-6	169	12.28	182
11.9-13	178	12.33-34	180
11.14-32	171, 178	12.35–13.9	180, 182
11.14-24	132	12.35-59	180
11.14-23	178	12.35-48	180
11.14-22	76	12.35-38	169, 180, 181
11.14-20	134	12.39-46	137, 180
11.14	173	12.39	181
11.15	132, 133	12.41-42a	172
11.19-23	86	12.42-48	181
11.19-20	77, 133	12.42	79
11.19	178, 121, 122, 124	12.54-56	130, 161, 162, 180
11.21-24	135	12.57–13.9	170
11.21-22	133	13.6-9	180
11.24-26	86, 178	13.8	140
11.27-28	178, 198	13.10-17	140, 170, 181, 183, 198
11.29-54	179	13.14	181
11.29	179	13.15-17	140
11.33-36	170	13.15	181
11.33	179	13.18-21	181
11.34-36	179	13.18-19	76, 139–40
11.37-38	198	13.18	139
11.38	161, 180	13.19	77, 140
11.39-52	123, 164, 179, 192	13.21-35	170
11.39-41	180	13.21	182
11.39	180	13.22–18.8	39
11.47-48	124	13.22-35	183
11.49-50	123	13.22-30	181, 182
11.49	123, 124	13.22	169
12.1–13.29	180–1	13.24	187
12	137	13.28-29	130, 160
12.1	161, 180, 181	13.30	31
12.1b–13.9	163	13.31-33	183
12.1b	161	13.31	183
12.2-9	180	13.33-35	181
12.2	181	13.33	169, 170, 183
12.5–13.9	180	13.34-35	86, 183
12.10	133, 135, 180	13.35	182
12.10a	136	14-17	184
12.10b	136	14.1-6	130, 170, 181, 183, 198
12.11-12	137, 180	14.1	183
12.13-34	170	14.4-32	164

14.5	130, 181	17.1-2	128
14.7-24	183, 184	17.1	190
14.11	31, 193	17.2	190
14.15–18.14	169	17.5-6	190
14.15-24	183, 192	17.5	130
14.15-16	81	17.6	160, 161, 190–1
14.18-20	184	17.7-10	191
14.21	99	17.10	164
14.23	187, 188	17.11-19	191, 198
14.25-35	187	17.11	169, 191
14.25-33	184	17.13	191
14.25-27	184	17.19	191
14.25	169	17.20-37	137, 191–2
14.26-27	184	17.20b-37	164
14.26	184	17.22-37	137
14.34-35	85, 128, 184	17.23	137, 138
15	187, 189	17.26-27	192
15.1-2	185	17.28-29	192
15.2	185	17.31	138, 139
15.3-7	169, 174, 185	18.1-14	170
15.4-32	163	18.1-8	192
15.7	31	18.7	192
15.8-32	174	18.8	192
15.10	31	18.9-14	193
15.11-32	169, 184	18.14b	31
16	185, 190	18.15-43	174
16.1-31	170	18.15-17	83, 193
16.1-12	186	18.15	193
16.1-7	185	18.18-30	170
16.8-13	185	18.18-25	186
16.9	31	18.31-33	170
16.13	86, 89	18.35	169
16.14-15	186, 187	19	137
16.14	185	19	137
16.16-31	186	19.11-27	26, 83, 85, 137, 169, 193
16.16-17	185, 186	19.12-27	164
16.16	32, 186–7	19.29	118
16.16b	188	20	83
16.17	186	20.1	83
16.18	186, 188	20.2	79
16.19-31	184–6, 189	20.20-26	80
16.21	189	20.32	77, 80
16.22	99	21	137, 192
16.25	189	21.5-24	192
16.29	186	21.8-36	163
16.31	186, 187	21.12-19	176
17	137	21.15	124
17.1-10	189	21.32-33	88–9
17.1-4	163, 189	22–23	83

22.1	83	5.12	79
22.24-30	161	7.42	95
22.28	161	11.1-2	177
22.29–23.01	193	11.1	209
22.30	130, 161	12.1-8	177, 209
22.47	81	12.34	79
22.54–23.1	83	18.38b	129
22.62	79	19.4	129
22.64	77, 78	19.6	129
22.66	79	21	141
22.69	118		
23.1-25	129	Acts	
23.2	129	1.1	11
23.3-5	129	1.8	117, 174
23.4	129	1.12	118
23.6-12	129, 198	1.14	170
23.11	129	2.14b-36	163
23.13-16	129	2.38	170
23.13	129	2.42	170
23.14	119	2.44-45	170
23.17-23	129	3.19-26	170
23.22	129	3.22-23	167
23.32-46	170	3.22	102, 177
23.53	129	4.32-35	170
24.1-9	193	6.4	170
24.4-6	119	7	195
24.6-7	118	7.2-53	163
24.7	79	7.30-31	170
24.9	119, 193	7.54-60	170
24.11-53	193	7.56	118
24.11	118	7.58–15.30	72
24.12	209	7.59	170
24.24	118, 209	8.4-25	174
24.27	186, 188	8.9	99
24.39	118	8.20	170
24.41	118	8.22-24	170
24.44	186	9.9	168
24.47	118	9.11	170
24.49	118, 119	9.16	170
24.50	118	9.33-34	72
24.51	118	10.2-4	170
24.52	119	10.9	170
24.53	117	10.30	170
		11.5	170
John		12.1-4	170
1.6-9	32	12.12	170
1.19-28	32	13.3	170
1.32	209	13.6b-41	163
3.22–4.3	32	13.11	122
3.24	209	13.15	186

13.24	170
14.19	170
14.23	170
15	19, 102
15.3	98
19.4	170
19.9	168
19.11-20	122
19.13-20	178
19.23	168
20.21	170
20.35	170
21.5	170
22.17	170
24.14	168
26.2-23	163
26.20	170
27.1–28.16	70
27.5	69
27.11	69
27.12	69
27.13-44	69
27.21-26	71
27.23-26	70
27.29	69
27.30	69
27.40	69
27.41	69
27.43-44	70
28.2	70
28.6	70
28.7	70
28.10	70
28.11-14	70
28.25-28	170
28.25	124
28.26-27	128

Romans
1.3	95
3.10-18	13
7.4-8	13

1 Corinthians
10.1-7	93
10.1-2	91
10.4	91
10.6-7	91

2 Corinthians
11.25	71

Galatians
1–2	72

James
3.4	69

Revelation
4.1	107
18.17	69
19.11	107

APOCRYPHA
Ecclesiasticus (Sirach)
35.11-22LXX	192

Tobit
5.16	59
11.4	59

PSEUDEPIGRAPHA
1 Enoch
106	97

Jubilees
2	97

LAB
9	97
9.10	92
25–28	98

Sibylline Oracles
11.140-71	72

QUMRAN
4Q41	41

RABBINIC LITERATURE
Exod. R.
12.4	47

PHILO
Migr. Abr.
1–100	52–4
85	123

Spec. Leg.		62–3	195
1.1-100	51–2	79	195
1.1-12	50	189–331	195
1.1	50	208–11	35
Vit. Mos.		*War*	
1.4	46	2.562-68	195
1.5-6	47	2.566–3.63	35
1.7	47	2.569-71	195
1.8	47	2.626-31	195
1.18	47	3.351-54	35
1.34	47	3.387-91	35
1.36-38	47		
1.44	47	CLASSICAL AND ANCIENT CHRISTIAN	
1.96-139	47	WRITINGS	
1.96-97	47	Augustine	
1.97-211	47	*De natura et origine animae*	
1.112	122–3	4.7.9	13
1.148-49	92		
1.155-56	92	Homer	
2.21-2	48	*Iliad*	
2.23-24	48	5.87-89	64, 66
2.53-56	48	20.273-352	62
2.57-58	48	20.302-308	62
2.59-65	48	22.93-96	63, 64, 66
2.66-186	48	23.226-897	60
2.175-86	48, 50	24.469-692	64
2.187-292	49		
		Odyssey	
JOSEPHUS		1–4	58
Ant.		2.11	59
1.5	35	3.1-484	60
1.17	35	3.388	42
2	33	4.1-619	60
2.205-238	97	5	70
2.205-237	92	5.255	69
2.205-234	92	5.270	69
3–4	36, 46	5.282-463	69
3.99	93	5.291-473	71
4	33	5.291-387	61, 62, 66, 68
5	33	5.315	69
7.53-89	38	5.330	69
12	33	5.333-352	70
		5.335	69
Apion		5.365-464	70
1.50	11	5.418	69
		5.465-93	70
Life		5.489-91	70
28–413	35	6.110-249	70
28–9	195	6.241-243	70

7.154-178	70		Pliny the Younger	
8.486-520	62, 64		*Letters*	
9.78	69		9.36.1-3	6
9.146-50	69			
9.546-47	69		Ps-Origen	
10.1-468	62		*Comm. Matt.*	
10.1-55	62, 66		5.14.4	186
11.20	69			
11.219	118		Quintilian	
11.465-540	64		*Inst.*	
11.504-540	64		1.8.8	69
12	61, 70		4.2.40-46	164
12.5-6	69		10.1-2	57
12.152	69		10.1.46-50	69
12.217	69			
12.230	69		Seneca	
12.305	69		*Epistles*	
12.402-55	71		84	56
12.403-453	69			
12.403-419	61, 66		Tacitus	
12.406-453	68		*Annals*	
12.411	69		1	57
12.412	69		1.61-62	57
13.1-92	70		1.64-65	57
13.93-24	70			
14.299-319	69		*Histories*	
15	58		2.70	57
17.62	59		5.14.2-5.15.2	57
24.349	42			
			Theon	
Horace			*Progymnasmata* (see n. 3 on p. 29)	
Odes			3 (5) [101]	30
4.2	56		3 (5) [103–4]	30
			4 (3) [75]	31
Lucian			5 (4) [79]	31
How to Write History			6 (7) [106]	29
15	58		10 (9) [112–3]	32
			16 [110]	29
Lucretius				
De Rerum Natura			Virgil	
1.280-9	64		*Aeneid*	
			1	62
Nicander			1.81-156	67–8
Theriaca			1.81-143	61
31–4	63		2	62
137–38	63		2.469-558	63, 66
359–72	63		2.469-475	63
389–92	63		2.469-99	195

2.473-475	66	*Georgics*	
2.494-499	63	3.426	63, 66
5.42-603	60	3.437	63, 66
8.102-584	60	3.439	63, 66
8.196-7	57		
10.850	57		
12.036	57		

Index of Authors

Achtemeier, P. 208
Adams, S. 11, 29, 32
Alexander, L. 8, 9, 10, 11, 36
Alexander, P. 9, 55
Allison, D. 20, 90, 91, 92, 93, 102, 110, 120, 128
Anderson, M. 13
Assmann, J. 8, 9, 16
Aurelius, E. 112, 165

Baban, O. 56
Baddeley, A. 13, 40, 194
Barker, J. 41, 42
Bauckham, R. 207
Beaton, R. 5
Begg, C. 38
Black, S. 78
Bonz, M. 72
Borgen, P. 50, 52
Boring, M.E. 80
Borman, L. 67
Botha, P. 8
Brodie, T.L. 2, 56, 57, 58, 59, 65, 68, 166, 168, 174, 175
Brown, R.E. 55, 78, 92, 93, 94, 98, 99, 100
Bruce, F.F. 69, 71
Bryan, D. 140
Burkett, D. 6, 21, 22, 24, 152–3
Byrskog, S. 15

Cairns, F. 60
Carlston, C. 86
Carr, D. 9, 11
Carroll, M. 87
Carruthers, M. 11, 13, 56
Casali, S. 61
Catchpole, D. 122
Croatto, J. S. 102
Crook, Z. 139–40

Damm, A. 20, 24, 29, 31, 32, 33, 57, 126, 165, 176, 179
Davies, M. 20, 76, 83

Davies, W.D. 20, 90, 91, 92, 93, 110, 120, 128
Dekel, E. 61–4
Delling, G. 47
Derico, T.M. 8, 87, 88
Derrenbacker, R.A. 1, 5, 26, 36–41, 73, 127, 146, 159
Derrett, J.D. 69
Dewey, J. 8
Donahue, J. 129
Downing, F.G. 1, 8, 9, 32–8, 41, 73, 78–9, 97, 108, 127, 131–8, 141–2, 159
Drury, J. 34, 96, 97, 99, 100, 101, 120, 167, 175, 178, 179, 180, 185, 191
Du Quesnay, I. 57
Ducharme, L. 197
Dungan, D.L. 170. *See also* McNicol, A.J.
Dunn, J.D.G. 25, 207
Dupertuis, R. 72

Egelkraut, H. 168
Elder, N. 20
Evans, C.A. 20, 121, 122, 123, 127
Evans, C.F. 109, 111, 121, 122, 123, 166, 167, 168, 187
Evans, P. 5
Eve, E. 1, 2, 8, 9, 10, 12, 13, 14, 15, 16, 20, 21, 24, 25, 31, 40, 41, 46, 47, 76, 78, 82, 121, 122, 125, 127, 131, 132, 135, 136, 137, 146, 159, 178, 207, 208
Eysenck, M. 13. *See also* Baddeley, A.

Fairclough, H.R. 63
Fantuzzi, M. 61
Farrer, A.M. 120, 136
Fayold, M. 151
Fine, G.A. 197
Finkelpearl, E. 56, 66
Fiske, G. 59
Fitzmyer, J. 135, 169, 188, 189, 190, 191
Fowler, R. 208
Franklin, E. 16, 96, 100, 120, 164, 167, 169, 171, 180, 181

Friedrichsen, T. 80, 84
Friesen, C. 72
Frolov, S. 58

Gallarte, I. 118
Garrett, S. 99
Gärtner, Ursula 61, 62
Goodacre, M. 20, 21, 36, 39, 76, 77, 78, 81, 84, 86–9, 94, 99, 120, 121, 126–7, 133, 139, 163, 164, 168–9, 174, 208, 209
Goodenough, E. 47, 49, 50
Gorman, H. 11, 122, 164
Goulder, M.D. 2, 9, 34, 38–9, 55, 67, 78, 79, 81, 84, 90, 91, 93, 94, 96, 98, 100, 101, 105, 106, 108, 109, 110, 111, 112, 113, 118, 119, 120, 122, 124, 127, 131, 135, 136, 139, 163, 167, 169, 174, 175, 177, 178, 179, 180, 181, 182, 183, 184, 186, 187, 190, 191, 192, 193
Green, H.B. 135, 137
Gregory, A. 2, 8, 13, 146, 186
Gundry, R. 84
Güttgemanns, E. 10

Harrington, D. 90, 91, 92, 93, 110, 129
Harstine, S. 69
Hauge, M. 31
Hexter, R. 61
Hock, R. 69
Hoffmann, P. 54
Holladay, C. 47
Holmberg, I. 61
Honoré, A.M. 77
Horsley, R. 8, 9, 10
Hurtado, L. 5, 8

Jaffee, M. 12
Jeffrey, D.L. 189
Jeffrey, G. 151
Johnson, L.T. 69, 122

Kahl, W. 77, 80, 83, 104–6, 108
Kartzow, M. 67
Keener, C. 41, 69, 71, 72, 102
Keith, C. 15, 16
Kelber, W. 5, 10, 16
Kellogg, R. 151
Kennedy, G. 29–32, 164
Kenny, E.J. 63–4, 66

King, K. 60
Kirk, A. 1, 7, 8–10, 12, 14, 15, 22, 24, 25, 40–6, 52, 54, 66, 73, 82, 113–14, 130, 131, 146–54, 156, 157, 159–61, 207
Kloppenborg (Verbin), J. 20, 25, 39, 41, 54, 86, 89, 95, 110, 117, 120, 121, 122, 125, 126, 127, 132, 135, 163, 207
Knauer, G. 55, 60, 62
Knoppers, G. 55
Kochenash, M. 72
Kuhn, K.A. 94

Landry, D. 67
Larsen, M. 23
Last, R. 7
Lear, J. 67
Licona, M. 29, 30, 32, 36
Lord, A. 8
Lummis, E.W. 82

MacDonald, D. 2, 55, 57, 58, 59, 67, 68–71, 72
MacEwen, R. 75
Mack, B. 5
MacKay, K.A. 60
Maclean, J. 69
Maddox, R. 168
Mainville, O. 118
Marshall, I.H. 110, 111, 121, 135, 161, 187, 188, 189
Martin, M.W. 11, 29, 31, 32, 121
Matson, M.A. 121, 145, 150, 164, 170, 179
Mattila, S. 6, 12, 35, 37, 41, 86
McAdon, B. 55, 57, 58, 59, 61, 67, 72, 94, 98, 103
McCane, B. 129
McIver, R. 87
McNicol, A. 170, 174, 175, 177, 187, 191, 192
Metzger, B. 78, 79, 81, 87, 119
Mitchell, M. 69
Moessner, D. 10, 129, 168, 169
Moles, J. 11
Moret, J.-R. 111
Morgan, T. 57
Morgenthaler, R. 86
Moyise, S. 13
Muller, M. 67
Murphy, F. 98
Murray, A.T. 63

Nassauer, G. 96
Neirynck. F. 76, 79, 84
Neville, D. 6, 22, 23, 24
Nickelsberg, G. 58, 59
Niehoff, M. 46, 47, 50, 52, 123
Nolland, J. 122, 187, 191
Norlin, D. 86

O'Leary, A. 58, 65, 67, 103
Olson, K. 121, 131-2, 137-8, 142
Ostmeyer, K.-H. 91

Padilla, O. 11
Park, I. 72
Parker, D.C. 78, 79, 118, 119, 206
Parry, A. 72
Parsons, M. 29, 31, 32, 188
Peabody, D. 170
Pelling, C.B.R. 6, 24, 35, 127
Perrin, N. 2, 208
Petersen, N. 208
Peterson, J. 1, 145, 169
Pitts, A. 56, 57
Poirier, J.C. 1, 16, 43, 87-9, 159
Praeder, S. 70, 71
Prince, D.T. 118
Proust, M. 13

Rajak, T. 35
Ramelli, I. 187, 188
Rastoin, M. 185
Reece, S. 11
Robinson, J. 54
Rodd, C.S.
Rodriguez, R. 5, 112, 197
Roose, H. 184, 189
Rubin, D. 13, 14, 88, 121
Russel, D.A. 56, 57

Sabin, M. 55
Sanday, W. 1, 5
Sanders, E.P. 20, 76, 83, 139
Sandnes, K. 56, 69, 95, 197, 198
Schacter, D. 13
Schippers, A.M. 56, 196

Schwartz, B. 15, 197
Shea, Chris 68
Shellard, B. 94, 209
Shelton, J. 165
Shuler, P. 46
Sim, D. 16
Simons, R. 100
Simpson, R.T. 136
Small, J. 6
Spong, J. 55
Stemberger, G. 14
Streeter, B.H. 20, 39, 76, 78, 107, 120, 145, 209
Styler, G.M. 20, 21

Tannehill, R. 71, 166
Taylor, N.H. 109, 111
Thatcher, T. 15
Torrance, M. 151
Troftgruben, T. 71
Tsagalis, C. 61
Tuckett, C.M. 39, 81-2, 84, 114, 120, 121, 124, 126, 131, 163

van Iersel, B. 129
Verheyden, J. 165
Vinson, R. 79, 80

Watson, F. 43, 90, 94, 97, 98, 112, 113, 114, 121, 154, 208
Wenham, D. 207
West, D. 65
Whitmarsh, T. 56
Wilkens, W. 86, 92, 105, 110, 111, 165, 176, 186, 187
Wilson, W. 155
Winn, A. 2, 59, 67, 68, 69, 65, 168
Winsbury, R. 6
Wire, A.C. 8
Wolfson, H.A. 47, 52
Woodman, T. 57, 58, 65
Wright, A. 58

Yates, F. 11

www.ingramcontent.com/pod-product-compliance
Lightning Source LLC
Chambersburg PA
CBHW072142290426
44111CB00012B/1950